*Lord, share out among us the tongues of your Spirit,
that we may each burn with compassion
for all who hunger for freedom and humanness;
that we may be doers of the word and so speak
with credibility about the wonderful things you have done.*

>*Lord, direct us in ways we do not yet discern and equip us
for the service of reconciliation and liberation in your
world.*

>*Break down the walls that separate us and unite us in a
single body.*

Acclamations II and III
(*Risk*, pp. 10, 11)

Oswald Russell, 1974

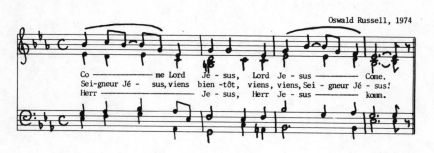

Co ——————— me Lord Jé - sus, Lord Je - sus ——————— Come.
Sei-gneur Jé - sus, viens bien -tôt, viens, viens, Sei - gneur Jé - sus!
Herr ——————— Je - sus, Herr Je - sus ——————— komm.

Dieter Trautwein, 1974

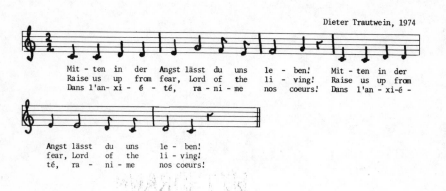

Mit - ten in der Angst lässt du uns le - ben! Mit - ten in der
Raise us up from fear, Lord of the li - ving! Raise us up from
Dans l'an- xi - é - té, ra - ni - me nos coeurs! Dans l'an - xi-é-

Angst lässt du uns le - ben!
fear, Lord of the li - ving!
té, ra - ni - me nos coeurs!

BREAKING BARRIERS
Nairobi 1975

The Official Report of the Fifth Assembly
of the World Council of Churches,
Nairobi, 23 November-10 December, 1975

Edited by
DAVID M. PATON

*Published in collaboration with
the World Council of Churches by*
SPCK, LONDON
WM. B. EERDMANS, GRAND RAPIDS

German version: BERICHT AUS NAIROBI, ed. Walter Müller-Römheld
and Hanfried Krüger, Otto Lembeck, Frankfurt
French version: ed. Marcel Henriet, to be published in August 1976

Library of Congress Cataloging in Publication Data

World Council of Churches. 5th Assembly, Nairobi, 1975.
 Breaking barriers, Nairobi 1975.
  1. Christian union—Congresses. I. Paton, David
MacDonald. II. Title.
BX6.W771975.A3B7 262'.001 76-6145
ISBN 0-8028-1639-8

S.P.C.K. edition: ISBN 0 281 02922 9

Contents

v

Preface

An Assembly of the World Council of Churches is necessarily a complex event. As a total experience within the fellowship of the member churches and of the whole ecumenical movement, it should be an occasion when the nature of Christians' joyful and yet painful community in Christ in this world is experienced and celebrated. It focuses upon the stage which the churches have reached at a particular point in their pilgrimage from division to unity, from self-concern to self-abandonment to God and to the needs of this world. It must reflect Christian loyalty to what God has given and Christian openness to what God will give. It must also express the joys, sorrows, hopes, and fears of the whole people of God. And it recognizes that all these things must be done together, in the Spirit.

The Fifth Assembly of the World Council of Churches which took place in Nairobi, Kenya, on 23 November-10 December, 1975, was a valiant attempt to realize this conception of an Assembly given by the Structure Report (1971). This Official Report is a full record of the Assembly.

Official Reports are often treated as documents for occasional reference. However, they are an indispensable way of preserving the memory of a big and many-sided event, and of setting out fully the challenges and tasks committed to the churches and the ecumenical movement for the ensuing years. This Report is further enlivened by the Personal Account of the Assembly which was written on the spot by the editor, Canon David Paton, a veteran of the ecumenical movement. He adds his own quick evaluation of the Assembly as a whole.

This Report is intended to be a working document for the churches and for the World Council. There is, first of all, the Message, which is a call to prayer, and was the result of the insights coming from the many small work groups which wrestled with the main theme, "Jesus Christ Frees and Unites", and with the addresses through Bible study and discussion. The reports of the six Sections, which dealt with some major issues facing the Church and the world today, are given in full together with brief accounts of the discussions on them in plenary session. These will be of special interest to readers because they contain a series of recommendations to the churches for future study and action.

An Assembly has to review the work of the World Council and indicate general guidelines for future programmes. Relations with ecumenical and confessional bodies are considered. Furthermore, the Assembly deliberates on current issues of international concern. All these are reported in this volume.

Addresses delivered at the Assembly are not included here for reasons of economy, but the major ones are published in the January 1976 issues of *The Ecumenical Review* and *International Review of Mission*, as indicated in the footnotes. Three reports made to the Assembly in plenary, namely, those of the General Secretary and the Moderator of the Central Committee and the Finance Report, are to be found in the Appendices.

We are most grateful to Canon David Paton, who acted as chairman of the Editorial Group as well as editor of the English Report, Dr. Walter Müller-Römheld, editor of the German Report, and M. Marcel Henriet, editor of the French Report, and all who assisted them, for the quick, efficient, and devoted work done.

I warmly commend this Report as a record of a new stage in the ecumenical movement. This Assembly was the most representative of the people of God in our churches. It expressed the impatient eagerness of the churches to be more deeply involved in the life of the World Council. It charged the churches and the Council to a new covenant relationship in which we can truly confess the Lord Jesus Christ who frees and unites us. Perhaps the mood of the Assembly can best be summed up in the sung refrain of an often used litany: "Break down the walls that separate us and unite us in a single body".

Geneva
30 January, 1976

PHILIP POTTER
General Secretary

Message: An Invitation to Prayer

As participants at the Fifth Assembly of the World Council of Churches, we send affectionate greetings to our sisters and brothers in our Lord Jesus Christ.

Representatives of many church traditions and cultures, we gathered together in Nairobi, Kenya. In a continent determined to be free, and moved by the joy with which African Christians celebrate the Lord, we tried to respond to the needs of the world. We had more representatives of the six continents than before and also more women, young people, and laity.

For eighteen days, we gathered under our common theme: Jesus Christ frees and unites. Listening to one another, we experienced the joy of unity across the barriers of culture and race, sex and class; we also experienced the pain of these deep divisions. Deliberation on our common witness in Bible study and prayer, in informal small group and large formal meeting, brought us closer together. Ideology and sharp contrasts in opinion and commitment pulled us apart. The Assembly report gives the direction of our thoughts. It will reach you soon.

Now we bring you these prayers and ask you to pray with us:

God, Creator and Author of Life, warned anew of the threats to human survival, we confess that the way we live and order society sets us against one another and alienates us from your creation, exploiting, as though dead, things to which you have given life. Separated from you we live in emptiness. We long in our own lives for a new spirituality of intention, thought, and action. Help us to struggle to conserve the earth for future generations, and free us to share together, that all may be free.

Kyrie eleison, Lord have mercy

God of Love, who through Jesus Christ shares our suffering, forgives our sins, and delivers from the bondage of oppression, help us to desire and nourish in ourselves sustaining community with our brothers and sisters everywhere. Give us courage to share suffering when it comes. Restore to us the joy of resurrection, that in the midst of situations we can hardly bear we may sing out:

Hallelujah, Praise be to you, O Lord

xi

God of Hope, whose Spirit gives light and power to your people, empower us to witness to your name in all the nations, to struggle for your own justice against all principalities and powers and to persevere with faith and humour in the tasks that you have given to us. Without you we are powerless. Therefore we cry together:

Maranatha, Come Lord Jesus

And grant that we may with one voice and one heart glorify and sing praise to the majesty of your holy Name, of the Father, the Son, and the Holy Spirit.

Amen

I
NAIROBI, 1975
A Personal Account

I
A Personal Account

1. INTRODUCTION

An Assembly of the WCC is more than the decisions it makes, the reports it prepares, and the programmes it approves. It is an experience of community in Christ. But while the experience is shared, it is also different for each participant. Moreover, how one perceives or understands this happening depends greatly on who and where one is.

This presents a problem for the writer of an account of an Assembly. It is acutest for the editor of the English-language edition, for he must try to serve not only the Anglo-Saxon churches from whom so many of the WCC's founding fathers came but also the churches of Asia of which relatively few are English-speaking but most use English as a regional *lingua franca*, plus the large and expanding churches of Anglophone Africa, plus more besides. And these differences are not only of race, language, or culture. There can be a world of difference between being less than 1% of the population (as in most parts of India) and being over 50% (as in some parts of Africa). There is a world of difference between the gaiety and self-confidence of rapidly expanding churches and the dour defensiveness of some of the older churches of the West. To say this much is merely to begin to indicate the immense diversity (not to say divisions) of our viewpoints.

One had best, therefore, try to indicate briefly the local and partial experience from which this personal account is written.

I was born into the ecumenical movement and cannot see it from outside; for me the ecumenical element is as integral to my Christian experience as the Anglican. English, but of Scottish origin, I was a missionary in China, and in the quarter-century since we left China have never for very long been wholly out of touch. A good deal of travel has brought me friends in many lands who have helped me to see and hear a little at least of what I would otherwise have missed. This was my third Assembly; and a WCC Assembly to me is a homecoming.

Even the phrase "an Assembly" has its difficulties; for the Assemblies

3

have all been different. At Amsterdam/1948 the WCC was founded and began to wrestle with the Cold War. Evanston 1954 brought into a single structure the various activities that had developed since 1948 and before, and introduced the WCC to the North American churches. New Delhi 1961 took us to Asia; the International Missionary Council was integrated into the WCC: the Russian Orthodox and other Eastern European Orthodox churches joined the Council, together with two Pentecostal churches from South America; and Roman Catholic official observers were present for the first time. Uppsala 1968 took the force of the wave of anti-racist, anti-colonialist feeling and responded with the new programmes to Combat Racism and Promote Development.

These four Assemblies were all different; and Nairobi was certain to be different again. Both membership and agenda were more genuinely worldwide, and more representative of the human race. Of 676 voting delegates, 107 were Africans, 92 Asians, 147 West Europeans, 97 East Europeans, 137 North Americans, 21 Latin Americans, 9 from the Caribbean, 42 from Australasia and the Pacific, and 20 from the Middle East. Of the 676, 152 were women (22%; Uppsala 9%), 62 under 30 years of age (9%; Uppsala 4% under 35), and 389 were clergy (42%; Uppsala 25%) and 287 lay. For about 80% of delegates Nairobi was their first WCC Assembly.

Added to the 676 voting delegates out of the 755 authorized to represent the 286 member churches were 95 fraternal delegates from related organizations, 35 delegated observers from non-member churches (including 16 Roman Catholic), 60 guests, 110 advisers, 180 stewards, 250 staff, and over 600 press.

The Structure Committee appointed by Uppsala and the Central Committee had worked at the idea of an Assembly which would have less business, less paper, more opportunities for friendship plus more celebrations. This, and the fact that we were meeting in Africa, were two further sources of novelty.

As we gathered for the Assembly we knew that its character and outcome were unpredictable. We hoped and prayed that we might be freed to speak truthfully in love, and that for all our divisions and hostilities we might be held together in unity, even in a deeper unity.

*   *   *   *   *

The Assembly took place in the Kenyatta Conference Centre in the centre of Nairobi. This is a large and splendid modern building; and the facilities were better than those offered to previous Assemblies. The original hope had been to hold the Assembly in Jakarta, Indonesia, but when it became evident that a large international Christian gathering in that country might create problems, the WCC and the church leaders of Kenya arranged a switch to Nairobi. A number of very large Christian gatherings have already taken place in Nairobi and smaller ones at Limuru not very far away, but nothing on the scale of a WCC Assembly. The Host

4

Committee had done quite a remarkable job of preparation in the short time available.

There are further reasons which render Kenya a particularly appropriate place for a WCC Assembly. Nairobi is the headquarters of the All Africa Conference of Churches, probably the largest and most active of the regional Councils of Churches associated with the World Council of Churches. And at Kikuyu the little wooden church still stands where there took place in 1913 at the close of a missionary conference on Christian Co-operation a united communion service in which two Anglican bishops shared with Methodists and Presbyterians. This created among Anglicans a rumpus of unexampled ferocity, which led in due course (the wrath of man being turned to God's praise) to the Lambeth 1920 Appeal to All Christian People about Christian Unity. But the wider effect was to ensure that the nascent Faith and Order movement did not become mainly an affair of academic debate on theological doctrine but had to include the sacraments and common participation in them. Kikuyu is thus an ecumenical holy place, and it is a pity that the Assembly did not make more of it.

And, thirdly, I think it is fair to say that the National Christian Council of Kenya is also of unusual quality and strength, notable for a varied and widespread network of social work through which the churches together contribute to the tasks of nation-building.

2. THE OPENING CELEBRATION AND THE ASSEMBLY'S WORSHIP

The Fifth Assembly of the World Council of Churches began with an Opening Celebration for which the participants gathered on the steps and balconies of the Kenyatta Conference Centre and the plaza in front of it. As the drums rose to a climax and then fell silent, the many personal conversations died away too; passages of the Scriptures were read by different voices from all the continents. An interruption by Pastor Glass and a colleague (allies of Dr Ian Paisley) from Glasgow shouting about "Anti-Christ" served only to rivet the attention of the company of 2,000 or more.

Then the General Secretary offered the following prayer which constituted the formal opening of the Fifth Assembly:

Almighty and everlasting God,
who by thy Holy Spirit didst preside
in the Council of the blessed Apostles,
and hast promised, through thy Son Jesus Christ,
to be with thy Church to the end of the world;

we beseech thee to be with the World Council of Churches
here assembled in thy Name and Presence.
Vouchsafe, we beseech thee, of thy great mercy
so to direct, sanctify, and govern us in our work,
by the mighty power of the Holy Ghost,
that the comfortable gospel of Christ
may be truly preached, truly received,
and truly followed, in all places;
till at length the whole of thy dispersed sheep,
being gathered into one fold,
shall become partakers of everlasting life;
through the merits and death of Jesus Christ our Saviour.

The participants "gathered from the nations" followed Archbishop Festo Olang' and singers of the African Israel Church of Ninevah into the great Meeting Room for the second part of the Celebration entitled "Gathered by the Lord". As the Assembly sang a musical acclamation, "Come Lord Jesus, Lord Jesus come", the leaders of worship entered, led by a Masai girl bearing a Swahili Bible ("the word of God which bears witness to him who frees and unites").

After the hymn "Praise to the Lord, the Almighty, the King of Creation", three voices (Ms Pauline Webb, Dr Roy Neehall, and Mr Bethuel Kiplagat) read passages on creation, light and darkness, interwoven from Genesis 1, John 1, and Colossians 1.

In a homily on 1 Peter 2.9 the Reverend Seth Nomenyo spoke in French of the darkness of our world, of a night of crises and judgement, and of "this rising sun, this Jesus Christ, this man who is *weak* before the powers of this world, because dead to sin and living for God he could not use the same means or the same weapons as his adversaries; but in his weakness God deployed his almighty, liberating power", and prayed that we might be given "grace to proclaim together in word and deed this joyous hope".

Another hymn (by Dr John Mbiti)

From north and south, from east and west,
The peoples of Almighty God
Converge to share a common life,
Traversing culture, race and wealth.

led into the intercessions in Swahili, Bahasa Indonesian, and English, and an Act of Commitment:

Risen Lord, by the power of your spirit we commit ourselves
to trust one another in this fellowship of your service
to be good stewards of the time and talents you have given us
to seek you within and beyond our confessions and cultures

6

to follow where you will lead us
to live for others as you died for all.
Lord, bless us, that we in turn may bless the world. Amen.

The choir, recruited from local churches (the word got around and the choir ended up much larger than planned), sang a Kalenjin song, asking Christ to chase away our fears. Archbishop Olang' pronounced the Benediction and exchanged the Grace with us. We exchanged the Grace or other greetings with our neighbours. After a postlude on drums by Morris Nyunyusa the Assembly slowly dispersed.

This was very different from the solemn ecclesiastical procession and the "traditional" ecumenical service of worship with which other Assemblies had begun, but which would have been inappropriate with a younger, more lay Assembly which also felt much more like a major church occasion in one's own home area.

But did the new form "work"? Not entirely. There were technical hitches with the microphones, and other hitches. Some would have preferred the familiarity of older forms. But for most it "worked", as it did for me, especially the most African bits, the songs and the drums. I was moved, and I prayed, and loved my fellow-Christians. It was for me what it has been hoped it might be, a celebration of the people of God.

And there was one delicious coincidence. The intercessions included prayer for the churches listed for the week in the WCC Cycle of Prayer. These turned out to be the churches of Scotland and Ireland which are the countries from which Pastor Glass and Dr Paisley come. Who denies the divine sense of humour?

Worship throughout the Assembly assumed the same varied, informal character. The Committee set up by the Central Committee to prepare the Worship of the Assembly had already published a double issue of *Risk* entitled "Leitourgia" which contained a variety of liturgical material, new and old. This together with the new and revised edition of *Cantate Domino* was in the hands of every participant.

Thus the first Business Session of the Assembly on Monday, 24 November, began with the singing of the acclamation "Come Lord Jesus, Lord Jesus come", followed by the recitation of the Nicene Creed and the reading of Philippians 2.1-2, 5. Then, after silence, there was a Prayer of Invocation of the Holy Spirit, the Lord's Prayer, and the hymn "All Praise to Thee". On Wednesday, 26 November, a somewhat shorter service of worship took place after the coffee-break and introduced Dr Payne's presentation of the Finance Report. Some of the presentations on the main theme were also set in a context of worship. An outstanding example was the Plenary Presentation on 27 November on "That all may be one", when Mrs Mercy Oduyoye of Nigeria led us in a service of worship that embraced in prayer and praise three short statements on the way in which

7

the disunity of the Church made worse the human disunity of Sri Lanka, Northern Ireland, and South Africa, and two longer statements on the nature of the unity we seek. This service, to which the music of the Peter Janssens Song Orchestra of Germany made a great contribution, was a satisfying unity of worship, reflection, and loving speech.

The Presentation on Friday, 28 November, on "Women in a changing world" concluded with a service, "Mary's story and ours". During this service a record of "I wish I knew how it would feel to be free" was interpreted in sign language by Mrs Claire Aca Manning, a member of the Shoshone-Paivte tribe. On 6 December morning prayers included a dance on the theme of the spiritual "He's got the whole world in his hands" performed by six stewards who had prepared the dance during the course of the Assembly under the direction of Mrs Shona Mactavish of New Zealand. An evening or two earlier on 4 December closing prayer for the day had ended with an Orthodox Easter hymn sung by the Russian, Greek, and Romanian delegations; and on 8 December a Bulgarian choir sang evening prayers. And I do not recall ever hearing Psalm 22 read as well as it was one morning by David Johnson (American Episcopal Church), who was chairman of the Assembly Worship Committee.

All this represented a fairly determined break with precedent. Worship has often been the weakest part of ecumenical meetings because it is the point at which, sometimes without recognizing it, we are most dependent on familiarity not only of liturgy and language but of style and even intonation. There is no possibility for most of us of complete freedom or unity here; and the absence of it is harder to take. The Worship Committee made a remarkable and imaginative effort to provide not a mixture of existing traditions but worship in an idiom which is partly new and partly scriptural and very ancient; and they relied heavily on Fred Kaan and Donald Swann (both of whom were at the Assembly) and other contemporary writers and composers.

The effort was not wholly successful. A good deal depended on where you were sitting, in a very large hall that did not lend itself to worship, and on whether your immediate neighbours were praying or gossiping. Some people, alas, made little attempt to join in the unfamiliar. The forest of microphones, cameras, and lights was distracting; but still worse were undisciplined delegates. The quality of leadership of worship also varied. In a liturgically unsympathetic building and a congregation too diverse for easy discipline, a strong voice, firm control, and an ear for silence were essential. We often had these things, but not always. Some felt, finally, that the hymns chosen lacked that specific quality in which the classical hymns are strong and modern products often weak—that of heartfelt and uninhibited adoration of the Triune God.

My own interim assessment would be that the Worship Committee offered us a potential feast of which for various reasons we didn't take full advantage either in plenary sessions or in smaller groups and subsections; but my own personal experience was mostly very positive.

There were also three eucharistic celebrations as part of the programme. The first of these, on Wednesday, 26 November, was arranged by the Oriental Orthodox churches. The basic structure of this composite liturgy was taken from the liturgy of St Basil (Coptic) with elements from the Ethiopian, Syrian, and Armenian liturgies, and the languages used were Coptic, Ancient Ethiopic, Ancient Syriac, Ancient Armenian, Arabic, English, French, and Malayalam. The main celebrants were the bishops from the three Asian churches (Syrian, Armenian, and Indian). Metropolitan Paulos Gregorios (formerly Paul Verghese) preached a sermon.

The second eucharistic celebration was on 3 December when a large company of African clergy led by Archbishop Festo Olang' celebrated the Eucharist, using the Liturgy for East Africa that had been prepared in the course of the Church Union Negotiations between Anglican, Presbyterian, Methodist, and Lutheran churches. Many hundreds of participants received communion standing behind their seats. This service was preceded by a short recital of his songs by Adrian Snell.

On the previous afternoon the plenary session had concluded with a "Service of Anticipation of Holy Communion", "a preparatory worship event for all eucharistic celebrations at the Assembly—those which have preceded it and those which will follow". This service, eucharistic in structure and led by Dr Eugene Carson Blake, gave thanks for the unity we have been given and looked forward to that which is still to come. As a climax there was a striking interweaving of Matthew 5.9, John 14.27, Hebrews 13.20, and Philippians 4.7 with the familiar prayer beginning "Lord, make us instruments of your peace . . . ". The Peace was then exchanged in a variety of ways in a subdued, affectionate, lively hubbub all over the hall, after which the leader said:

> O Lord our heavenly Father, you have gathered us from many nations into the fellowship of this place, into the fellowship of one faith, one hope, and one salvation. We thank you for the many manifestations of your Kingdom that allow us to anticipate with joyful hearts the splendour of the world to come. We thank you for the togetherness you are granting us now, at this very moment, for the love with which you have loved us so that we in turn may love one another. We thank you for your whole creation that is longing to be redeemed and made free and made new, through Jesus our brother, the risen Christ, who made us bold to pray:

and we all said the Lord's Prayer in our own language.

On Monday, 8 December, the Holy Eucharist was celebrated according to the Liturgy of St John Chrysostom by Bishop Emilianos Timiadis of the Ecumenical Patriarchate, Protopresbyter Vitaly Borovoy, and the Rever-

9

end Bogdan Soiko, all of the Russian Orthodox Church, with Russian and Greek choirs from among Assembly participants.

On Sunday, 30 November, participants in the Assembly and many of the Christians of Nairobi attended an Advent Rally in Uhuru Park. This was a very simple service of African dancing, singing, and drumming with prayers and two lessons (John 8.31-59 and Ephesians 3.14-21)—the latter chanted in Japanese and English by Bishop Sayama (Orthodox). The sermon, by the Anglican Bishop Festo Kivengere of Kigezi, Uganda, was a full-dress evangelistic sermon in the classical evangelical tradition, given in English by a natural orator and translated sentence by sentence into Swahili. It was, however, a good deal firmer and sharper in its secular references than much evangelical preaching: "Your inner fragmentation, your racial animosities, your denominational conflicts, your ideological prejudices, your sex discriminations, your tribal feuds, are now finished", because of the victory of Christ won on the Cross.

It was an informal, colourful, relaxed occasion; but in its own way dead serious. I found myself rather happy, taking it in slowly.

On Sunday, 7 December, participants in the Assembly were invited to join in the worship of the congregations in and around Nairobi, who also entertained their visitors to lunch after the service. This hospitality enabled many of us to have our first experience of the ordinary congregational church life of our generous hosts.

This necessarily selective account of the Worship of the Assembly would not be complete without mention of the chapel created in one of the smaller of the Kenyatta Conference Centre meeting rooms, and the eucharistic celebrations and other forms of worship and private prayer that took place daily.

3. PRESENTATIONS ON THE MAIN THEME

The main themes of the Assembly were presented in a variety of ways at eight plenary presentations.

JESUS CHRIST FREES AND UNITES

The first of these, on "Jesus Christ frees and unites", was a presentation of the Parable of the Two Sons (Luke 15.11-32) by the United Bible Societies in a medley of biblical exposition, discussion, drama, and song. The Archbishop of Canterbury, Dr Donald Coggan, was an informal compère rather than a presiding officer, and Donald Swann was at the piano with a locally recruited choir.

In the first part probing questions were asked of American, Asian, and

African families about why children leave home and how families should react. (Some objected that this, exegetically, is not what the parable is about.) The second part asked still more searching questions about the situation after the prodigal's return, and included defences (in a court-room manner) not only of the elder brother who had after all manfully defended decent moral standards, but also of the father against the charges of losing control of both his sons and of acting without proper dignity.

This presentation, whose methods were at times of a Sunday School simplicity, even naivety, which some regretted, left most participants with a good deal to think about. Anyone, for example, who wants to be with the father must accept that there will always be a brother, and that occasions will arise when there is a celebration by some of events which others find morally objectionable. What, in fact, must happen in order that the father may keep both his sons *and* be the same father?

This was an exposition of the main theme which, by functioning at several levels, offered a disconcerting perspective on the divisive issues before the Assembly.

The next presentation, "African challenge", raised many of the same issues in an indirect way.

AFRICAN CHALLENGE

The African member churches had been asked to prepare a session under this title. After much discussion, it was decided to ask Mr Joe de Graft, a Ghanaian at the University of Nairobi, to write and direct a play that would pose the challenge Africa makes to its own peoples as well as to the rest of the world. A play entitled *Muntu* was the result, and we saw its première. The play is about the African sense of the original harmony of mankind with his cosmic environment, and about the disharmony, oppression, and alienation that men and women experience in history.

The play begins with the children of Muntu—the name means "man" in many African languages—asking their father about the days when Nyambe, "he of the thousand names, whose essence is brightness", sustainer of creation, seemed near and real to them. Time is still marked by the rhythm of the seasons—sowing, hunting, harvesting, and feasting—but already the Age of Innocence is past.

Journeying to a new country, the children send out messengers to test the friendship of their neighbours. Most of them return with the good news of welcome and acceptance, but the second son has made a new discovery. There are enemies as well as friends, and family and possessions must be defended—by violence, if necessary. He returns with bodyguards and a new note in his voice; he is sceptical about his father's assurance that life is based on harmony.

Muntu leaves his children and they have to find their way in a world of increasing alienation. Second Son gives his younger sisters to his body-

11

guards as mates. At the same moment strangers arrive—from the desert and from over the sea.

After this the play traced the story—largely but not wholly brutal and sordid—of the exploitation of Africa by the "Desert-men" (Arab slave traders) and "Water-men" (colonialists and missionaries); of the African struggle for independence. In the conduct of Second Son, who became the brutal arbitrary ruler of an independent African state, it was impossible not to see a comment on neighbouring Uganda.

The mood of the first part was slow and lyrical, and this note never wholly disappeared. The second part was as ruthless in its criticism of present-day follies and tyrannies in independent Africa as of the slave trade or the imperialist carve-up. The play ended with a question mark. How *does* Africa—or the rest of the world—recover harmony?

WHO IS THIS JESUS CHRIST WHO FREES AND UNITES?

Third came a major but unusual theological set-piece, "Who is this Jesus Christ who frees and unites?" by Dr Robert McAfee Brown (USA, Presbyterian).

Dr Brown began with Matthew 16.13-15 and a wide variety of voices illustrating the answers men and women give today to the question: "Who do men say that I am?" Voices similarly offered some of today's answers to "Who do you say that I am?" and contemporary comments on Peter's recognition and Peter's rebuke. The variety of answers inside and outside the Church, said Dr Brown, should not discourage us. It is a sign that the living Christ cannot be imprisoned in a formula. It is both threatening and liberating to realize that our understanding of Jesus as well as our understanding of ourselves will be changed as we share more fully our backgrounds, questions, anxieties, and answers. We are forced to realize the limitations of our perspectives, and Dr Brown was forced to realize that many would regard him, a white, male, affluent American, as a symbol of racism, sexism, classism, and imperialism. To confess publicly the sins of his own country (as Dr Brown did) was not a "white guilt trip" nor to imply that "to live in the third world is automatically to be endowed with virtue". It is to recognize how things are. There was loud applause when he moved from English into Spanish for the rest of his address, in token of solidarity with that large majority in a world gathering who have to try to understand and express themselves in a language not their own.

Remarking that one of the lessons we may learn from the Caesarea Philippi passage (and from other places in the Gospels) is that we may know the words but miss the meaning, Dr Brown moved to an extended discussion of Jesus the Liberator, Jesus the Divider, and Jesus the Unifier. Negatively, he said, Jesus frees us from the false securities by which we try

12

to make our lives secure; and positively, he frees us for the possibility of seeing the world through eyes other than our own. The eyes he gives us are those of the hungry, the exploited, the tortured—the non-person whom the world ignores and discards. We do not live by bread alone, but Jesus never pretended we can live without it. His words and deeds were full of feasts, and he left a meal as sacrament of his ongoing presence. So he frees us also for struggle with and on behalf of those others, the poor and the dispossessed. But Jesus is also the Divider. He came to bring not peace but a sword. Talk about Jesus the Liberator seems to some to betray the gospel by making Jesus too political; but others feel that this Jesus is not political enough. Moreover, good news for the poor is bad news for the rich, and letting my people go from Pharaoh is not good news for Pharaoh.

Such an analysis divides a North American both from the oppressed who deem him as one of their oppressors and from his own North Americans who are outraged by such an exposition of the gospel. It divides him also from God, for he is also on the wrong side in a struggle in which God has taken sides with the oppressed. Yet Jesus is also the Unifier. This must be said, but not too quickly. If some think the WCC has been infected by Marxism, others may think it has been infiltrated by the CIA. But within the Christian community, such postures are provisional, transitional. If Jesus is provisionally the Divider, he is not finally the Divider. He liberates us from these attitudes. He is the Unifier. If so, "we have to demonstrate that we have been sufficiently *freed* to go beyond our *divisions* and begin to embody the *unity* to which Jesus the Unifier beckons us. The path of repentance, confession, and new common obedience is the only way open to us; and because God's healing grace can reach across our divisions, the final note of the gospel is not division or ambiguity or tension or condemnation, it is joy."

Dr Brown's speech was greeted with loud and prolonged applause. In the discussion that followed some fifteen persons made contributions and a further twenty-six were unable to do so for lack of time.

The first speaker, a Latin American Pentecostal, praised Dr Brown's "almost complete speech" as the message of "a full and complete gospel", the message of the complete liberation of the whole man, contrasting sharply with the cautious and fearful attitude of many preachers. Where Dr Brown was at fault was in restricting his confession of the sins of oppression to his own USA. "There are other oppressors and other imperialisms." This speech, of unusual courage and humour, was in assonance with the logic of the play *Muntu* and with much else that seemed to be stirring in the Assembly that might lead to a common mutual recognition, in the midst of our divisions, as a "community of the pardoned".

"Confession of sins is never easy for any of us and I have wondered to what extent each of us could make the same sort of confession without being threatened as soon as he goes home" (Congo).

13

The same speaker thanked Dr Brown for "the new word" of Jesus the Divider: "We must take these divisions and support all the consequences of them. At the same time we must add that Jesus Christ unites us first to God and then to men. Without this there can be no unity on the human level." Other speakers queried this idea, or urged caution in its use. "I agree that Jesus divides, but in what sense? He divides because of sin and evil, and this division is a temporary one, a deviation" (Russian Orthodox). Dr Brown in replying to the debate agreed; but he insisted that our divisions had to be taken seriously and not easily glossed over: but, finally, Jesus Christ is the Unifier.

A speaker from East Germany said that the Church there had lost a million members since Uppsala: this was the loss of "a million potential missionaries". They had left for reasons of spirituality—they had not discovered what the Lord meant for their daily life. Similarly, from South Africa: there are many people who want the liberating word of God. But this word only seems important when we provide the Church with an area of service and action where the Church expresses practically its concern.

But there were others who thought that "making liberation central and not peripheral" was to blur the identity of the Church and the uniqueness of the gospel. "We need a new doctrine of God and of creation. . . . Christ sets his sisters and brothers free in all human contexts; but working for these objectives is not essentially the same as preaching that Christ frees and unites. Is it accidental that the main themes of the last three Assemblies have not referred to God?" (Norway).

THAT ALL MAY BE ONE . . .

The next plenary presentation on unity questions had a rather different character. "That all may be one . . ." (which was led by Mrs Mercy Oduyoye of Nigeria) was a service of worship, in which three short statements and two longer addresses found a natural context of intercession, confession, and praise.

A voice from Sri Lanka (Wesley Ariarajah) spoke of the betrayal of the gospel when, in a country divided by caste, language, culture, and creed, the divided Church fails to express the oneness that Christ brings. A voice from South Africa (Manas Buthelezi) spoke of the ways in which dividedness of the Church manifests itself; he concluded: "How can the Church minister pastorally to those of its members who are polarized in a situation of military confrontation? Should the Church take sides and forget that it has a pastoral responsibility even to those who have decided to be guerilla fighters? What shape should such a pastoral responsibility take? How does one maintain church unity among members who are fighting one another on the battlefield?" He asked for prayer and action. So did Gordon Gray, the voice from Northern Ireland. He spoke of the painful lesson they had

14

learned that the Christian Church must not ignore social and political injustice: to do so is to invite a holocaust. Moreover, church division is a breeding-ground for other sectarianism: "Divided churches cost lives." The unity we seek must be one in which "we hold to our conscientious differences but hold still more to Jesus Christ and his Cross and *so to one another* until Christ gives us true repentance and genuine reconciliation".

In the first of the longer addresses, Fr Cyrille Argenti (Dean of the Greek Orthodox parish, Marseilles, France) spoke first of the secular elements in our disunity which go deep into our subconscious. We are more intensely aware of being Greek, Irish, or Boer than of being Orthodox, Catholic, or Calvinist. Our confessional label serves simply as an alibi to justify or conceal our real motives which contrive to be those of the old man who still lingers in all of us. Our Christianity is skin deep. We must pray for conversion to the Kingdom and be its citizens in exile in our respective native lands in this world.

Fr Argenti then moved on to an exposition of the mystery of the Body of the Risen Christ as the foundation of Christian unity and of the eucharistic assembly as the laboratory which transforms the community of believers into the Church. It is this same mystery which is the foundation of our witness to the world. The Church is a witnessing community because it identifies itself with the Body of the crucified and risen Christ. It is to this goal that all our efforts for unity must be directed. What defines the Church is what the creative Word of its Lord incessantly summons it to become, not the caricature of it that its clergy too often present.

So also because Christ, the head of the Church, is Alpha and Omega, the Lord and Creator of the world, the unity of the Church prepares the way for the unity of the world. The Church is made for the world and the world is made for that Kingdom which has been ready since the world was made. Into this fullness of Christ the Church must grow; and the quality of Christian unity, in its inner completeness, is at least as important as the quantity of Christians assembled. A true "Council" of the Church is really the visible expression of a unity of faith already lived out.

An inter-confessional Assembly such as Nairobi is not a Council of the Church but it can and must display every sign of heralding a Council; and Fr Argenti concluded thus:

May I express the wish or rather the prayer that:

Through the participation in the World Council by all the Christian Churches and in particular by the very ancient and venerable Church of Rome our elder sister and all the Holy Churches in communion with her

Through the deeper growth in Christ of all the member churches, present and future

15

Through the action of the Holy Spirit, the Spirit of Truth, the unifying Spirit,

if not the 5th or 6th Assembly of the World Council of Churches, then at least the nth Assembly will be recognized by the whole Christian people as the Eighth True Ecumenical Council of the One Holy Catholic and Apostolic Church of Christ.

This was a deeply Orthodox statement of a kind which many other Christians could largely make their own, with gratitude. In a quite different but strikingly complementary way, Professor John Deschner (Professor of Theology at Southern Methodist University, USA) spoke of "visible unity as conciliar fellowship".

Dr Deschner began by analysing the successive ecumenical attempts to describe the unity we seek as local (New Delhi), diversified (Uppsala), and a sign of coming human unity (Uppsala), and the current attempt in the emphasis on "conciliar fellowship" to do more justice to the universal aspect.

A number of questions arise, which Dr Deschner discussed not abstractly but by means of an examination of the Council at Jerusalem reported in Acts 15 and Galatians 2. He noted six points:

1. That meeting was not routine, but called to deal with an emergency; and in the emergency local churches with different views reached out towards one another.

2. The delegates of Antioch are recognized *and welcomed* at Jerusalem as representatives of a controversial sister church.

3. Nothing is said about the Eucharist, but "surely this Council's central act was an offering of this controversy to God in common worship, else how could they write of their decisions that 'It seems good to the Holy Spirit and to us'?"

4. There is very frank debate; there is silence and listening; and a clarifying decision. Paul has stood for a free mission, Peter for unity, and James for God's will to have both.

5. There is a real decision, expressed in the right hand of fellowship and in the sending of people as well as a document to Antioch. There will be difference and even controversy but it is not to divide the Church.

6. There was no "problem of communication". The churches needed the meeting and heard its results with joy.

Between us and that vision of the conciliar fellowship, said Dr Deschner, lie these things: local churches really striving to express afresh the common faith; a desire to reach out in need to one another; a true recognition and welcoming of one another's representatives; a common Eucharist; true debate leading to a common bond and action of witness; a

16

welcome of this witness in each local church as the expression of the Spirit and the mind of the whole.

"That is a vision of visible unity worth praying for here, together." And after a hymn we dedicated ourselves anew:

In gratitude for the love of Christ
We dedicate ourselves anew to work for unity
In the life of the Church Universal and for the sake of all humanity
Trusting in the guidance of the Holy Spirit
Who gives us unity within the bonds of peace.

THAT THE WORLD MAY BELIEVE

The fifth plenary presentation followed naturally on the other half of the text. In "That the world may believe", after a hymn and prayer, Bishop Mortimer Arias (Methodist, Bolivia) gave a major address to which Ms R. Andriamanjato (Reformed, Madagascar), Archbishop Samuel Carter (Roman Catholic, Jamaica), and Dr John Stott (Anglican, UK) made responses.

Dr Arias recalled the missionary origins of the Ecumenical Movement, and confessed that we have not always been faithful to this calling or to the priorities it implies, though he also insisted that we could "acclaim and affirm the missionary and evangelistic potential" of the programmes of the WCC. "Everything the Church does has an evangelical dimension" but often the evangelical dimension is not translated with evangelistic intention; the implicit often does not become explicit.

Dr Arias therefore proposed a "holistic" approach—the whole gospel for the whole man for the whole world, rejecting equally a reduction of evangelism to "saving souls" and of the gospel to a programme of service or social action. Social justice, personal salvation, cultural affirmation, and church growth are all integral parts of God's saving acts.

Evangelism, then, must be integral in content as well as in form, in the inseparable union of word and action; and it must be contextual. There are times and places where we must hold our tongues and let our witness speak through our presence and action, but such an extreme situation must not be considered normal or normative. There comes a moment when we must name the Name and proclaim the Word. There may also come times and places where we are forced to recognize that those whom we meet have more of Christ in them than we who speak in his Name: all that is missing is the naming of the Name. The gospel cannot be authentic unless it is faithful both to the Scriptures and to real people in real contexts. Evangelism is inescapably vulnerable—"a beggar telling another beggar where both could find bread" (D. T. Niles)—and most difficult where we are best known, at home. But churches which have lost the will to evangelize cannot remain in that state; and renewal comes not before mission but in mission.

Evangelism is local: its medium is the Christian and the Christian community. Evangelism is free: it goes from person to person, from community to community. This is not so much a case of John Wesley's "The world is my parish" but "My parish is the world". Mission is centrifugal, begins in a given place, and seeks the ends of the earth. Yet God has his time which is not our time, and there are today masses of human beings who are inaccessible to the missionary work of the rest of the world. But it remains a basic right of every human being to know God's purpose for his life revealed in Jesus Christ. We are sustained in the evangelistic task not only by the horror of a world without Christ, or by gratitude, but above all by the all-powerful intercession of him who prays "That they all may be one that the world may believe".

In responding Archbishop Samuel Carter expressed his general and cordial agreement with Dr Arias' address and illustrated it from a wealth of recent Roman Catholic experience and reflections and especially the meeting of the Synod of Bishops on "Evangelization".

Ms Andriamanjato regretted that Dr Arias had not included in his list of WCC missionary activity its labours for the improvement of the status of women in church and society or dwelt on the failure of the Church to live up to the words of St Paul to the Galatians that in Christ there is neither male nor female. She considered further that the credibility of the gospel in Africa required a much more determined attack on the manifold evils of racism and colonialism; and that a "moratorium" in missionary work in Africa should be regarded by the sister churches, formerly called the giving churches, not as a hostile act but as an appeal to each of them to break with tradition and bear witness to Christ the Liberator in each country on a new basis, and become the instruments through which Christ makes all things new. Finally, Ms Andriamanjato believed that it was not Christian disunity but the failure of the Church to bring deliverance to the captives that was the most serious obstacle to mission.

It was unfortunate that time allowed neither for Dr John Stott to give the whole of his response nor for the discussion which his firm but courteous statement would have provoked.

Dr Stott, while in agreement with much that Dr Arias had said, believed that the WCC needed to recover five things:

1. A recognition of the lostness of man. According to the New Testament, men and women are not "anonymous Christians" already in Christ and only needing to be told so. They are "dead in their trespasses and sins". Universalism is a deadly enemy of evangelism.

2. Confidence in the truth, relevance, and power of the gospel of God.

18

3. Conviction about the uniqueness of Jesus Christ. Of course there is truth in other religions and ideologies. But Paul's argument in Romans is not that this knowledge of God saves men but that they are without excuse because they suppress it.

4. A sense of urgency about evangelism which might begin by trying to agree on vocabulary. It seemed to Dr Stott that mission is the comprehensive word to include both socio-political action and evangelism. The Lausanne Covenant drew clear distinctions not only between evangelism and social action, but also between salvation and political liberation. Dr Stott was neither urging the WCC to drop its social and political concerns nor to "administer a fresh dose of opium to the oppressed" but to be truly concerned with the *total* demands of justice and love and with the *fullness* of God's freedom.

5. A personal experience of Jesus Christ: the greatest of all obstacles to evangelism today is the poverty of our own spiritual experience.

He ended: "We are all conscious, I think, of the wide gap of confidence and credibility which exists today between ecumenical leaders and evangelicals, between Geneva and Lausanne. What can be done about this gap?

"Ecumenical leaders genuinely question whether evangelicals have a heartfelt commitment to social action. We evangelicals say that we have, but I personally recognize that we have got to supply more evidence that we have. On the other hand, evangelicals question whether the WCC has a heartfelt commitment to world-wide evangelism. They say they have, but I beg this Assembly to supply more evidence that this is so."

WOMEN IN A CHANGING WORLD

The next plenary presentation on Friday, 28 November, ran into even more serious problems of time—and, in fact, exceeded its allotted time by an hour or so. But, if the Assembly became somewhat inattentive at one point, the situation was saved by Dr Sylvia Talbot's observation that their concerns had "filled up and spilled over" the too strait limits of space allotted.

In introducing "Women in a changing world", Mrs Takeda Cho (President), presiding, traced the history of the WCC's concern and recalled some of the women who had contributed to its work; but she noted all the same that "In the life of the WCC, this is the first time that a plenary has been held in which women can speak clearly, fully, and radically out of our concrete situations to the whole Assembly. In this sense, this plenary has great significance." The occasion was historic and not an isolated event to appease a particular group. With great insight, Mrs Takeda Cho quoted a prayer of Reinhold Niebuhr, before she asked Dr Talbot to take over:

O God,
Give us serenity to accept what cannot be changed;
Courage to change what should be changed;
And wisdom to distinguish the one from the other.

Dr Talbot greeted the Assembly in Swahili and then briefly described the consultation in June 1974 in Berlin on "Sexism in the '70s" in which 160 women from forty-nine countries had explored together their experience of discrimination in society and church, and their longing to share their alienation and to experience the promise of a new humanity in Christ.

She then introduced the three women who were to speak about what it meant to be a woman in their own circumstances. Ms Dorothy Mc-Mahon, a teacher active in the Australian Council of Churches and the Methodist Church, in the Australian Labour Party and in Mothers and Others for Peace, examined her identity, asking whether she was defined by her relationships, by what she did, by other people's ideas of what a woman is like, by class, race, and national background, and sorrowfully confessed: "I have not been able to find in the Church enough ways to share the pain and confusion of that struggle, nor enough celebration to express the hope I feel as I go through the resurrection process of finding myself."

Ms Teny Simonian, an Armenian social scientist on the staff of the Near East Council of Churches, analysed the struggle for women's rights in its social context, as the product of social change, and its impact on our institutions as society evolves from the agrarian to the industrial, and a conflict develops between the role of women within the family and their new roles in economic and academic and other institutions. "The issue is born of a combination of challenged male ego and societal affluence. It is not arbitrary, and I look to the future with calm determination."

Dr Julia Ojiambo, M.P., of Kenya, spoke as a woman who operates in a man's world as a politician. (She is a nutritionist who is now Assistant Minister of Housing and Social Services.) Down to earth and pragmatic, denying that there was anything special about being both politician and homemaker, she also had found the influence of social change. "As a woman politician, one surprising fact is that not only am I expected to listen to various problems of people as men do, but I am also called upon in my constituency to act as an elder, a role which, traditionally, was not a woman's. This is in itself a clear indication of the acceptance of new forms and values. . . . It is a role I personally perform with great respect and satisfaction, despite the fact that it is a new challenge to the Kenya female."

There followed a panel in which three women spoke less personally and more analytically. Ms Prakai Nontawassee, Principal of the Thailand Theological Seminary, spoke of the role of the Church in a culture where the traditional position of women is summed up in the proverb, "Men are the front legs of the elephant and women are the back legs"—which rules out the need for women to have a conscience, and therefore sterilizes their minds and obstructs their self-understanding. Men and women in the Church, in contrast, should confront each other, discuss each other's strong and weak points, and become a "socialization model" for the society as a whole. "The role of women in my country is to heighten the awareness of the dignity of being born as women in the image of God in a world of men."

Dr Mrs Justice Annie R. Jiagge, a member since 1969 of the Supreme Court of Appeal in Ghana, and for some years a leading member of the UN Commission on the Status of Women, spoke at somewhat greater length and with great authority on the actual disabilities under which women labour in many societies—in employment, marriage law, property law, and so on—a sad catalogue of which men, for the most part, are unaware. She then moved on to demonstrate the connection between the status of women and the problems of development and over-population. ". . . whenever women are advanced and a large number have economic pursuits outside the home, the population growth rate drops with or without incentives. But wherever women are illiterate, ignorant, house-bound, and dependent on men, the growth rate increases even with the best possible incentives for a decrease." There is required, therefore, a new policy in favour of higher education and better jobs for women; and this requires a change in attitudes—the re-education of public opinion.

Lastly, Dr Una Kroll (UK) spoke with great insight and compassion of the social and psychological factors which prevent men and women from relating to each other as partners, and of the roles of behavioural conditioning, and of plain ignorance and superstition, and of fear. "We fear that if the space between men and women becomes too narrow, we shall lose some of the 'mystery' that clothes the other and makes them so attractive. . . . But if we prevent either men or women from following their vocations for fear they might lose their distinctiveness, we fail to trust God and become prisoners of fear and perpetrators of grave injustice."

Finally, Dr Kroll analysed the malign influence in this sphere of the seven deadly sins of pride, covetousness, lust, anger, greed, envy, and sloth.

The panel was followed by a ten-minute animated film, made in America for the WCC, which in a series of images traced the subjection of women, their revolt, and the tentative feeling out towards one another of the two sexes in hope of a new way to be. The presentation ended with a service of celebration entitled "Mary's story and ours".

FROM THE SHACKLES OF DOMINATION AND OPPRESSION

The seventh plenary presentation was a major address by the Hon. Michael Manley, Prime Minister of Jamaica since 1972. A "humanist by instinct, an egalitarian in social philosophy, a Christian by faith, a democratic socialist by political commitment, and finally a member and spokesman of the Third World by force of circumstance and by active involvement", Mr Manley began by analysing the way the need for social order produces societies sometimes based on domination rather than consensual authority, and how these turn to imperialism; and then turned to a full-scale attack on capitalism.

"At no point in history has an economic system reflected the process of domination in political, social, psychological, and ultimately even in philosophical terms more completely than under capitalism." Within that system the workers have struggled through the Trade Union movement to establish minimum conditions for survival; and others have been so brutalized as to accept charity with gratitude rather than ask how the need for charity arose in the first place. The notion has arisen that man exists to serve private property and that the law exists to protect "that morally inverted relationship". Capitalism has divided society into permanent categories of master and servant, proprietor and propertyless. "If capitalism was the engine that lifted man to new levels of economic and technological progress it was equally the burial ground of his moral integrity." But the extreme reaction to the total state ownership and control and the bureaucratic centralism it promotes does not much help. "These new models often involve a new form of oppression to maintain what is in reality state capitalism."

We must seek, therefore, to establish economic orders which are based on public participation and democratic consent; in our economic enterprises there should be workers and no masters; the creation of a society free of all entrenched privilege. We must seek a total freedom, including the freedom to explore one's relationship to the universe and walk the rocky road of personal salvation—and "the agnostic must be left secure in his right to doubt". Internationally, the current struggle for a new international economic order is a "critical part of the total process of liberation".

Churches have a clear duty to make common cause with the Third World in the search for a new world order. Christendom cannot cease from struggle until outrages that violate our faith are ended. The Third World needs to be clear about its moral foundations and set its own house in order by tackling the internal injustices among its members.

"I am convinced, therefore, that whereas the churches must first be concerned with Christian witness as it relates to personal salvation, they have also an historical mission to assist in the definition, validation, and articulation of just political, economic, and social objectives"; and the "men of God" ought to equip themselves to help the political leader renew his moral insights.

Mr Manley ended his address with an eloquent appeal for action to liberate the victims of oppression now; and was greeted with a prolonged standing ovation.

In the short discussion that followed there was some critical reaction to Mr Manley's own critical use of Marxist ideas. The Reverend R. Holloway (Episcopal Church in Scotland), a democratic socialist born in a poor working-class home, thought there had been "a quiet revolution" in the West, but that there is alienation on the factory floor both in Russia and in Glasgow. We must address ourselves to a total renewal. Dr N. Benedyktowicz (Methodist, Poland) said that we could co-operate with radical revolutionary forces only in some situations. Mr G. Bebawi (Coptic Orthodox, Egypt) and Professor J. Mohapeloa (Lesotho Evangelical Church) were both concerned with the relations between the struggle against racism and other struggles for justice. Canon Burgess Carr (All Africa Conference of Churches) spoke of being often driven to despair by the lack of democratic consensus in so many of the independent African states, and by the fact that the AACC is responsible for the care of more than a million refugees. How can we be a moral force? he asked.

Replying, Mr Manley said that he thought it essential to work for social control by way of co-operatives, land control, and so on: workers' participation in decisions is essential. In response to Canon Burgess Carr, he said that he did not underestimate the bleak side, but "Do not be ashamed. It's not much different in other parts of the world. We must make a political climate in which bad leadership is impossible."

In thanking the Prime Minister, Dr Payne said, "You have come very quickly into a warm relationship with this Assembly. We pray that God's blessing rest upon Jamaica and the part that the Caribbean may in the future play in the cause of justice."

CREATION, TECHNOLOGY, AND HUMAN SURVIVAL

Professor Charles Birch of Sydney University began by relating his theme to the Assembly's proximity to what seems to be the cradle of human life in Kenya. His subtitle was "Called to replenish the earth", and after a chillingly detailed analysis of the threats to human survival, whose total impact is so serious that there is demanded the positive "de-development" of the rich developed world, he asked what positively we could do, for if we cannot permit technology to have its head, we cannot do without it. Our goal, therefore, must be a just and sustainable society; and this demands a fundamental change of heart and mind about humankind's relation to nature.

"If", said Dr Birch in conclusion, "we are to break the poverty barrier for almost two-thirds of the earth's people, if we are to continue to inhabit the earth, there has to be a revolution in the relationship of human beings to one another. The churches of the world have now to choose whether or not they become part of that revolution." (Prolonged applause.)

Dr Kosuke Koyama (University of Otago, New Zealand) in response analysed with reflective spirituality the implications of technology for civilization, especially that "wounding and healing" Western civilization with its dynamic spirit of reorganization to which all peoples everywhere have to react; for the theological task of understanding what speed of change is tolerable; and for the cultural task of replacing a technocratic society which only lifts up its eyes to the hills to mine them for some ore with an attitude which looks for refreshing replenishment.

Metropolitan Paulos Gregorios drew a sharp distinction between the Limits to Growth People (LGPs) and the Technological Optimism People (TOPs). They could, however, agree to put their best minds and efforts together to control the four elements of population explosion, resource depletion, environmental deterioration, and nuclear war. But success will depend on a new economics and a new science and technology; and these can only grow in a climate of thought and life which takes seriously the deep religious questions about our relationships with the Transcendent, with one another, and with nature. "There *is* balm in Gilead, and the Physician is waiting for us."

4. HOW THE ASSEMBLY WORKED

The bony structure of the Assembly can be described in some such fashion as the following. Most of the first week was spent in two ways. One of these was in plenary session where the main theme of the Assembly, "Jesus Christ frees and unites", together with the record of the past seven years and some reflections upon it were all fed into the minds, hearts, and imaginations of participants. The other was in small (8-15 people) work groups.

By the Thursday when the Committees began and the Friday when the Sections began, participants had received an input of a fairly sizeable and varied sort and had had a chance of absorbing it and reflecting upon it in a group small enough for confidence and friendship to grow. The theory was that they would then be ready to start to think about it in depth in the Sections and to begin to grapple with the practical policy questions in the Committees.

The theory was not, of course, fully reflected in what happened. The presentations were varied in style and relied far less exclusively on a succession of long addresses or papers. Even so, some objected to the number of solid addresses they were expected to assimilate. It is difficult, however, to see how a large heterogeneous body would be able to do anything much more than exchange experiences and (almost certainly) verbal fire from entrenched positions, if it was not presented with a sizeable bloc of common material to digest and react to. Most of us are

24

familiar in our own churches with debate which because there is no input amounts to little more than the well- or ill-tempered exchange of prejudices.

THE WORK GROUPS

Insofar as the Work Groups succeeded, they undoubtedly helped to contribute to the cheerful and human atmosphere, and the firm but civilized way in which contentious issues were generally handled. (The self-service arrangements for lunch, with tents provided for shelter from sun or rain, also helped.) Not all Work Groups were a success; and not all participants went to them. It is impossible to give a general account, so I content myself with a summary account of the one I went to. It included an Armenian bishop from London, an Australian university teacher, an Anglican bishop from Uganda, a senior Kenyan Salvation Army officer, an Indonesian medical practitioner, an American Presbyterian pastor (white), a water filtration engineer from Detroit (black), a leader of the Women's Guild in the Church of Scotland, a Swedish missionary bishop in Central India, a Roman Catholic priest-journalist from Belgium, and some others who attended irregularly. I think that I was the only regular who had been to an Assembly before.

In the six sessions in the first week we did some serious Bible study on Mark 9, and also on Mark 8, Galatians 2, and other passages. We also had some sharp and thoughtful exchanges on dialogue with other religions and the uniqueness of Christ; on racism; on oppression, rebellion, and violence; and on the relation of the WCC to the member churches. In the process we learned a good deal about one another and through one another about the world. We were about ready for some more sustained thought in our Sections.

It is also fair to say that about this time one becomes aware that the operators were beginning to make their dispositions. This can be discreditable, as when staff move to protect entrenched positions or delegates come with preconceived plans for which they intend by one means or another to secure support. But some activity of this kind is inevitable if a large body is ever to *do* anything; and in a community of this kind there is a large enough majority who are competent, alert, and charitable to keep sin and its consequences down to tolerable levels. The daily publication for the Assembly of *Target*, the local Christian weekly, also helped. In fact, it was all a sign that we were ready to get down to business. It was already noticeable that "participants" were for the most part keen to participate. For example, in addition to those who were heard, twenty-six others sent up their names to speak in the debate after Dr Robert McAfee Brown, and thirty-six in the debate after the General Secretary's report and the Finance Report.

The Work Groups were for most participants probably the most satisfying item in their experience of the Assembly. They continued at intervals till near the end; some at least of those who were not involved in committees, or drafting section reports, continued to meet with a work group which had by now become a group of friends. The two workshops on youth and on spirituality also became continuing fellowships.

THE SECTIONS CONSIDERED

The work of the Sections stands or falls by the Reports that are printed later in this book together with a short account of the plenary sessions debate upon them. They embody the results of the Assembly's corporate thought upon the six themes entrusted to them; and in their second report each section offered some practical recommendations upon the basis of its statement of principle.

The reception accorded to the drafts of the Section Reports when they came before the plenary sessions is briefly noted before each Section Report later in this volume. I venture here a few comments, of which the first is that there is a certain lack of clarity about the purpose of the Sections.

In consultations of more or less expert people, Section discussions are a useful way of finding out what qualified people think about a subject, and their reports can be useful expressions both of a consensus and of the remaining differences. They are less useful when the membership is widely representative and difficult new ideas are not in prospect. Nor was the connection between the Sections and the Work Groups sufficiently clear. At the same time, the compulsion to try to say something together is a valuable discipline. This is a question for the staff and the Central Committee to think about—and the churches too. Do the churches know (or care?) what they are letting their delegates in for?

On the Section Reports themselves I would make only the following observations. Section 1 represents part of the mind of the Assembly on the question which Dr M. M. Thomas raised right at the beginning—the modern concept of evangelism. Section 2 answers the question "Is Faith and Order dead?" with a firm "No", and outlines the agenda for the next period. Both this and the Report of Section 3 should be useful in local situations which are multi-denominational and multi-racial.

The reception accorded to Section 3 needs some interpretation. I take the meaning of the critical reception of the first report to be this: the Assembly knew that within and outside the member churches people were asking if the WCC is sound on the gospel; the Assembly was affirming its central Christian orthodoxy. In the second debate it was saying: We hold the faith, but we are not narrow-minded about it or contemptuous of others.

There was also beginning to surface a feeling that churches for which dialogue was not a real need were churches in which there was no real meeting with the outside world. If Indian churches cannot avoid a dialogue with Hinduism or Sri Lankan churches with Buddhism, what is the state of North Atlantic churches who seem to notice neither atheistic existentialism nor secular humanism nor Marxism? They can no doubt do revival meetings among lapsed or slack Christians, but is genuine *evangelism* possible to them? The Reports of Sections 5 and 6 need to be studied in connection with the debates on related public affairs in the reports of Policy Reference Committee III (pp. 161ff.). I take them to mean fundamentally that the Assembly was saying quite firmly that it intended to stand behind the Uppsala positions and the actions since then: there was, for instance, no weakening on the issues of the Programme to Combat Racism and the Special Fund. But the Assembly was also saying that it wanted to understand this commitment to action on behalf of the weak and oppressed in a more deeply evangelical way.

A related point arises out of the public affairs debates. The attentive reader will observe that on several occasions an attempt was made by some third party to gloss over a tricky situation and protect those involved from critical scrutiny. She or he will also observe that this attempt was resisted by the Assembly as a whole, but if those concerned (who might really be at serious risk) asked the Assembly to be cautious, it was ready to do as asked. This was an Assembly which recognized that the gospel does, as our Lord said, put us all at risk; but that it is the responsibility of Christians in each situation to determine their own course of action, listening to the Spirit in the whole Body.

The *Sections* in this respect overlapped somewhat with the *Hearings*.

THE HEARINGS

In former Assemblies each department of the World Council had been examined by a Committee, whose report was presented to and adopted by the whole Assembly; and every delegate was in a Committee as well as a Section. The Structure Committee was persuaded that this involved an intolerable burden of committee work on participants without much compensation in the form of control by the member churches through the Assembly of the actual programmes of the WCC, since it was not easy in six to eight meetings for people coming fresh to the subject to acquire a sufficient mastery of the material.

At Nairobi, therefore, a series of four Hearings was arranged, one on each of the Programme Units of the Council (I Faith and Witness; II Justice and Service; III Education and Renewal) and one on the General Secretariat and the parts of the structure directly related to it. These provided an opportunity for those interested to make points or ask questions.

The Hearings had five sessions. The discussions in the earlier sessions seem generally to have been appreciated. But when it came in the later sessions to formulating priorities for the consideration of the Programme Guidelines Committee, there was a certain tendency to express enthusiasm for all the Council's existing work and more besides, and to recoil from the distasteful task of selecting what was held to be of the first priority—distasteful because it implies the corollary that other work can at a pinch be discontinued. This embarrassment was at its most acute during discussions on the future of the Ecumenical Institute at Bossey.

It therefore seemed altogether too likely that the responsibility would be handed to the Programme Guidelines Committee and the Finance Committee (which might be held to give them too much power) and even possible that they and the Assembly would in time shuffle off the responsibility on to the Central Committee. It is neither surprising nor shameful that Christian bodies should come with such reluctance to difficult decisions when decision means, in fact, the end of activity and employment which one's fellow-Christians have loved. (And yet, on the other hand, those parables about the hard choice and clear decisions remain in the Gospels.)

For the most part the Hearings did not produce recommendations so much as a considerable body of ideas and reactions. They were set up to enable people to say their piece rather than to arrange the pieces once said in order of priority. A very large mass of records of the proceedings of the Hearings will be considered by the Central Committee. A 21-page summary report of the Hearings was attached as an appendix to the Report of the Programme Guidelines Committee, and is reprinted in this volume as Appendix 10.

It has, I think, to be said that the problem of how an Assembly can control the actual work of the World Council of Churches has not yet been solved; and it may in fact be insoluble. The ordinary delegate found himself participating in a small work group and in plenary session, and (in between the large and the very small) at an intermediate level in a Section, a Hearing, and (for some) a Committee. It may be that a further simplification is required at this intermediate level. Certainly a good deal of the matter in the summary Report of the Hearings overlaps with the recommendations in the second parts of the Sections.

There are, however, three themes that recurred again and again in this context or that. The first of these is the overmastering importance of deepening and improving the quality of relationship between the WCC and its member churches (remembering, however, that these member churches are infinitely more varied in their gifts and needs than any one of them finds it easy to recognize!). The second is the desirability of simplifying the budget structure of the WCC's finances; the third is the importance of serious commitment (which need not and indeed should not be uncritical) to the ecumenical task on the part both of individuals who get involved and the local churches to which they belong. It will be perceived that these three points are connected.

Since the world exists, and the Christian family exists around the world, the WCC is a necessity; and if it did not exist, it or something very like it would have to be invented. Since it is necessary, it has to be worked at and paid for, even in times when most churches are short of resources in money and people.

The consequences of these plain necessities will have to be worked out by the Central Committee; and that the Central Committee should have in addition to its Finance Committee a permanent Review Committee was one of the brighter practical ideas to be thrown up at Nairobi. All the same the Central Committee's task is formidable.

THE COMMITTEES

By the second Friday evening (5 December) the Sections had all submitted their first reports to the Assembly, the Hearings were over, and the Committees were well under way.

The Committees were as follows:

The *Programme Guidelines Committee*, whose work has already been indicated.

The *Finance Committee*.

The *Nominations Committee*, charged with nominating the new Presidents and Central Committee.

Three Policy Reference Committees:

1. dealing with the reports of the Moderator and the General Secretary, and the revision of the Constitutions and Rules of the WCC;

2. dealing with relationships—new member churches, relationships with the Roman Catholic Church and the World Confessional Families, and the like;

3. dealing with public affairs.

The Assembly's handling of the work of these Committees is reported in "The Business of the Assembly" and "The Future of the World Council of Churches".

There were also a *Credentials Committee* (dealing with a few uncertainties about representation); a Committee to try to keep track of the Assembly's thinking and feeling and distil from it a *Message* to the Churches; and Committees on *Worship, Press, and Broadcasting*, and *Assembly Business*, whose essential work was reflected rather in the life of the Assembly than directly in the form of reports.

By 5 December people involved in these Committees could see clearly their deadline approaching, and the tempo quickened somewhat.

29

NO OVERMASTERING ISSUE?

At the same time, no overwhelmingly important issue, new or old, had emerged to preoccupy the Assembly and polarize its passions. Those who looked for excitement did not find it; those who longed for an enemy to fight looked in vain.

There were indeed a number of contentious issues. A major one was susceptible of many descriptions: Evangelicals versus Ecumenicals, the "vertical" versus the "horizontal" dimensions in Christian discipleship; Evangelism or Social Action; Prayer or Politics; Lausanne or Bangkok; Dialogue and the Uniqueness of Christ. It cropped up all over the place.

Another was about Human Rights. An appeal for support by the WCC had been received from two Soviet dissidents, circulated, and widely discussed. Officially the question formed part of the business of Section 5; unofficially it ramified everywhere; not least into consideration of the work of the Nominations Committee.

But neither on these nor on other questions did the passionate confrontations many expected take place. The Assembly did not polarize between the Third World and the North Atlantic or between East and West. Insofar as it had after a fortnight polarized at all it had become a case of the rest against the management (sometimes confused with the different question of the member churches against the WCC establishment). This came out in the loud and prolonged applause that greeted a proposal from a UK delegate that a paragraph in a Section criticizing the structures of the churches should include a like criticism of the structures of the WCC. When the General Secretary spoke in reply and indeed rebuttal, a surprising number of people applauded him; and some, on their own admission, were on both sides of that encounter.

Shrewd and experienced observers were puzzled. Was it that we knew that our divisions, deep and tragic as they are, must yet be held in the one Body, and therefore that though the struggle for truth and justice was deadly serious, stridency and violence were out of place? Were we giving ourselves to the truth in love? That would be a splendid thing, presaged by much in the Assembly from the play *Muntu* onward. There was of course another possibility—that we had been overcome by one of the deadly sins: sloth.

And so we came to the last weekend—spent in frantic drafting or committee meeting if you were one of the much-criticized elite, or (if you were not) with the churches of Nairobi, or on a short "safari" (there's a game park just on the outskirts of the city), or with friends.

But before we get to the climax of the final day, there is one further element to sketch in—the milieu in which we met.

30

5. THE MILIEU

Kenya and Nairobi were important to the Assembly. This has been indicated more than once in this account, and what has been said must suffice. But the Kenyatta Conference Centre itself was full of varied attractions. There were snack bars and restaurants; a bank, a post office, and various shops and stalls; some of these were set up by church bodies and sold the attractive wares that were provided by the social work of the churches and the community at large. Upstairs, there was in the Delegates' Lounge a striking paraphrase-with-pictures of the Ten Commandments. Other exhibits illustrated the Programme to Combat Racism, the United Bible Societies, the All Africa Conference of Churches, or Radio Voice of the Gospel. "Media Walk" ("pop in during gaps in the official programme") was an imaginative and varied exercise in audio-visual presentations of many themes. The East African Christian weekly *Target* became a daily and offered an unofficial commentary on the Assembly's proceedings and a forum for criticism of them. So—more sharply—did a stretch of notice-board on which a Dutch believer in personal encounter and his Mexican cartoonist colleague offered a running and pungent critique of the WCC ecclesiastical system; and where these led many others followed. As well, then, as its culture, the Assembly had also its counter-culture. There was also a multitude of subsidiary meetings—for Anglicans or Orthodox, for Americans or Germans, for alumni of a particular university or seminary, for people interested in this or that—and musical events of all sorts. And with a lengthy lunch break and the late evening free, there was time for friendship.

This description of the milieu and the counter-culture has been perhaps too cursory. Let me expand it by saying a little more about music and the arts, about *Target*, and about the counter-culture.

MUSIC AND THE ARTS

The Assembly's life was greatly enriched by the presence, for part of the time, of Donald Swann and David Amram (the first "composer in residence" of the New York Philharmonic Orchestra) and especially of the Peter Janssens Song Orchestra. They contributed to the worship of the Assembly and also gave concerts and sparked off more informal occasions. Participation in the Spirituality Workshop along with advisers such as Fred Kaan and Doreen Potter and Shona Mactavish led to the development during the life of the Assembly and from among the participants of a dance group, the writing of a new song used in the closing Service, and the setting to music by Peter Janssens of the litany "Break down the walls that separate us and unite us in a single body."

31

TARGET

Target for its part printed most of the letter from two Russian dissidents which had a considerable effect on the life of the Assembly. It provided a forum for people who wanted to give expression to their frustrations, and performed the usual journalistic liturgy of sticking pins into the establishment. It also on one happy day cheered up the *cognoscenti* with such offerings to a revised ecumenical lexicon as the following:

Parameter: an instrument carried in the right hand by WCC staff members to dig out grass roots in the ecumenical centre.

Ecclesiology: finding out what a church is, as in the sentence "the eschatological perspective introduces a revolution in comparative ecclesiology", i.e., "Jesus is coming so let's get together".

COUNTER-CULTURES

There were not one but two counter-cultures. One consisted of those who stayed firmly within their national and confessional tradition and took some care to avoid being affected by the Assembly experience, except negatively. The other sought to participate more directly; and its methods were the wall-newspaper and the "Red Strippers"—participants who had accepted an invitation to add a red strip to their Assembly badge and who met informally to be, as they put it, open to one another, coming out from behind the masks imposed on the person by the dehumanizing mass of words and paper and rigid structures. The wall-newspaper contained, day by day, many admirable cartoons and pointed bits of satire. There was, however, as time went on a certain predictability about the content of these protests, which were mostly directed against metropolitans, bishops, general secretaries, and other big shots. I was myself therefore moved to scrawl "Why not take the mickey for a change out of young lay persons?" Nor do I believe that "personal encounter" can always take the place of hard work and disciplined thought—at any rate in this vale of tears and soul-making.

STEWARDS

The elderly crack above against the young should be balanced by a reference to the stewards. These were 180 stewards, and a large number laboured away with long hours and (generally) good humour, not merely to see people into the right place and keep them out of the wrong one, but above all to distribute the documents to the delegates, making sure that each got what was needed and in the preferred language. Many an ecumenical leader has begun his career as a steward. It was a moving moment when in the final session they crowded on to or about the platform and one saw the face of the Ecumenical Movement of the future. But more: it was an eschatological vision of the reversal of Babel by the happy collaboration of the nations in bringing their varied glories into the Kingdom.

CONFUSION OF TONGUES

And so to Babel. The World Council had initially three "official languages"—English, French, and German; to these were added *de facto* Russian and Spanish. At Nairobi there was also some interpretation into Portuguese and Swahili; and in worship many more languages were used. There is of course no final solution while Babel endures. But it is now time for a serious reconsideration of WCC language policy—and this was well ventilated in one of the Hearings.

6. THE CLOSING SERVICE

The Closing Service of Advent and Farewell was called "He came into the world to free and unite". The gap before it began was occupied by a hymn sing in which under the leadership of the Peter Janssens Song Orchestra we practised the hymns. The Service itself began with the singing by an Orthodox choir of an Introit of Praise and the ancient evening hymn *Phos Hilaron*, which occurs in some English hymn books in a different version beginning "Hail, Gladdening Light". (In passing, it may be remarked that biblical words and Orthodox song and the contemporary hymns and prayers fitted together surprisingly well; and that the Assembly was remarkable for the absence of the classical "preaching service" that has been the staple of Protestant worship for four centuries. What does that mean?)

Then we moved into a Call to Worship: the first verses of Hebrews read in Swahili, a new Litany of Liberation, the Advent Collect (in Portuguese), and the hymn "O Come, O Come, Emmanuel". The Scripture lessons were read: Isaiah 42.1-9 (in Hebrew), the Magnificat (in English), Titus 2.11-15 and 3.3-8a (in Latin), and the Gospel (Luke 2.25-40, in Greek) preceded by a modern Christmas hymn written and composed in Germany in the Nazi period.

There followed a Syrian Orthodox Affirmation of Faith and a Musical Offering of African music by a local choir, during which a collection amounting to Shs.K. 22,000 was taken for the poor and handicapped of Nairobi and the neighbourhood. Then there was a period of free prayer and silence, the hymn by Doreen Potter and Fred Kaan, "Help us to accept each other as Christ accepted us", the praying of the three prayers from

33

the Message and the Our Father said each in his or her own tongue (but on these occasions out of an old solidarity I myself always use Chinese).

Then there was another offering, this time the exchange of a tiny Christmas present with people sitting in front and behind, while we sang a new song composed by Fred Kaan and Doreen Potter during the Assembly and on the Assembly theme:

> *Love has come among us!*
> *Christ is on our side.*
> *Lead us into freedom.*
> *Life is high and wide.*
>
> Refrain
> *Free and One make Life.*
> *Love is bread and cup.*
> *One and Free make Sense.*
> (Rhythmical clapping)
> *It all adds up.*
>
> *Jesus, emptied, broken,*
> *makes his people whole,*
> *fills up with his fullness,*
> *helps us fill our role.*
>
> *Christ, triumphant, living,*
> *makes us fall in love*
> *with his world of people,*
> *world of share-believe.*
>
> *God-and-man among us,*
> *Christ is all in all:*
> *love incarnate figures,*
> *freedom rings a bell!*

Then in Korean came an invocation of the Holy Spirit followed by a Litany from *Risk*, "Break down the walls that separate us and unite us in a single body", set to music and interpreted in dance by members of the dance workshop. Singing this haunting refrain and led by the Worship Leaders and Officers, we streamed out into the plaza, which was by now dark, for a Scripture Litany of Departure (read in languages that I do not remember—services are no time for note-taking—but one at least was Polish). And so to the Blessing and for some of us the utter family-and-local-church-familiarity of *Adeste fideles*. The stewards, I am told, sang Christmas carols in the bus all the way home to their hostel on the outskirts, and I can well believe it. I shall not easily forget the sense of community as we moved from the hall to the plaza, both experiencing and

34

expecting the peace of God among men; or the ever-green beauty of *Adeste fideles* in the darkness illuminated by the lights in the great tower block of the beautiful modern African/Scandinavian Conference Centre— serving as a kind of technological Christmas tree.

7. TENTATIVE EVALUATION

There were whirlpools and eddies of all kinds, some highly personal, others quite artificial. On 24 November, for instance, one news agency put out a detailed story about a Third World attempt, led by the All Africa Conference of Churches, to pack the Assembly Committees, which had been foiled by a European/American alliance. This story was totally untrue; and I am told that other games of this kind were played.

More moderately, there were misunderstandings or tendentious accounts of statements by leading figures, including the WCC General Secretary and the Archbishop of Canterbury. Not everyone remembered all the time that words and styles that are effective or at least inoffensive at home can sound and look very odd in an international milieu; and few of us appreciate other people's hang-ups.

National or confessional delegation meetings could also stir things up. And people could be made as weary by the feeling that they weren't getting anywhere as by being told that their church, their country, their theology, their leader, was under attack by some person or persons deficient in Christian love.

Such were the eddies and the whirlpools. But was there a stream and was it going anywhere?

The first thing to say is that to me at least it seemed that in its final days the Assembly found ways at last of declaring its mind on controversial issues and of doing so without stridency or the lust of battle or wanting to go on and on about things. It wanted to be clear and it wanted to be economical of time and words.

A very wise and loving Roman Catholic said this was "An Assembly of Consolidation". There was nothing specially new in the way of ideas. The ideas and causes were still for the most part those that had erupted at Uppsala or earlier. But they were stated less shrilly and more firmly, and they were understood more religiously.

Dr Robert McAfee Brown quoted the Evanston slogan "We intend to stay together". A number of people had come with the hope that the Assembly might be about the world's real needs and divisions but that we might tackle them not by way of a slanging match but as brothers and sisters in a solidarity of guilt and forgiveness. Put together, these thoughts became too long for a slogan; but I believe that such a statement as "We intend to struggle together in love for truth and justice as a community of the pardoned" would not be too far off the mark.

Another shrewd and dear friend rather callously described the Message to me (he knew that I had been a member of the Committee) as "the dampest squib of all time", and thought that the Message should have been "A Call to Maturity".

I am not sure that we got that far; and when we consider how immature is so much of the churches' handling of serious secular matters, it is not surprising. An impossible but thought-provoking phrase cropped up in a debate in the Message Committee (no, not a "a debate"; rather, "a conversation"—there were about a dozen of us). We noted that we were meeting in Advent and that if delegates took the Message home and did anything with it, it would be shortly before Christmas. But we also thought that we were, at our best anyway, awaiting in prayer, thought, and action the descent of the Spirit in power. Someone said, "A sort of Advent, but before Pentecost." "Advent for Pentecost" is an impossible phrase. But, taken with the other phrases in these paragraphs, it's as near as I can get to indicating what was going on.

*   *   *   *   *

An Assembly is an objective phenomenon. The participants came in identifiable categories from identifiable churches and countries to talk and act together for eighteen days in a particular place; and the results, as objectively presented as the limitations of space, time, and intelligence permit, are in this volume.

But in another sense, the Assembly is a subjective experience differing for every participant. Dr M. M. Thomas interrupted the final session from time to time to present a rose to Ms Cynthia Wedel, Ms Takeda Cho, and Ms Pauline Webb and also ("lest I be accused of sexism") to Dr Visser 't Hooft and Dr Eugene Carson Blake, thus illustrating the truth of Dr Potter's remark that he had as Moderator displayed an Indian resistance to the tyranny of Robert's *Rules of Order*. He went on to say: "The Ecumenical Movement is an adventure in the exploration of the will and meaning of Jesus Christ for our time. This is an exciting adventure and nothing is more significant than to participate in an exciting adventure. I must thank you for the opportunity you gave me to serve the Ecumenical Movement. There is a world community of friends which sustains the Ecumenical Movement, the life-full work-groups of the Ecumenical Movement."

My own share in the Movement has been vastly less than M. M.'s; but I would want to make his words my own. It is from this perspective that I have seen and reported the Assembly, and I cannot pretend to an "objectivity" which I do not feel, and believe in fact to be unattainable and undesirable. I love my own church and return to its life of assured graceful worship with peace and joy. But when I seek to discern the signs of these global times and to struggle in faith for the meaning and truth of the gospel, I get more help from the WCC community of friends than from the Church of England. I have friends in other churches who say the same; and in my own church I am most helped by those who allow themselves to be influenced by the Ecumenical Movement.

Let me finally in grateful affection list the other members of that "life-full work-group" who were known as The Minutes and Report Team: David Craig, Shelagh Friedli-Dobell, Marcel Henriet, Victor Koilpillai, Walter Müller-Römheld, Marcelo Perez Rivas, Sheila Ray, Irene Smith, Robbins Strong, Heather Stunt, and Veronica Vaz.

Nairobi
15 December, 1975   DAVID M. PATON

Karibu! African dancers welcome delegates to the Kenyatta Conference Centre, Nairobi.

The Assembly gathers: the choir of the African Israelite Church of Ninevah prepares to lead the Assembly into the meeting hall and to lead the Assembly in the opening worship of the Fifth Assembly.

Muntu, *by Joe de Graft, raised the question: How does humanity recover harmony?*

Nyunyusa, the blind drummer, concluding the worship of the Assembly.

Metropolitan Paulos Gregorios talking with Masai tribesmen at the Conference Centre.

Mee Jomo Kenyatta, President of Kenya, welcoming guests at the garden party in the grounds of State House.

Peter Janssens at the piano with his Song Orchestra practises one of the hymns composed for the Assembly by Doreen Potter (centre).

Women in a changing world: Dorothy McMahon, Teny Simonian, and the Honourable Julia Ojiambo.

Some issues were caricatured by the Mexican cartoonist Zapata.

Dr Sylvia Talbot greets delegates.

Professor Robert McAfee Brown: Who is this Jesus who frees and unites?

John Gatu

The Honourable Michael Manley, Prime Minister of Jamaica.

Philip Potter, the General Secretary of the World Council of Churches.

Plenary Session.

II
The Reports of the Sections

II
The Reports of the Sections

Introduction

The first Section Reports were presented by the Moderators of the Sections in Plenary Deliberative Sessions on 5 and 6 December.

Rule XIV.6 *Deliberative Sessions* states that the Assembly shall sit in deliberative session when the business before it (which specifically includes Section Reports) is "of such theological or general policy nature that ... they ought not to be amended in so large a body as an Assembly". The procedure is therefore that each Section Report is presented and debated. At the conclusion of the debate, the report is either referred back to the Section for reconsideration and revision in the light of the debate, or approved in substance by the Assembly (subject to amendment by the Section's officers and Drafting Committee in the light of the points made in the debate) and commended by it to the churches for study and appropriate action.

At Nairobi, the Section Reports were submitted in two parts. In the first and longer part the Section reported its fundamental thinking; in the second, submitted later, its practical recommendations for action. In this chapter, the reports of the Sections are printed in their *final* form; and to each is prefixed a relatively brief account of the debates in Plenary Session, which usually took place on several different days. Any explicit comment on the debates or interpretation of the underlying issues or tensions is made in the personal account above, and not here. (It must, however, be admitted that an element of interpretation is inevitably involved in the composition of a very brief summary of the debates.)

SECTION I: CONFESSING CHRIST TODAY

In introducing the report, Dr William Lazareth (Lutheran, USA) acknowledged the help received from the reports of the Bangkok Conference on

"Salvation Today" (1973), of the Lausanne Congress on "The Evangelization of the World" (1974), and of the Synod of Bishops of the Roman Catholic Church on "Evangelization in the Modern World". He spoke briefly on the way in which the report moved from a bold confession of Christ alone as Saviour and Lord to emphasize the Confessing of Christ as an Act of Conversion. There are many different cultures in which the one Christ was to be confessed, and in them Christ is confessed especially by the Confessing Community of the Church in its Witness and Life. The report ends with a call to confess the whole gospel to the whole person and the whole world by the whole Church, urgently, intelligently, and imaginatively.

In the discussion Dr John Deschner (USA, Methodist) asked for a fuller definition of the content of the whole gospel, and Dr Manas Buthelezi (Lutheran, South Africa) said that if the gospel was to inspire real hope as distinguished from resignation, more needed to be said. Professor Todor Sabev (Orthodox, Bulgaria) objected to the mentioning in the same sentence of socialistic and capitalistic structures as obscuring the gospel; the Reverend Neil Gilmore (Churches of Christ in Australia) thought there was not enough about the way in which the culture in which the Church lives can trap it into blunting the edge of the gospel; Metropolitan Emilianos Timiadis (Ecumenical Patriarchate) insisted that in spite of cultural conditioning there is a permanent and universal way of reading the Scriptures. Dr Coggan (Church of England) pointed out that though the issue of a "moratorium" on the sending of missionaries and money from one part of the world to aid evangelization in another had not been raised in the report, it had obtained serious and constructive attention in the relevant Hearing.

In replying, Dr Lazareth said that the officers of the Section were in agreement with almost all that had been said and would make the necessary corrections.

The substance of the Report was *approved and commended to the churches for study and appropriate action.*

The Reverend Edwin Taylor (Methodist Church, Bahamas) presented the Second Report of Section I, and moved that the Assembly approve the substance of the recommendations.

The Reverend J.A. Kirk (Anglican, Argentina) moved to delete paragraph 14 and replace it with new wording which would not suggest that there are two classes of Christians. The Reverend Dr Gerhard Linn (United, German Democratic Republic) moved to add to paragraph 21(a) the words "especially with regard to realms of life and social levels neglected so far in their witness and service". Pastor M. Demaude (Reformed, Belgium) moved a rewording of paragraph 19. Bishop Michael (Russian Orthodox) moved that in paragraph 2 the ecclesiastical structures should be mentioned first.

All these amendments were accepted by the Committee.

The Report as amended was unanimously approved by the Assembly.

SECTION I: CONFESSING CHRIST TODAY

Introduction

1. Today's world offers many political lords as well as secular and religious saviours. Nevertheless, as representatives of churches gathered together in the World Council of Churches, we boldly confess Christ alone as Saviour and Lord. We confidently trust in the power of the gospel to free and unite all children of God throughout the world.

2. Amid today's cries of anguish and shouts of oppression, we have been led by the Holy Spirit to confess Jesus Christ as our Divine Confessor. Confident in the Word of God of the holy Scriptures, we confess both our human weakness and our divine strength: "Since then we have a great high priest who has passed through the heavens, Jesus, the Son of God, let us hold fast to our confession" (Heb. 4.14).

3. As our high priest, Christ mediates God's new covenant through both salvation and service. Through the power of the cross, Christ promises God's righteousness and commands true justice. As the royal priesthood, Christians are therefore called to engage in both evangelism and social action. We are commissioned to proclaim the gospel of Christ to the ends of the earth. Simultaneously, we are commanded to struggle to realize God's will for peace, justice, and freedom throughout society.

4. In the same high priestly prayer which bids "that they may be one", Jesus also discloses the distinctive life-style of those who have been set apart to serve in the Church's universal priesthood. While we are "not of" the world, even as he was not of the world, so we are also sent "into" the world, just as he was sent into the world (John 17.16, 18).

5. Christians witness in word and deed to the inbreaking reign of God. We experience the power of the Holy Spirit to confess Christ in a life marked by both suffering and joy. Christ's decisive battle has been won at Easter, and we are baptized into his death that we might walk in newness of life (Rom. 6.4). Yet we must still battle daily against those already dethroned, but not yet destroyed, "principalities and powers" of this rebellious age. The Holy Spirit leads us into all truth, engrafting persons into the Body of Christ in which all things are being restored by God.

6. Our life together is thereby committed to the costly discipleship of the Church's Divine Confessor. His name is above every name: "that at the name of Jesus every knee should bow, in heaven and on earth and under the earth, and every tongue confess that Jesus Christ is Lord, to the glory of God the Father" (Phil. 2.10-11).

CONFESSING CHRIST AS AN ACT OF CONVERSION

The Christ of God

7. Jesus asks: "Who do you say that I am?" At the same time he calls

43

us into his discipleship: "If anyone would come after me, let him deny himself and take up his cross and follow me" (Matt. 16.15, 24). We confess Jesus as the Christ of God, the hope of the world, and commit ourselves to his will. Before we confess him, he confesses us, and in all our ways, he precedes us. We therefore confess with great joy:

8. Jesus Christ is the *one witness of God*, to whom we listen and witness as the incarnate Son of God in life and death (John 14.8). "You are my witnesses. . . . I am the first and the last. There is no God except me" was said to Israel (Isa. 43.8-11). So we are the witnesses of Christ and his Kingdom to all people until the end of the world.

9. Jesus Christ is the *true witness of God* (Rev. 3.14). Into the world of lies, ambiguity, and idolatry, he brings "the truth that liberates" (John 8.32). And as God has sent him, so he sends us.

10. Jesus Christ is the *faithful witness to God* (Rev. 1.5). In his self-offering on the Cross he redeems us from sin and godless powers and reconciles creation with God. Therefore, we shall live for God and shall be saved in God. "There is no condemnation for those who are in Christ Jesus, who walk not after the flesh, but after the Spirit" (Rom. 8.1ff).

11. We believe with certainty in the *presence and guidance of the Holy Spirit*, who proceeds from the Father and bears witness to Christ (John 15.26). Our witness to Christ is made strong in the Holy Spirit and is alive in the confessing community of the Church.

Our Discipleship, His Lordship

12. In our confessing Christ today and in our continuing conversion to the way of Christ, we encourage and support one another.

13. *Confessing Christ and being converted to his discipleship belong inseparably together.* Those who confess Jesus Christ deny themselves, their selfishness and slavery to the godless "principalities and powers", take up their crosses and follow him. Without clear confession of Christ our discipleship cannot be recognized; without costly discipleship people will hesitate to believe our confession. The costs of discipleship—e.g. becoming a stranger among one's own people, being despised because of the gospel, persecuted because of resistance to oppressive powers, and imprisoned because of love for the poor and lost—are bearable in face of the costly love of God, revealed in the passion of Jesus.

14. We *deplore* cheap conversions, without consequences. We *deplore* a superficial gospel-preaching, an empty gospel without a call into personal and communal discipleship. We *confess* our own fear of suffering with Jesus. We are afraid of persecutions, fear, and death. Yet, the more we look upon the crucified Christ alone and trust the power of the Holy Spirit, the more our anxiety is overcome. "When we suffer with him, we

44

shall also be glorified with him" (Rom. 8.17). We revere the martyrs of all ages and of our time, and look to their example for courage.

15. We *deplore* conversions without witness to Christ. There are millions who have never heard the good news. We *confess* that we are often ashamed of the gospel. We find it more comfortable to remain in our own Christian circles than to witness in the world. The more we look upon our risen Lord, the more our indolence is overcome and we are enabled to confess: "Woe to me if I do not preach the gospel" (1 Cor. 9.16).

16. We *deplore* also that our confessing Christ today is hindered by the different denominations, which split the confessing community of the Church. We understand the confessions of faith of our different traditions as guidelines, not as substitutes, for our actual confessing in the face of today's challenges. Because being converted to Christ necessarily includes membership in the confessing body of Christ, we *long and strive* for a world-wide community.

17. *In confessing Christ and in being converted to his Lordship, we experience the freedom of the Holy Spirit and express the ultimate hope for the world.* Through his true and faithful witness Jesus Christ has set us free from the slavery of sin to the glorious freedom of the Spirit. Within the vicious circle of sin, death, and the devil are the vicious circles of hunger, oppression, and violence. Likewise, liberation to justice, better community, and human dignity on earth is within the great freedom of the Spirit, who is nothing less than the power of the new creation.

18. We regret all divisions in thinking and practice between the personal and the corporate dimensions. "The whole gospel for the whole person and the whole world" means that we cannot leave any area of human life and suffering without the witness of hope.

19. We regret that some reduce liberation from sin and evil to social and political dimensions, just as we regret that others limit liberation to the private and eternal dimensions.

20. In the witness of our whole life and our confessing community we *work* with passionate love for the total liberation of the people and *anticipate* God's Kingdom to come. We *pray* in the freedom of the Spirit and *groan* with our suffering fellow human beings and the whole groaning creation until the glory of the Triune God is revealed and will be all in all. Come, Lord Jesus, come to us, come to the world!

MANY CULTURES, ONE CHRIST

Search for Cultural Identity

21. In all societies today there is a search for cultural identity; Christians around the world find themselves caught up in this quest. The

Bangkok Conference on Salvation Today (1973) asked: "Culture shapes the human voice that answers the voice of Christ. . . . How can we responsibly answer the voice of Christ instead of copying foreign models of conversion . . . imposed, not truly accepted?"

22. In our sharing with one another we have discovered that the Christ who meets us in our own cultural contexts is revealed to us in a new way as we confess him. Further, since Christ shares in a special way with all who are exploited and oppressed, we find when we meet with them that our understanding of him is enlarged and enriched.

23. We affirm the necessity of confessing Christ as specifically as possible with regard to our own cultural settings. We have heard him confessed in that way at this Assembly by Christians from all parts of the world. In partial answer to the question raised by the Bangkok Conference, we can say that Jesus Christ does not make copies; he makes originals. We have found this confession of Christ out of our various cultural contexts to be not only a mutually inspiring, but also a mutually corrective exchange. Without this sharing our individual affirmations would gradually become poorer and narrower. We need each other to regain the lost dimensions of confessing Christ and even to discover dimensions unknown to us before. Sharing in this way we are all changed and our cultures are transformed.

24. There is great diversity in our confessions of Christ. Nevertheless, through the illumination of the Holy Spirit, we have been able to recognize him in the proclamation of Christians in cultural situations different from our own. This is possible because we confess Christ as God and Saviour *according to the Scriptures.* And although our reading and interpretation of the Scriptures is to a certain extent itself culturally conditioned, we believe that it is part of the mystery of Christ that even as we confess him in different ways it is he who draws us together.

25. We believe that in addition to listening to one another, we need to know what people of other faiths and no faith are saying about Jesus Christ and his followers. While we cannot agree on whether or how Christ is present in other religions, we do believe that God has not left himself without witness in any generation or any society. Nor can we exclude the possibility that God speaks to Christians from outside the Church. While we oppose any form of syncretism, we affirm the necessity for dialogue with men and women of other faiths and ideologies as a means of mutual understanding and practical co-operation.

Structures That Obscure the Confession of Christ

26. We recognize that there are power structures and social factors that obscure the Christ we seek to confess. It is difficult for a black Christian, for example, to believe that the Christ whom he or she confesses

is the same Christ whom white Christians confess. The structures of racist oppression have obscured the image of Christ. It is difficult for a woman to confess a Christ who frees and unites when she has been taught subordination to men—in church and society—in the name of this same Christ. The structures of sexism also obscure the image of Christ. Religious expression is severely restricted both in states that pretend to be Christian and others which do not. In both kinds of societies there may be political structures that can and do obscure the confession of Christ. In such societies Christians are called to be as committed in their confession of Christ as are those who may seek to oppose or undermine their confession.

27. Economic structures may also obscure the confession of Christ. In consumer economies, whether capitalistic or socialistic, there are different forms of stress upon productivity, competition, and materialistic values. This increases the gap between the industrialized nations and the Third World and further decreases the quality of life in the industrialized societies. Thus while we confess a Christ who frees and unites, the economic structures in which we live tend to enslave to wealth and divide.

28. How do we meet this materialism which obstructs the confession of Christ and leads to uncaring societies? We find hope where churches, whatever the cultural context, confess Christ by standing for that which is truly human, where Christians "bear the marks of Christ" among suffering humankind, where churches address public issues in the name of Christ, and where communities of Christians are radically changing their life style as a sign of their discipleship.

29. In our discussions with one another we were also sensitized to the fact that a kind of nationalism can develop which is a distortion of the legitimate search for cultural identity and can obscure our confession of Jesus Christ the Unifier. We want to testify that in this Assembly we have found it possible to meet others of different national and cultural traditions and yet remain ourselves because we all belong to him.

30. We also know that it is not only societal power structures that can obscure the confession of Christ. Sometimes the institutional structures of the churches themselves are oppressive and dehumanizing; often they uncritically reflect the values of their own culture. Where churches are identified with wealth and privilege both the preaching and the hearing of the gospel are hindered and Christ is obscured. Unless we who belong to the Church have met him in our own lives and been changed by him, we shall not be able to name his name with power and authenticity. In this connection the issue of a "moratorium" in mission funding has been raised and is receiving serious consideration in other sections of this Assembly.

31. Despite all of our cultural differences, despite the structures in society and in the Church that obscure our confession of Christ, and despite our own sinfulness, we affirm and confess Christ together, for we

47

have found that he is not alien to any culture and that he redeems and judges in all our societies. Our common confession is Jesus Christ frees and unites.

THE CONFESSING COMMUNITY
Community in the Spirit

32. Confessing Christ is not only intensely personal; it is also essentially communal.

33. Those who take part in the life of Christ and confess him as Lord and Saviour, Liberator and Unifier, are gathered in a community of which the author and sustainer is the Holy Spirit. This communion of the Spirit finds its primary aim and ultimate purpose in the eucharistic celebration and the glorification of the Triune God. The doxology is the supreme confession which transcends all our divisions.

34. Through word, sacrament, and mutual care he transforms us, makes us grow, and leads us to the integration of worship and action. This power fills our weakness.

35. Confessing Christ *today* means that the Spirit makes us struggle with all the issues this Assembly has talked about: sin and forgiveness, power and powerlessness, exploitation and misery, the universal search for identity, the widespread loss of Christian motivation, and the spiritual longings of those who have not heard Christ's name.

36. It means that we are in communion with the prophets who announced God's will and promise for humankind and society, with the martyrs who sealed their confession with suffering and death, and also with the doubtful who can only whisper their confession of the Name. The confession of Christ holds in one communion our divided churches and the many communities, new and old, within and around them.

37. When the Holy Spirit empowers us to confess Christ today, we are called to speak and act with concern and solidarity for the whole of God's creation. Concretely: when the powerful confess Christ, the suffering must be enabled to concur; when the exploited confess Christ, the rich should be enabled to hear in such confession their own freedom announced.

38. Within the communion of the Church, we witness in our time the emergence of many new communities: missionary orders, ecumenical experiments, communes and action groups, which are trying out age-old or spontaneous and new forms of worship and action. All these groups represent attempts to find answers to the fragmentation of our societies and to the loneliness which results from the disintegration of traditional community life. They also express the lasting strength of the call of the gospel to communion and mutual care, which the Spirit instills in everybody who is touched. Despite the problems these groups often give to the

institutional churches, we recognize a creative challenge in them. We urge the churches to be sensitive towards such groups, to respect the search for authenticity which they represent, and not to reject them, lest such groups turn away from the larger communion and lose the opportunity to share their discoveries and spiritual fruits with all the others.

39. Again: all Christian community life is a creation of the Spirit of Christ, nourished by his word and sacrament, held together by love, and pushed forward by hope. Worship is its anchor and the source of its energy. So, through informed intercessions, naming people far away and close by, they live in solidarity with the whole community of grace and also, irresistibly, with all those who suffer and yearn for dignity. Through these prayers and through old and new forms of direct *diakonia*, they forge links which embrace the earth, breaking through man-made divisions of race and class, power and exploitation.

Prayer and Suffering

40. Worship, especially the Eucharist, is the instrument through which all these communities open themselves up to God and his creation; thus it breaks down walls of divisions and stimulates creative forms of solidarity. In worship we are constantly reminded of the age to come and made to live in anticipation of the messianic kingdom; thus confidence and urgency are wedded in one common life. It is our lasting shame and pain that we have not overcome our divisions at the Lord's table, where we experience God's salvation for and on behalf of all humanity. In many of our churches growing numbers of people disregard the theological and juridical barriers which make common celebration of the Eucharist impossible. Here we are not in agreement in our reaction to such developments, but we find a strong common bond in the recognition of the urgency of the call of our Lord for full unity.

41. Confessing Christ in communion means confessing the suffering and the risen Lord. We should not refuse his Cross. He will not refuse us his life.

42. We know that the acceptance of the suffering Christ is the only way to overcome our feelings of powerlessness over against evil. We also know that this acceptance would make us once again credible in the eyes of the world. We therefore pray that our churches will again and again return to the reality and the promise of the Cross, so that together we may find ourselves the stewards of the new life in Christ.

CONFESSING CHRIST IN WORSHIP AND LIFE

Facing Reality

43. "Confessing Christ" or "Christian Witness" describes, above all, that continuous act by which a Christian or Christian community pro-

claims God's acts in history and seeks to manifest Christ as "the Word that was made flesh and dwelt among us" (John 1.14). Our confessing Christ today would deny God's incarnation if it would be limited to only some areas of life. It concerns the wholeness of human life: our words and acts; our personal and communal existence; our worship and responsible service; our particular and ecumenical context.

44. All this is done under the guidance of the Holy Spirit in order that all may be reconciled and be gathered into Christ's one and only Body (Col. 1.18; Eph. 1.22-23) and attain life everlasting—to know and love the true God and him whom he has sent (John 17.3).

45. Confessing Christ is an act of gratitude for God's faithfulness and his liberating presence in our life. His is the power and the glory. At the same time, Christian witness has to do with Christians struggling against the power of evil within themselves, within the churches, and in society. This power expresses itself in many ways—in temptations of various kinds, in prejudices nurtured in us by birth, sex, class, race, religion, or nationality; in dehumanizing political and socio-economic forces; in hostility which disrupts human relationships; in selfish ambition which thrives on the misery and sufferings of others; in sicknesses which have no cure. In the midst of such reality each of us is called in our baptism to confess Christ according to the special gift (*charisma*) which one has received from God.

46. Liturgical worship, an action of the Church centred around the Eucharist, in itself thankfully proclaims the death and resurrection of the Lord "until he comes again" and incorporates people into mystical union with God, because in the act of baptism they have been identified with that death and resurrection. Confessions of faith and creeds are expressions of the communion of the Christian life both of yesterday and today. Our witness is rooted and nourished in that communion. Yesterday flows into today, the present engages the past, in continual dialogue. We approach our biblical and confessional heritage with questions that arise from contemporary involvement. At the same time, we gratefully receive from that heritage both criticism and encouragement for concrete service and fellowship.

Christian Authenticity

47. Though it seems flat and even naive on paper, we insist on repeating that the key to authentic confession is the Christian who indeed is a Christian within the community of faith. Authentic Christians live the death and resurrection of Christ by living the forgiven life in selfless service to others, and believe in the Spirit by whose power alone we are able to live our life of discipleship (1 Cor. 12.3). Especially in a secularized environment or in situations where religious commitments are scorned or

50

even attacked, the primary confessors are precisely these non-publicized, unsensational people who gather together in small, caring communities. They remain free to proclaim Christ even out of their self-acknowledged condition of weakness and sin. Their individual and communal life-style provokes the questions: "What is the meaning of your life, and why do you live as you do?" One must name the Name. Yet shared experiences reveal how often today Christ is confessed not in loud and frequent words or in massive programmes of varied activities, but in the very silence of a prison cell or of a restricted but still serving, waiting, praying Church. Today, as always in the Church, we are blessed by confessors, martyrs "even unto death".

48. Indeed, in those milieux which seem so hardened to any religious confession or in areas which for centuries have seen so little "success", confessing Christ may rest in the very hope that flows from our incorporation through the Spirit into the mission, death, and life of Jesus Christ. Only that hope holds us, only that hope never abandons us.

49. The call to confess Christ is a vocation also to that *common* witness in each place which the churches, even while separated, bear together. By sharing resources and experiences in mission, they witness to whatever divine gifts of truth and life they already share in common. Such witness should proclaim together the content of Christian faith, as fully as possible. Furthermore, such ecumenical faithfulness of the churches in each place includes fidelity to the needs of the local churches which elsewhere are also striving to give common witness.

50. For many Christians in very diverse situations, confessing Christ amounts almost to the same thing as involvement in struggles for justice and freedom. In many instances, Christian faith has become a dynamic force, awakening the conscience of the people and bringing new hope to hopeless situations. In this way, confessing Christ is liberated from mere verbalism which renders the life and ministry of the Church stagnant, introverted, and contentious.

51. What are our hesitations about explicitly confessing our faith before others?

(a) A loss of confidence in the God we proclaim and in the power of the gospel so that we lack confidence in our mission as Christians?

(b) By not experiencing deeply enough the joyful, healing love of God so that we are unable *honestly* to give an account of the hope within us?

(c) An unreadiness to be different before those to whom the good news is heard as bad news?

(*d*) By misunderstanding our belief in the uniqueness and finality of Jesus Christ as "arrogant doctrinal superiority", and not understanding it as the humble and obedient stewardship of the Church which knows it has been "put in trust with the gospel"?

52. We confess Christ in the perspective of the coming Kingdom. His Spirit is the Spirit of the New Age. This vision makes us both sober and hopeful. None of the achievements as individuals, churches, societies will in themselves inaugurate the messianic era. Never can women and men be justified by works. Yet the promise of the Kingdom is valid and encourages Christians to respond in prayer and action. Confessing Christ shall not be in vain.

A CALL TO CONFESS AND PROCLAIM

53. We do not have the option of keeping the good news to ourselves. The uncommunicated gospel is a patent contradiction.

54. We are called to preach Christ crucified, the power of God and the wisdom of God (1 Cor. 1.23, 24).

55. Evangelism, therefore, is rooted in gratitude for God's self-sacrificing love, in obedience to the risen Lord.

56. Evangelism is like a beggar telling another beggar where they both can find bread.

The Whole Gospel

57. The gospel is good news from God, our Creator and Redeemer. On its way from Jerusalem to Galilee and to the ends of the earth, the Spirit discloses ever new aspects and dimensions of God's decisive revelation in Jesus Christ. The gospel always includes: the announcement of God's Kingdom and love through Jesus Christ, the offer of grace and forgiveness of sins, the invitation to repentance and faith in him, the summons to fellowship in God's Church, the command to witness to God's saving words and deeds, the responsibility to participate in the struggle for justice and human dignity, the obligation to denounce all that hinders human wholeness, and a commitment to risk life itself. In our time, to the oppressed the gospel may be new as a message of courage to persevere in the struggle for liberation in this world as a sign of hope for God's inbreaking Kingdom. To women the gospel may bring news of a Christ who empowered women to be bold in the midst of cultural expectations of submissiveness. To children the gospel may be a call of love for the "little ones" and to the rich and powerful it may reveal the responsibility to share the poverty of the poor.

58. While we rejoice hearing the gospel speak to our particular situations and while we must try to communicate the gospel to particular

52

contexts, we must remain faithful to the historical apostolic witness as we find it in the holy Scriptures and tradition as it is centred in Jesus Christ—lest we accommodate them to our own desires and interests.

The Whole Person

59. The gospel, through the power of the Holy Spirit, speaks to all human needs, transforms our lives. In bringing forgiveness, it reconciles us to our Creator, sparks within us the true joy of knowing God, and promises eternal life. In uniting us as God's people, it answers our need for community and fellowship. In revealing God's love for all persons, it makes us responsible, critical, and creative members of the societies in which we live. The good news of Jesus' resurrection assures us that God's righteous purpose in history will be fulfilled and frees us to work for that fulfilment with hope and courage.

The Whole World

60. The world is not only God's creation; it is also the arena of God's mission. Because God loved the whole world, the Church cannot neglect any part of it—neither those who have heard the saving Name nor the vast majority who have not yet heard it. Our obedience to God and our solidarity with the human family demand that we obey Christ's command to proclaim and demonstrate God's love to every person, of every class and race, on every continent, in every culture, in every setting and historical context.

The Whole Church

61. Evangelism cannot be delegated to either gifted individuals or specialized agencies. It is entrusted to the "whole Church", the body of Christ, in which the particular gifts and functions of all members are but expressions of the life of the whole body.

62. This wholeness must take expression in every particular cultural, social, and political context. Therefore, the evangelization of the world starts at the level of the congregation, in the local and ecumenical dimensions of its life: worship, sacrament, preaching, teaching and healing, fellowship and service, witnessing in life and in death.

63. Too often we as churches and congregations stand in the way of the gospel—because of our lack of missionary zeal and missionary structures, because of our divisions, our self-complacency, our lack of catholicity and ecumenical spirit.

64. The call to evangelism, therefore, implies a call to repentance, renewal, and commitment for visible unity. We also deplore proselytism of any sort which further divides the Church.

65. Yet, even imperfect and broken, we are called to put ourselves

humbly and gladly at the service of the unfinished mission. We are commissioned to carry the gospel to the whole world and to allow it to permeate all realms of human life. We recognize the signs that the Holy Spirit is in these days calling the Church to a new commitment to evangelism, as evidenced by his voice to the Bangkok Conference on "Salvation Today" (1973), the Accra conference on "Giving account of the hope that is within us" (1974), the Lausanne Congress on "The Evangelization of the World" (1974), and the Synod of Bishops of the Roman Catholic Church on "Evangelization in the Modern World" (1974). Clearly this is a common mandate which deserves common support.

On Methodology

66. In our times many churches, Christian individuals, and groups find themselves under pressures and challenges which demand a clear choice between confessing or denying Christ. Others, however, face ambiguous situations in which the question arises: When is the appropriate time to confess and how should we do it? This leads to the question of education for mission. Programmes of lay training ought to be encouraged in order to equip lay workers for communicating the gospel at their particular place in everyday life, including those who, for professional reasons, cross cultural frontiers.

67. Never before has the Church universal had at its disposal such a comprehensive set of means of communication as we have today—literature, audiovisuals, electronic media. While we need to improve our use of such media, nothing can replace the living witness in words and deeds of Christian persons, groups, and congregations who participate in the sufferings and joys, in the struggles and celebrations, in the frustrations and hopes of the people with whom they want to share the gospel. Whatever "methodologies" of communication may seem to be appropriate in different situations, they should be directed by a humble spirit of sensitivity and participation.

68. Careful listening is an essential part of our witness. Only as we are sensitive to the needs and aspirations of others will we know what Christ is saying through our dialogue. What we should like to call "holistic methodology" or "methodology in wholeness" transcends mere techniques or tactics. It is rooted in God's own "strategy of love" which liberates us to respond freely to his call to union with him and our fellow human beings.

A Sense of Urgency

69. We need to recover the sense of urgency. Questions about theological definitions there may be. Problems of precise implementation will arise. But neither theoretical nor practical differences must be allowed to dampen the fires of evangelism.

70. Confessing Christ must be done *today*. "Behold, now is the acceptable time; behold, now is the day of salvation" (2 Cor. 6.2). It cannot wait for a time that is comfortable for us. We must be prepared to proclaim the gospel when human beings need to hear it. But in our zeal to spread the good news, we must guard against fanaticism which disrupts the hearing of the gospel and breaks the community of God. The world requires, and God demands, that we recognize the urgency to proclaim the saving word of God—today. God's acceptable time demands that we respond in all haste. "And how terrible it would be for me if I did not preach the gospel!" (1 Cor. 9.16).

RECOMMENDATIONS

71. We, the delegates of the Fifth Assembly of the World Council of Churches, meeting in Nairobi, have shared a moment of time in a great ecumenical experience to confess and to proclaim Jesus Christ as Lord and Saviour under the theme "Jesus Christ frees and unites".

72. We invite all our brothers and sisters around the world to consider some of the concerns voiced at Nairobi, and to join us as we continue in this ongoing process. We urge all people committed to Christ's discipleship to share with us in confessing him in this ecumenical movement initiated by the Holy Spirit.

73. In this spirit of ecumenical discipleship to which we are committed we invite our fellow-Christians to share with us the following concerns, which *we recommend to the WCC member churches:*

73.1. That the churches utilize for study within local congregations the report of Assembly Section I on Confessing Christ Today, translating the report into the language spoken within their country or region;

73.2. That the churches and local congregations find ways to relate the content of the report on Confessing Christ Today to their own ecclesiastical, cultural, social, political, economic structures so that the whole gospel may be proclaimed to all persons in every situation;

73.3. That the churches encourage and support the study of intercultural communication and the processes of communication applicable to matters of faith and the interpretation of Scriptures, and that they give special attention to the question as to how their own interpretation of the Bible is culturally conditioned;

73.4. That regional or local clusters of churches engage in reflections based on Bible study and common experience, on the common content of their faith, in order to produce educational materials related to their particular situation;

73.5. That the churches use the best talents inside and outside the church to write hymns, prayers, and other liturgical texts which relate to vital contemporary concerns and issues, and to share such texts widely within the ecumenical movement;

73.6. That the churches develop ways in which those suffering in the name of Christ are included by name in the intercessions of all congregations and that the faithful are informed about the situations of people thus mentioned. No one—imprisoned, tortured, harassed, or persecuted—should escape the vigilance of the praying Church;

73.7. That the churches increase their efforts to overcome the barriers which hinder common celebration of the Eucharist;

73.8. That the churches encourage and promote broader participation on all church levels in ecumenical studies pertaining to confessing Christ, such as the study on "Giving account of the hope that is in us";

73.9. That the churches share with each other and with national/regional ecumenical councils to which they belong statements of faith and theological reflection on actual concerns so that they can help each other assure that in such statements the interests of the poor and the discriminated can be heard, and the powerful and rich may hear their liberation announced. In so doing, churches may be helped in their own attempts to confess Christ;

73.10. That the churches study and practise continuous efforts at developing fresh and communicable methods of expressing their confession of Christ today, learning especially from the universally understood methods of modern art in theatre, film, and other artistic expressions;

73.11. That theological training programmes should include studies in mission and evangelism as a normal part of their curriculum;

73.12. That the churches examine the relationship between Christian and national identity in their particular contexts so that members may gain the courage to give priority to their Christian identity;

73.13. That churches within "consumer societies" encourage and even establish "counter-cultural communities" where persons are accepted without being "productive" or "successful", and in this way help the members to change their consumer-oriented life styles;

73.14. That the churches encourage all Christians to witness to Christ by a holy life and by their daily participation and struggle along with others for a just order in Church and society as means of broadening the scope of the Church's ministry with all people;

73.15. That the churches assist groups and communities of Christian concern, inside and outside the ecclesiastical structure, to relate to each other and to the churches, to meet, exchange, and develop common planning and action;

73.16. That the churches recognize the need to hear and see Christ confessed by Christians from other parts of the world, particularly those churches which have traditionally sent missionaries to other countries, but have never received missionaries; we need to encourage a cross-cultural mission in six continents and to share our gifts and our best models for evangelism;

73.17. That the churches examine the extent to which their missionary structures obscure the confession of Christ, and study the reasons for and the different aspects of the call for a moratorium which has been extended by some churches in their concern for greater effectiveness of mission;

73.18. That the churches provide means of exchange and mutual feedback between church leaders and congregational members (i.e., hearings or consultations on crucial issues for the laity) to enrich the common confession of Christ;

73.19. That churches recognize, stimulate, and make use of evangelistic gifts in individuals and voluntary groups for the benefit of the whole local church and community;

73.20. That churches with different cultural backgrounds within multi-cultural societies not only speak to one another about confessing Christ, but proclaim Christ together;

73.21. That churches in a local situation co-operate in:

(a) studying their given situation and the challenge in it to the Church, especially with regard to realms of life and social levels neglected so far in their witness and service;

(b) serving the needs of the community in ways that lead towards self-help and wholeness;

(c) suffering in solidarity with those whose plight they cannot change (e.g., the bereaved) or whose plight they are struggling to change (e.g., victims of discrimination).

SECTION II: WHAT UNITY REQUIRES

In introducing the Report, Bishop Kenneth Woollcombe (Church of England) emphasized that the Report was incomplete; much work remained to be done in which the Section sought the assistance of the rest of the Assembly. Part II of the Report, he hoped, took the discussion about "conciliarity" and "local churches" somewhat further; Part III explored several aspects of the context of church unity; Part IV asked why progress was so slow.

In the debate, Fr Pierre Duprey (Roman Catholic delegated observer) praised the Report as showing that conciliarity is that which expresses the unity of local churches and that unity in the sacraments could be achieved without sacrificing welcome diversity in theology and liturgy. Metropolitan Paulos Gregorios (Syrian Orthodox, India), from a tradition which has managed without a Council for 1640 years, raised questions about Councils and conciliarity.

A second theme, that of the relation of the search for the unity of the Church to the social and political context, was raised in different ways by Professor N. Young (Methodist, Australia), Archbishop O. Sundby (Church of Sweden), and Bishop Wölber (Evangelical Church, German Federal Republic).

Sister Elena Gundyaevna (Russian Orthodox) said that the fact that women are not ordained in the Orthodox Church is not to be regarded as an historical or cultural matter of discrimination against women. A change should be made in the text.

Dr I. B. Bokeleale (Church of Christ in Zaïre) said that in African eyes a brother is one who eats with you, and it was painful to be called a brother and denied communion. Could not a day be set aside at the next Assembly when all present could come together at the Lord's table? Others spoke of the pain felt by those whose principles disallowed the open table. Professor N. Nissiotis (Orthodox, Greece) agreed that in the next seven years the problem of intercommunion must be faced and that the future of the WCC depends on our working at this and other signs of visible unity.

Responding to the debate, the Moderator thanked the Assembly for their comments and asked that the Report be referred back to the Section for revision.

The Report was *referred back.*

Bishop Kenneth Woollcombe (Church of England) later introduced the revised version of the first Report of the Section together with the Recommendations. He reminded the Assembly that the goal is visible unity, and that this makes demands upon us now; and drew attention to the changes in Part III and especially the concern for the handicapped in paragraph 8. There was much that should and could be done; it was a time not for disenchantment but decision. Archdeacon Pawley (Church of England) hoped that more work would be done on the idea of conciliar fellowship; on the definition of "local churches"; and on the status of our existing denominational divisions. Archbishop Frank Woods urged the delegates to work at the idea of conciliar fellowship. Giving thanks for what he owed to the WCC, he asked for the blessing of God as we moved towards conciliar fellowship.

The first Report as presented was unanimously accepted and recommended to the churches.

On the *Recommendations,* Fr Borovoy (Russian Orthodox) stressed the importance of the paragraph headed "Decisions which contribute to an advance towards unity" and moved an addition, which was accepted, to the final sentence concerning the continued study of Baptism, the Eucharist, and the Ministry. Mr B.M. Pulimood (Mar Thoma, India) said that some churches could help others by the sharing of personnel. Dr W.M.S. West (Baptist, UK) spoke from his own experience of the importance of fostering relationships between the churches and the converts of churches and the growing small informal interconfessional groups.

The Recommendations were adopted by unanimous vote.

SECTION II: WHAT UNITY REQUIRES

I. FOREWORD

1. We thank God for his presence with us in our Assembly. Our gathering, more than any of our previous Assemblies, has been representative of the nations and the total membership of the Church—younger and older, men and women, lay and ordained. The privilege of meeting in Africa has enhanced our awareness of the rich diversity of God's family. Meeting in small groups for Bible study, we have been guided and comforted by the word and presence of our living Lord. Through music, praise, and prayer we have been knit together in adoration of our God. We have learned to know him better as the one who frees us for unity in himself and as the one who unites us in his freedom. He himself precedes both the freedom for which he sets us free and the unity which binds us together; it is as we are in him that we find the liberty which does not tear us apart from one another and a unity which does not impose uniformity upon desirable diversity. We are grateful also for much that has happened in the wider life of the Church, for fresh signs of the presence of the Holy Spirit, for the advance in mutual understanding, theological agreement, closer bonds, and in some cases even unions among the churches. For all this, God be praised!

II. UNITY REQUIRES A COMMONLY ACCEPTED GOAL

2. We believe that we are called to the goal of visible unity and have therefore struggled, as previous Assemblies have done, to describe more fully that goal. We recall and reaffirm the statement made at the Third Assembly at New Delhi which described God's will for unity in terms of one fully committed fellowship of all God's people in each place, in all places, and in all ages. The Fourth Assembly spoke of a deeper internal dimension of unity which is expressed by the term "catholicity". "Catholicity", the Assembly said, "is the opposite of all kinds of egotism and particularism. It is the quality by which the Church expresses the fullness, the integrity, and the totality of life in Christt.... The Church must

express this catholicity in its worship by providing a home for all sorts and conditions of men and women; and in its witness and service by working for the realization of genuine humanity" (*Uppsala Speaks*, pp. 13, 14, paragraphs 7 and 9). True catholicity involves a quest for diversity in unity and continuity. In its catholicity the Church "is bold in speaking of itself as the sign of the coming unity of mankind" (*ibid.*, p. 20).

3. The Faith and Order Commission at its meeting in Louvain made a considered attempt to describe the unity which we seek in terms of "conciliar fellowship". The Conference at Salamanca on "Concepts of Unity and Models of Union" has recommended the concept in the following terms: "The one Church is to be envisioned as a conciliar fellowship of local churches which are themselves truly united. In this conciliar fellowship, each local church possesses, in communion with the others, the fullness of catholicity, witnesses to the same apostolic faith, and therefore recognizes the others as belonging to the same Church of Christ and guided by the same Spirit. As the New Delhi Assembly pointed out, they are bound together because they have received the same baptism and share in the same Eucharist; they recognize each other's members and ministries. They are one in their common commitment to confess the gospel of Christ by proclamation and service to the world. To this end, each church aims at maintaining sustained and sustaining relationships with her sister churches, expressed in conciliar gatherings whenever required for the fulfilment of their common calling" (cited in *Uppsala to Nairobi*, p. 79).

4. The term "conciliar fellowship" has been frequently misunderstood. It does *not* look towards a conception of unity different from that full organic unity sketched in the New Delhi statement, but is rather a further elaboration of it. The term is intended to describe an aspect of the life of the one undivided Church *at all levels*. In the first place, it expresses the unity of church separated by distance, culture, and time, a unity which is publicly manifested when the representatives of these local churches gather together for a common meeting. It also refers to a quality of life within each local church; it underlines the fact that true unity is not monolithic, does not override the special gifts given to each member and to each local church, but rather cherishes and protects them.

5. True conciliar fellowship presupposes the unity of the Church. We describe this unity in different ways. One description given in our meeting, in which we all share, even though it is not yet expressed in the language of all, is the following: "True conciliarity is the reflection in the life of the Church of the triune being of God. It is that unity for which Christ prayed when he asked the Father that his disciples might be one *as* the Father and the Son are one. The source of the Church's unity, as of her faith and her joy, is the meeting of the Apostles with the risen Christ who bears the marks of his cross, and the continued encounter with the disciples today with his living presence in the midst of the eucharistic fellowship. He

brings its members into the communion of the Holy Spirit, and makes them children of the Father. Thereby, they share a common participation in the divine nature and become living members in the one living Body of the risen Christ. Though different members in each local community, and different local communities, do and should manifest a rich diversity, and develop their own proper personality, nevertheless no cultural, sociological, psychological, political, or historical difference can alter the integrity of the one apostolic faith. By the working of the Holy Spirit, the One Living Word and Son of God is incarnate in the One Church, the One Body of which Christ is the Head and the true worshippers of the Father the members. They commune with him who said: 'I am the truth.' This Living Truth is the goal towards which all churches who seek for unity tend together. Conciliarity expresses this interior unity of the churches separated by space, culture, or time, but living intensely this unity in Christ and seeking, from time to time, by councils of representatives of all the local churches at various geographical levels to express their unity visibly in a common meeting."

6. Our present interconfessional assemblies are not councils in this full sense, because they are not yet united by a common understanding of the apostolic faith, by a common ministry, and a common Eucharist. They nevertheless express the sincere desire of the participating churches to herald and move towards full conciliar fellowship, and are themselves a true foretaste of such fellowship.*

7. It is because the unity of the Church is grounded in the divine triunity that we can speak of diversity in the Church as something to be not only admitted but actively desired. Since Christ died and rose for all and his Church is to be the sign of the coming unity of humankind, it must be open to women and men of every nation and culture, of every time and place, of every sort of ability and disability. In its mission it must actively seek them wherever and whoever they are, and in its company they must find their true home. It follows that, in order to be faithful to our calling to unity, we must consider this calling within the wider context of the unity and diversity of humankind. It is because we have often failed to do this that many have dismissed the quest for church unity as irrelevant to their real concerns.

III. UNITY REQUIRES A FULLER UNDERSTANDING OF THE CONTEXT

8. *The Handicapped and the Wholeness of the Family of God.* The Church's unity includes both the "disabled" and the "able". A Church

---

*Some examples of the way in which the Church might experience more fully the foretaste of which we speak are given in Part II of this report and are developed on pp. 34-36 of *What Unity Requires.*

which seeks to be truly united within itself and to move towards unity with others must be open to all; yet able-bodied church members, both by their attitudes and by their emphasis on activism, marginalize and often exclude those with mental or physical disabilities. The disabled are treated as the weak to be served, rather than as fully committed, integral members of the Body of Christ and the human family; the specific contribution which they have to give is ignored. This is the more serious because disability—a world-wide problem—is increasing. Accidents and illness leave adults and children disabled; many more are emotionally handicapped by the pressures of social change and urban living; genetic disorders and famine leave millions of children physically or mentally impaired. The Church cannot exemplify "the full humanity revealed in Christ", bear witness to the interdependence of humankind, or achieve unity in diversity if it continues to acquiesce in the social isolation of disabled persons and to deny them full participation in its life. The unity of the family of God is handicapped where these brothers and sisters are treated as objects of condescending charity. It is broken where they are left out. How can the love of Christ create in us the will to discern and to work forcefully against the causes which distort and cripple the lives of so many of our fellow human beings? How can the Church be open to the witness which Christ extends through them?

9. *The Community of Women and Men and the Wholeness of the Body of Christ.* The Church's unity includes women and men in a true mutuality. As a result of rapid cultural, economic, and social change, women (and many men) reject the passive or restrictive roles formerly assigned to women, and search for fuller participation in the life of the Church and in society at large. The relations of women and men must be shaped by reciprocity and not by subordination. The unity of the Church requires that women be free to live out the gifts which God has given to them and to respond to their calling to share fully in the life and witness of the Church. This raises fundamental dogmatic issues on which we are not agreed, but which are further pursued in the study, "The Community of Women and Men in the Church", which will include the significance of the Virgin Mary in the Church and the question of the ordination of women. It will be important for the churches to discuss the implications of this study for their teaching on family life and on religious vocation.

10. *Organization and Personal Community in the Unity of the Church.* The Church's unity enhances and does not hinder personal freedom and community. Church unity is often misunderstood as implying larger bureaucratic structures incompatible with spiritual freedom and personal community. In essence, the Church is not bureaucratic, but gathers God's people in each place and in all places around the personal presence of Christ in the ministry of word and sacrament acknowledged and accepted by all. The heart of any proposal for church union is the

integrity of this fundamental personal community. The fresh search, especially among young people, for an authentic spirituality and a sense of community can contribute to that "fully committed fellowship" which is intended by the term "organic union". It is true that there is no community without structure, but structure must serve and facilitate good church order, which is itself essentially and properly the expression of committed personal fellowship in Christ. Organic union of separate denominations to form one body does mean a kind of death which threatens the denominational identity of its members, but it is dying in order to receive a fuller life. That is literally the "crux of the matter".

11. *Political Struggle and the Unity of the Church.* The Church's unity is lived in the tension of political struggle. The Church is called to discern and attest God's purpose of justice in history and in the created world, but it is frequently tempted to remain silent in order to preserve "unity", or to divide in a crusading spirit for or against some particular cause. On these difficulties, we have three things to say:

(*a*) Christians are sinners judged and forgiven, accepting one another as such in Christ. At the Eucharist we are all equal, a company who have no righteousness of our own but who receive by faith and in love the righteousness of God. The Church is thus the place where people with sharply opposed commitments can meet at the foot of the cross within the divine mercy which sustains them all.

(*b*) But the Church is also a company under Christ's discipline. We are not permitted to ignore or to compromise with sin. We are called to open and vigorous mutual criticism, bearing the pain of controversy, openly testing ethical decisions (including political ones) under the truth of Christ, and seeking always the way of obedience in each concrete situation. Individual Christians may and often should take more radical positions than the Church as a whole can or should do. But there are political issues on which the Church itself must speak and act on behalf of the dignity of God's creatures. To do this is not to "politicize" the Church. Rather, the Church is politicized when it is so tied to a party or a government, a class or an ideology, that it is not free so to speak and act.

(*c*) Open and honest controversy on political issues may lead to agreement or it may lead to polarization. When all things are brought into the light, some will find their refuge in a retreat into darkness. The Church has to learn to distinguish in the light of God's Word between sin which can be exposed and forgiven, and apostasy which rejects God's forgiveness and must therefore be rejected by the Church. How can we learn to exercise this discipline and this discernment in situations where our churches are involved in racism, in social, political, or religious oppression, and in economic exploitation?

12. *The Search for Cultural Identity and the Oneness of the Church Universal.* The Church's oneness has to include and to transcend every culture, but the gospel cannot be wholly separated from those cultures through which it has in fact come to us. For the sake of witnessing to the gospel of Christ the Church is free to ground itself firmly in the culture and life style of every people to whom it is sent. Otherwise it would die like a potted plant with no roots in the local soil, rather than find life as a seed which dies to bear fruit. There is no single culture peculiarly congenial to the Christian message; each culture is to be both shaped and transcended by that message. But cultures change, and the Church's alertness to cultural development is essential to healthy oneness.

No church should become so identified with its own or another particular culture, present or past, as to frustrate its critical dialogue with that culture. When a church's loyalty to a given culture becomes uncritical, the oneness of the Church Universal suffers. Indeed, there may be situations of dependence between churches where, for the sake of the integrity of a church's witness in its own culture, there should be a temporary moratorium on existing dependencies in order to prepare for a more mature independence. Yet, the people of God will always find their first and primary identity through their baptism into the one Body of Christ. How does this understanding of culture and unity shape our life in liturgy and mission, increase our understanding of diverse theological understandings of the One Faith, free us in situations, such as Ireland, where cultural identification has become an imprisonment making it profoundly costly for the churches to exercise their ministry of reconciliation?

IV. UNITY REQUIRES COMPANIONSHIP IN STRUGGLE AND HOPE

13. There are some who question the wisdom of placing the discussion of issues of church unity within the wider context of the secular struggles of humankind for peace and justice, just as there are those who question the relevance of the decades of patient theological work which have brought us to the place where we are. To the first we must say that the purpose for which we are called to unity is "that the world may believe". A quest for unity which is not set in the context of Christ's promise to draw all people to himself would be false. To the second we say that it is only within the reality of a forgiven community that humankind can find true liberty. It is as a community which is itself being healed that the Church can be God's instrument for the healing of the nations.

14. The healing of our divisions is a slow and complex process which has many elements. Councils of churches at all levels are drawing the churches together for various tasks. Union negotiations between churches proceed at varying speeds. Bilateral conversations between confessional

bodies continue at various levels. These diverse activities do not always assist and enrich one another, and sometimes they are in tension with one another. Within the common commitment to unity one can speak broadly of two tendencies which are not mutually exclusive. There are on the one hand those whose primary stress is upon the necessity for faithfulness to the truth as it has been confessed in the past and as it is embodied in the received traditions. This emphasis leads them to give priority to the bilateral and multilateral conversations between representatives of different traditions, seeking a common understanding of the one tradition of the gospel. There are others whose primary stress is upon faithfulness to the calling of the Church to be the sign, instrument, and foretaste of Christ's purpose to draw all people to himself. They therefore seek above all to find a form of unity in each nation or region which will enable the Church to be such a sign. Many of these, especially (but not only) in the younger churches of Asia, Africa, and Latin America, find that the language which earlier generations used to confess the one faith does not help them to confess the same faith in the language of their own peoples. They find that the truth they confess in common as they witness to their neighbours is more important than the separate formulations of an earlier time and another culture. In many places united churches have been formed by the action of separated churches in surrendering their separate identities in order to become one. This surrender has been costly, but those who have experienced it testify that it has been the way to new life. The Conference of United Churches in Toronto in the present year has borne witness to this experience of new life through the surrender of the denominational identities which had separated them (cf. *What Unity Requires*, pp. 18-29). These two ways of approaching unity must be complementary and not competitive. Local or national unions of churches could fall into confusion and error by not taking seriously enough the issues of the continuity with the past which are involved in the dialogue between the confessional families. This dialogue could become sterile if it does not take seriously the urgency of God's will to show forth the oneness of his Church. Both must seek to enable the Church in each place to be, and to be seen as, the one family gathered into one eucharistic fellowship.

15. Yet at the end of this Assembly we have to ask what progress we have made. We have had true companionship. In the broader context which this Assembly has provided there has been a fresh opportunity to undertake the ancient and often difficult conversation between the Eastern and Western traditions in the Church. The presence of many voices from Asia and Africa has helped to give this ancient dialogue a new intensity—and therefore both a new pain and a new hopefulness.

16. But we must also record deep and continuing disagreements, as a

result of the sin which divides us. In some respects we are still far apart, and even where there is theological consensus, the churches are slow to act on it. There are conflicts about the whole shape of theology as the churches of Asia, Africa, and Latin America challenge the long dominance of Greek and Latin forms of thought. There is disagreement about the extent to which diversity in credal formulations is acceptable to the one Church. Above all, there are sharp questions which demand answers not in words but in decisions by the member churches: Why does the visible, organic union of churches in the same region move so slowly? Why—after so many decades—have we not reached that common understanding of the faith which would enable us to share together in the Eucharist at this Assembly where we have confessed Christ together and known his presence in our midst? Why—if we speak in terms of conciliarity—do we not move more rapidly from our present pre-conciliar stage to a fuller conciliar fellowship in a shared Eucharist? And, if the answer is "Because we are not yet united", the question comes again: "Then why do we not unite?"

17. These are not only the questions of impatient men and women; they may also be the questions put to us by our common Lord. If so, they call for an answer not at some future time determined by us at our leisure, but in the day of his mercy which is given to us today.

18. Meeting in the Advent season we ask the churches to consider these questions. The Lord who has come to free and unite us will come also as our Judge. But with judgement there is hope. In reporting to this Assembly the Churches' Commission on International Affairs says: "We have found that the specificity or uniqueness of any Christian contribution can only be found in the basic conviction that there is 'a hope beyond hope'." It is in that hope that we call the churches to go forward.

V. IMPLICATIONS AND RECOMMENDATIONS

19. *We Recommend a Common Effort to Confess Christian Truth and to Share More Fully in Witness and Mission.*

(a) *A common effort to confess Christian truth.* We ask the churches to undertake a common effort to receive, re-appropriate and confess together, as contemporary occasion requires, the Christian truth and faith, delivered through the Apostles and handed down through the centuries. Such common action, arising from free and inclusive discussion under the commonly acknowledged authority of God's Word, must aim both to clarify and to embody the unity and the diversity which are proper to the church's life and mission.

(b) *A more common witness and mission.* We ask the churches to recognize their common responsibility for mission by planning together not only the tasks which they have to accomplish jointly, but also the tasks which they have to do separately. But mission involves more than joint planning, and we believe that the churches should move towards a greater degree of joint action and witness.

20. *We Recommend a Fuller Sharing among the Churches of Experience, Personnel, Resources, and Support.* Recognizing that it is one of the most pressing and immediate ecumenical tasks to develop more truly sustained and sustaining relationships among the churches, as they look towards the time when they can enjoy full conciliar fellowship, we recommend:

(a) *Mutual intercession.* That all churches should encourage and assist their members in regular and informed intercession for the other churches.

(b) *Reciprocal visitation.* That reciprocal visitation among the churches be accepted as a normal part of their responsibility. Visits by church delegations should be regularly arranged for the purpose of sharing in each other's liturgy, theology, and spirituality, and for mutual pastoral help, counsel, and encouragement. Churches should also arrange wherever possible that when their members visit other areas in the course of secular duty advantage be taken of such visits for personal contacts with the churches there.

(c) *Solidarity in suffering.* That whenever any church is passing through suffering, the other churches must find ways of expressing solidarity with them in their suffering, both by prayer and visitation, and by courageous action in publishing the facts and making appropriate protest.

(d) *Sharing of personnel and finance.* That concerted efforts be made to share personnel and finance in ways which promote both the proper freedom and the proper interdependence of all the churches. This sharing must be mutual. True sharing within a mature partnership means that churches are free to use personnel and financial aid in accordance with their own priorities; they can also decline any support which they feel would not further the cause of the gospel in their area.

(e) *Growing together in each place.* That neighbouring churches in the same locality should find ways of closer reciprocal encounter in the bond of truth and love, offering correction to one another, and being open to the witness of the many small interconfessional groups which are created by a common social or political concern, a common charismatic experience, a common search for a new spirituality and life style or a common theological research. These groups merit and need the active pastoral support of the churches. They are in many places real points of ecumenical growth and must not be pushed to the margin of the Church's concern.

(f) *Shared pastoral responsibility.* That the churches engage more seriously together in fulfilling their pastoral responsibility towards those who enter into mixed marriages, and to the organized groups of those who have contracted such marriages.

21. *A Fresh Review of Ecumenical Commitments*

(a) *A reappraisal of ecumenical commitments.* The vision of conciliar fellowship at all levels represents a challenge to the present ecumenical situation, and raises a sharp question about the extent to which our ecumenical commitments actually contribute to a resolute quest for unity. We ask the churches to review the pattern and degree of their present commitment to the ecumenical structures at local, national, regional, and global levels, and ask themselves whether these structures are functioning as means towards unity or as a substitute for unity.

(b) *Greater interdependence between ecumenical initiatives.* The vision of conciliar fellowship emphasizes the importance of interdependence among our various ecumenical efforts. The quest for visible unity is being pursued in many ways at different levels: regional, national, and local "councils", union negotiations, bilateral and multilateral conversations at international, regional, and national levels, and local initiatives in collaboration. We ask the churches by concerted action to ensure that these efforts support, influence, and encourage one another.

(c) *Decisions which contribute to an advance towards unity.* The vision of conciliar fellowship urges us to move beyond mere common dialogue and study to identify and make those decisions as churches which will generate movement towards that goal. While it is important for us to report to our churches about WCC Assemblies, and to develop more effective channels of communication and support, the essential need is for actions by the churches which strengthen the development of true conciliar fellowship. We ask the churches for such actions: deliberate steps towards a fuller fellowship with other churches. As an example of one such decision, we ask the churches to consider the three agreed statements on "Baptism, the Eucharist, and a Mutually Recognized Ministry", compiled after many years of study and consultation by the WCC Commission on Faith and Order. These statements indicate a growing convergence among the churches in these three areas. We ask that the churches study these texts and transmit their responses to the Faith and Order Commission by 31 December, 1976, and that further study of these issues be taken on the basis of their replies. *In responding, the churches should not only examine whether the agreed statements reflect their present teaching and practice, but indicate the ways in which they are prepared to contribute to the common advance towards unity.* On the basis of the replies the study on baptism, the Eucharist, and the ministry should be continued and deepened.

22. *We Recommend Study of the Following:*

(a) *Integration of the disabled.* We ask the churches to participate fully in the proposed WCC study of the Church and the disabled, to take account of the findings of the Faith and Order Commission on this subject at Louvain (*Study Encounter,* no. 17, 1971), and to do everything possible to integrate the disabled fully into the life of the Church at every level.

(b) *Women and church unity.* Recognizing that the catholicity of the Church requires the community of men and women in its life, we recommend that the churches participate fully in the study on the Community of Women and Men in the Church, with consideration of issues of theology, Scripture, tradition, and ministry. We ask the churches to engage in serious theological reflection on these issues, especially in relation to the issue of the nature of the unity we seek.

(c) *Conciliar fellowship.* We ask the churches to provide opportunities for a careful study and evaluation of the concept of conciliar fellowship as a way of describing the unity of the Church, and for this purpose we recommend the following documents: "Conciliarity and the Future of the Ecumenical Movement", *Faith and Order* (Louvain, 1971); "The Unity of the Church—Next Steps", the report of the Salamanca Consultation, *What Kind of Unity?* pp. 119-30; *Orthodox Contributions to Nairobi* (WCC, 1975), especially pp. 10-13 and 31-33; the report of the Orthodox Consultation at Etchmiadzin, *Study Encounter,* vol. 11, no. 4 (1975); "What Unity Requires—A Comment", *What Unity Requires* (WCC, 1975), pp. 14-17; and "What Unity Requires", report of Section II, WCC Fifth Assembly, Nairobi. This study must clarify the varied meanings given to the phrase "local church", and the relation of the local church to the full reality of the Church. It must also take up the issues concerning the Eucharist, ministry, and authority.

SECTION III: SEEKING COMMUNITY:
THE COMMON SEARCH OF PEOPLE OF VARIOUS FAITHS, CULTURES, AND IDEOLOGIES

Before introducing the Report, the Moderator of the Section, Metropolitan Paulos Gregorios (Syrian Orthodox, India), spoke with gratitude of the contribution of five guests belonging to other faiths:

Professor K. L. Seshagiri Rao, Hindu, Professor of Religious Studies, Virginia, USA

Professor L. G. Hewage, Buddhist, Professor of Education, University of Sri Lanka

Rabbi Dr Arnold J. Wolf, Jew, Director of the B'nai B'rith Hillel Foundation and Jewish Chaplain at Yale University, USA

Dr Harun Hasution, Muslim, Rector of the State Islamic Institute, Jakarta, Indonesia

H. E. Dr Gopal Singh, Sikh, High Commissioner of India to the Republic of Guyana.

Amidst applause, Dr M. M. Thomas greeted and thanked them.

Introducing the Report, Metropolitan Paulos Gregorios reminded the Assembly that the Christians, even if united, would be a minority within humanity, and that the wider human community really matters. The questions are, therefore, first: What in our faith makes it possible to say that God, the Father, Son, and Holy Spirit, is working within the whole of creation and humanity? Second: What is the right relationship between Christians and people of other faiths and ideologies? Third: With cultures all interacting, how do we find a world in which all cultures learn to make a common response to the problems confronting humanity?

Dr Albert van den Heuvel (Netherlands Reformed Church) characterized the Report as cautious, and some others agreed; but the majority of speakers were not happy with it and believed that it would be understood as spiritual compromise (Dr Per Lønning, Church of Norway) or opposition to the mission of the Church (Bishop Michael, Russian Orthodox). There were a number of detailed criticisms, in particular to paragraphs 4 and 5, which stated that Christians should not allow their faith to add to the divisions of humanity because, as fellow-creatures of God, we are linked together. To this, Bishop Lesslie Newbigin (United Reformed Church, UK) replied: "The one holy reason we have for seeking community is that God has become man and reconciled man to God. What separates us is our sin. It is on this basis that we have to seek for community for all men."

Replying to the debate (to which twelve others had wished to contribute), Metropolitan Paulos Gregorios offered to draft a supplementary page to cover the points made. Dr Lønning, however, felt that the objections were so serious that the Assembly should see a revised version before voting. By a large majority, the Report was *referred back* to the Section for reconsideration.

Dr Principal Olle Engstrom (Mission Covenant Church, Sweden) later introduced the revised text of the Section Report to which had been added a preamble. He noted that for many member churches the search for a wider community is not an academic but an existential issue, and asked that those who are a bit further away from direct encounter should listen carefully to those churches for which it is a primary concern.

Principal Russell Chandran (Church of South India) said that the report was weak and uncommitted, and the new preamble made it still more cautious. He therefore felt bound on behalf of many others to ask for a more definite endorsement of the dialogue approach. After reviewing the history of the question from Edinburgh 1910 to the Tambaram Conference in 1937 and the debate occasioned by Dr Hendrik Kraemer's "The Christian Message in a Non-Christian World", Dr Chandran continued:

In this debate not only the first-hand experience of those who have lived and moved with people of other faiths but also the deeper theological understanding of the gospel, Jesus Christ, the Holy Spirit, the doctrine of the Trinity, and the meaning of revelation, led many to modify or abandon the Kraemerian approach and to adopt the approach of dialogue. It was this development which led to the establishment of the WCC Secretariat on Dialogue following the Uppsala Assembly. The Second Vatican Council also led the Roman Catholic Church to establish a secretariat for relations with other faiths. Both the WCC-sponsored and the Roman Catholic studies and consultations in recent years have only been deepening the theological insights and convictions about the presence and work of Christ and the Holy Spirit in other religions and cultures.

This development is not simply the consequence of human considerations of tolerance, religious harmony, and peace. On the contrary, it is deeply rooted in our confession of Jesus Christ as Lord and Saviour and our commitment to the trinitarian faith. The theology of creation affirms the presence and the work of God in all cultures. Our confession of Christ as Lord is an affirmation that he is Lord, not only of Christians but of all peoples. He is the Logos who holds all things together. He is the light which lightens everyone. It is in him all things and all peoples are to be united.

We also need to acknowledge that we have not yet fathomed the depths of the unsearchable riches of Christ and our knowledge of him must never be absolutized or identified with the fullness of the reality of Christ. It is the Holy Spirit who leads us into all truth. He does this by interpreting Christ to us and by helping us to learn from one another's experience of Christ. In a genuine sense, our knowledge and experience of Christ is enriched by the response of the people of other faiths. Witnessing to Christ is, therefore, a two-way movement of mutual learning and enrichment.

The Church which evangelizes is also evangelized in the sense that its knowledge and experience of Jesus Christ and his gospel is deepened by the response of those to whom the gospel is proclaimed. This is true also because Christ whom we proclaim and witness to is greater than our knowledge and experience of him. We do not possess him. He possesses us and all peoples. Discerning and making manifest his presence in the faith and experience of others is also part of the process of our witnessing to him. Therefore those who preach Christ to people of other faiths should also be willing and expectant to learn about the fullness of the reality of Christ by listening to what they have to say in witness of their faith. Only through such dialogue can we grow into the presence of Christ and deepen and enlarge the catholicity of the Church.

We would like our brethren who are concerned about the commitment to the great commission of our Lord and the dangers of syncre-

71

tism to be willing to listen to the testimony and insights of those who have more intimate knowledge of our faiths and are in no way less committed to Jesus Christ and his mission. We plead that they avoid the mistake of making judgements on the basis of traditional doctrines, without the knowledge of other peoples and their faiths, and thus failing to grow into the fullness of Christ.

Dr Lynn A. de Silva (Methodist, Sri Lanka) spoke as Director of a Study Centre with many years of experience in promoting dialogue, which is accepted as essential for the unity and integrity of the life of the nation:

There are many misgivings, fears, and anxieties that have been expressed by some members in this Assembly about dialogue with people of other faiths. I have good reason to believe that these arise mainly in the minds of those who have not encountered people of other faiths nor ever lived among them. Let me therefore make a few statements about the significance and importance of dialogue in the Asian context which I hope will allay such fears. These have risen out of my own experience of actual dialogue during many years.

1. Dialogue does not in any way diminish full and loyal commitment to one's own faith, but rather enriches and strengthens it. Many have borne testimony to this fact.

2. Dialogue, far from being a temptation to syncretism, is a safeguard against it, because in dialogue we get to know one another's faith in depth. One's own faith is tested and refined and sharpened thereby. The real test of faith is faiths-in-relation.

3. Dialogue is a creative interaction which liberates a person from a closed or cloistered system to which he happens to belong by an accident of birth, and elevates him to spiritual freedom giving him a vision of wider dimensions of spiritual life by his sharing in the spirituality of others.

4. Dialogue is urgent and essential for us in Asia in order to repudiate the arrogance, aggression, and negativism of our evangelistic crusades which have obscured the gospel and caricatured Christianity as an aggressive and militant religion. As a result of this Jesus Christ appears in the eyes of people of other faiths as a religious Julius Caesar, as one of our honoured guests from another faith present in this Assembly put it in one of our Section's meetings. Let us remind ourselves that Jesus Christ was not a Christian—he belongs to all—but we have made him appear as a Western Christian of an affluent society, somewhat like a Julius Caesar.

5. Dialogue is essential to dispel the negative attitude we have to people of other faiths, which makes proclamation ineffective and irrelevant. A negative attitude invites a negative response; if we are not prepared to accept the others in love they will not accept us. (In many instances Christianity has been rejected because it has rejected other religions.) If we are not prepared to listen to people of other faiths they will not listen to us. In such a situation effective proclamation of the gospel will not be possible. Dialogue therefore is essential in order to dispel the misunderstandings and prejudices of the past created by our negative attitude to other faiths and thereby create a healthy atmosphere where we can receive as well as give, listen as well as

proclaim. Above all, dialogue is essential for us to discover the Asian face of Jesus Christ as the Suffering Servant, so that the Church itself may be set free from its institutional self-interest and play the role of a servant in building community—the community of love or the Kingdom of God.

Dr Roger Mehl (Reformed, France) thought that the Report was not too cautious but even more incautious and that Christianity could not without critical study absorb the spirituality of other religions. The new preamble was criticized by Ms Carmencita Karagdag (Philippine Independent Church), the Reverend W. Ariarajah (Methodist, Sri Lanka), Dr David Stowe (United Church of Christ, USA), and Dr E. Nacpil (Methodist, Philippines).

Others spoke in favour of the document as a whole, and after a brief reply by Principal Engstrom, the motion to commend the Report of Section III to the churches for study and appropriate action was carried.

SECTION III: SEEKING COMMUNITY: THE COMMON SEARCH OF PEOPLE OF VARIOUS FAITHS, CULTURES, AND IDEOLOGIES

Preamble

1. We are all agreed that the *skandalon* (stumbling block) of the gospel will always be with us. While we do seek wider community with people of other faiths, cultures, and ideologies, we do not think there will ever be a time in history when the tension will be resolved between belief in Jesus Christ and unbelief. It is a tension that divides the Church from the world. It is a tension which also goes through each Christian disciple, as each is unable to say that his or her faith in Jesus Christ is perfect.

2. We should also make a proper distinction between the division created by the judging Word of God and the division caused by sin.

3. We are all agreed that the Great Commission of Jesus Christ which asks us to go out into all the world and make disciples of all nations, and to baptize them in the Triune Name, should not be abandoned or betrayed, disobeyed or compromised, neither should it be misused. Dialogue is both a matter of hearing and understanding the faith of others, and also of witnessing to the gospel of Jesus Christ.

4. We are all opposed to any form of syncretism, incipient, nascent, or developed, if we mean by syncretism conscious or unconscious human attempts to create a new religion composed of elements taken from different religions.

5. We view the future of the Church's mission as full of hope, for it is

not upon human efforts that our hope is based, but upon the power and the promise of God.

Introduction

6. The Christian gospel creates community. It has always done so. It does not create "Christianity" as a philosophy or a system, but leads to the formation of the Church, i.e. a community of persons. The gospel calls men and women from diverse families, tribes, castes, classes, parties, nations, races, cultures, etc. into a new community. Over the centuries Christians have deepened and elaborated this fact in various doctrinal affirmations (ecclesiologies), and millions of Christians have thanked and do thank God for the support and joy they found in the community that God gave them through Jesus Christ in the fellowship of the Holy Spirit.

7. This community of ours (even if all Christians come together in one community) has always been a minority within humanity. Our generation has become keenly aware of the religious plurality of the world. This plurality is augmented and criss-crossed by further differences between ideologies and cultures. Even in the old Christian countries of the West with their relatively homogeneous Christian culture and established churches, the presence and awareness of other religions is growing rapidly—often with shock effects. Such awareness does not require travels—the mass media do shrink the world.

8. But there is more than a new and sharper awareness of other faiths and communities of faith. There is a great urgency for seeking a community beyond our own. Whether we like it or not, we find ourselves thrown in with all of humanity in a common concern for peace and justice. We have been thrown together in an interdependent world, in which the urgency is that of survival or extinction.

9. In that world we cannot allow our faith, the gift of our sense of community in Jesus Christ, to add to the tensions and suspicions and hatreds that threaten to tear apart the one family of humanity. We cannot allow our faith to be abused for such demonic purposes. We must seek the wider community, without compromising the true *skandalon* of the gospel.

10. We all agree that we have one solid basis, one holy reason for seeking community with others: as fellow-creatures of God we are linked to each other, although in a fallen creation sin and unbelief divide. Many of us believe and some witness to the actual experience of a common ground far beyond that of our common humanity. They have found that Christ sets them free to explore a community under God with men and women of other faiths. We believe that in this as in all matters the gifts are different. Some seem to be called to bold pioneering, adventures and risks beyond the confines of present ecclesiastical and theological structures.

Others acknowledge an equally exacting calling to deepen the time-honoured understanding of the community that is ours in Christ.

11. We are grateful to our guests of other faiths who were gracious enough to come and be with us, and that, so to say, on our terms. They were not official representatives of their faiths, but revered exponents and expositors thereof. Their presence and their contributions gave us indispensable reminders of the reality of plurality, and the need for letting each community of faith speak its own language, and define its own identity.

12. For practical purposes our Section met in three sub-sections, somewhat arbitrarily assigned one of the three foci: Faiths, Cultures, and Ideologies. It is worth noting how different are the reports of the sub-sections; what better demonstration of the plurality of which we speak? The search for community thus must be widely different in different parts of the Church. There are different agendas and different timetables in different parts of the world.

13. Thus it is imperative to recognize that our unity in Christ is so deeply rooted and grounded in God's love (Eph. 3.17) that we are set free from all fear as we follow the various paths that God opens up ahead of us (1 Cor. 16.9; 2 Cor. 2.12; Col. 4.3) in the various parts of the world and according to the various conditions of peoples and societies.

FAITHS AND THE SEARCH FOR COMMUNITY

14. What kind of community are Christians committed to seek? Some clarification of the word "community" was sought. There is the community within a church or denomination and between the churches as pursued by the ecumenical movement. We then discussed a different dimension of community—that is, community with people of other faiths and convictions, and, in the widest sense, the community of all humanity. Some felt that this could be described as "wider ecumenism". Others, however, felt that the term was better avoided because it might create confusion. For the time being the term "ecumenical" should perhaps be used of inter-Christian dialogue, while the wider dialogue should be referred to as "inter-religious". In any case, it should be noted that this wider community is one of people with people, not of religions with religions or systems with systems, and that it is experienced or blocked in local and regional situations. Community is specific, for instance, the community of people living in the same village or district, working in the same factory or office, being fellow-citizens in the same state, sharing the task of building the same nation.

15. Almost everywhere Christians live together with neighbours of other faiths and we are all part of the world community. We live in one world and have a common calling to work for its survival and betterment.

All of us, Christians and others, are also open to being addressed by neighbours of a faith different from our own concerning the truth and the attractiveness of that faith. We all, therefore, have to learn to receive such an address without regarding it as an aggression by our neighbours of differing faith. We have to seek a community of common searching.

Starting Points in the Search for Community

16. But is there also a theological basis on which Christians should seek community with their neighbours of other faiths and convictions? Several answers were given to this question. Many stressed that all people have been created by God in his image and that God loves all humanity. Many believed that in a world broken by sin it is the incarnation of God in Jesus Christ which provides the basis for the restoration of the creation to wholeness. Others would seek this basis for community in the trinitarian understanding of God. Still others find theological meaning in the fact that history has removed and is removing geographical and cultural barriers which once kept us isolated and so is moving us towards one interdependent humanity. In all this discussion we encountered the question of a possible double basis for our search for community. Christians have a specifically theological basis for such a search. Is there also a common basis which should be mutually acceptable to people of differing faiths and ideologies? Considerable difficulty was experienced about this and no agreed conclusion reached. It would appear, however, that in practice in particular situations men and women of various cultures, faiths, and ideologies can enter into community together, although their own understandings of their motivations will vary.

17. The question was discussed whether we can posit that Jesus Christ is at work among people of other faiths. Here opinions differed. Some stated as their conviction that Jesus Christ as Saviour is not present in the other religions, although they accepted the idea of a natural knowledge of God. Others acknowledged the presence of *logoi spermatikoi* (scattered seeds of truth) in other religions but stressed that only in Jesus Christ do we receive fullness of truth and life. Others gave first-hand testimony that their own faith in Jesus Christ had been greatly deepened and strengthened through encountering him in dialogue with those of other faiths. The point was also made that the Spirit works among people outside Israel and outside the Church, and that this Spirit is one with the Father and with the Son.

18. Two points emerged:

(*a*) We should not talk about religions in general but take account of the specific nature of each religion. We are unable to say that all religions pursue the same aims or witness to the same truth nor that everything in any religion is good.

76

(b) In the last few centuries a new situation has arisen. The gospel has been made known all over the world and people of various faiths and convictions have been faced with the person and teaching of Jesus Christ. This has worked as a ferment widely outside the borders of the Christian community and in that sense Christ's work is not confined to the limits of the Church.

19. At this point our Hindu guest drew attention to the fact that while it is true that Jesus Christ has worked as a ferment among the people of other faiths, it is also true that insights from such religions as Hinduism and Buddhism, etc., are working as a ferment among some Christians and others in Europe, the USA, and elsewhere.

Dialogue as a Means towards Community

20. Many stressed the importance of dialogue in view of the necessity of co-operation of all people in order to establish a righteous and peaceful society. Dialogue helps people in their search for community. Authentic dialogue is a human and a Christian undertaking in its own right. It should not be seen as an alternative for mission and it should not compromise our faith.

21. Further, we cannot speak about dialogue in general. Dialogue is affected by at least two sets of circumstances which make a difference to the ways in which it will be understood and undertaken:

(a) The situation in various areas of the world is very different. In some pluralistic societies a dialogue and a living-in-community has been going on for a long time; in other societies great tensions between different religious communities hamper dialogue and at the same time make dialogue the more desirable; in other situations again dialogue is almost impossible because a dominant group is not interested in it.

(b) Dialogue also varies in accordance with the nature of the partner. There is a very special relationship between Christianity and Judaism. The three West Asian religions, Judaism, Christianity, and Islam, have a close historical relationship and theological interconnections. The relation between Christianity and East Asian religions has a different history. Traditional religions in Africa and elsewhere have yet another kind of relationship to Christianity.

22. Depending on the partners and the situation, a dialogue might sometimes start with common concerns in society and ways of working together in tackling these problems; sometimes theological issues could be the basis for dialogue. Very often these are interrelated.

23. The terms "spirituality" and "sharing" need clarification in the context of dialogue. "Sharing in spirituality" need not mean entering into common worship. For some, it implies seeking to understand with empa-

thy the dimensions of worship, devotion, and meditation in the religious tradition and practice of the partners.

CULTURES AND THE SEARCH FOR COMMUNITY

24. We met and introduced each other to our differing cultural and social contexts, where we are called as Christians to seek community with our fellow human beings. We experienced a bewildering, though exciting, mosaic. We felt challenged to grapple anew with the question of culture and the search for community.

The Diversity of Culture

25. When we speak of culture, we speak of a very involved phenomenon. Culture includes the world-view and way of life of a people. It has its roots in history and is subject to continual change and revision. Culture is dynamic, not static. Culture embodies a people's style of life, religion, technology, literature, and the arts. People are bound up with culture. To each, culture is a fact, a challenge, and a blessing. Different peoples have different cultures, and, as peoples meet, cultures interact. There is, however, a conserving element in culture which makes people resistant to change. In the process of the interaction, the dialectics of culture become apparent. On the one hand, there is the reality of arrogance as apparent in cultural imperialism. On the other, there is the danger of egoism reflected in cultural isolationism.

26. The universal and the particular can oppose one another and can promote one another. Universality can grow out of openness to change and exchange among cultures. It grows also through the deepening of particularity which is received through increasing awareness of the distinct riches in one's own culture. There are even in the culture of one people particularities of time and place, such as rural or urban. In all this we recognize that varying cultures reflect the richness and diversity of humankind.

27. Today we recognize the wide-ranging effects of the technological culture. It manifests itself in "secularity" in post-Christian milieux in both East and West. It is apparent in "urbanization" in cosmopolitan world capitals. Technological culture reflects men's and women's ability to shape the future. But it also implies dangers of dehumanization, particularly when it clashes with traditional cultures. Special attention should be drawn to people everywhere who are at the crossroads of impinging cultures, such as Aborigines in Australia, native Americans (Amerindians), migrant workers in Europe and elsewhere, and peoples involved in the rural exodus in Africa and Latin America.

28. Thus, though technological culture is international, it is not the final answer to the quest for wider community.

Christ and Culture

29. Is there a specific Christian culture? The question is pertinent, and loaded with the cultural imperialism associated with missionary history. Sharing our Christian commitment in different cultural contexts we realized joyfully that Jesus Christ both affirms and judges culture. As our Jewish guest affirmed, Jesus was an historical person, sharing a specific culture. At the same time Christian experience affirms that no culture is closer to Jesus Christ than any other culture. Jesus Christ restores what is truly human in any culture and frees us to be open to other cultures. Resources for world community are no Christian monopoly. We must be ready to acknowledge the presence of such resources wherever they are found. He offers us liberation from attitudes of cultural superiority and from self-sufficiency. He unites us in a community which transcends any particular culture.

The Church as a Community

30. As Christians with widely differing cultural history we belong to that community which is the Body of Christ, the Church. The Church, too, should become embodied in every culture. It is called to fellowship in worship, freedom, and service, sustained by a foretaste of God's Kingdom. As such a community the Church is called to relate itself to any culture critically, creatively, redemptively. That means that within the Christian community each member should be open to the other, respecting the authenticity of his or her particular cultural form of obedience to the gospel, in the one Church. Commitment to Jesus Christ takes different cultural forms. This is an expression of the Church's catholicity.

Christians' Search for Wider Community?

31. The Church manifests itself in scattered communities in varying cultures where, too often, egoism and arrogance, even between Christians, threaten the wider community. Christians are themselves caught up in the world-wide confrontation between technological and traditional cultures. It is in such situations that Christians are called to face common responsibilities with fellow human beings of different religions or ideological persuasions. The need to reconcile local tensions calls for commitment to wider community. This need not endanger the identity of the Christian Church.

32. We were encouraged when we heard of creative acts of solidarity, of the will for dialogue, and of the search for community in situations of grave tension. We heard, for instance, of reconciling initiatives from both sides in the Christian-Muslim conflict in Mindanao. We heard also of fresh attempts to make rural people the world over aware of their resources and responsibilities.

33. It is now widely recognized that cities are not "melting pots".

Within a city people can find their own "villages", namely communities within which they may express their identity and humanity more fully. Despite the risk of ghettoism, the search for identity is often necessary. Also the opposite tendency manifests itself: for example, in New York there is a group of women of different religions and ethnic backgrounds who pursue the search for further openness, mutual trust, and active co-operation. In New Delhi local Christians are attempting to make of a religiously pluralistic housing estate a community where people can live together in mutual trust. It is a battle against anonymity and isolation, a battle for community. The search for a wider community also involves Christians in entering into dialogue, especially in seeking to relate to the cultures of urban secularism.

34. In all these situations where ventures are made to seek wider community a necessary prerequisite has proved to be an honest recognition of the cultural integrity of different groups.

35. In local situations, these resources are released for wider world community. There is a necessary relationship between the local and the global. As "the new community in Christ", the Church is called upon to prefigure that world community, but, alas, the present disunity of Christians makes a mockery of that model.

IDEOLOGIES AND THE SEARCH FOR COMMUNITY

36. By way of introduction, the following issues were posed:

(a) What are the actual forms of encounter between Christian faith and ideologies?

(b) Can we distinguish between faith as transcendental and ideology as temporal and historical?

(c) What is our understanding of ideology? Is it valid to distinguish between socialism and capitalism, as political praxis, from the ideologies that undergird them?

(d) Should we seek community with adherents of secular ideologies? Can deep differences be transcended?

37. We took particular note of the variety of situations in which we live and in which religions and ideologies are engaged in the struggle to defend or transform existing social structures.

The Content of Institutional Ideologies

38. First, there are those of us who come from societies where Marxist socialism has been institutionalized, i.e., the eastern European countries and Cuba. In these countries, the Christian churches face radically new situations and have lost most of their former privileges. Some of

these churches, like churches elsewhere, came to see that they had often taken the wrong side in social upheavals and, sometimes, had even sanctified the oppressive structures in the name of Christian principles. This can explain partly why institutionalized Marxist ideology is opposed to religion. Therefore, Marxist socialism has posed a serious challenge to the churches and their understanding of Christianity. In some eastern European countries, the churches no longer withdraw into isolation, but have been led to go to the sources of their faith for a more creative approach to their situation. They have begun to respond to the challenges with which every ideology confronts them. In so doing, they witness to the wholeness of humanity, of men and women, of individuals and communities.

39. However, this reconciling element in the Christians' search for community together with people of ideological convictions should not be taken to mean ideological convergence. The churches are called to witness in a divided world and cannot remain neutral in the struggle for justice. But they do not necessarily take sides ideologically. Dialogue with Marxists has taken place not only on the theoretical level but still more over practical issues. This has been possible because, while atheism is contrary to Christian faith, atheism is only one part of the Marxist ideology.

New Forms of Ideology

40. Those of us, meanwhile, who came from the poor countries of Asia and Africa were concerned that little attention had been given to the varieties of ideological components. We would be preempting the ideological debate if we saw it exclusively in terms of institutionalized forms, whether liberal capitalism or Marxist socialism. In the Philippines, Dahomey, and Tanzania, for instance, ideology is seen more as a necessary tool in the struggle for a more human and just society.

41. In Asia, particularly, traditional feudal systems are now being challenged by state philosophies such as Indonesian Pantja Sila or by ideologies such as Chinese Maoism. This challenge as so many others is faced by other people of other religions as well as Christians. Repressive, technocratic states based on Western capitalism are confronted by varying forms of ideologies advocating human rights, social justice, and people's participation. African socialism, as in Tanzania, makes use of traditional elements while basing itself on the principles of justice and self-reliance. Rediscovery of traditional cultural values in many countries in Africa had led to Christians questioning an uncritical acceptance of the division, made by some Western Christians, between good and bad ideologies.

42. Within this context, socialism in the Third World countries assumes a variety of expressions. Hence the ideological challenge in the Third World must be seen in terms of where the Church as an institution is located within the wide spectrum of political and economic and ideological positions.

43. Some of us in the Western, capitalist, pluralist countries, for example the United States, Great Britain, and Belgium, called attention to the ideological presuppositions implicit in the capitalist system, e.g. individualism and consumerism. These are often masked as pragmatic values as opposed to ideological ones.

44. In the West, especially the United States, ideology has often taken on a derogatory meaning and it is not recognized as undergirding every political and economic option. Many often erroneously associate the term "ideology" only with Marxism. Christians in the West, as elsewhere, ought always to scrutinize sensitively and critically their own, perhaps unconscious, ideological presuppositions.

45. As Christians, we find that no person or group should fail to come to terms with the challenge of ideologies. We accept the responsibility to judge critically and openly the ways in which our Christian faith may interact with various cultures and ideologies.

The Relationship between Faith and Ideology

46. Out of these varying situations a few points have emerged:

(*a*) The growing recognition of the ideological presuppositions in the life of churches and local congregations has helped to destroy the oversimplifications and prejudices that have traditionally beset the ecumenical movement. Increasingly, ecumenical programmes are open to change.

(*b*) There is need to explore in some detail the relationship between faith and ideology. Are they mutually exclusive, demanding absolute loyalty from adherents, or are they, in some situations, in dialectical tension with each other, not only between groups but within individuals as well? Can we speak of a pure Christianity, isolated from an ideological milieu, whether it be Marxist, humanist, or some other?

(*c*) The question must be asked again: Is Christian community possible despite ideological diversities? Conflicting ideologies and deepening and violent ideological struggles within the same system threaten from within and from outside the unity in Christ which we proclaim. Yet, as we commit ourselves to struggle for community and as we affirm that Jesus Christ frees and unites, we find in him the vision and the hope which help us to transcend these divisions.

Note: The specific countries mentioned in this report often reflect the way in which these countries happened to be represented in a particular sub-section.

RECOMMENDATIONS TO THE CHURCHES

The following proposals arising out of the Section III report are commended to the churches in their varying contexts as Christians seek community with people of various faiths, cultures, and ideologies.

47. *Preparations within the Churches*

a. Study of the Bible as well as of the traditions of the churches in order to illuminate the meaning of wider community and to clarify the basis in our faith for seeking community with all peoples. This study should help us to relate the uniqueness of Christ to God's larger work among all peoples and in the whole creation. Such study should also help us to avoid confusion or compromise, and to inspire critical openness to others.

b. Sympathetic and critical studies on the faiths and ideologies of people with whom the temporal destinies of Christians are intertwined, including other peoples' understandings and misunderstandings about Christian claims.

c. Examining and revising wherever possible with the assistance of people of other faiths our catechetical, liturgical, and theological materials. The aim is to remove all caricatures and misrepresentations of other people's faiths, cultures, and ideologies, and in the teaching about other religions in theological seminaries.

d. Study and reflection on the mutual impact and interpenetration of the Christian faith and indigenous elements in each religious and cultural setting.

e. Continued reflection, on a regional and local basis, on the relation between dialogue and evangelism, taking into account experiments in actual dialogue with people of various faiths and ideologies.

f. Acquainting the members of our churches with the wide spectrum of the Christian spiritual heritage, ranging from the ancient Oriental Christian traditions of Asia to the contemporary spiritual practices, for example, of African independent churches.

48. *The Search for Community*

a. Actually promoting dialogue and collaboration, on a selective and experimental basis, with people of other faiths and ideologies, on common concerns, and evaluating the experience gained, in order to improve the quality and widen the scope of dialogue and collaboration.

b. Building up the freedom and unity of the Christian fellowship in local congregations by removing all cultural, age, sex, class, and race barriers within the fellowship, in order to create a new atmosphere of understanding between various cultures, religions, and ideologies, as also between old and young, men and women.

49. *Involvement in Dialogue*

a. Establishing the principles and basis for dialogue in each cultural and geographical context, such as comparable levels of education and attitudes of participants, commitment to one's own faith and conviction while maintaining sympathetic openness to others, clear definition of agenda or theme, starting point and objectives, etc.

b. Learning from the experiences of others who have already engaged in dialogue.

c. Preparing people adequately for dialogue and collaboration.

50. *Sharing in Spirituality*

a. In a world where Christians are increasingly exposed to the disciplines and practices of East Asian religions and traditional or primal religious heritages, the churches should help Christians both to evaluate correctly the significance and consequences of these, and to go back to the forgotten or neglected aspects of the Church's own spiritual heritage, in order to reappropriate what is valuable in it in the current context.

b. The preparation of Christians to discern what could be seductively demonic or dangerously misleading in any religious or spiritual traditions.

c. Pastoral concern both for those who feel threatened by the hazards of sharing spirituality, and for those who claim enrichment of their Christian faith through experiences of such sharing, with mutual dialogue between the two groups.

51. *Ecumenical Reflection about Faiths, Cultures, and Ideologies*

a. Clarification of terminology: for example, is it wise to adopt terminology like "wider ecumenism" for seeking wider community beyond the churches, or is it open to confusion and misunderstanding?

b. Encouragement of Christian communities in various countries to affirm and express their cultural identity, but also to evaluate it critically. The results of such studies could be shared ecumenically.

c. Deeper analysis and perceptive understanding of the causes of mutual mistrust between faiths and ideologies; examination of ways of promoting mutual trust without abandoning caution, the need to promote both identity and openness.

d. Examination of tensions created within the Christian fellowship on account of conflicting ideological commitments and the promotion of inner dialogue within the churches between different ideological camps.

e. Actual collaboration between peoples of differing faiths, cultures, and ideologies, in commonly organized programmes in a specific area of promoting social justice and human dignity; this may be organized either between people of different religious convictions or ideological persuasions, or both, or depending on the circumstances.

52. *Requisite Church Structures*

a. Living-in-dialogue may often be more important than organized dialogue. Organized or occasional dialogue may lead to a situation of living-in-dialogue, where religious communities may seek to resolve conflicts arising between them in an atmosphere of mutual trust and peaceful negotiations.

b. Churches could produce or subsidize educational programmes (including text-books and curricula) to promote inter-religious understanding and collaboration on certain specific and existential issues. In certain countries churches could influence the governments to produce such programmes. In some cases such programmes may be jointly sponsored by different religious communities, in order to achieve fair and accurate presentations of the views of each religion by its adherents.

c. The services of the WCC Sub-unit on Dialogue with People of Living Faiths and Ideologies are at the disposal of the churches: to transmit experience gained in one region to other regions; to promote and prepare local or regional dialogues; to gather information and experience and make them available to the churches; and to encourage study projects or practical ventures at all levels of society.

SECTION IV:
EDUCATION FOR LIBERATION AND COMMUNITY

The Report was introduced by Mr Harry Ashmall (Church of Scotland), Moderator of the Section, and Principal of a large comprehensive school in Scotland. The Report was not a finished document but rather a basis for the practical recommendations that would follow later. The discussion, to which fourteen people contributed, dealt largely with matters of detail rather than with its general point of view, though Fr Aram Keshishian (Armenian Orthodox) thought that it wholly failed to understand Christian education in its context of the traditions of the Church, and Ms Benita Johanson (Church of Finland) thought it inadequate in that respect and in its definition of the duties of the Church, and moved that the Report be referred back for redrafting.

This was resisted by the Moderator of the Section. He pointed out that since conditions varied so widely from country to country, the Report had inevitably to be general: the member churches must insert their own particularities. When Ms Johanson's motion was put it was defeated. The motion that the Report be approved in substance after minor amendment and commended to the churches for study and appropriate action was carried.

Mr H. Ashmall, Moderator, presented the Second Report of Section IV.

The Report was criticized by Professor K. Osipov (Russian Orthodox) for failing to face deepening materialism with a still deeper spirituality; and Fr Argenti (Ecumenical Patriarchate) was surprised that there was no emphasis on the teaching of the faith. Canon P. H. Boulton (Church of England) moved that the fourth group of recommendations begin with a new paragraph: "Provide the means for teaching a spirituality for life". Mr Knut Lundby (Church of Norway) moved that there be added to the end of the Report a reference to its connection with Section I. These were accepted by the Committee. A proposal by Dr B.M. Pulimood (Mar Thoma, India) to add a paragraph on drug abuse was resisted by the Committee but approved by the Assembly. Ms Barbara Thompson (Methodist, USA) proposed an amended version of the paragraph about the right use of full-time ministers, which was accepted.

The Report as amended was put to the vote and accepted.

SECTION IV:
EDUCATION FOR LIBERATION AND COMMUNITY

THE CONTEXT OF EDUCATION*

1. We live in a world of great suffering and disunity; a world shackled to the domination and oppression of human beings by other human beings; a world which persons exploit for their own ends, disrupting the stability of nature; a world in which the major threats to survival now come from human beings themselves given through education the power to be more threatening.

---

*Note: For the purpose of this report the English term "education" is used very broadly, to include the wide range of planned intentional actions designed to influence and inform persons or train them in skills. It includes formal education, the systems of schools at various levels; non-formal and informal education, what the French language calls *formation*, the German *Erziehung* and *Bildung*, and the formative processes often called "socialization".

The term "liberation" derives from the saving work of Jesus Christ who frees and unites. It involves both the personal and the corporate-

2. In obedience to the commandment of Jesus Christ to love our neighbour, we are called to work for the creation of a society in which humanity, justice, openness, and freedom reflect the will of God for his creation. It is Jesus Christ who gives us the vision and the promise of the new world, and provides the basis and the force for renewal in both personal and community life. To say that he is our hope and basis is not to claim that we are free from sin ourselves.

3. We live our lives in this hope, daily engaged in a whole series of realities which shape our society. The informal influences of family, friends—and enemies—impinge on our lives. Radio and television, meetings and discussions, as well as formal education, have a strong influence on our attitudes. Humanity learns many lessons from schooling, and outside it, and so we are required to evaluate critically the forces which liberate and those which enslave.

4. None of us can claim expertise for this. We are ourselves the products of the educational conditioning which we now question. When we speak to the world, we speak also, and first, to ourselves.

ALIENATION FROM AND ASSIMILATION INTO OUR CULTURE
AND OUR HISTORY

5. We cannot be liberated if we are divorced from the culture which bred us and which continues to shape and condition us. Many are taught to despise their culture, many are not participants—except by omission—in the shaping of it. Some educational programmes play a large part in creating false images: prejudice, fear, hatred are instilled into persons through selective and biased curricula and teaching, and this situation is aggravated by the false expectations which people derive from the influences of social organizations. Education policies in many countries serve development strategies that are harmful to their societies. We are not romanticizing indigenous culture: it too can have elements which enslave and degrade, but we advocate that people be brought to a critical awareness of the strengths and weaknesses of their own culture for the development they desire for themselves, rather than being disruptively separated from it to serve the purposes of others.

6. As we search for and stress indigenous values, we must also affirm

---

structural, as does the concept of sin and death from which Christ brings liberation. It also includes the full biblical and theological meaning of the liberated life for persons and communities to which God calls us.

The term "community" combines all the richness of biblical and theological understandings of *koinonia* and of God's *oikoumene* over the whole inhabited earth, the unity which Christ is bringing to creation and to his Church.

that there is a universality in Christianity and a growing awareness of the global nature of problems which calls for an education which both informs and transcends the local. The danger of imposing our own values when we engage in the situations of others has to be guarded against, but it must not become the excuse for staying with only the local and familiar in a world which is becoming increasingly interdependent.

7. The voice of alienation has come to us most strongly from the countries of the Third World. To their long history of economic exploitation has been added the serious imbalance between the skills generated by the educational system and their actual needs. In many of these countries the system was simply an expansion of that of their former colonial rulers. In nearly all of these countries the failure of the system to meet their needs is accentuated when the institutions borrow from developed countries and have not developed an indigenous character. Western patterns of teaching, evaluation, and accreditation persist still and even proliferate, and pupils (and people and teachers) face a double alienation: the one from the westernized model and the other from their own culture.

8. In affluent countries consumer-orientation all too often breeds a competitiveness and selfishness which is anti-Christian: actively opposed to the human values revealed in Christ Jesus. A personal malaise and search for identity characterizes many lives. The lost, the lonely, and the frightened are no strangers in the so-called "developed" world. Increasingly the effects of this consumer-orientation are being felt in developing nations as well.

9. The educational system and institutions are all too often mirror images of society, reinforcing by their practices the values which society holds. Though not plagued as severely by the drop-out problem which blights the educational provision of some developing countries, the developed countries share with them in the provision of an education which disqualifies the large majority from "success". Content becomes more theoretical and abstract, the practical is degraded, experience counts for little, the cognitive becomes increasingly emphasized over other values and virtues, until in higher education it is the pre-eminent if not the only concern.

We are aware of a deep and pervasive sense of anxiety about systems of formal education in many parts of the world. The formal education system is itself in ferment. The naive utopianism which equates technological development with progress is being abandoned. This is paralleled in the education system which serves that development, with the abandonment of the view that more and more schooling is a good thing in itself.

10. This criticism of formal education is not to deny the value of certain highly developed intellectual skills and processes which conserve the best in traditions and values from the past. The debate is rather

whether the production of the few who obtain these skills should be obtained at such expense to the many who do not; and whether the values attached to these skills in schools, and the rewards given to them in society, do not distort the values of the whole education system.

11. The link between school and society and the relationship between dominant economic and social values and the educational system leads many to hold the view that education cannot itself be reformed until the political and economic systems which it serves and which support it are also reformed or radically transformed. Education in too many societies is a consciously used instrument of power: designed to produce those who accept and serve the system; designed to prevent the growth of a critical consciousness which would lead people to want alternatives. In many places disenchantment with the system and with its unwillingness to reform itself leads groups to infiltrate actively and consciously the educational institutions, to erode the structures so that they change more rapidly, and incorporate more of the non-formal and the informal in their methods. Where societies perpetuate racism through separate systems of schools, churches should actively combat such a system.

12. Within the system of education new possibilities are, however, emerging.

13. Attempts are being made to develop greater participation in the control of education so that decisions are made by the people and not only by an elite; though the problem of educating the new controllers is made the more difficult because they were trained by the same system.

14. Attempts are being made to secure a two-way community movement in relation to the schools. On the one hand, the introduction into schools of those who bring in from the community their often more practical skills encourages relevance and enriches the curriculum. On the other hand, the participation of the school in the affairs of the larger community encourages awareness and involvement.

15. Curricula are being reviewed and revised so that they attempt to deal honestly and effectively with such things as:

(a) attitudes of prejudice and the creation of stereotypes;
(b) the indigenous cultures to replace the foreign;
(c) the development of community;
(d) the spiritual life;
(e) the development of the emotional life;
(f) more vocational, relevant training;
(g) a value system;
(h) the reinterpretation of history where this has been distorted;
(i) injustices in social, economic, and political systems.

16. While this section has concentrated on alienation from culture

and history, we recognize other equally important forms, especially the alienation of persons from persons, and the alienation of human beings from nature. Further analysis of these other forms of alienation will contribute to education for liberation.

17. The dynamic nature of society means both assimilation into a culture and alienation from it. This Section has raised some of the more evident examples of this process and we stress the need for a deeper study of the whole effect of cultural changes as they relate to Christianity and education.

THE CHRISTIAN COMMUNITY AS A SIGN OF LIBERATION

18. The Christian community is placed in the human community to present the. total message of Christ and to be a sign of God's liberating power. Yet we as Christians are painfully aware that we must confess our failure to live in such a manner. Too often our Christian communities are signs not of liberation and community, but of authoritarianism and narrow parochialism. An urgent question for the churches to answer is how they can become the sign of liberation to the people: the guide to service and witness to and for the world.

19. In some countries, where church communities do not have opportunities for religious involvement in formal education, they depend upon the nature of their communal life, the life style of its members and various informal types of Christian nurture. In these situations, the life style of Christians is the primary form of witness and manifestation of God's care and concern for the world.

20. The entire life of the Christian community is educative, and the quality of its worship and work as a whole determines the quality of the nurture of its members. Each local congregation is called to be a community—a *koinonia*—which reflects the care and love of God for all people. In such a fellowship all members have their part and must contribute to the life of the whole. Christian education is a vital part of this, for it belongs to the whole Church and is the responsibility of all its members.

21. Through Christian education the Church builds up itself and its members. Specific programmes of study in Sunday schools, confirmation classes, and other settings, training for discipleship and mission, help concentrate awareness on specific issues, assist in certain developmental tasks as mature persons, and create group identity which can support individuals and the groups. They enable parish participants to relate to the Triune God, to find their place as individuals and groups in God's plan, and to nurture the spiritual reality. Through Christian education the story of human redemption is transmitted to each generation. The interpretation of the essential message of the Bible and tradition is one of the central

educative tasks of the Church. Churches must always avoid isolating Christian education from life. Through all these efforts they must help their members, children, young people, and adults, develop in their discipleship.

22. At the centre of the learning experience in the Church stands worship and the liturgy. This is the joyous expression of the Christian's dependence on God and Christ's presence in the life of his community. We must constantly examine church practices to see if they divorce liturgy from life. The liturgy must lead us to participate in the fellowship of God and guide us to service and witness in and to the world.

23. The Church is more than a local congregation. It meets in denominations and dioceses, and gathers in the larger fellowship of national, regional, and international conferences and councils. At each of these gatherings we must ask what message is conveyed and by what style of work. Do such gatherings hold the promise of liberation for those who are oppressed or do they speak of triumphalism and power?

24. The educational process of this 5th Assembly of the World Council of Churches is itself not exempt from scrutiny. We have spoken of the relationship of education to people's concerns and needs. We have indicated an education that is open and bars no questions. The development of liberation and community in large assemblies is a difficult task.

25. Our experience in an ecumenical gathering like this Assembly, with its diversity of cultures, values, styles, practices, and languages, proves to us how limiting has been our education, how difficult it is to be patient and listen carefully to what is strange or new, and how closed our cultural and educational conditioning has made us to the rich potential of engagement and interchange in the name of Christ.

DOING THEOLOGY

26. The Church has always placed a high priority on critical theological reflection on the meaning of the gospel because such reflection enables the Church in a particular time and place to witness to Christ in a way that is both faithful to the universal gospel and meaningful to men, women, and children in the culture and social conditions of that time and place. This struggle for the meaning of the gospel for today must never cease and is an activity of the whole people and not only professors and clergy.

27. The tradition of theological teaching will continue to be an integral part of training for the ordained and other specialized ministries, but the diversified needs of the Church require alternatives. Particularly restrictive has been reliance on Western models of theology and the adoption in other places of Western models of theological education. The new alternatives in extension programmes, field work programmes for

theological students, lay institutes, and the provision of continuing theological education are urgent priorities today. As many societies become more multi-cultural, another urgent priority is the need for a theological training which allows dialogue to be opened up at all levels with those of other faiths, no faith, or faiths which are anti-Christian.

28. The aim of theological education is to contribute to growth in Christ through community. Such growth takes place through conscious intellectual reflection, the nurturing of spiritual awareness, the proclaiming of the good news of human redemption, and the involvement of the people in the total liberation process.

29. Personal acts of spiritual discipline and repentance also contribute to this growth. We learn theology by reflecting on the total revelation of God and its relationship to our experiences in church, community, and society. If we engage with Christian commitment in the divisions of society, the struggles for a fully human life, the concern for the liberation of certain groups of people, and in the various power struggles, we gain fresh consciousness of God, and critical awareness of his world.

30. This learning is accelerated as we encounter cultures other than our own. Each culture bears witness to other cultures. As we enter into dialogue with persons of other faiths and of no faith, or speak with representatives of counter-cultures, or learn the attitudes of minority cultures, so we discover more fully our own identity and integrity. Our ecumenical encounters with those of other Christian groups greatly assist us in understanding our own faith.

31. It is the task of theological education to create opportunities for such experiences and to give an opportunity for those involved to reflect on the experiences and see their theological relevance.

32. Theological education belongs to the whole people of God in the equipping of them for ministry. The times are witnessing changes in the development and organization of the ordained ministry, the development of more kinds of specialized ministries, and ministries open to a greater variety of persons in a greater variety of situations than ever before. The Church needs to respond to this situation of divergence with other than a single mode of theological education, if it is to respond adequately. Ministry is the task of the whole Church and the training of Christians in a living theology should be seen as part of the total educational work of the Church.

A CREATIVE LIFE STYLE FOR COMMUNITY

33. In seeking to emphasize the inherent educative nature of the total Christian experience and the whole Christian community, we recognize

that the Church teaches by its life style. Despite the inspiring example of individual persons, the Church has many times failed to evangelize, simply because it has failed to be a community of those who find freedom and awareness in Christ. Many cannot hear what we say when our style of living interferes with and contradicts the message we are trying to communicate. Those outside the Church would learn of Christ through our life style, if we made his Word flesh and dwelt among them, not over and against them.

34. The local congregation in each place should begin to take seriously its life style and to ask what witness this is giving to the world and what nurture it is giving to its members. The local congregation proclaims its message to the rich in affluent suburbs and to the poor in villages and slums. It celebrates its worship in some of the most lavish buildings of the world as well as in miserable hovels. In each situation the Church must examine its style of life to find what that life style is saying to the world: to learn whether what it portrays in its life is contradicting the gospel message, which brings judgement to the rich and hope to the poor.

35. The struggle to find a new and creative life style is at the heart of many of our current discussions. There is value in the individual response, but the Church is the Body of Christ—its members called to live in harmony with and not in blatant contradiction of each other. The Church as a Christian community demonstrates whose side it is on by the way it appears to its neighbours. Each local congregation must ask itself critical questions about its use of buildings and land and the salary scales of its workers—not because inflation is causing a re-evaluation, but because our relationship to the gospel and to the world demands it. In some situations, the Church is being challenged to be more faithful to the message of the gospel, by the new and radical life styles being lived by groups of people.

36. If we are to reflect the Kingdom of God in our own lives that others may be led to salvation, we must develop and express in each Christian community that quality of life which is sensitive to the whole community and to the whole created universe. Each local congregation, separate denomination, diocese, and each gathering of church fellowship has to become a sign of hope to the society in which it belongs and a reflection of that global community to which we all belong.

POSTSCRIPT

37. We feel called to bring education to the notice of the Assembly. The hopes and aspirations of much of what the other Sections would wish to see achieved in the Church and in the world will be frustrated or enabled by education. It is time that all of us accepted our responsibility to create and participate in the educative community.

RECOMMENDATIONS

38. We ask the churches to recognize that the assumption underlying the foregoing Report is that they should give priority attention to educational activities, because their hopes for the Church and for the world will be frustrated or enabled by the kinds of educational provision available to their members and others in society, the ways in which it is reviewed and reformulated, and the extent to which it serves the people.

39. We encourage the churches in their own life to consider how and where they can:

1. provide intensive cross-culture experiences for all age groups, to increase awareness of the options for human development;
2. develop ways which not only create a growing awareness of the global nature of problems but also secure action in local situations;
3. assist the family to be the fundamental educative group, securing liberation and community for its members;
4. distinguish between those elements in local cultures which enrich and those which impoverish, and especially to study the interrelationships of Bible, tradition, and culture;
5. create a diversity in the provision of contextual theological education to match the variety of ministries;
6. evaluate the contribution of present programmes of theological education to the discipleship of the whole people of God and to assess the amount of expenditure of church resources, capital and recurrent, for the training of clergy compared with the amount devoted to the theological education of the whole people of God, and redress any imbalance;
7. reappraise whether the training of persons to fulfil full-time paid ministries and their present deployment are being implemented within the principles of a good stewardship of resources;
8. create ecumenical programmes of theological education for laity and clergy at all levels including the local situation;
9. engage with other Christian traditions whose modes of activity and thought are strange or appear threatening, in order to challenge familiar and restricted modes of apprehension and behaviour and secure a fuller growth in discipleship;
10. engage with those of other faiths and no faith, so that the minds of Christians are not closed to the variety and richness of God's human and natural creation;
11. create education programmes which have regard to the unique qualities of children as learners and contributors to parish life;
12. re-examine the traditional Christian views of human sexuality, and extend awareness of the issues related to it;
13. constantly act to show their solidarity with the poor, the handi-

capped, the prisoners of injustice and any local situations of injustice and oppression;

14. take advantage of their unique situation to overcome inter-generational alienation;

15. take note of the problem of drug addiction among the youth and help them to come out of this in co-operation with psychiatrists and social workers.

40. In the provision of education by other agencies we urge the churches to consider how and where they can:

1. attempt to co-operate in the creation and development of education policy and its implementation so as to encourage participation and equality;

2. affect the distribution of resources into the various kinds of education so that the resources are distributed where they secure the greatest benefit to the greatest number and eliminate disadvantage;

3. make use of ecumenical resources in order to deal effectively with the public sector of education;

4. work to ensure curriculum revision in formal education which eliminates bias and prejudice especially with regard to sexism and racism;

5. seek ways by which the curriculum in formal education relates more to the experience of the participants and uses people with special gifts and the total life of the community as educational resources;

6. encourage the development of informal and other modes of education concerned with such things as nutrition, vocational education, and community organization;

7. enable all educational processes to secure the development of the whole human being in which the emotional, the physical, the mental, and the spiritual are related to each other, and in which none of them is developed at the expense of the others;

8. attempt to secure a fuller coverage and truthful analysis by the secular and religious media of the issues and problems in God's world;

9. help growth in awareness of the effects of radio and television programmes, and develop the ability to influence their open and hidden messages;

10. study advertising messages and other media which create and reinforce materialist values and stereotyped responses, in order to affect their operation and influence;

11. prevent education from serving patterns of development which stress economic and technological growth at the expense of human development, and divert resources to those programmes which involve the participation of people and work for social justice;

12. raise consciousness about the dangers of militarism and search for creative ways of educating for peace;

13. enable disengagement from those educational practices which because of their alien nature are inconsistent with nation building.

41. In their own educational provision to their members and to others we urge the churches not only to adopt the practices they propose to others but also to consider how and where they can:

1. provide the means for teaching a spirituality for life;

2. work with the least of Christ's sisters and brothers so that the powerless share power and the voiceless are heard;

3. concentrate educational attention on the processes by which personal and social values are formed and maintained, and contribute to the continuing clarification and amendment of these processes in the light of the Christian gospel;

4. stimulate education for development so that those in affluent countries become aware of the root causes of injustice between nations and seek to change the situation;

5. have a special concern for education in political awareness which encourages community development and experimental forms of community organization, is based on an action and reflection mode of learning, and involves collaboration with other groups in society who are concerned with political freedom;

6. work in hope even in societies where Christians are a minority and the state has responsibility for education, to secure free space for their own provision of education to supplement that which the system inadequately provides, such as basic literacy, nursery provision, adult education;

7. motivate those who at present hold power, and those who will hold power, to have a concern for and involvement with those other than themselves, which is expressed in working with them for their liberation;

8. be particularly concerned with securing the provision of continuing educational opportunities throughout the life span, especially for women and for acquiring new skills;

9. make their own educational institutions models of communities which are non-elitist, and provide alternative life styles to competitive and individualistic learning;

10. train and retrain teachers to break with professional stereotypes, and enable them to reach out to society, and enable its members to overcome alienation;

11. study the stewardship of their present buildings with a view to considering a moratorium on new educational buildings, until they have secured maximum and multiple use of the facilities which they have.

42. We ask that at all levels the churches consider establishing special

groups to consider their educational provision and their life style; and make available for interchange through the WCC Office of Education and to each other their experience in establishing new models.

43. We ask that all groups consider the extent to which the forces affecting educational provision (in operating not only at the local and parochial level, but also at national, regional, and world levels) require the churches' response to be made at these levels also, and to be made ecumenically.

44. We ask all churches to seek for ways to strengthen and develop the effectiveness in the field of education of ecumenical instruments such as national and regional councils and the World Council.

45. It is recommended that the Report and the Recommendations from this Section be studied in close context with the Report of Section I on Confessing Christ Today.

SECTION V: STRUCTURES OF INJUSTICE AND STRUGGLES FOR LIBERATION

The Moderator of the Section, Dr John Gatu (Presbyterian Church of East Africa) introduced the paper which dealt with three principal topics—Human Rights, Sexism, and Racism.

In the discussion, Fr R. Beaupère (Roman Catholic delegated observer, France) and other speakers criticized as inadequate some of the theological formulations, especially in the first part of the Report. Professor Jan Lochman (Swiss Protestant Church Federation) and other speakers commended the section on human rights and wished it could be strengthened, Dr David Russell (Baptist, UK) drawing attention to the recent report of Amnesty International concerning prisoners of conscience.

Ms Jean Hendrickse (United Congregational Church, South Africa) thought that the liberation of women must be taken seriously and seen in the light of the liberation of all oppressed people, which included children and (Professor T. Hopko, Orthodox, USA) the unborn. Mr I. Gelev (Orthodox, Bulgaria) disagreed with the statement that racism can be seen everywhere, and desired the paragraph containing it to be reformulated.

Dr Russell Chandran (Church of South India) drew attention to the subtleties of oppression which required a sophisticated appreciation of the situation by the churches.

Mr N. Wright (Church of England), praising the Report for its even-handedness ("Beyers Naudé and Solzhenitsyn need to be seen together"), drew attention to the clauses concerning the right to dissent and the right of groups to be involved in the decision-making process. He thought that the WCC, as well as the churches, needed to take this to heart, and that the Assembly's style showed that the WCC could create its own structures of injustice. (Loud and prolonged applause.)

97

In replying to the debate, Dr Gatu said that in revision every attempt would be made to meet most of the points made; but the statement that racism was to be found everywhere in the world had been carefully and seriously discussed, and the Section thought it should stand.

The Report was approved in substance (subject to revision) and commended to the churches for study and appropriate action by a substantial majority.

Forty-three persons who had sent in their names had not been able to speak, and further time was requested for discussion. Dr Potter said that the programme of the Assembly had been designed in the light of the desires expressed by the member churches and rejected charges of staff manipulation. (Applause.)

It was subsequently announced that a further discussion period on the Report would be held on 5 December at 6 p.m., and several hundred participants attended.

In presenting the Second Report of the Section, Dr John Gatu (Presbyterian, Kenya) thanked Dr Ernest Payne for moderating the extra hearing and thanked all those who had submitted points in writing. It was agreed that debate should take place on the three parts of the Report—Sexism; Human Rights; Racism—separately.

Dr Una Kroll speaking in favour of the Report noted, however, that if sexism is treated on its own, some of the most urgent moral issues may be lost sight of. Metropolitan Paulos Gregorios (Syrian Orthodox, India) proposed two minor amendments to the paragraph on language which were accepted. He went on to propose the deletion of paragraph II 4. There was an extended discussion out of which a drafting group including Archbishop Sarkissian (Armenian), Ms Jean Powers (Methodist, USA), and Professor N. Nissiotis (Orthodox, Greece) produced by agreement the following text:

> Those member churches which have agreed in principle to the ordination of women to the priesthood/ministry, to take immediate action to admit women to all their ordained ministries, taking into serious consideration that there are other churches of our WCC fellowship that are not in agreement with this practice.

This part of the Report was approved by a large majority.

On the second part of the Report, on Human Rights, a considerable debate was begun by the Reverend R. O'Grady (Christian Conference of Asia) who moved the following as a new paragraph between paragraphs 15 and 16:

> In many parts of Asia today, authoritarian forms of government are being established. There is martial law in the Philippines and Taiwan (Republic of China); military rule in Bangladesh; emergency rule in Korea and India; one-party states in the People's Republic of China, North Korea, Vietnam, Cambodia, and Laos. Where these governments violate human rights in the name of economic development or national security, we believe it poses serious questions about the mission of the Church. We therefore urge the churches to work for the rights of fuller participation of the peoples of Asia in their own development.

The amendment was supported by Professor R. McAfee Brown and a speaker from Korea, and criticized by Dr S. Jacobson (Lutheran, Canada) and Dr E. Nacpil (Methodist, Philippines) who thought that no names of countries should be mentioned unless all could be. Metropolitan Paulos Gregorios criticized the assumption, e.g., that a one-party state was necessarily evil. The Reverend Oscar McCloud (Presbyterian, USA) identified his own government as involved in oppression but said that we were at the Assembly as representatives of churches not countries.

A motion to refer the amendment to a small drafting group of those most concerned was carried by 248 to 174.

The section of the Report on Human Rights was approved, subject to the rewording of the amendment, by a large majority.

Dr Margaret Mead was invited to address the Assembly. She spoke about the relations in the Assembly of delegates (especially new delegates), advisers, and staff, and asked delegates to realize the extraordinary complexities with which the WCC is struggling. (Applause.)

On the section of the Report on Racism, Dr David Russell (Baptist, UK) regretted that there was not more definite guidance from the Assembly for the future of the Programme to Combat Racism and its Special Fund. He recommended that detailed guidelines for the Programme and criteria for the Special Fund be submitted to the Central Committee in 1976.

The General Secretary said they could be put to the new Central Committee on 11 December.

After some discussion, Bishop Philip Russell (Anglican, South Africa) moved a resolution to insert the following after the first of the Recommendations on Racism:

> We recommend that the churches do not support the Programme to Combat Racism and the Special Fund unless an assurance is given that no assistance will be given from the Special Fund to organizations that at the time of their application are such that their course of action is likely to cause the inflicting of serious injury or the taking of life.

Professor W.B. Sidjabat (Protestant Christian Batak, Indonesia) criticized the amendment as too negative. Dr G. Stalsett (Church of Norway) said that PCR had had full support in the decisions of Central Committee from 1971 onwards and ought not to be weakened or limited. It will undermine the whole programme (Reverend W. Ariarajah, Methodist, Sri Lanka). Bishop R.C. Nichols (African Methodist Episcopal Church, USA) was against the amendment as making judgement impossibly difficult, in a context that already contains violence. Moreover, "peace is not the absence of war but the presence of justice". The Reverend R.T. Van der Veen (Reformed, Netherlands) said that his church had recently had a meeting with representatives of the four Dutch Reformed churches—White, Black, Coloured, and Indian. They expressed the following conclusions:

1. The humanitarian support from PCR should be continued unless it can be proved that this support has been used for the support of violent action.

2. If this support were to be withdrawn, it would be regarded in South Africa and elsewhere as a capitulation to the white DRC and an abandonment of the cause of the victims of racism.

When Bishop Russell's amendment was put to the vote, 62 were for, 325 against, and 22 abstained.

Mrs W.W. Button (Church of the Brethren, USA) moved an amendment to amend paragraph 2 to read as follows:

Of primary importance to the churches' involvement in the struggle against racism is theological reflection on the subject of racism and on the methods of combating racism. We therefore draw to the churches' attention the ongoing joint project of the PCR and Faith and Order and its report on a recent consultation, "Racism in Theology and Theology against Racism" (WCC, 1975). We also encourage the study and implementation of the statement entitled "Violence, Non-violence and the Struggle for Social Justice" (adopted by ECC Central Committee, 1973).

This was accepted by the Chairman.

The Report as a whole was carried by a substantial majority.

The following text of the amendment on Human Rights in Asia was accepted unanimously:

Many changes are taking place in Asian governments. There is martial law in Taiwan; crisis government in the Philippines; emergency rule in India and South Korea; military rule in Bangladesh; one-party states in such countries as the People's Republic of China. In all other countries of Asia (e.g., Malaysia, Singapore, Australasia, New Zealand, Indonesia, and Japan) there are also violations of human rights. Whenever human rights are suppressed or violated by any Asian government, churches have a duty to work for the defence of human rights especially of the oppressed. We believe that the whole mission of the Church is involved in this issue and urge churches to work for the right of the people of Asia to participate in their own development.

Canon Burgess Carr spoke of the gratitude of the African churches to all outside Africa who have supported the PCR and so helped to give credibility to the churches' efforts on the continent of Africa.

Mr G. Habib (Orthodox, Lebanon) said that he hoped that the fact that the Middle East had not been mentioned in the text on the discussion did not mean that there was a conspiracy of silence. "There is no nation where there is not some kind of racial discrimination. I hope we can deal with this in the future. There are still misunderstandings but we value our unity more than anything in the world. The WCC should keep this on its agenda."

Mrs Bobrova (Russian Orthodox Church) spoke of her distress at the action earlier on the amendment concerning the ordination of women, which she felt to be putting a divisive pressure on the Orthodox churches.

SECTION V: STRUCTURES OF INJUSTICE AND STRUGGLES FOR LIBERATION

Preamble

1. Structures of injustice and struggles of liberation pose a formidable challenge to the Church today. In striving to meet it, the Church has no other foundation on which to stand than it has in Jesus Christ. From him it has received its mandate: to witness to the truth which judges and to

proclaim the good news which brings about freedom and salvation. In seeking its particular place in today's struggles for social justice and human liberation, the Church needs to be constantly guided by its divine mandate.

2. Whenever a Christian is confronted by structures of injustice and takes part in struggles for liberation, he or she is bound to experience the grip of destructive forces which are at work throughout the human family. Such forces give a taste of the "principalities and powers" of which Paul spoke.

3. The gospel brings us a message of God's total identification with humanity which is suffering under sin and other destructive powers. God's own solidarity with human beings is expressed in the reality of the servant Christ who humbled himself to take up human form, who was born into poverty, who accepted the path of rejection, and who finally met his death on the cross. The vicarious suffering of Christ is the supreme manifestation of God's love. God in Christ took upon himself the whole burden of human sin and weakness.

4. God calls his Church, a community of forgiven sinners, to follow Christ on the same path committed to the cause of the poor, oppressed, and rejected, to declare the love of God by word and by the whole of life and to accept the cross.

5. The meaning of human suffering in itself is ambiguous. It both reflects the evils which plague the human race and it opens us to God's redeeming activity. In suffering for the cause of justice and for the sake of the gospel, the Church may participate in the vicarious suffering of Christ himself.

6. Is there readiness for suffering in our churches today? Or are our church structures built for our own protection and security and have they therefore become barriers which prevent us from sharing suffering in obedience to Christ and from receiving or reflecting God's redeeming love?

7. Christians who suffer together for the cause of justice and liberation find a deep experience of community with each other and with Christ. This community transcends differences of ideology, class, and Christian tradition. It is knit together by the power of forgiveness and love. It reflects the life of the ultimate community of the Triune God, and the expression of its deepest solidarity with the suffering and sinful humanity is the sharing of the Eucharist.

8. Suffering, however, is not the goal: beyond the cross is the resurrection. Christ has overcome the power of sin and death and broken the grip of the principalities and powers now still seemingly self-reinforcing and outside the control of persons involved. The victory of Christ therefore brings a tangible and deepened hope to those engaged in actual

struggles against oppression and dominance. Moreover, his victory promises that the vicious circle in which injustice breeds more injustice and one form of oppression gives way to another form is being broken.

9. We realize that those who operate the structures of oppression are dependent on the people they oppress and that both are equally in need of liberation and God's forgiving love. In this fallen world, however, it is far more likely that the will and strength to end oppression come from those who bear the brunt of it in their own lives rather than from the privileged persons, groups, and nations.

10. Structures of injustice and struggles of liberation cannot be separated from each other. For practical purposes, however, we have divided this Report into three main sections: Human Rights, Sexism, and Racism.

HUMAN RIGHTS

Introduction

11. Our concerns for human rights are based on our conviction that God wills a society in which all can exercise full human rights. All human beings are created in God's image, to be equal, infinitely precious in God's sight and ours. Jesus Christ has bound us to one another by his life, death, and resurrection, so that what concerns one of us concerns us all.

12. Thus God's will and his love are intended for all and the struggle of Christians for human rights is a fundamental response to Jesus Christ. That gospel leads us to become ever more active in identifying and rectifying violations of human rights in our own societies, and to enter into new forms of ecumenical solidarity with Christians elsewhere who are similarly engaged. It leads us into the struggle of the poor and the oppressed both within and outside the Church as they seek to achieve their full human rights, and frees us to work together with people of other faiths or ideologies who share with us a common concern for human dignity.

13. In working for human rights we are often tempted to deal with symptoms rather than root causes. While we must work for the abolition of specific denials of human rights, such as torture, we must remember that unjust social structures, expressed through, e.g., economic exploitation, political manipulation, military power, class domination, psychological conditioning, create the conditions under which human rights are denied. To work for human rights, therefore, also means to work at the most basic level towards a society without unjust structures.

14. In our fallen world, there is no nation where human rights have been fully achieved. Because of discrepancies between what we profess and what we practise it is crucial for the churches to move from making

declarations about human rights, to working for the full *implementation* of those rights. As Christians we affirm that the gospel brings about a human dignity which transcends our own human potential.

15. The world community has agreed upon certain high principles which are embodied in the Universal Declaration of Human Rights and the International Covenants on Human Rights. The recent Helsinki Declaration on Security and Co-operation in Europe* gives, particularly for its signatories, a new potential for the implementation of these standards. These principles and standards largely coincide with our current Christian understanding about what makes up a just society.

16. Our chief task is to work for the realization of these enunciated rights *where we are*, but when there are those elsewhere who are powerless to cry out, we are called to be the voice of the voiceless and the advocates of the oppressed. In order to do this we must base our actions on accurate information. For this, open channels of communication are vitally important.

17. Common to all expressions of human rights is the right to self-determination by individuals, groups, and nations. The balance between these claims is always precarious, and their creative interrelationship may differ in various times and places. A distinction can be made, for example, between the limitation of rights due to all and the limitation of privileges available only to a few. Christians will need to assess different structures carefully, championing the rights of the individual when they are threatened by unjust structures and defending the rights of the majority when they are threatened by the tyranny of the few, and always bearing in mind that rights involve responsibilities.

18. Within this overall framework there are a number of specific human rights to which attention must be directed.

The Right to Basic Guarantees for Life

19. No rights are possible without the basic guarantees for life, including the right to work, to adequate food, to guaranteed health care, to decent housing, and to education for the full development of the human potential. Because women have the lowest status in most world communities their special needs should be recognized.

20. The ever-widening gap between rich and poor nations and between rich and poor within many nations has created today a highly explosive situation in which millions are denied these rights. This is due to a number of contributing factors, including the following:

---

*See the document "Final Acts of the Conference on Security and Co-operation in Europe", signed by all European governments (except Albania) plus USA and Canada.

(*a*) The present international economic structures are dominated by a few rich countries who control a large proportion of the world's resources and markets.

(*b*) Transnational corporations, often in league with oppressive regimes, distort and exploit the economies of poor nations.

(*c*) National economies are controlled in many cases by a small group of elites who also often give special access to transnational corporations.

(*d*) Patterns of land ownership are often exploitative.

21. The right to the basic guarantees for life involves guarding the rights of future generations, e.g., through protection of the environment and conservation of the earth's resources.

The Rights to Self-Determination and to Cultural Identity, and the Rights of Minorities

22. All people have the right freely to determine their political status and freely to pursue their economic, cultural, and social development. These rights are often violated by foreign governments and power systems, and through internal oppression and discrimination.

23. The churches should condemn such violations and take active part in efforts to ensure national sovereignty and self-determination for people who are deprived of them.

24. The churches must also defend and promote the rights of minorities (including that of migrant workers), be they cultural, linguistic, religious, ideological, or ethnic. Efforts to ensure that the Helsinki declaration be implemented could be of great importance in this context, especially for minorities in countries who have signed it.

25. The churches must closely scrutinize the reasoning of people in power when they seek to justify the violation of human rights for what they deem to be overriding concerns. Even in times of public emergency, fundamental rights such as the right to life and personal dignity, as defined by the Universal Declaration of Human Rights and the Covenants, should under no circumstances be derogated from.

The Right to Participate in Decision-Making within the Community

26. Participation of groups and individuals in the decision-making processes of the various communities in which they live is essential for achieving a truly democratic society. As a precondition, there must be created an economic and social foundation which is in the interests of all segments of society. All members of the community, especially the young and women, should be educated in a spirit of social and political participation and responsibility. The structures of government on the national and local levels, within the religious communities, educational institutions, and

in employment, must become more responsive to the will of all the persons belonging to these various communities, and must provide for protection against manipulation by powerful interests.

27. Women, because of their particular experience of oppression and the new insights they are receiving in the process of liberation, can often make a special contribution regarding participatory decision-making. They are exploring styles of shared leadership in which power and decision-making is horizontal rather than hierarchical, fluid rather than static. The Church, like the community, needs to receive this contribution, if it is to develop unifying and freeing structures.

28. Churches should participate in developing activity through which local communities of poor people, industrial and rural workers, women, minority groups, and others who suffer from any form of oppression can become aware of their condition and influence the course of the society.

The Right to Dissent

29. The right to dissent preserves a community or system from authoritarian rigidity. It is essential to the vitality of every society that the voices of dissenters be heard and that their right to hold opinions without interference, to freedom of expression, and to peaceful assembly be guaranteed. Christians, as followers of Jesus Christ, have a solidarity with the people who suffer because of their religious faith and practice and because of their stand in favour of political and social justice. Christian solidarity means a definite choice on the side of prisoners of conscience and political prisoners and refugees. The churches should make all efforts in their witness and intercessions, and by providing remedial assistance, to support those fellow human beings who suffer.

30. In readiness to reassess and to change their own structures and attitudes wherever necessary, the churches and the World Council of Churches itself must give all due attention within their communities to men, women, and young people who take a critical stand towards the predominant views and positions of their churches and of the World Council of Churches.

The Right to Personal Dignity

31. In many countries represented in this Section, evidence has been cited of gross violations of the right to personal dignity. Such violations include arbitrary arrest and imprisonment, torture, rape, deportation, child-battering, enforced hospitalization in mental hospitals, threats to families, and denial of habeas corpus. In some cases, prisoners and refugees are denied contact even with their families, thus becoming "non-persons". In other cases, arrested persons either disappear or are executed summarily.

32. The basic causes for these violations are to be found in the unjust social order, the abuse of power, the lack of economic development, and in unequal development. This leads to violations of unjust laws and rebellion by the dispossessed, to which political and military forces of "law and order" respond with cruel repression. In some cases, the churches themselves have actively supported the oppressors or even become involved in the oppression itself, out of misguided convictions and/or attempts to safeguard their own privileges.

33. We also observe the increasing role, both nationally and internationally, of security police and para-police forces in the violation of the human right to personal dignity.

The Right to Religious Freedom

34. The right to religious freedom has been and continues to be a major concern of member churches and the WCC. However, this right should never be seen as belonging exclusively to the Church. The exercise of religious freedom has not always reflected the great diversity of convictions that exist in the world. This right is inseparable from other fundamental human rights. No religious community should plead for its own religious liberty without active respect and reverence for the faith and basic human rights of others.

35. Religious liberty should never be used to claim privileges. For the Church this right is essential so that it can fulfil its responsibilities which arise out of the Christian faith. Central to these responsibilities is the obligation to serve the whole community.

36. The right to religious freedom has been enshrined in most constitutions as a basic human right. By religious freedom we mean the freedom to have or to adopt a religion or belief of one's choice, and freedom, either individually or in community with others and in public or private, to manifest one's religion or belief in worship, observance, practice, and teaching. Religious freedom should also include the right and duty of religious bodies to criticize the ruling powers when necessary, on the basis of their religious convictions. In this context, it was noted that many Christians in different parts of the world are in prison for reasons of conscience or for political reasons as a result of their seeking to respond to the total demands of the gospel.

Human Rights and Christian Responsibility

37. Churches and other Christian communities carry, on the basis of the gospel, a special responsibility to express in word and deed their solidarity with those people whose human rights and fundamental freedoms are denied.

38. During its deliberations, the Section made frequent reference to the report of the consultation on "Human Rights and Christian Responsibility" held in St Pölten, Austria, October 1974.

SEXISM

39. For the sake of the unity of the Church and humankind, the concerns of women must be consciously included in every aspect of the deliberations of the WCC. The liberation of women from structures of injustice must be taken seriously as seen in the light of the liberation of all oppressed people and all forms of discrimination.

40. At Amsterdam (1948) it was stated that "The Church, as the Body of Christ, consists of men and women, created as responsible persons to glorify God and to do God's will". Dr W.A. Visser 't Hooft has added that "this truth, accepted in theory, is too often ignored in practice".

41. Despite efforts of the WCC in the past,* the position of women, in both the Church and the world, has not changed significantly. As long as women are largely excluded from decision-making processes, they will be unable to realize a full partnership with men and therefore the Church will be unable to realize its full unity.

We wish to identify three areas in which change is necessary:

The Area of Theology:

42. A thorough examination needs to be made of the biblical and theological assumptions concerning the community of women and men in church and society.

43. Particular attention should be paid to the relationship of cultural assumptions and the way we understand the Word of God. Women and men in the Church are in need of clarification of the various biblical texts relating to the role of women in the story of creation and redemption.

These and other theological dimensions of our faith need to be re-examined, drawing heavily on the investigations of women as well as of theologians and scholars.

44. Language in many instances and the connotations of language in other instances fail to reflect the depth of the mystery of God who transcends all human metaphors and images. It is important that our language about God be inclusive (e.g., Isa. 49.15; 46.3-4; Matt. 23.37) to be true to the original biblical text. As the mother of Jesus, Mary embodies

---

*For the latest efforts see the report on "Sexism in the 1970s" (1974) and "The Community of Women and Men in the Church" (1975).

particular significance for Christian women and men. Her openness and willingness to respond to the call of God, in ways which were totally unexpected, proclaim to all people their responsibility to be free from any preconceived understandings as to how God works in and through people.

45. Also, it is important that the member churches of the WCC examine their liturgical language and practices with a view to eliminating sexist patterns so that women may join fully in the worshipping community.

The Area of Participation:

46. In order to be truly free, all people must participate in working towards their own liberation. This can be seen in all struggles for human rights and to overcome oppression.

47. The WCC must recognize the dimensions of powerlessness that affect women in the political, economic, social, and ecclesial areas of life. It should therefore continue its work, the work begun in International Women's Year, in working on the ten-year plan for action.

48. The model for this work should aim at providing funds for self-development and self-help programmes. We draw attention to the following vital areas:

(a) The urgent need to secure water supplies for women who are responsible for obtaining water for their community—in rural situations and others where water is not in easy supply;
(b) the need to facilitate indigenously-based self-help programmes which particularly relate to the needs of women, including the need to educate all women about the importance in all questions concerning their reproduction functions and the rights of their unborn children, and also regarding nutrition;
(c) the need to examine the relationship women hold to the law—both judicial and customary law (e.g. dowry systems), family law, inheritance law, contract and loan law. Women also need to be helped to understand their rights under present legal systems;
(d) the need to recognize that where racism is involved women are the most disadvantaged group of all.

The Area of Relationship:

49. A third area of urgent concern is the interrelationship of women and men who frequently exploit one another. This exploitation often takes the form of misuse of power over each other which is linked with lack of understanding of their mutual identity.

50. People need to feel independent, valuable, and secure in the totality of their identity as men and women before they can relate to each other in mutual interdependence.

51. For this to happen it is essential that women unite in supportive groups to find solidarity with their sisters, and a new sense of worth. Such a discovery of worth is essential for the full development of equal partnership.

52. We recognize that men and women together form one corporate body in Christ and that they cannot be seen in separation from each other; nevertheless, evidence shows that in many marriage relationships women and men are unable to develop their full personhood. The Christian Church is in a key position to foster and support the partners to marriage in their search for mutuality.

53. The Church is in the same unique position in respect to persons living in different life situations (e.g. single people living in isolation, single parents), extended families, and persons living in communal patterns. There is evidence that these people are not fully accepted by many societies and are often ignored by the Church.

54. In the social relationships between women and men, the dynamics that are set up by oppression are such that women have a particular understanding of, and interest in, reconciliation of confrontation and conflict. They are emphatic that those who are liberated from oppression should not become the oppressor in the same structures. This can only prevent true liberation and perpetuate conflict.

55. Recognizing that small advances in the position of women in church and society have been made, we are nevertheless convinced that it is vital for the WCC and the member churches to open all service opportunities to women and to encourage the study, by both men and women, of a deeper and more thorough participation of women in church life with special attention to the question of ordination and the employment of women in the Church.

56. The freedom and unity of Jesus Christ includes both halves of the human community; therefore it is imperative to the unity of church and society that the full participation of women be given urgent consideration and immediate implementation.

RACISM

Fundamental Convictions

57. Racism* is a sin against God and against fellow human beings. It is contrary to the justice and the love of God revealed in Jesus Christ. It destroys the human dignity of both the racist and the victim. When

---

*A working definition of racism for the WCC is to be found in the *Uppsala '68 Report*, p. 271.

practised by Christians it denies the very faith we profess and undoes the credibility of the Church and its witness to Jesus Christ. Therefore, we condemn racism in all its forms both inside and outside the Church.

58. When we again try to deal with racism at this Assembly we cannot but begin by confessing our conscious and unconscious complicity in racism and our failures to eradicate it even from our own house. In previous Assemblies we have many times affirmed as churches our common rejection of racism. Yet, we still find ourselves only at the beginning. We stand in need of God's forgiveness and grace which will free us from our complicity and failures, towards a new commitment, to strive for the justice that will bring an end to all racism.

59. The past years of struggle against racism have shown that we as churches need a more profound understanding of the nature and of all varied manifestations of racism. We need to confront it with the fullness of the biblical message, to see more deeply its demonic character, and also to comprehend its psychological, economic, and social impact on persons and communities and its roots in societies. However, although our understanding needs to grow, we already know more than enough to participate in obedience to Christ in the fight against the manifestations of racism in politics and in the Church.

60. Concerning the methods to be used in the fight against racism, we join the agonizing search for guidelines on how to deal with the inevitable question of violence and non-violence. A helpful contribution to this search has been made in the paper "Violence, Non-violence, and the Struggle for Social Justice" (commended by the WCC Central Committee, 1973).

The Scope of Racism—a Litany of Shame

61. Racism can be seen today in every part of the world. No nation is totally free of it. Its victims cross the paths of most of us daily. Yet, it is obvious that some of our countries are more visibly plagued by it than others, e.g., where racism is legally enforced. We heard in the Section from every continent a series of passionate pleas to draw the common attention of the churches here to the outrageous expressions of racism in their respective countries, like a litany of shame of the whole human family. However, it brought home the growing urgency of the problem of racism on every continent.

62. There is much evidence that racially oppressed communities are rapidly becoming aware of the injustices to which they are subjected and that they more and more refuse to endure indignity and exploitation. Consequently, they are increasingly determined to liberate themselves and thereby affirm their humanity. We need to express our solidarity with them.

63. It also became obvious that racism is a factor in numerous

violations of human rights and fundamental freedoms as dealt with in another part of this Report.

Racism in Churches

64. To our shame, Christian churches around the world are all too often infected by racism, overt and covert. Examples of it include the following:

(*a*) churches and congregations have been and are still being organized along racially exclusive lines;

(*b*) congregations welcome to their fellowship warmly those who are like the majority of its members, but easily reject those who are different;

(*c*) many argue that they are free of racism as if its reality could be undone by ignoring it;

(*d*) churches frequently contribute to the psychological conditioning of the racially oppressed so that they will not sense the racism imposed upon them;

(*e*) they are more willing to support struggles against racism far from home than to face the racism which is practised on their doorstep;

(*f*) churches often reflect the racially prejudiced attitudes of their governments, their elites, and self-pretensions, while presuming that their own attitudes arise out of Christian faith;

(*g*) in leadership privileges and in programmatic priorities churches tend too easily to indulge in racism without even recognizing it.

65. We recognize that the Spirit of God does break through structural and other barriers so that Christian communities do from time to time rise to challenge their own racism and to seek models of commitment to a non-racist Christian faith, even if for every such sign of hope there remain too many examples of denial.

Institutional Racism

66. Pervasive as individual attitudes and acts of racism may be, the major oppressive racism of our time is imbedded in institutional structures that reinforce and perpetuate themselves, generally to the great advantage of the few and the disadvantage of many. Examples of this:

(*a*) racism openly enforced by law;

(*b*) predominantly white North Atlantic nations create trade patterns and preferences that militate against other racial groups;

(*c*) strong military powers and other industrialized countries supply sophisticated arms and assistance to racist regimes;

(*d*) powerful countries, without regard to their social system, often entrench themselves in supporting racial repression under the pretence of legally justified defence of their own national self-interest;

111

(e) continued patterns of settler colonialism contribute to racial oppression;

(f) the powerful in affluence, education, ecclesiastical position, or secular authority, tend to protect their systems of privilege and to shut out of the decision-making any influence of the weak and the subordinate. Moreover, they tend to overlay their racist privileges all too often with an aura of kindliness and service.

67. Institutionalized racism, in its many structural forms, resists most challenges with careful concessions calculated to preserve its power. We reject a conspiratorial theory of history that oversimplifies the complex struggles of humanity for liberation by describing all institutions with power as pernicious and all powerless peoples as virtuous. This does not, however, make us blind to the evident inclination of current power structures to perpetuate racism. All these institutional forms of racism need to be carefully analysed and as Christians we need to attack them with prophetic word and action.

Interdependence of Oppression

68. We lift up for special attention the fact that across the globe racist structures reinforce each other internationally. Self-serving policies of transnational corporations operate across boundaries with impunity; weapons or mercenaries are supplied internationally to local elites; the worldwide communications networks are manipulated to reinforce racist attitudes and actions. It is precisely because of this world-wide web of racist penetration that the churches must seek out policies and programmes at ecumenical and international levels. Such programmes can expose international systems which support racism and provide an effective counter-response to them.

69. In this connection it should be noted that churches and their foreign mission agencies in the West ought to re-examine their use of human and material resources so that they can effectively support liberation efforts and contribute to human dignity in developing countries in ways that are beyond the scope of traditional patterns of giving and receiving.

70. The multinational character of racist structures also makes necessary a constant vigilance by Christians so that they are ready to speak and act and that the pressure of international challenges to racism is felt and felt strongly, and the victims of racism may know that they are not abandoned and that their liberation is essential to the liberation of all.

The Urgency of the Task of the Churches

71. The grip of racism is today as acute as ever because of its institutional penetration, its reinforcement by military and economic

power and because of widespread fear of loss of privilege by the affluent world.

72. This gives a special urgency to the task of the churches both in facing and eradicating racism within themselves and their home countries and in strengthening their international efforts against racism.

73. Southern Africa deserves continued priority in the churches' combined efforts because of the churches' own involvement in the area and because of the legal enforcement of racism there. African delegates brought forcefully before us the need of churches to practise what they preach. What is at stake is the faithfulness to the fullness of the message entrusted to the Church.

RECOMMENDATIONS

ON SEXISM

74. Whereas a thorough examination needs to be made of the biblical and theological assumptions concerning the community of women and men in the Church, *it is recommended that* the WCC shall commend the study document "The Community of Women and Men in the Church" (1975) to its member churches and invite their active participation in a three-year study in which:

1. priority be given to a theological study of sexuality, taking into account the culture of the member churches;

2. women theologians and scholars be invited to participate fully in the study;

3. care be taken in translations of the word of God, which always comes in human language, so that they reflect the gender used in the original language, and to consider developing principles for the elimination of sexist terminology, if any, in our languages.

75. Whereas there is ample evidence that the expertise and gifts of women are not being fully used by any Church, *it is recommended that* the WCC shall urge:

1. member churches to consider making available funds for theological education of women (especially advanced study);

2. member churches to ensure full participation of women in all decision-making bodies;

3. those churches that ordain women to give them the same opportu-

nities and pay as men, according to the measure of their gifts (1 Cor. 12);

4. those member churches which have agreed in principle to the ordination of women to the priesthood/ministry to take immediate action to admit women to all their ordained ministries, taking into serious consideration that there are other churches of our WCC fellowship that are not in agreement with this practice;

5. those member churches which do ordain women and those which do not continue dialogue with each other and with non-member churches about the full participation of women in the full life of the Church including ordained ministries, according to the measure of their gifts.

76. Whereas men and women in some parts of the world are living at subsistence level, while others are living at adequate and more than adequate levels; and whereas women have special responsibilities for bringing new life into the world, nurturing and rearing children, *it is recommended that* the WCC shall urge its member churches and those present at this Assembly to encourage women and men to:

1. realize that all those who benefit from the economic exploitation of other people in any part of the world have to share the responsibility for such exploitation, even if they are not directly involved; and to act to bring pressure on governments, transnational corporations, and other bodies whenever they are oppressive;

2. participate fully in the ecclesial, political, economic, and social structures of their own societies at all levels to change these structures towards a more just society;

3. help local congregations and communities to study and implement the UN Ten Point World Plan of Action (cf. 47);

4. support women by facilitating and funding specific projects such as:

(a) securing safe water supplies (cf. 48(a));

(b) fostering indigenously-based self-help programmes (cf. 48(b));

(c) educating women about their legal rights (cf. 48(c));

(d) establishing programmes in congregations to study and implement the proposals of the WCC's Consultation on Sexism in the '70s as found in the report, "Discrimination Against Women", published in 1975;

(e) supporting those organizations which are working to eliminate discrimination against women in political, economic, social, and ecclesial areas of life (cf. 47).

77. Whereas we recognize the urgent need to examine ways in which

114

women and men can grow into a partnership of mutual interdependence, *it is recommended that* the WCC urge its member churches to:

1. affirm the personhood and mutual interdependence of individuals in families;

2. affirm the personhood and worth of people living in different life situations (cf. 53);

3. act upon these affirmations so as to enable women to realize their potential in every area of life;

4. actively support programmes which investigate the exploitation of human sexuality for gain and seek to assist individuals who are exploited.

78. Whereas these recommendations have such important implications for the Church, *it is further recommended that:*

all member churches, especially their women's organizations, shall be urged to support women's concerns through special funds earmarked for the Women's Desk and to ask the WCC to appoint an additional staff member to co-ordinate the work.

ON HUMAN RIGHTS

Education and Conscientization on Human Rights

79. The churches should:

1. seek to raise Christian and public awareness of violations of human rights and their causes, developing educational materials for this purpose;

2. educate their constituencies, particularly at congregational levels, to their rights and the legal recourses available to them;

3. develop further technical expertise on human rights, perhaps through the creation of human rights institutes related to national and regional ecumenical bodies and providing scholarships for the study of human rights;

4. in the light of the increasing incidence of torture and inhuman treatment of prisoners in many parts of the world, promote instruction on human rights and moral responsibility in the training of police and military personnel;

5. include human rights in the formation of pastors, priests, and lay leaders, and in the curricula of other church training centres, such as development education institutions.

Information and Contacts

80. The churches should:

1. gather and disseminate information on different approaches to human rights, and on the bases of human rights;

2. gather reliable information on human rights violations in their own societies and elsewhere;

3. analyse such violations in order to discover their causes, reminding their constituencies regularly of how specific injustices reflect unjust social structures and seeking to avoid complicity with them;

4. develop effective channels of communication with one another, through personal contacts or otherwise, in order to ensure reliability of information and real effectiveness of active expressions of solidarity;

5. recognize, as a priority, that in the Middle East the rights of the Palestinian people under occupation should be implemented and work towards that end;

6. where the rights of entire peoples are violated through colonial domination; undue political, economic, or military interference in their national affairs; occupation of their lands by foreign powers; expulsion from their homelands; self-imposed racist, military, or other oppressive regimes—look beyond the propaganda of the offending power to the realities of those who suffer and help Christians and others to understand the true nature of their plight and struggles for their just rights. In co-operation with regional ecumenical bodies, the WCC should assist the churches in this task.

Legal Machinery for the Protection of Human Rights

81. The churches should:

1. help create new, improve existing, and facilitate access to legal institutions for the defence and promotion of human rights at community, national, and international levels;

2. seek access to prisons, camps, and other places of detention in order to obtain complete and accurate information about the treatment of inmates and conditions of detention, and defend the prisoners' rights to regular contact with family, friends, and legal counsel.

Action at Local, National, and Regional Levels

3. The struggle of the people themselves for their own rights is fundamentally important. Local congregations should become more active in identifying, documenting, and combating violations of human rights in their own communities. They and their national churches should seek ways to support the struggles of peoples, groups, and individuals for their own legitimate rights, helping them to form networks of solidarity to strengthen one another in their struggles.

4. Particular attention should be given to the special needs of political

prisoners and refugees. In some cases, pastoral care becomes an act of courage, yet Christ calls us to minister both materially and spiritually to those in prison and to the outcasts as well as to their families.

5. Many changes are taking place in Asian governments. There is martial law in Taiwan; crisis government in the Philippines; emergency rule in India and South Korea; military rule in Bangladesh; one-party states in such countries as the Peoples' Republic of China. In all other countries of Asia (e.g. Malaysia, Singapore, Australia, New Zealand, Indonesia, Japan) there are also violations of human rights. Wherever human rights are suppressed or violated by any Asian government, churches have a duty to work for the defence of human rights, especially of the oppressed. We believe the whole question of the mission of the Church is involved in this issue and urge churches to work for the rights of the people of Asia to participate in their own development.

6. Regional ecumenical bodies should help their churches to become more active in responding to the human rights needs of their societies. Work like that of the Christian Conference of Asia, and the consultation on "Human Rights and the Churches in Africa", sponsored by the All Africa Conference of Churches in collaboration with CCIA should be encouraged and pursued, and work like that of the interpretation programme of the MECC.

7. The report of the consultation on "Human Rights and Christian Responsibility" is commended to the churches for appropriate study and action (St Pölten, Austria, October 1974).

Responsibility of the WCC

82. The WCC should:

1. aid the churches in the above tasks;

2. gather and disseminate information about human rights violations within the limits of its possibilities;

3. help strengthen church leaders and Christians to perform the difficult tasks which face them, and to execute conscientiously their prophetic role in the face of abuses of power and inhuman practices in their churches, communities, and national societies;

4. provide a place for mutual challenge of the churches to become better servants; a place where the churches come together to give one another pastoral and material support as they become more courageously engaged in the struggle for human rights where they are; and a place to share strategies for struggle;

5. when necessary and appropriate, send pastoral and/or information-gathering teams to places where Christians and others are in need of support and encouragement in their own struggles for human rights;

6. use its consultative relationship with the UN, its possibilities to approach regional inter-governmental bodies and individual governments, and its co-operation with other non-governmental organizations in efforts to bring an end to human rights violations;

7. directly or through the CCIA issue public statements on violations of nations', groups', or individuals' human rights where this could serve those directly affected and, through clarifying the issues involved, contribute to the elimination of the root causes of such violations;

8. aid, materially and otherwise, groups and individuals who, because of their efforts to act out their Christian faith in defending human rights and in struggling for justice in their societies, have become the objects of harassment, repression, imprisonment, or persecution.

ON RACISM

83. We commend the Programme to Combat Racism to the member churches, and urge them to ensure that their members receive accurate information about the whole programme. We ask for further support of the Programme in terms of increased commitment, prayer, and finance, in order that the various aspects of the Programme, e.g. theological reflection, action-oriented research, information, Annual Project List and Special Fund, may be even more effective.

84. Of primary importance to the churches' involvement in the struggle against racism is theological reflection on racism and on methods of combating it. We therefore draw to the churches' attention the ongoing joint project of the Programme to Combat Racism and Faith and Order and its report on a recent consultation, "Racism in Theology and Theology against Racism" (WCC 1975). We also encourage the study and implementation of the report on "Violence, Non-violence, and the Struggle for Social Justice", commended to the member churches by the Central Committee (Geneva 1973).

85. We urge member churches to ensure, wherever possible, the active participation of representatives from minority and racially oppressed groups in decision-making concerning their welfare and well-being within the life of churches and of society.

86. We urge member churches to provide factual information, gained from the oppressed groups themselves, so that Christians can learn the extent of their involvement in structures that perpetuate racial injustice and have recourse to specific proposals for responsible ecumenical action.

87. South Africa, which highlights racism in its most blatant form, must retain high priority for the attention of the member churches. Apartheid is possible only with the support of a large number of Christians

there. We urge member churches to identify with, and wherever possible initiate or activate, campaigns to halt arms traffic; to work for the withdrawal of investments and the ending of bank loans; to stop white migration. These issues have already been urged by the WCC and we recommend these for urgent action by the member churches. Their implementation would be an effective non-violent contribution to the struggle against racism.

88.   Racism, as a world problem, however, also demands the churches' attention in other particular situations, including

(a) the plight of the Korean minority in Japan;

(b) the condition of the native peoples of North and South America;

(c) the situation of the aboriginal peoples of Australia and ethnic minorities in New Zealand;

(d) growing racism against black people and migrant workers in Europe.

89.   Churches everywhere should beware that their commendable zeal for combating racism and other forms of ethnocentrism in distant lands should not lead to ignoring its manifestations in their midst.

90.   In all this, churches should be making a conscious effort to be themselves models of non-racist communities.

SECTION VI: HUMAN DEVELOPMENT:
AMBIGUITIES OF POWER, TECHNOLOGY, AND QUALITY OF LIFE

Ms Birgitta Hambraeus (Church of Sweden), Moderator of the Section, introduced the Report, and read certain parts to highlight their importance. The discussion (eleven speakers) ranged over the wide field covered by the Report, dwelling mainly on particular points. Among these were: the importance of class difference in Asia and Africa (Mr Habre Tsegaye, Ethiopian Orthodox); multinational and state corporations (Mr H.-B. Peter, Swiss Protestant, and Mr M. Chandler, Church of England); the New International Economic Order (Reverend J. Blanc, Reformed, Algeria, and Dr Grohs, EKD, Germany); the sanctity of human life (Dr J. R. Nelson, Methodist, USA); the drink trade (Dr K. Greet, Methodist, UK); the responsibility of the developed countries for pollution (Reverend A. Nyemb, Reformed, Cameroun); the nature of the churches' power (Dr Kyaw Than, Baptist, Burma); the food crisis (Dr R. V. Moss, United Church of Christ, USA).

In view of the importance of the last issue raised, Ms Hambraeus asked that the Report be *referred back* to the Section, as proposed by Dr R. V. Moss.

This was agreed.

Ms B. Hambraeus, Moderator of the Section, asked Dr H. de Lange (Remonstrant Brotherhood, Netherlands) to present the revised First Report of the Section.

Dr de Lange drew attention to the section on the Food Crisis and the Quality of Life which had been requested in the earlier discussion. The Committee had considered the alcohol question but decided not to handle it. He drew attention to the work done by the British Council of Churches.

Mr G. McManus (Disciples of Christ, USA) thought the paragraphs on economic power quite inadequate, especially about transnational corporations. This was contested by Dr de Lange and Dr Philip Potter.

The Report was adopted unanimously.

Dr de Lange presented the Recommendations of Section VI.

The Reverend N. Gilmore (Church of Christ, Australia) moved an amendment to clause 1 to support a 2% appeal to which others also wished to speak. This amendment was accepted by the Committee.

Dr B. Sidjabat (Batak Protestant Church, Indonesia) moved an amendment to replace the phrase "the restoration of creation" with "for the good management and maintenance of creation" on the ground that man could not *restore* creation. The Committee believed that humankind had been invited to be co-workers with God and resisted the amendment, which was defeated.

Ms J. Hendrickse (United Church of Christ, S. Africa) moved an amendment to include a reference to the abuse of resources for alcohol; a further, stronger version was moved by Commissioner H. Williams (Salvation Army). Dr de Lange said the Committee would like the Assembly to decide. The amendment was carried by a large majority. Other amendments, to include a further definition of development, and attacking multinational corporations, were defeated.

Mr M. Chandler (Church of England) moved an amendment concerning the International Disaster Relief Fund. This was accepted by Dr de Lange.

The Recommendations were accepted by the Assembly as amended and were commended to member churches.

Dr W.F. Keesecker (United Presbyterian, USA) wished it to be recorded that he voted against the Report of Section VI.

SECTION VI: HUMAN DEVELOPMENT: AMBIGUITIES OF POWER, TECHNOLOGY, AND QUALITY OF LIFE

Introduction

1. There are four revolutionary and powerful elements which will affect the processes of change in the next decade. They are:

1. the demands of two-thirds of the earth's people;

2. the food and ecological problems that threaten present and future generations;

3. the misuse of power and the struggle of the powerless;

4. the questioning of the growth-oriented affluent societies and the consequences of this for the rest of humankind.

2. Therefore, there is urgent need to define new goals for both national and international societies.

3. What are the basic reasons and the motivations for the deep and long-standing involvement of the ecumenical movement, Christians, and churches in society? The first is the human suffering in almost all continents, nations, and regions: suffering from hunger and misery, from violence and oppression, from working conditions, and from tasks which are too heavy for those who have responsibilities in politics, education, industry, and services. Reshaping societies to minimize suffering is a process of humanization which the ecumenical movement could stimulate.

4. The second motivation is the demand for a renewal of society. There is no point in merely surviving in this world with its injustices. We think that the processes of liberation could be improved and the world could be made more human. Our motivation is that we are looking forward to the kingdom that has been promised to us and that we have been called to witness to it.

5. The third reason is God's permanent demand for justice to restore all broken relations. Human relations are disturbed by sin and guilt not only at the individual level but also in specific economic and political developments. Justice is a way of relating both to God and to other people. Its consequences are seen first in the poor, the humiliated, the exploited, and the oppressed. The search for a more just world and more just relations between nations, peoples, and generations brings us together as a uniting force.

6. A fourth reason is that as Christians we have been invited and challenged to be stewards of God's creation on the basis of love for all.

7. A fifth reason is that Christians must be prepared to help to transform despair into hope and uncertainties into positive certainty, to point out courageously the many positive and unexpected opportunities for significant moves towards a more just order and conditions for a more helpful development process—"Faith is the assurance of things hoped for, the conviction of things not seen" (Heb. 11.1).

NEW DIMENSIONS IN THE QUEST FOR DEVELOPMENT

8. Since the Uppsala Assembly, churches in all parts of the world have taken many initiatives to participate in the development process. The World Council also has taken several fresh initiatives including the establishment of the Commission on the Churches' Participation in Develop-

ment to co-ordinate the various efforts and to take further measures to promote the development concern.

9. And yet today, more than ever before, we find it difficult to articulate our understanding of the development concept and consequently to decide on the patterns of participation in the development process. In the past few years there have been many conscious efforts to give human development a conceptual clarity that it lacked, but the relation between the concept and reality seems to become more diffused and more evasive. The uncertainties and ambiguities resulting from this situation are made more pronounced because of the few certainties that cannot be evaded: that after two decades of efforts to remove poverty and reduce inequality there are today more people in the grips of dire poverty and the gap between the rich and the poor has widened; that in a world with tremendous technological possibilities, there is the persisting threat of famine; that in the spaceship earth the expenditure on armaments is steadily mounting; that in numbers mankind is continuing to grow at an unprecedented rate. In the quest for development, thus, we find ourselves caught in a pensive mood, raising many questions and finding few answers. This is a hopeful sign. It urges us to re-examine the positions of the past, to learn from our mistakes, and to move forward with renewed vigour.

10. Recurring famines and incipient mass malnutrition in many parts of the world and the recent World Conference on Food in Rome have once again brought up questions relating to hunger, food production, agricultural policy, and trade and aid relationships between nations. The malnutrition among children, in particular, results in irreparable body and brain damage robbing them of a full life and impeding the national development. The issues involved here are very complex and churches should resist all attempts to settle complex problems through simple solutions. Natural calamities frequently result in food scarcity, but the problem of hunger in the world is essentially man-made. In what are often referred to as Two Thirds of the world, the many are hungry because the few own the land, control trade, and determine crucial policies pertaining to the production of food. In many such countries the governments are the representatives of such vested interests and hence public policies including the utilization of international aid often get deflected to favour the rich and the powerful. It must be noted also that in the past international aid whether from governmental or non-governmental agencies, even when moved by humanitarian considerations, has tended to strengthen such groups. The long-term solution of the hunger problem must come primarily from within these countries. The churches must be responsive both to present-day hunger problems and to the difficult long-term solutions.

11. Some of our uncertainties are the result of our rejection of the certainties of the past. The affirmation at Montreux that development

must be thought of as including social justice, self-reliance, and growth was a rejection of a view of development that was clearly comprehensible, but narrowly limited. The broader vision of development that we now have must be used to look at old problems in a new perspective. The Church's concern for development has arisen primarily from the concern for the poor. But how does the Church express its solidarity with the poor and fight along with them for liberation and justice? In this quest we are led to new understandings of the problem and of our tasks. Poverty, we are learning, is caused primarily by unjust structures that leave resources and the power to make decisions about the utilization of resources in the hands of a few within nations and among nations, and that therefore one of the main tasks of the Church when it expresses its solidarity with the poor is to oppose these structures at all levels. Unjust structures are often the consequence of wrong or misdirected goals and values. This makes it necessary to examine critically the economic and social goals, the patterns of resource ownership and decision-making processes in the local and national situations, as also at the international context to reject all patterns that oppress the poor and to work for those which release the creative powers of people to satisfy their needs and decide their destiny.

12. If this is the essential task of development, in many situations the primary responsibility for the development process will be exercised by secular bodies. The role of Christians and the churches will be to assist in the definition, validation, and articulation of just political, economic, and social objectives and in translating them into action. Specifically it will involve:

1. joining hands with all who are engaged in the task of organizing the poor in their fight against poverty and injustice;

2. educating the more privileged to co-operate in the establishment of new socio-economic orders with changed wealth and income distributions enabling a production pattern and use of technology favouring the needy;

3. searching for new structures for human beings to live together in justice, freedom, and peace.

13. In recent years the development concept has been seriously challenged by the "limits to growth" debate. While controversies still remain about the immediacy of the depletion of physical resources, the debate has brought to light the excessive utilization of the resources of the world by a small affluent minority. It has also been shown that "growth" in an economic order based on the so-called "free market" system has a built-in exploitative tendency where resources are unevenly distributed. In this context Christians are called upon to examine carefully the patterns of utilization, control, and ownership of resources.

14. Discussions to provide alternatives to the free market system at the international level have led to the recent proposals for a new international economic order (NIEO). The forum that the United Nations and its agencies provide for countries of the world to question international orders of domination and dependence and the power that at least the oil-producing countries have recently acquired to challenge old patterns of trade were contributing factors in the formulations of the NIEO proposals. As an effort to restructure patterns of international trade, transfer of resources, and technology, to bring about monetary reforms, and to change patterns of decision-making in international economic affairs, all geared to ensure that the poorer countries of the world have a fairer share in these matters, the NIEO deserves to be studied carefully. However, we must not forget that at the international level there are yet no political processes to implement any radical change in the economic order and that changes in *international* economic orders alone do not go to the roots of the problems of poverty and underdevelopment. The question is: Can a new (i.e. a more just) international economic order really be built on the basis of the present one or should it at the same time be accompanied by changes at the national level?

15. One of the biggest shames and tragedies of our times in the matter of the utilization of resources is the big share claimed by armament production in all parts of the world. The tendency for defence expenditure to claim 50 per cent or even more of national budgets is not uncommon today in rich and poor countries alike. Apart from the fact that such expenditures reflect a gross distortion of priorities, they also lead to increasing concentration of economic power which often becomes the basis for oppressive political structures especially in the poor countries. Churches all over the world must raise their voices against the growing militarism and call upon public opinion to bring about necessary changes in national economies so that the armaments race can be effectively stopped and general disarmament promoted.

16. Another question that is frequently raised and must continue to be raised is regarding population growth. The discussions about the ecological imbalance and the depletion of global resources have shown the urgency to reduce the unprecedented population growth of the past few decades with its attendant economic and social consequences. At the same time it is becoming increasingly clear also that the control of population growth cannot be achieved as a goal in itself. The Chinese experience shows that there is a very close relationship between an economic policy aimed at social justice and participatory self-reliance and an effective population policy. It is therefore necessary to examine how a policy to curb population growth can be made part of a broader approach to human development.

17. A new aspect in the development debate today is that not only the methods of development, but also the goals of development are being brought into question. Many factors have contributed to this mood of questioning. The growing weariness with consumerism in affluent societies, the warnings about the depletion of the natural resources and the dangers of the technological gap, the tensions between economic and political aspirations and the new leads in theological thinking, have all forced on us questions about development as it is related to a meaningful life. In this search the churches have an opportunity to speak to mankind at large in their prophetic role supported by a "theology and spirituality for combat". In this sense the churches must favour an economy "as if people matter".

SOCIAL RESPONSIBILITY IN A TECHNOLOGICAL AGE

Introduction

18. It is the considered view of many scientists and technologists that the world is on a catastrophic course leading to mass starvation, global depletion of resources, and global environmental deterioration. The responsibility that now confronts humanity is to make a deliberate transition to a sustainable global society in which science and technology will be mobilized to meet the basic physical and spiritual needs of people, to minimize human suffering, and to create an environment which can sustain a decent quality of life for all people. This will involve a radical transformation of civilization, new technologies, new uses for technology, and new global economic and political systems.

19. The new situation in which humanity now finds itself has been created in less than a generation. There is even less time to create the transition to a sustainable global society if humanity is to survive.

Technological Assessment and the Criteria for "Appropriate Technology"

20. The world has reached the end of a triumphalist era in the use and deployment of science and technology. The time has come to exercise discriminating choice in favour of those technologies which conform to simplicity in design, are easily maintained, which reduce the overall impact on the environment, and are compatible with indigenous materials and culture. The technology should also conform to ecologically sound "development". The human costs of technology have to be assessed as in many cases they appear to outstrip the apparent advantages. A movement towards a more diverse pattern of technological development must also be encouraged.

125

21. *The assessment of risks.* The increase in the scale of technology has introduced the possibility of a new order of catastrophe, e.g., the vulnerability of "the green revolution" and of large centralized systems of production, such as chemical plants. There is need to examine the ethics of choice as between calculable risks in say coal mining and the possibility of a catastrophe in nuclear power production. This demands a discipline and integrity of purpose that is unlikely to exist under conditions of social disorder. The introduction of any new technology may be challenged on these grounds alone. The principle should be established that the community must be given the opportunity to share in the planning of safeguards and in the ultimate choice between technologies.

22. *Energy conservation.* The immediate priority is to reduce the conspicuously high patterns of energy consumption in those countries which make the largest demands on the world petroleum market. This would extend the limited life of presently known recoverable reserves. Policies for energy saving include a shift to smaller cars and public transport, reduction of fuel used in food production and processing, better insulation of buildings, decentralized electricity generation, eliminating the use of electricity for space heating, reduced packaging and recycling of products.

23. *Nuclear energy.* Increasing pressures on the world petroleum market bring the prospect of rapid expansion in the construction of nuclear power stations in countries at widely differing stages of development. This poses ethical dilemmas in view of (*a*) the inevitable coupling of nuclear energy for electricity generation and the production of nuclear weapons (how to limit the use of nuclear energy only for peaceful purposes of development, and avoid the possibility of using nuclear energy in nuclear weapons); (*b*) the hazards involved in the storage of nuclear waste for long periods; and (*c*) the problems of theft and sabotage. The ecumenical discussion of these issues has just begun and needs to be continued. Discussion should concentrate on the effectiveness of the monitoring and control of the nuclear fuel cycle at the international level, ratification of the Non-Proliferation Treaty by all countries possessing nuclear technology, the drift towards a plutonium fuel economy and its consequences, and the political and military implications of the further spread of nuclear technology.

24. *Alternative energy technologies.* During the next decade, there will be increased research and development of alternative systems of energy production. The world is now entering the transition between dependence upon petroleum and dependence upon other sources of energy, e.g., solar, wind, water, and geo-thermal. Priority must be given to ensure that research on alternative energy sources is funded at a high level, especially as these technologies will be of direct benefit to developing countries.

126

25. *Military technology and the use of resources.* A large proportion of the world's wealth and scientific and technical manpower goes into weapons and military technology. The Church must openly work against the increasing deployment of these resources to such destructive purposes and it must assist in making the full facts widely known.

26. *Social consequences of the uses of modern technology of human communication.* Modern technology makes increasingly possible the invasion of privacy by eavesdropping devices and computer banks of information. The control of radio, television, and publication by relatively few people has reduced the capacity of individuals to make responsible social judgements.

The Allocation of Common Resources Not Yet Claimed by Particular Nations

27. A possible way of driving a wedge between the present pattern of resource "ownership" and the long-term demand for a more equitable distribution is to ensure that the regions currently beyond the control of national governments and transnational companies be protected for the future prospect of a fairer distribution of the oil and mineral resources they contain. There is urgent need to ensure that yet another resource exploitation is not handed directly to those countries possessing the necessary and available technology. A new taxation scheme on commercial and state enterprises in the "international commons" such as the sea bed would help to channel revenues to developing countries on the basis of need. A clear ethic of control of natural resources will be required if such a taxation system is to be introduced.

Agricultural Technology and Food Crisis

28. The short-term issue is concerned with the establishment of an emergency food programme which could be utilized in the event of widespread crop failure or other types of natural disaster. The long-term issue involves the need to develop food technologies on a sufficiently large scale that are both ecologically sound and compatible with policies of self-reliant development. The changing pattern of agricultural development and food technologies in major food-exporting areas of the world, such as North America, Australia, and New Zealand, will also need to be adjusted to meet the requirements of sustainable long-term production.

Ethical Problems in the Transition to a Sustainable and Just Society

29. Today new emphasis is being put on the goal of a sustainable society, where each individual can feel secure that quality of life will be maintained or improved. For the developed countries it means in the first instance a sustainable core of economic activity relating to patterns of indigenous resource consumption, for example, land use, food supply, and

energy production, in a far longer time frame than suggested by trends in current commodity markets. It implies a substantial reallocation of power controlling the patterns of world trade in essential resources. It also implies increased participation by workers in the decision-making process in industry.

30. For the developing countries, it means emphasis on production for essential human needs, including food and energy; the search for the technologies which will guarantee this result, and which will at the same time avoid a continuing dependence on technology imported from industrialized countries, which is in direct conflict with social and cultural identity.

31. There is a need to investigate ways of ameliorating the adverse effects of the impact on less industrialized nations of the stabilization of production and consumption of the industrialized world, and the effects on employment in the industrialized world. This will involve the search for alternative development strategies for less industrialized countries, new patterns of optimal international division of labour, the use of foreign capital and expertise, international control of such matters as resource rationing and pollution. The basic goal remains: nobody should increase his affluence until everybody has his essentials.

Ethical Dilemmas Arising from the Application of Modern Biology to Human Problems

32. Throughout Christian history the practice of abortion and the advocacy of contraception and euthanasia have posed ethical and theological dilemmas and remain controversial issues. Recent discoveries in the biological and medical sciences raise fresh ethical questions in uncharted areas. We accept that each individual life is infinitely precious in the sight of God, and the Christian responsibility is to preserve the sanctity of human life. This responsibility is challenged by the following developments and obliges the churches to reinterpret historic Christian teaching on the sanctity of human life.

1. Experimentation on human foetuses, including the transplantation of ova fertilized outside the body (prenatal adoption).

2. Artificial prolongation of human life in the comatose patient.

3. Recognition of biological death as a process, and its relationship to the practice of organ transplantation.

4. Possibility of controlling the sex of offspring.

5. Genetic engineering. This involves the future possibility of direct manipulation of human genes for the purpose of replacing deleterious genes by "normal" genes. Present experimentation in genetic engineering is largely done on viruses and bacteria. They present the hazard of

unintentional transformation of harmful viruses and bacteria into lethal ones. The churches should be involved in the risk-benefit analysis and in the problem of reducing risk in such experimentation. The possible application of genetic engineering to people raises the critical questions of experimentation on people.

6. Behavioural control. The use of drugs, electrical stimuli, psychosurgery, and psychological methods of behaviour modification to control socially disapproved behaviour raises many unanswered ethical questions.

7. The misuse of studies on animal behaviour in interpreting human behaviour. These studies raise in a new context the question "What is man?"

The Encounter of Science and Faith

33. The encounter of science and faith takes place in two areas. One is in ethics. The application of scientific discoveries to human affairs raises ethical issues which science alone cannot resolve since science itself does not prescribe the good.

34. The second area is the challenge of the Christian view of the creative activity of God in the world to the dominant scientific view of reductionism and materialism. The need is for a new working out of a common Christian conception of the creation which seeks to save the personal and which at the same time incorporates valid insights of modern science into the nature of the creation.

TOWARDS ACKNOWLEDGEMENT OF POWER

35. Since the Uppsala Assembly, the member churches of the WCC, through their commitment and action-research, have acknowledged the importance of power in decisions about development, understood as a liberating process geared towards social justice, self-reliance, and economic growth. This implies a sharp correction of the prevailing understanding of development as mere economic growth. Through the action-research carried out by the WCC, it has become increasingly clear that power is to be conceived as the capability to orient and to implement decisions. This capability can be of economic, political, ideological, and/or military nature, being all these components in a dynamic interrelation among themselves.

36. The assessment of different components which constitute power can only be undertaken in concrete, historical, geographical, and sociopolitical situations. There are different concepts of power expressed in the different capitalist and socialist systems. Control of power in these differ-

ent political systems will require specific methods of people's organization. This can only be developed in concrete national situations.

37. As Christians and churches we cannot speak about nor work for a new world order in the midst of situations of domination and structures of oppression without referring to the liberating power of Jesus Christ. He liberates us from sin, both personal and social. We recognize that the gospel expresses this liberating strength. The prophetic word of Yahweh's drawing near to the humble, to the powerless, finds an echo in fundamental passages of the Gospels (Luke 4.17-21; Matt. 25.31-46, etc.). The gospel *has been* brought to the poor, to the powerless, to the oppressed, to the captives, to the sick. In the person of Jesus, Yahweh has put himself decidedly in the place of the poor; he has searched for those who are "nothing" (1 Cor. 1.26-31). The word "nothing" refers not to intrinsic moral quality but to the very fact that the poor are marginal, leaving their very destiny to the powerful.

38. One implication is that Jesus is our liberator inasmuch as:

1. he calls on us to follow him upon that role which brought him face to face with those who use religion as a means of domination;

2. he gives us a hope, i.e., he affirms the right to life and the triumph of life against cynicism and fatalism of the pure politics of power. To believe in him is not to renounce participation in the struggle for justice and liberation. It means, on the contrary, that in spite of our apparent powerlessness we must keep alive faith so that we hasten the day when "justice will flow like water";

3. he indicates to us that the way through which the community of believers is called to overcome the ambiguities of power is the way of love and the Cross. We are not faithful to Jesus Christ when we submit to the powers that be: at that moment we become captives of the powers that have been defeated by Christ.

39. Another implication is that power manifested through weakness requires of the churches a review of their social behaviour, of their sometimes hierarchical and non-participatory structures, of their styles of life and decision-making processes.

40. Power can be used by dominating minorities or by democratic forces. Given the relevance of this issue, and in order to provide to the churches some operational instruments for action, we can only indicate some perspectives which seem the most important concerning the present constellation of powers.

Economic Power

41. The desire for control over resources all over the world has always been and still is a basic reason for the exercise of economic power and the establishment of exploitative structures of domination and dependence.

Colonialism was the classic form of such domination. Overt forms of colonialism are rather rare today, but there are many subtle forms of neo-colonialism which result in the rich countries exploiting the poor countries. They represent a concentration of economic and technological power in the hands of a few. They play an important role in shaping the world economy not only in countries based on the principle of private ownership of means of production, but also in relation to trade with the socialist world. These corporations claim to bring capital and technology to the countries where they operate and thereby to create employment and income. But, essentially, their aim is to take advantage of the cheap labour that is available in the host countries and to draw out profits from them, making use of the immense control they exercise over world trade and prices. It must be mentioned that their operations in the poorer countries are with the approval of national governments and often in active collaboration with local private business enterprises. But the type of goods they produce is meant invariably to satisfy the needs of an elite class, the technology they use is ill-suited for the needs of these countries, and the employment they create and the incomes they generate are only to the advantage of the higher income groups in the host countries.

42. Increasingly they also disrupt the ecological equilibrium in the host countries and pollute the waters and the air. Transnational corporations are a typical example of the ways in which capitalist forces in the international and national spheres join together to oppress the poor and keep them under domination. Measures to check the activities of the transnational corporations are now under discussion, but because of the immense control they exercise over the channels of the "free-market" international economy, it is very difficult to envisage any effective measure which will eradicate their innate exploitative patterns.

Political Power

43. On the one hand, in many countries of the world the minority which controls and orients the use of international capital, being unable to give an adequate answer to the development challenge, has become allied to national oligarchies of countries of Africa, Asia, Latin America, and the Middle East. This minority tries to improve a political project of international domination. This coalition of forces confronts with totalitarian regimes popular forces who look for the defence of their rights. When liberal democracies are no longer sufficient for guaranteeing the profits of the privileged, in some cases and in increasing manner, they resort to totalitarian regimes for whom torture and terror have become usual means of government. They do not hesitate at instigating subversion, political intervention for the purpose of consolidating their hegemony.

44. On the other hand, it is possible to observe an accumulation of political power by political apparatus in countries where there is a cen-

trally planned economy. In this case, there is evidence that not all freedoms are guaranteed to collectivities and individuals.

Ideological Power

45. On the ideological level, a new cultural power is being developed through the control of mass media, the educational system, and others. Unrestrained consumption, imposition of dominant values are constitutive elements of an ideology established by dominant powers. Particularly oppressive is the power exercised by some governments over mass media to their advantage and with no regard for freedom of the people, among whom Christians are one part.

Military Power

46. The maintenance of zones of influence by the super-powers has been a decisive element for the increasing importance of this component of power. Moreover, the cost necessary to support such situations has made the war industry a prominent sector of some industrialized countries, both in the capitalist and in the socialist world. It ensures all kinds of orders for an industry whose immense productive potential is not always fully utilized, and it absorbs a large slice of the surplus produced, which could receive a more appropriate use for the development of the poor.

Within the framework of the present balance of power, history has shown that arms are used in the territories of Africa, Asia, Latin America, and the Middle East. One of the consequences of the prevailing logic of the dominant systems is the use of military equipment for the repression of popular forces. Thus the cycle is complete: the arms produced in the metropolis become tools of control and domination, within the respective zones of influence, of the peoples of the dependent countries.

47. It must be noted that because of the increasing importance of this sector in the contemporary constellations of power, militarists are playing more than ever before in modern history a determinant role in processes of economic growth and social organization, especially in countries of Africa, Asia, Latin America, and the Middle East. However, this trend is proving in most of the cases not to be the appropriate means for full liberation of people.

People's Power

48. In developed as in underdeveloped countries as well, people are struggling for justice, development, and more human life, although their methods of action are not always acceptable for all. The existence of people's movements actively involved in the struggle against dominating powers is understandable. These movements express the aspiration to overcome situations and structures of domination and dependence, both among and within countries.

132

49. It must be recognized that in some developed countries, in spite of the de-mobilizing role which sometimes workers' organizations play, the combative mood of the working classes and their capability to set objectives which are not of economic nature, are in progress. People's movements are developing also, and in a more dynamic way, in underdeveloped nations. They are growing up in contexts where culture, history, vision, and hopes are nourishing their struggles. Among the components of people's power are: awareness of the situations of dependence and domination that have to be overcome; clarity of goals that have to be achieved; and commitment for organization and action. Among the latter, accumulation of forces seems to be a need which requires a policy of alliance and unity among underprivileged sectors of society. In this sense, the struggle for human rights—including people's rights—and the movement for liberation of women have to be seen as contributions of historical importance. But the real importance of people's power is related to the process of creation of self-reliance, as a fundamental element in the struggle against poverty and for development.

The Role of the Churches

50. It is impossible to ignore in this analysis the role and the power of churches. As social institutions they are engaged at all levels of social life. Some churches are landowners, related to feudal, capitalistic, and neo-capitalistic structures. Sometimes this alienates them from the poor and the oppressed. They are also involved in financial powers, i.e., shares, banks, investments, holdings. Equally various churches are influential elements of political power, either as active agents or as media of the establishment. Moreover, they are particularly influential at the ideological level in sharing and reinforcing dominant ideologies through religious teaching, shaping public opinion. Nevertheless, we cannot ignore through the whole history of the Church the existence of committed people and churches for whom to be faithful to Jesus Christ has implied and still implies to share with the oppressed their struggles for liberation. The participation of the Christian community in the struggle against poverty and oppression is a sign of the answer to the call of Jesus Christ to liberation. When this happens, the churches can no longer be considered as unconditional allies of the rich. On the contrary, they can be instruments of the renewing work of Christ whose strength is made known in weakness. The sufficiency of the Church to participate in tackling problems of such magnitude is based only on the sufficiency of the grace of the one who is the crucified and risen Lord.

QUALITY OF LIFE

51. A discussion on "quality of life" must recognize at least two levels of human existence. On the most primary level, human beings need

to survive. But mere survival is hardly life with quality, or life as it should be. For human beings, as God's most precious creatures, must fulfil God's purpose. This fulfilment, history and the Christian revelation have shown us, comprises three dimensions: freedom, community, and total obedience to God. That is, we need to be free; yet, at the same time we need to belong. This is the root of life's ambiguity. In order to transcend this ambiguity and thereby attain true freedom and true community, human beings must individually and communally give themselves to God and to their fellow human beings.

52. In order to survive, men and women need food, clothing, shelter, and medical care. Moreover, men and women need to belong and be at home, to love and to be loved, to be significant and to have a sense of dignity, to develop and express God's gifts, and to participate in decision-making and other processes of life.

53. Being implies having. But there exists in humanity a fatal tendency to let having gain the rule over being, to be trapped by the things we possess, to think and believe that having is more fundamental in life. Thus, having becomes pathological and demonic. The corruption of obsessive having is called "consumerism": the need to consume conditioned by external motivation. The structural expression of this disease has been called "giantism". Its consequent productive processes throw up enormously powerful institutions which now have global impact. In this context, human creativity and control have been seriously preempted if not entirely blocked.

54. We are spiritual beings. It is the despiritualizing impact of this process which dismays us. It has resulted in a serious diminishment of the quality of our experience of life. At home and at work, life is increasingly depersonalized and functionalized. We have been alienated from our neighbour, nature, cosmos, and God. For many, a glory has passed from the earth. While not pleading for an impossible return to some imagined age of pre-technological innocence, we must assert our autonomy and control over the machines we have created. We must make them instruments and not master. In short, we must discover ways of satisfying our basic needs and our spiritual and cultural creativities by creating structures which are appropriate to people and on a human scale, not industrial "gods" which only consume those who create them and depend on them. For example, the enrichment of our being through arts and music is a determinant element of our quality of life.

55. There is also another side of the absurdity of human life today: the perennial corruption of deprivation. Starvation and poverty are the clearest expressions of this corruption. We recognize that the root cause of not having enough to live by on the part of the poor is the same as over-consumption on the part of the affluent. That is the human sin of

self-seeking and the will to dominate. This sin has local, national, and international character.

56. The quality of life problem is at root a theological problem. It concerns the nature of humanity as made in the image of God. In the biblical tradition, being human is not dependent upon human achievement or success. Rather, our worth is dependent upon acceptance by God, in spite of our shortcomings. God wills for us to be his faithful stewards, enjoying and caring for his creation. At the same time, he also wills for us to be his agents, promoting love, peace, harmony, reconciliation, and justice, within individuals, among neighbours, within societies, between nations, and in the cosmos. The basic Christian principle in this regard is faith in God, love towards him and our neighbours, and hope for salvation in Christ through the Holy Spirit.

57. We call the churches to a joyful and vivid reaffirmation of our Christian faith in repentance. We have abused our relationships with each other and with the whole of creation because we have forgotten who we are and whence we come. Creation is the overflow of God's creative love, the "bodying-forth" of the very life of the Trinity. It was meant to be an expression of the very life of God. The harmony of creation is an image of the family-life of God. As such, humanity would have been at one with creation. Humanity's original sin was to choose to be self-centred, rather than to seek meaning and fulfilment in relationship with God in creation. This is still our sin, the root of our alienation from one another, from nature, from the cosmos, and from God. The causes of our alienation and the lack of quality of life lie within ourselves.

58. Christ calls us to conversion, to a radical recognition of our human predicament, and to a new orientation in which we would be open to each other, to nature, and to God. He calls us out of bondage of our own obsessive self-seeking to a true liberty of the children of God, once more "at home" in creation. He calls us to be free in community, in the pursuit of holiness, wholeness, relatedness, meaningfulness, self-giving love and joy. This is the meaning of recreation or restoration. It is only from such a spiritual foundation that a true Christian witness and service can spring.

59. Christ also calls us to a proper asceticism: to a recognition that the quality of life does not consist in the abundance of *more having* but in our *being* in relationship with the Father and with our brothers and sisters. In Christ's resurrection, God restored and transfigured Christ's broken humanity as a symbol that God intends to restore the whole creation. It is the vocation of Christians to participate obediently in this work of restoration.

60. While they must rejoice in the joy and beauty of life and the

135

glory of human relationships, Christians know that here they have no Abiding City. There is a quality of life which is known in its fullness only in our eternal life with the Divine Trinity. This makes us aware of the provisional nature of our life and existence. Furthermore, it liberates us from bondage to material things. If we possess all things and lose God, we lose everything; but if we lose everything except God, we lose nothing.

61. In summary, we as Christians must recognize that the ultimate test of the quality of life on earth is the obedient sacrifice of costly Christian discipleship. And as such, Christians live according to an ethic of self-giving and self-limiting, as fully exemplified by our Lord Jesus Christ who is both divine and human.

RECOMMENDATIONS

PARTICIPATION OF CHURCHES IN DEVELOPMENT PROGRAMMES

62. If poverty and oppression are the manifestations of complex economic, social, and political processes, responsible participation in the struggle against these evils *must* necessarily involve the churches in investing the time and effort to understand the complexity of the problem. We must avoid the dangers of becoming too simplistic or moralistic. Equally, the results of such detailed study must be disseminated so that the churches become educated for mobilization of resources in appropriate action.

63. The struggle against oppression and injustice inevitably necessitates confrontations with powers and the handling of power. Churches have, in the past, underestimated the dimensions of these aspects even when they have marginally recognized them.

64. The churches' involvement in these struggles for liberation and development will vary in nature according to the local context. In some cases, the churches' role will be one of leadership. In others, it may involve joining hands in co-operation with secular forces. In yet other situations, the churches may not have a struggling but a serving role to play. But in no case should they retreat into the comfort of socially uninvolved "otherworldiness".

65. What are then the possible patterns of the churches' participation in development? We see the answer to this question as having two aspects: the first relates to the identification of the *priorities* for involvement in the given situation; the second relates to *methods* of involvement.

66. Therefore we make these recommendations:

1. We urge the member churches to plan their participation in development to be primarily in support of the poorest of the poor, the rural sector and its spillover into urban squatters and slums.

2. We also call the attention of member churches to approach the population problem as an aspect of comprehensive development involving social justice and self-reliance.

3. We ask the member churches and the WCC, through its appropriate units and sub-units, to pursue and deepen education for development in co-operation with member churches from all countries as a sign of a world concern.

4. In this connection we renew the appeal made by the WCC to the member churches to set aside 2% of their regular income for development efforts, not only as a means of providing money for development but also as an educational instrument to ensure fuller understanding of the development process and wider participation of people at the local level. This appeal is also addressed to groups and Christian movements.

67. *Methods* of involvement in development are necessarily varied and depend upon the local situation. Participation in development calls, above all, for imagination and sensitivity to the local context. But some possibilities might include:

1. The influence of churches on their own governments, and power structures at the local level (e.g. schools, trade unions, newspapers, etc.).

2. Direct implementation of development programmes by churches or ecumenical bodies (such as National and/or Regional Councils of Churches, and the WCC) at the local, regional, or national levels.

3. Churches' action in partnership with secular bodies and people's movements involved in development work, including governments and UN specialized agencies. For example: motivator's training for development; popular education programmes; mobilization of public opinion in order to influence governments, etc. These are actions which can be undertaken by churches in their participation in development programmes. Christians also could join efforts with persons of other faiths and ideologies in people's movements.

4. The encouragement by the churches of proposals for the creation of an international disaster relief fund.

68. Finally, we recommend that churches that are members of the World Council of Churches urge their respective governments to support the immediate creation of a food reserve for emergency purposes, under international control, to back the recommendations of the 1974 World

Food Conference at Rome, particularly the massive transfer of capital and appropriate technology to support developing countries in their efforts to improve food production and become more self-reliant in dealing with hunger, and that whatever the aid, care be taken to avoid new patterns of dependency. The churches are called to engage in dialogue with their governments on measures to control drug abuse, especially the greatest of these—alcohol. Further, we recommend that the churches of the WCC continue to urge their constituents to contribute to non-governmental agencies and to international agencies that are concerned with the relief of hunger.

SOCIAL RESPONSIBILITY IN A TECHNOLOGICAL AGE

Energy Conservation

69. It is recommended that the churches in the industrialized countries should challenge present patterns of energy consumption in order to extend the useful life of non-renewable energy resources and to assist the movement towards a low-growth energy economy in those countries.

Nuclear Energy

70. As far as nuclear energy is concerned the churches at the national level should lobby for more effective safeguards in the control and operation of the nuclear fuel cycle to ensure that there is a reduced risk of diversion of strategic weapon materials; in addition there is a need to press for more serious investigation of the long-term disposal of radioactive wastes by those responsible for the management of nuclear power programmes. The churches are further urged to register their reactions to the findings of the Ecumenical Hearing on Nuclear Energy, Sigtuna, Sweden, 1975. (See Report on Nuclear Energy, Anticipation, no. 21.)

Alternative Energy Technologies

71. Since there are inevitably grave ethical problems involved in the application of nuclear energy, we recommend that the churches and individual Christians seek to promote sufficient funding and moral support for research and development of renewable sources of energy, e.g. solar and wave energy.

Ethical Obligations in the Sustainable and Just Society

72. We recommend that the churches should examine very carefully the implications of a movement towards a sustainable and just society as this embodies many significant structural changes in the patterns of food production, energy consumption, employment, population, housing, and transport, in both developed and developing countries.

73. It is important that the churches encourage scientists and technologists to develop socially responsible new directions for modern societies. This encounter should focus on issues of science and faith and on the ethical implications of specific and technical activities.

Ethical Dilemmas in Biology

74. We recommend to the churches and the Christian Medical Commission of the WCC further study of the ethical dilemmas and theological perspectives relating to recent discoveries in the biological and medical sciences. This study should include a fresh consideration of the meaning of the concept of the sanctity of human life.

POWER AND JUSTICE

75. In order to make sure that the elitist and non-participatory structures which exist in society are not duplicated in life style, preaching, teaching, decision-making of the churches, we call the churches to a serious self-criticism of their economic, political, and ideological role in their own societies. Moreover, we fraternally appeal to all churches to examine their interest in and concern for:

1. social justice;

2. peaceful coexistence of nations;

3. participation in people's organizations;

4. participation in educational process which will develop critical awareness in order to begin to shape the features of a new society.

76. The present constellation of power requires a rethinking of the relationship between Church and State as this was stated at the Oxford Conference, 1937. We therefore recommend the churches throughout the world to search for ways by which they may fully exercise their priestly and prophetic role and, at the same time, contribute to a more just and free society.

77. We witness with hope the increase of commitment to a more just and human society within many churches and Christian organizations all over the world. We recommend the churches and the WCC to continue to clarify and articulate the theological criteria of this engagement, taking into account recent regional experiences.

78. We request the churches to co-ordinate efforts with the WCC—through its appropriate sub-units—in order to continue research and dialogue and to develop documentation on the role of the transnational corporations. In this sense we ask the WCC to aid the member churches to undertake or pursue this research at local, national, and regional levels in

order to enable people to participate in the shaping of a new economic order.

79. In view of the increasing world-wide trend to militarism which in itself is contrary to the Christian view of a world of justice and peace, and its tremendous negative impact in the process of development geared towards social justice, self-reliance, and economic growth, we strongly recommend that the churches and the WCC should make concrete the warnings they have already pronounced against militarism. We therefore recommend to the WCC to convene a special consultation on the nature of militarism as a preparation for a Programme to Combat Militarism.

QUALITY OF LIFE

80. We call the attention of the churches to the growing concern over the consequences of modern science-based technological developments with their accompaniment of a deterioriating environment and debased and alienating forms of human communities. This has resulted in a new call to consider the "quality of life". This is an emphasis on the quality rather than the quantity of material things and on the obligation of the affluent both to provide basic necessities for all the people of planet Earth, and to modify their own consumption patterns, so as to reduce their disproportionate and spiritually destructive drain on earth's non-renewable and renewable resources, excessive use of energy resulting in contamination of the sea and air, and urban concentration and rural poverty that are breeding grounds of starvation, crime, and despair.

81. In solidarity with all who share our concern for quality of life, we encourage churches and Christians to take action to alter those structures and practices which hinder the achievement of an appropriate quality of life.

82. We ask all Christians to take costly and exemplary actions to show by deeds and words their solidarity with and concern for those who are deprived of adequate quality of life.

83. We urge Christians, individually and corporately, to pray for grace and courage to persist in the task of working obediently for the restoration of creation.

84. Recognizing that many groups are today engaged in a search for a new life style which enhances quality of life, we urge all Christians and churches to engage in a genuinely open dialogue with, and to support, such groups. It is important in this sense to be sensitive to meet life styles of the younger generations.

85. One of the main issues taken up by International Women's Year was the crucial contribution of women in relation to problems of develop-

ment and quality of life. Issues of malnutrition, starvation, family size, etc., all these ultimately focus on what women do as overseers of the nutritional needs of their families and the education of their children. Therefore it is incumbent on the churches to take note of this and to see that women are included at all levels of decision-making regarding these critical and global issues that affect the work, education, legal rights, and contribution of women.

A FINAL WORD

While the above recommendations are addressed to the member churches of the WCC, and also to the NCC itself, we hope that individuals, groups, and local congregations study and discuss these recommendations towards local involvement and appropriate action.

III
The Business of the Assembly

III
The Business of the Assembly

1. OPENING ACTIONS

Monday, 24 November

WORDS OF WELCOME AND THANKS

After opening prayers conducted by Ms Pauline Webb (Vice-Moderator of the Central Committee), the Assembly *in General Session*, with Dr W. A. Visser 't Hooft (Honorary President) presiding, received addresses of welcome from African church leaders.

Bishop L. Imathiu said:

Mr Chairman:

On behalf of the Local Arrangements Committee, the Kenya Member Churches of the WCC are very delighted to welcome you all to Kenya. I bring you greetings from the Member Churches and wish to assure you that the general public (here we call them *wanachi*) are happy indeed that the WCC decided to hold its 5th Assembly here in Nairobi.

We wish you a very pleasant stay and hope that in addition to the hard and demanding schedule ahead of you, you will find time to see Kenya and its people. Our country is working tirelessly on development and improvement of standards of living and character building to which the churches in this country are fully committed. It is in this connection that many of the delegates here have known and been in contact with the National Christian Council of Kenya, commonly referred to as NCCK.

It is my added pleasure to say as Chairman of the NCCK how we have appreciated your partnership in support and understanding of our projects for all in need. The general secretary of the NCCK and his staff send their greetings to you all. They are also happy to show you some of the work you may be interested in during your stay in Kenya, and particularly those who can stay a little longer after the meeting of the 5th Assembly are assured of our attention.

In case you find any shortcomings I beg to take this opportunity to apologize to you all, Mr Chairman. I believe you will also give us your understanding that eleven months' notice was not long enough to polish up some of our arrangements, but no doubt you will find Kenyans warm-hearted and friendly.

(At this point Bishop Imathiu amidst applause introduced Mr John Kamau, General Secretary of the National Christian Council of Kenya, who spoke briefly on behalf of his colleagues.)

We are convinced in our hearts that the Church is called by God as an instrument of peace, hope, and love to the world, and every delegate and guest and visitor is expected to accept this responsibility. Today the Church is challenged to show the world through her prophetic role how mankind can live. If we do not answer our calling, God will use another way.

May God bless you.

The Reverend John Gatu said:

Mr Chairman, my brothers and sisters:

On behalf of the Kenya Member Churches of the World Council of Churches, namely, the Church of the Province of Kenya, the Friends, the Methodist Church in Kenya, the Presbyterian Church of East Africa, and the Salvation Army, it is my great and honoured duty to welcome you to our beautiful city and secondly to our beautiful country. As you come in from the airport you may have seen the notice board which reads "Nairobi, the city in the sun". While many of you have noticed only rain since your arrival, I am sure you will not find it as cold as some of the countries from which you have come at this time of the year. We will give you our warm hearts.

When the urgent request came to the Kenya Member Churches as to whether this Assembly could meet in Nairobi, we were caught, as you normally say, "red handed". For instead of receiving the call in any of the church offices in Nairobi, the message was phoned to the State House, Nakuru, where a delegation was meeting His Excellency the President on domestic matters. So apart from the members of the delegation the second other person who received the message was His Excellency the President of our Republic, who straightaway said, If you want to invite them here, tell them they are most welcome. I know that His Excellency will have his opportunity to greet the members of the Assembly and so I shall not dwell on this point.

The history of Christianity in East Africa can be traced, in terms of modern history, to the year 1489 when Vasco da Gama landed at Malindi on the Kenya coast, in the company of several Roman Catholic missionaries. In 1844 a German Lutheran employed by the Church Missionary Society of London arrived at Mombasa, thus starting the new era of Christianity.

The missionary movement, however, changed radically after the beginning of the colonial era, especially with the building of the railway line. Many missionary groups arrived and by the time the railway line reached Nairobi about 1899, Protestant missions sprang up in every direction. Today in this country we have any number of church denominations, whether you categorize them as Catholics, Orthodox, or Protestants.

It did not take time, Mr Chairman, before we had what were called in those days independent churches, now commonly known as locally founded churches. The disparity between the first and this second group and lack of fellowship remained with us for many many years. It is a matter of praise to God that today that gap is closing up and the membership of such bodies within the National Christian Council of

146

Kenya and the presence of their students in at least one theological college of the established churches augurs well for the future of our ecumenical relationships in this country.

Mr Chairman, there is another reason why we, the Kenya Member Churches, feel so privileged that you did accept our invitation to meet in Nairobi. For sixty-two years ago, in 1913, a conference was held in one of the Presbyterian mission stations in those days. Their terms of reference could be rightly summed up as those of the World Council of Churches, and probably these must have had a lot of impact in the birth of the Ecumenical Movement. I refer particularly to the fact that they were seriously discussing the closer working together and the relationship of the mission churches working in the country then, with a hope that in the end there probably could be a one Church of Kenya and that all may believe that we are one in Christ.

It is only to be lamented, Mr Chairman, that up to this day, we do not have a Church of Kenya united organically to welcome you, but we can assure you without any shadow of doubt that the Member Churches of WCC along with a few others who may not be officially members of WCC have very happy and cordial relationships, so that we can extend a word of welcome to you on their behalf also.

While we do not have a state church as you may have been used to in some of your countries, the Kenya community is a religious community and consequently the place of the Church is not without recognition. It is in this connection that, for the coming fortnight or more, the eyes of all Kenyans and indeed of all the world will be looking at this Assembly with great anticipation. In the past, we have warned other groups not to make Kenya "a religious battlefield", and while undoubtedly this is not your intention, we nevertheless wish to pass on this word of caution also.

And finally, Mr Chairman, we welcome you to Kenya which has been termed archaeologically the cradle of mankind. For only a few hundred miles from here in Lake Rudolf the earliest fossil of man was discovered. We hope that if you have not done so already, you will spare yourselves some time to see something of the beauty of our land, our people, and our heritage. In conclusion, we bid you welcome to our homes, to our churches, to our congregations, and for those of you who do not come from Africa, we welcome you to Kenya, the cradle of mankind and of your ancestors.

Peace!
Pray God of our Fathers for
Peace! Peace! Peace!
Peace be with us all.

Canon Burgess Carr said:

On behalf of the Member Churches and Councils of the All Africa Conference of Churches, and in my own name, I extend to all of you a most cordial welcome to Africa. Happily you are meeting in the African city where our headquarters happens to be located, and this gives us added joy. We are glad that you have come among us to declare, affirm and celebrate the gospel message that JESUS CHRIST FREES AND UNITES.

Not all of you are strangers to Africa. Many of you come from churches that have had and still have close relationships with the churches in Africa. Indeed, many of the churches in Africa owe their origins and their development to the sacrifices of faithful men and women who came from many of your lands to preach the gospel among our peoples. It is appropriate at this time to pause and remember them, to thank God for their obedience and witness, and to acknowledge our gratitude to all those who enabled and sustained their mission with prayers and other resources.

The All Africa Conference of Churches is one of the regional ecumenical conferences in fraternal relationship with the World Council of Churches. We comprise 114 member churches and councils, and represent approximately one-third of the total Christian population in Africa. Our numbers are always growing. We have in our constituency, not only those churches which have emerged out of the modern missionary enterprise, but the ancient churches of Egypt and Ethiopia and the nascent African Independent churches as well. We stretch across thirty-one countries from Morocco to Malagasy, and from Cairo to the Cape of Good Hope.

The affirmation in our theme has been a central preoccupation of the All Africa Conference of Churches ever since it was founded. The theme of our first Assembly which met in Kampala in 1963 was FREEDOM AND UNITY IN CHRIST. In this the AACC seeks to bring the relevance of contemporary African concerns to bear upon our Christian profession. For every single African is today preoccupied with freedom and unity.

As such the theme of this Assembly has a special importance for us. Our empirical experience as African peoples demonstrates that Jesus *detains* and *divides*. Witness the horrifying injustices that have been perpetrated and are still being perpetrated in Africa even today in the name of "Christian civilization"; but witness also the unflinching diplomatic, economic, and military support from those same countries whose churches have sent scores of missionaries to evangelize Africa. Witness further the rivalry among denominations and the conditioning of Africans to place greater priority upon their confessional allegiances than on their common unity in Jesus Christ. Fortunately in the All Africa Conference of Churches we have reached a fairly wide measure of consensus against *spiritualizing* the freedom and unity bestowed by Jesus Christ.

We believe and we affirm that JESUS CHRIST FREES BEFORE HE UNITES. Therefore the *liberation* aspect of this theme is of primary significance for the churches in Africa. Unless we are first liberated, we cannot be united. I would like this to be clearly understood by every single participant in this Assembly. It is against this background that our total and unequivocal support for the WCC Programme to Combat Racism must be understood. The assistance channelled through this programme to the liberation movements in Africa, in particular, has enhanced the credibility of African churches. We are committed to ensure that this Assembly confirms its support for that programme—without any modifications whatsoever, except those which would give it greater effectiveness in speeding up the total elimination of white racism and colonialism from our continent.

I am done. I will conclude by reminding you that you have gathered in that region of our continent where archaeologists and palaeontologists have discovered the oldest human fossils going back 250 to 350 million years. The evidence is fairly conclusive that human life began here on the continent of Africa. From here men and women wandered across the earth, through the kindness of nature and of grace. It is significant to us that in this age when human beings are groping again for community and inter-independence, for fellowship and for peace, the Church of Jesus Christ from across the whole inhabited earth gathers in this place to affirm that it is neither race, nor economic status, nor social class, nor sex, nor confessional creed and liturgy—but JESUS CHRIST who frees and unites.

All of the peoples and nations of Africa will be listening to hear from this Assembly how we here work out the implications of this solemn affirmation in word and in deed.

In reply, Dr Visser 't Hooft spoke gratefully of the "marvellous job" done by the Local Arrangements Committee in a short time and contrasted the Kenyatta Conference Centre with the Concertgebouw in Amsterdam where the WCC had been founded in 1948 and which now seemed to him to be "a kind of log cabin". Dr Visser 't Hooft spoke also of the contributions that the churches of Africa had made and would make, and looked forward to "a much more fruitful meeting between African Christianity and the Ecumenical Movement".

ADOPTION OF AGENDA AND APPOINTMENT OF COMMITTEES

In Business Session, with Dr M. M. Thomas (Moderator of the Central Committee) presiding, the Assembly accepted the proposed Agenda and the proposed Assembly Officers and Committee members. (The Assembly Programme and the Officers and Committee lists are printed as Appendices 1 and 2.)

THE REPORT OF THE MODERATOR OF THE CENTRAL COMMITTEE

In the afternoon, *in Business Session*, Ms Pauline Webb presiding, Dr M. M. Thomas presented *The Report of the Moderator of the Central Committee to the Assembly of the World Council of Churches*. This is printed as Appendix 3.

Dr Thomas spoke of the background of this Assembly in the life and work of the WCC described in *Uppsala to Nairobi*. The WCC had always been concerned with and for the world, for theology is only active at the cutting edge between the Word and the world. Nevertheless since 1961 there has been a change.

The integration of the International Missionary Council with the WCC at New Delhi had introduced a new interaction between the ecumenical concerns for unity, mission, and service; this in turn had resulted in a fresh discussion on the meaning and practice of evangelism in the modern world

149

as evidenced by the conferences at Bangkok 1973, Lausanne 1974, and the Synod of Roman Catholic Bishops 1974.

Secondly there had been a reflection at Uppsala of three new developments. The many churches from eastern Europe and from the Third World that had come into the Council brought with them the hopes, aspirations, and struggles of their peoples, races, and nations. We had also listened with a new sensitivity to the poor, the oppressed, and the marginalized. Thirdly, we had been helped by theological and secular experts to take more seriously the secular context and the tasks of justice and development. These also had had a profound theological and spiritual effect on the Council.

Dr Thomas then proceeded to analyse in some depth the effect of the interrelational approach of "contemporary ecumenism" on church unity and evangelism on the one hand, and on the quality of life, world service and development, and human liberation on the other.

Time allowed of only a brief discussion.

Tuesday, 25 November

In Business Session, Dr W.A. Visser 't Hooft (Honorary President) presiding, Dr Philip Potter presented the proposed allocations of participants to Work Groups, Sections, Hearings, and Workshops, and suggested that those who had strong objections should put them in writing. The list of allocations was approved.

(The rest of the day was spent on the address by Dr Robert McAfee Brown on "Who is this Jesus Christ who Frees and Unites?" and on the first meeting of the work groups.)

Wednesday, 26 November

THE REPORT OF THE GENERAL SECRETARY

In Business Session, with Dr M.M. Thomas presiding, Dr Potter presented his report as General Secretary. Before doing so, he drew attention to the fact that the first four years of the period under review had been under the General Secretaryship of Dr Eugene Carson Blake, who was invited onto the platform amidst applause. Dr Potter paid tribute to the courage and pertinacity with which Dr Blake had carried out the policies of the Council and to his comradeship with the staff. Dr Potter also pointed out that the only survivor of the Stockholm Conference of 1925 in our midst was Dr Visser 't Hooft, who had attended it as a delegate of the World's Alliance of YMCAs.

Dr Thomas had analysed primarily the thought of the World Council. Dr Potter, in a complementary fashion, indicated how in the fifty years since Stockholm 1925 the Ecumenical Movement had tried to help the churches to discern the issues that called for action and to act together upon them, and spoke in particular of the things that have preoccupied the WCC in the last seven years.

Dr Potter then turned to the manner of the Church's action at the world, regional, national, and local levels, and of the new trend towards popular participation which is marred by an increase in violence and oppression, and a growing malaise of the human person. To all these crises of faith our theme, "Jesus Christ frees and unites", is a challenge of faith. It is also a challenge to the way in which the Council functions; and Dr Potter ended by dissecting some of the practical questions about the future of the Council with which the Assembly would have to deal—the proposed new statement of functions and purposes; the gap between the WCC and the member churches; the priorities in its life and work; its finances; and its relations with the Roman Catholic Church and the progress of Faith and Order discussions of visible unity.

The General Secretary's report is printed as Appendix 4.

A short discussion followed, to which five speakers contributed, while many others could not speak because of lack of time.

THE FINANCE REPORT

In Business Session, Ms Pauline Webb presiding, Dr Ernest A. Payne (President) presented the Finance Report on behalf of the Earl of March, Moderator of the Finance Committee, who was unable to be present but had sent a cable of greeting and support. Also in the hands of delegates were the Finance Report and Accounts of the WCC for 1974 together with a detailed *Composite Statement of Needs for 1975 and 1976.*

In a detailed and technical report, presented with great skill, Dr Payne (who had been a member of successive Finance Committees since 1954) first surveyed the financial operations of the WCC, and the present critical position caused largely by inflation and the value of the Swiss franc against the dollar. He then turned to the questions and suggestions which the Assembly should consider: the establishment of priorities and the reduction of expense; the seeking of new and increased income and the shape of support; and the seeking of improved budget procedures and presentation.

The discussion that followed (eight speakers) dealt with both reports; and some speakers referred also to the addresses of Dr M.M. Thomas and Dr Robert McAfee Brown. Two issues were prominent. One of these concerned the relation between the controversial confrontation with injustice and oppression in the programmes of the Council and the revelation of God in Christ and our personal commitment to him. There was applause for a black South African who put it in this way: "We work for liberation because of our understanding of, and encounter with, God as revealed through Jesus Christ and understood through the Holy Spirit in the eucharistic fellowship of the Church. The horizontal involves the vertical and *vice versa*. My plea is that this be more thoroughly and eloquently explicated as the basis for all we say and do."

The other theme concerned the uncertainty and bewilderment felt in some churches about the character and policies of the WCC, and the gap between the WCC and the ordinary church member in almost all member churches—and the implications of this for financial support.

Bishop Athanasios (Coptic Orthodox Church, Egypt) expressed regret that the General Secretary had not consulted the churches in the Middle East before issuing the statement about the recent UN resolution on Zionism.

In replying to the debate Dr Payne answered two specific questions arising from the Accounts and the composite statement. The Finance Report was referred to the Finance Committee. It is printed as Appendix 5.

Dr Potter in replying to the debate insisted that the WCC is a fellowship of service to the churches and the world; that if the churches saw and practised their own work in the same light the relation between the member churches and the Council would be more creative; and that it was on those who represented the member churches in Assemblies and other WCC meetings that a prime obligation of commitment and integrity rested. "There is a tendency to put on our ecumenical hats here but to take them off when we return home to put on local ones.

"In these times, we cannot afford two hats. The WCC has persistently been misrepresented. I hope and pray you will be honest in reporting what we stand for."

The Report of the General Secretary was referred to Policy Reference Committee I.

It was agreed that the Moderators of the two Workshops (on Spirituality and on Youth) should be added to the membership of the Assembly Business Committee; and that the Workshop on Youth should be asked to select a person under 30 to be its member on the Assembly Business Committee.

Friday, 28 November

MESSAGES OF GREETING

In Business Session, Dr M.M. Thomas presiding, the Assembly received messages of good wishes.

The General Secretary read a message from His All Holiness the Ecumenical Patriarch Dimitrius I:

From His All Holiness the Ecumenical Patriarch Dimitrius I to the Fifth Assembly of the World Council of Churches.

Dimitrius, by the Grace of God, Archbishop of Constantinople, New Rome and Ecumenical Patriarch.

To the participants of the Fifth Assembly of the World Council of Churches, Grace and Peace be with you.

Truly free in the freedom of Christ and united with Him in His unity with the entire human race; bound by this freedom and yet free from all prejudice; we greet the Fifth Assembly of the World Council of Churches and its convocation on the soil of Africa.

In this continent Christianity, in our view, has the following two important characteristics. It is at once primitive and modern; very close to the ancient Church and yet very near to the demands of humankind which are addressed to the Church at this moment. In Christianity space and time, though not absolute categories, are nevertheless factors contributing to the development of the life of the Church and the creation of Tradition. In this sense it can be said that African Christian Tradition is ancient and at the same time recent.

It is for this reason that we believe that the member churches of the World Council of Churches, gathered together in prayer and seeking a deeper consciousness of their duty towards their Lord, the One Church and the world, should proclaim the message of freedom and unity arising from a true and right Christian basis. This is especially necessary in these days when these two existential dimensions of life are often misunderstood and misplaced.

As this Fifth Assembly of the World Council of Churches gathers in Africa and deals with the subject of Christ freeing and uniting, it undertakes a major responsibility in the history of the Ecumenical Movement and the life of the contemporary world. It would be a pity if it fell into demagogy. It would be a pity if it secularized the freedom of Christ. It would be a pity if it reduced unity in and through Christ to slogans of temporary expediency.

In addressing this message to you from this our ancient see of the Ecumenical Patriarchate in full contact with the problems and the agonies of modern man, we wish full success for the work of the Fifth Assembly of the World Council of Churches and invite all to prayer with us and work for the freedom and unity of all in Christ.

22 November, 1975   *PATRIARCH DIMITRIUS*

The General Secretary read a message from His Holiness Pope Paul VI:

To the Reverend Dr Philip Potter
General Secretary
World Council of Churches

The ecumenical importance of the celebration by the World Council of Churches of its Fifth Assembly at Nairobi moves us to address you with words of friendship, encouragement and Christian greetings.

Because your desire for unity and reconciliation coincides with our own, we have been happy to appoint sixteen Catholic observers who are with you on this occasion. And to give further evidence of the confidence which it awakens in us we are asking our brother Cardinal John Willebrands to tell you at greater length of our interest in the Assembly and of our warm good wishes for its successful outcome.

We hope that the Assembly will indeed have an important influence on the life of the World Council of Churches, on its member Churches and on all who are committed to the ecumenical movement.

We trust that the efforts which the Catholic Church has made and will continue to make to promote the ecumenical movement and, wherever possible, to collaborate with the World Council of Churches will continue and grow even greater with God's help. May the assurance of our fraternal solidarity hearten you for the years ahead.

Be assured that our thoughts and fervent prayers are with you in these days. May God grant you courage and faithfulness and joy in doing his will, and the strength to move steadily forward, through the assistance of the Holy Spirit, towards the fulfilment of Christ's prayer to the Father: ". . . that they may be one, even as we are one" (John 17:11).

From the Vatican, 20 November, 1975   POPE PAUL VI

The Reverend Dr Philip A. Potter
Secretary General of the
World Council of Churches

Dear Dr Potter,

I am greatly privileged to be charged by His Holiness Pope Paul VI to write to you at this moment.

The year of the Lord 1975 is undoubtedly most significant in the history of the Church because of several great spiritual events which it is witnessing. A major one is the Fifth Assembly of the World Council of Churches, called together in order to consider in the light of Christ, who illumines all nations and is the good news for all men, the problems and pains and sorrows of the contemporary world. Above all it seeks to further ecclesial unity among all Christians. From the beginning this goal has inspired the World Council of Churches in its studies and activities so that a common witness to Jesus Christ as God and Saviour may be given to the world and his prayer may be fulfilled: "May they all be one. Father, may they be one in us, as you are in me and I am in you, so that the world may believe it was you who sent me" (John 17.21).

This year the Catholic Church is celebrating a Jubilee or Holy Year which "provides a special opportunity of repentance for the divisions which exist among Christians; it offers an occasion for renewal in the sense of enlightened experience of holiness of life in Christ; it allows progress towards the reconciliation we hope for by intensified dialogue and by concrete Christian collaboration for the salvation of the world" (*Apostolorum limina*, VII).

As this same year ends, we are celebrating the tenth anniversary of the Second Vatican Council during which the Catholic Church responded in a new way to the longing "for the one visible Church of God, a Church truly universal and sent forth to the whole world" (*Unitatis Redintegratio*, 1) and committed itself to take part in that ecumenical movement which is "fostered by the grace of the Holy Spirit for the restoration of unity among all Christians" (*Unitatis Redintegratio*, 1).

Now as the World Council of Churches assembles the delegates of its member Churches in Nairobi to celebrate the Fifth Assembly, the opportuneness and importance of this moment move us to address ourselves to you.

More striking than the events in themselves and their coincidence are the similarity of the themes chosen for these celebrations: the theme "Jesus Christ frees and unites" is the inspiring motive of the Assembly, the theme "Renewal and Reconciliation" is the goal of the Holy Year. Jesus Christ came to loose the bonds of sin and death, to free from oppression and the limitation of our mortal condition every man and woman in their individual lives, in their life in society, and in their membership in the human family as a whole. Jesus Christ is the source and centre of communion for all who are Christians, their only and firm hope of being able "to fulfil together their common calling to the glory of the one God, Father, Son and Holy Spirit" (Basis WCC; cf. *Unitatis Redintegratio*, 2) to be "a lasting and sure seed of unity, hope and salvation for the whole human race" (*Lumen Gentium*, 9). Here surely is a point of contact with the content and perspective of renewal and reconciliation as it was described in the Bull of Indiction of the Holy Year: "It is in the depths of the heart therefore that there must take place conversion or *metanoia*, that is, a change of direction, of attitude, of option, of one's way of life". and, "For the whole world: . . . liberty, justice, unity and peace" (*Apostolorum limina*, 1).

As Catholics our best ecumenical efforts are directed both to removing the causes of separation that still remain, as well as to giving adequate expression to the communion which already exists among all Christians. We are sustained and encouraged in this task because so many of the most significant elements and endowments "that are Christ's gifts to his Church are the common source of our strength" (*Unitatis Redintegratio*, 3). In this context we acknowledge gratefully the work done by the Joint Working Group between the Catholic Church and the World Council of Churches. With complete loyalty to the principles and methods of both partners it is an instrument of reflection and of planning that has promoted authentic ecumenical activity.

For these reasons, then, as we Catholics give thanks for the ecumenical emphasis given by the Second Vatican Council and the ten subsequent arduous years of implementing its decrees, I address this brotherly word of hope and encouragement to you our Christian brethren and to the Churches and Communities which gather in the fellowship of the World Council of Churches. For us in the Catholic Church it is a moment of re-dedication to the task of enabling the spirit and principles of the Vatican Council to penetrate the structures and the living tissue of the Church's life. So that an important part of our concern meets yours as you gather in Nairobi—to renew commitment to the principles by which ecumenical activity is guided, looking to the future, joining, wherever possible, our initiatives with those undertaken by you, our brethren (vid. *Unitatis Redintegratio*, 24), intent on going forward "without obstructing the ways of divine Providence, and without prejudging the future inspirations of the Holy Spirit" (*Unitatis Redintegratio*, 24).

May almighty God bless your deliberations and guide your decisions so that this Assembly will kindle new hopes and find new ways for freedom and unity in Christ, "pouring forth words of wisdom and giving thanks to the Lord in prayer" (Sirach 39.6).

21 November, 1975   *JOHN CARDINAL WILLEBRANDS*

The General Secretary read a message from His Holiness Abuna Theophilus, Patriarch of Ethiopia:

From His Holiness Abuna Theophilus, Patriarch of Ethiopia

This is indeed a unique moment in the life of the African churches, and we consider it a great honour and recognition to the continent as a whole and to the Christian people inhabiting it in particular that the Fifth

Assembly of the World Council of Churches is being held in the renowned city of Nairobi. As one who has had the divine permission and guidance to lead a delegation of the Church of Ethiopia to every one of the World Council Assemblies so far held, I have unbounded joy to associate myself in according to each and every one of the Assembly participants a hearty welcome to our continent, and to send you all the warmest greetings of the Ethiopian Orthodox Church and of myself.

As the Assembly of the World Council of Churches is meeting in Nairobi, we should recall the fact that Christianity is not a newcomer to this continent, neither is it in any way a negligible religious tradition among its people. As you all know, Christianity reached Africa at the very beginning of its history, and some of the most renowned churches of the Christian world have existed and flourished in this land. Moreover, during the early centuries of Christian history, it is the churches of Africa that laid a lasting foundation in theology and spirituality for the entire Christian movement, so that there is practically no Christian tradition in the world which has not been directly or indirectly influenced in some way by those contributions of the African Church. We may make mention here of the churches of Alexandria and Egypt, Carthage and North Africa, and Axum and Ethiopia. The memorable contributions, as much of the Theological School of Alexandria with men like Clement and Origen at its head, as of the famous theologians and church fathers in the persons of St. Athanasius and St. Cyril, do still live in the Church everywhere, and particularly in the East. In a similar way, men of the calibre of Tertullian, St. Cyprian, and the great Augustine expounded the faith of the Church, in their times, so memorably that their achievements constitute a tradition which has been indelibly integrated with the life and teaching of the Church, particularly in the West. The Church of Ethiopia can feel gratified to have developed its own traditions in many areas of church life within the cultural and social conditions of the Ethiopian people, without simply following traditions evolved elsewhere. In this way, the Ethiopian Orthodox Church constitutes a forerunner to the movement of indigenizing Christianity to African conditions. As the Assembly of the World Council of Churches meets in Nairobi, it is our duty and privilege to call to mind the many luminaries and pillars of the Church whom Africa has produced. They have bequeathed to us a noble heritage which we should follow in our life-situation of today, facing our Christian responsibility.

Africa has Christian traditions both of the Roman Catholic Church as well as those derived from the Reformed churches of the West. These have made significant contributions in many ways to the life of the African people. Thus, in fact, almost all of you coming from whatever Christian background anywhere in the world will find in our land communities of men and women belonging to your particular brand of Christian tradition. In addition to all these, Africa has communities of Christians who seek to bring into being religious traditions that are genuinely Christian and African at the same time. They do this by trying to express their Christian faith and life-patterns within their own cultural milieux.

This brief word about African Christianity will show that there is as much need for the ecumenical spirit here as anywhere else in the world. It is therefore in the fitness of things that the World Council of Churches, with its emphasis on Christian unity, is holding its Assembly here. Christians of this continent are called upon to live together and work in harmony for the spiritual, moral, and material well-being and prosperity of the people of our continent as a whole. In this context, we should make

156

mention of the All-Africa Conference of Churches, which is trying to help the churches of Africa to engage themselves in this very job. The strengthening of the All-Africa Conference of Churches as a concrete and immediate expression of the ecumenical spirit represented by the World Council of Churches is the task of every Christian community in Africa. We should come closer to one another and work together in all possible ways. We want to have stability for the Christian communities, but we do not seek it to the exclusion of the African people belonging to other faiths and religious or secular ideologies. Ours is an endeavour together to make a viable Christian contribution to the life of the people of Africa as a whole. It is a well-known and recognized fact that Africa needs to advance in the realm of education, medical service, and economic and other areas far beyond the condition in which it exists today. In the march towards progress which Africa should undergo, we do not exclude any people, neither do we as Christians seek to monopolize anything. We believe, on the other hand, that in the light of the gospel and the faith of our fathers, we have something of lasting value to offer men and women, both as individual beings and as communities of people.

In seeking the well-being of the African people, we do not try to live in isolation from the rest of the world, neither do we maintain that Africa should belong exclusively to the indigenous people of the continent. We believe that man is man wherever he lives and whatever his race, language, nationality, or culture. But we witness before our eyes in this continent people of one race or class oppressing those of others. This indeed is a contradiction of the Christian faith which those people themselves claim to hold, and we Christians of this land solemnly express our solidarity with the oppressed and down-trodden. It is our conviction that Jesus Christ, the Saviour of mankind, is present with them in their struggles, as also with man anywhere under the conditions of injustice and inhuman treatment, and that He is offering them courage and strength which they need. We are glad that this Assembly brings to us the message of freedom, unity, and liberation which Jesus Christ is giving us every day.

On this auspicious occasion, we deem it our duty and privilege to place on record our profound appreciation to churches and Christian agencies in the world who have expressed their concern for Ethiopia in the hour of her dire need. It is well known that Ethiopia is one of the African countries gravely affected by the drought disasters, and we are gratified that Christian brethren came forward with their memorable assistance. This serious calamity has cost us the lives of men and women in thousands. The scattered nature of village life in Ethiopia and the lack of roads and other communication facilities aggravated the problem even more. Many expatriate philanthropists who volunteered to help the victims have lost their lives while fighting the deep gorges and the rugged mountain ranges. This indeed is the highest form of sacrifice which man can offer. In return for it, the only thing we can do is to pray that the Lord may reward them in His own way. The problem is still far from over. The nation is consistently engaged in combating the effects of drought in all possible ways, and the international community also continues with its support. We, on our part, should give a sincere expression of gratitude to all those who have extended to Ethiopia, and who still extend their sympathy and assistance.

We should recall on this occasion the many changes that take place in the living conditions of the people of this continent. The Church has a significant part to play in these developments as well as for the well-being of the people as a whole. We believe that history does not stay static; history moves and we should make it a movement forward. Holding to our faith in God and trusting in His living power, the Ethiopian Orthodox Church will take part wholeheartedly in helping the nation in its development forward. To this end, we request your prayers that it may play its part ably and ungrudgingly.

Being deeply inspired by the spirit of the theme of this Assembly, may we raise our hands in prayer and supplication, that man everywhere will transcend the limitations of geography and join in the struggle for freeing all mankind from ignorance, disease, hunger, and all forms of oppression, "because the creature itself shall be delivered from the bondage of corruption into the glorious liberty of the children of God" (Romans 8:21).

The Ethiopian Orthodox Church has great joy in wishing the meeting of this Assembly and the World Council of Churches every success in the promotion of its manifold programmes of activities in the world, and we pray that God may bring His children into the unity of His Church, so that they may all in union praise and glorify the Holy and Blessed Trinity, for ever and ever.

The General Secretary also referred appreciatively to a message from the Patriarch Pimen of Moscow and All Russia, the text of which had been circulated to all participants.

The General Secretary said that messages had also been received from the following:

The Greek Evangelical Church, Athens
The Mar Thoma Syrian Church of Malabar
The Evangelical Church in West Irian, Indonesia
The Evangelical Lutheran Church of Latvia
The Presbyterian Church in Taiwan
Comicion Evangelica Latino-Americana do Educacion Cristiana (CELADEC)
The National Christian Council of Burma
The Christian Peace Conference
The National Andean Evangelical Lutheran Church, Peru
The Cherubim and Seraphim Church, London
The Youth Committee of the National Council for the Lay Apostolate of the Roman Catholic Church in England and Wales
The Nazareth Christian Community, Nazareth
Mr L.-B. Demonge, Arnhem, Netherlands
The Committee for Freedom of Word and Service in the Church, West Germany
Mr Jairo A. Asila, Emareryo Church of God, West Bunyoro, Maseno, Kenya
Dr Billy Graham
Dr Pedro Pires, Premier Ministre, Republique Cap Vert
Dr Egon Bahr, Bundesminister für Wirtschaftliche Zusammenarbeit, Federal Republic of Germany
Dr Luiz Cabrah, President du Conseil d'Etat, Guinea-Bissau

The Assembly agreed to send special greetings to the Presbyterian Church in Taiwan and to the member churches and the National Christian Council in Burma. Delegates had not been able to travel from either of these countries; the Church in Burma had been able to appoint Dr Kyaw Than (now teaching at Yale University in the USA) as a delegate. The General Secretary was asked to respond to the other messages.

THE CREDENTIALS COMMITTEE

The Credentials Committee presented its report. No problems had arisen requiring the attention of the Assembly. The report was accepted.

GREETINGS

Apologies for absence were received from three of the Presidents: Patriarch German of Serbia, Bishop A.H. Zulu, and Dr John Coventry Smith. It was agreed to send them greetings from the Assembly.

The following Special Guests were welcomed onto the platform amidst applause.

Dr Eugene Carson Blake
Dr Martin Niemöller
Dr Akanu Ibiam
Mrs Martin Luther King

It was reported that Dr Billy Graham (who had been present at the four previous Assemblies) had been invited but had cabled that he was prevented by illness from attending.

Dr Thomas welcomed on behalf of the Assembly Mgr Charles Moeller, General Secretary of the Secretariat for Promoting Christian Unity, Mgr Andria di Montezemolo, General Secretary of the Pontifical Commission Justice and Peace, and the sixteen delegated observers appointed by the Roman Catholic Church.

Dr Thomas also welcomed the fraternal delegates from associated National Councils of Churches and the world confessional families; the advisers; the observers from other churches not members of the WCC and from international organizations; the visitors; the press; and, last but not least, the Host Committee in Nairobi, who stood in their places amidst applause.

ADMISSION OF NEW MEMBER CHURCHES

Dr Alan Brash presented the applications for membership of the Council as recommendations from the Executive Committee.

By unanimous vote of all the member churches present the applications of the following churches were approved:

159

The Church of the Province of the Indian Ocean
    (Anglican)   (one delegate)
African Christian Church and Schools, Kenya

                                                 (one delegate)
The Cook Islands Christian Church
    (Reformed)   (one delegate)
The Methodist Church in Tonga

                                                 (one delegate)
The Progressive National Baptist Convention, USA

                                                 (two delegates)
The Church of the Lord (Aladura), Nigeria and other countries of West
Africa, UK and USA

                                                 (three delegates)
The African Israel Church, Ninevah, Kenya

                                                 (one delegate)
The Moravian Church in Surinam

                                                 (one delegate)

Dr Brash presented the applications for associate membership of the
Council as recommendations coming from the Executive Committee.

By unanimous vote of all member churches present the applications
for associate membership of the following seven churches were approved:

The Church of Bangladesh
The Evangelical Methodist Church of Costa Rica
The Methodist Church of Samoa
The Protestant Church in Sabah, Malaysia
The Disciples of Christ, Argentina
Punguan Kristen Batak, Indonesia
African Church of the Holy Spirit, Kenya

The Assembly noted that at present churches with fewer than 25,000
members are eligible only for associate membership, but that no criteria
have been defined regarding minimum size for associate membership.

The Assembly referred the question of criteria of membership to
Policy Reference Committee I.

The following were officially greeted as delegates from new member
churches:

The Reverend Mugo Mwangi—African Christ Church and Schools
Mr Nga Rain—Cook Islands Christian Church
The Reverend Dr Sione Havea—Methodist Church in Tonga
Dr Nelson Smith—Progressive National Baptist Convention
The Reverend Dr E.O. Ade Adejobi, Miss Claire Meadows, and Mr
Jacob Sofolahan—Church of the Lord (Aladura)
Mr Albert Nyangor—African Israel Church, Ninevah

Dr Adejobi responded on behalf of all the newly accepted member churches.

GARDEN PARTY AT THE STATE HOUSE

On Tuesday, 2 December, the officers and delegates of the Assembly were the guests of His Excellency the President of the Republic of Kenya and Mama Ngina Kenyatta at a Garden Party in the grounds of the State House. They were entertained by displays of dancing and singing and the music of drums and a silver band.

In a short gracious speech of welcome President Kenyatta thanked the WCC for coming to Kenya and urged all participants to make themselves thoroughly at home—especially if they were able to take time to do so on a visit to the rural areas of the country. "We like visitors to stay a long time. Thank you very much for coming."

In responding on behalf of the delegates Dr W.A. Visser 't Hooft spoke with gratitude of the way in which the Republic of Kenya and the City of Nairobi had provided "the right atmosphere exactly" for the fifth WCC Assembly to be held in Africa. Recalling the President's words about the history of African Christianity at the laying of the foundation stone of the new headquarters for the All-Africa Conference of Churches, Dr Visser 't Hooft said that in the Council's confrontation with Africa one dimension at least of Christianity would become clearer to us—that of joy.

The WCC was always concerned with public life and had been reminded by the Prime Minister of Jamaica of the importance of the spiritual factor in public affairs. We greatly valued, therefore, a relationship with the Head of State at this, as indeed at all previous Assemblies. "Our hearts are full of gratitude. Thank you ever so much."

2. PUBLIC AFFAIRS

THE REPORT OF POLICY REFERENCE COMMITTEE III

The Report of Policy Reference Committee III was presented and debated in stages on 8, 9, and 10 December. General Simatupang (Indonesian Christian Church), Moderator, gave a general introduction to the Report in which he explained that out of the multitude of themes that could have been taken up, they had selected four—the Middle East; Disarmament and the Helsinki Declaration; Southern Africa including Angola; Latin America. Work groups had been appointed to deal with each of these, and a further small group was working on East Timor. The Committee had decided not to present a single report, and the sections would be presented by the Reporter of the groups who had prepared them.

THE MIDDLE EAST

Dr W.P. Thompson (United Presbyterian, USA) presented the draft statement on *The Middle East.*

In an extended debate a number of amendments were proposed, with the purpose either of strengthening paragraph 3(*c*) by a more explicit reference to the desires of the Palestinian people, or of eliminating or qualifying the word "terrorism" in paragraph 6. Both Dr George Bebawi (Coptic Orthodox, Egypt) and Ms Jean Zaru (Friend, Israel West Bank) insisted that self-determination in their homeland was of great significance to the Palestinian people. The document did not give them sufficient hope. Another amendment was moved on the subject of Israel's need for a clarification of the intentions of the Palestine Liberation Organization's views on Israel's future. These were all opposed by the Committee and defeated.

A further amendment, moved by Dr André Pieters (Reformed, Belgium) proposed to add to paragraph 2 of the draft the words "... and stress the necessity for the great world powers to cease furnishing the arms which maintain and aggravate the tensions". This was opposed by the Committee but carried by a large majority.

Bishop Sarkissian spoke of the grievous situations in Cyprus and Lebanon, and expressed the hope that at least the Assembly might be able to pass a resolution of sympathy and concern. It was agreed that the officers of the Committee should authorize the drafting of a suitable resolution.

The Report as amended was adopted; the text follows.

The Middle East

1. The World Council of Churches has expressed concern regarding the situation in the Middle East on previous occasions. Events which have occurred in the area during the meeting of the Fifth Assembly in Nairobi have demonstrated anew that tensions persist there unabated.

2. We are concerned at the continued escalation of military power in the area which can only aggravate the threat to world peace from the unresolved conflict; and stress the necessity for the great world powers to cease furnishing the arms which maintain and aggravate the tensions.

3. We recognize that an international consensus has emerged as the basis for peaceful settlement on the following:

(*a*) Withdrawal by Israel from territories occupied in 1967.

(*b*) The right of all states including Israel and the Arab states to live in peace within secure and recognized boundaries.

(c) The implementation of the rights of the Palestinian people to self-determination.

We are encouraged that the parties to the conflict seem to be progressively willing to accept these principles.

4. We recognize the Second Sinai Disengagement Agreement as a means of reducing tension between Egypt and Israel. However, since it is not addressed to the fears and distrust among Israel, other neighbouring states, and the Palestinian people, this Agreement must be followed soon by resumption of the Geneva Peace Conference for reaching a total settlement on the basis of the principles mentioned above. The Geneva Conference should necessarily involve all parties concerned, including the Palestinians.

5. We note that some Arab states have recently declared their readiness, with the participation of the Palestine Liberation Organization, to seek agreement with Israel based upon these principles.

6. Although the parties have not trusted one another sufficiently until now to engage in dialogue, full mutual recognition by the parties must be seen not as a precondition to, but rather as a product of, the negotiation. We call upon all parties to take those steps essential to negotiations with hope for success. Among these steps, we emphasize the cessation of all military activity, both regular and irregular, including terrorism.

7. Peace in the Middle East must be based upon justice and security for all concerned. The well-being of each party depends upon the well-being of all other parties. We urge the churches to help their constituencies to have more accurate information on and more sensitive awareness of the various discussions of the Middle East conflict. The churches could thus help to promote natural trust among the parties and to develop a responsible involvement in peaceful solution on the part of their members and the government of their countries. This opportunity is open to churches within the area and the churches outside the area as well.

General Simatupang, Moderator, later read a letter received from Archbishop Sarkissian:

Given the very short time and heavy schedule of the work of Policy Reference Committee III, it was not possible to draft a statement on the situations in Cyprus and Lebanon.

I feel there is a need for further study of the situations themselves. Therefore I do not wish to press my motion, hoping that the General Secretary will keep these two situations in vigilant concern. I thank the Assembly for its sympathetic response to my proposal.

The Assembly agreed that this letter should be recorded in the minutes.

Dr W. P. Thompson introduced the draft Report on the *Jerusalem Area*, which had been prepared with the assistance of a message to the General Secretary from the Ecumenical Patriarchate. After the defeat of three minor amendments, the Report was put to the Assembly and *adopted* by an overwhelming majority. The text follows.

Jerusalem

1. For many millions of Christians throughout the world, as well as for the adherents of the two great sister monotheistic religions, namely Judaism and Islam, Jerusalem continues to be a focus of deepest religious inspiration and attachment. It is therefore their responsibility to co-operate in the creation of conditions that will ensure that Jerusalem is a city open to the adherents of all three religions, where they can meet and live together. The tendency to minimize Jerusalem's importance for any of these three religions should be avoided.

2. The special legislation regulating the relationship of the Christian communities and the authorities, guaranteed by international treaties (Paris 1856 and Berlin 1878) and the League of Nations and known as the Status Quo of the Holy Places must be fully safeguarded and confirmed in any agreement concerning Jerusalem. Christian Holy Places in Jerusalem and neighbouring areas belong to the greatest extent to member churches of the WCC. On the basis of the Status Quo none of the church authorities of a given denomination could represent unilaterally and on behalf of all Christians the Christian point of view, each church authority of a given denomination representing only its own point of view.

3. Many member churches of the WCC are deeply concerned about the Christian Holy Places. However, the question of Jerusalem is not only a matter of protection of the Holy Places, it is organically linked with living faiths and communities of people in the Holy City. Therefore the Assembly deems it essential that the Holy Shrines should not become mere monuments of visitation, but should serve as living places of worship integrated and responsive to Christian communities who continue to maintain their life and roots within the Holy City and for those who out of religious attachments want to visit them.

4. While recognizing the complexity and emotional implications of the issues surrounding the future status of Jerusalem, the Assembly believes that such status has to be determined within the general context of the settlement of the Middle East conflict in its totality.

5. However, the Assembly thinks that apart from any politics, the whole settlement of the inter-religious problem of the Holy Places should take place under an international aegis and guarantee which ought to be respected by the parties concerned as well as the ruling authorities.

6. The Assembly recommends that the above should be worked out with the most directly concerned member churches, as well as with the Roman Catholic Church. These issues should also become subjects for dialogue with Jewish and Muslim counterparts.

7. The Assembly expresses its profound hope and fervent prayers for the peace and welfare of the Holy City and all its inhabitants.

SOUTHERN AFRICA

Mr Antony Wilson (Society of Friends, UK) presented the draft Report on *Angola: Independence and Intervention* and in his introduction traced the history of Angola and of the present conflicts. Several amendments were proposed to strengthen or weaken the references to South Africa and other outside powers. These were opposed by the Committee and rejected by the Assembly, as was a proposed amendment advising the Angolan parties not to hire foreign volunteers. After a motion to close the debate, the Report was *adopted* unanimously. The text follows.

Angola: Independence and Intervention

1. On the eve of the independence of Angola, the General Secretary of the World Council of Churches issued a statement which expressed solidarity with the Angolan people and churches in their aspirations for a nation united in seeking to build a just and peaceful society. The statement expressed concern over the exploitation of the situation by outside powers supporting particular movements in order to further their own political and economic interests.

2. The Portuguese left the country without handing over power to any legally constituted authority, the transitional government which included the representatives of the three liberation movements having failed to function. In the past few weeks further suffering has been inflicted on the population as a result of massive military intervention by several foreign powers. Some of the powers now actively involved in Angola had previously been supporting the Portuguese regime in its repression of the people. There is a grave danger that the conflict in Angola may escalate into a major war on the continent of Africa: the international rivalry of several powers poses a serious threat to world peace. The WCC strongly deplores all foreign intervention in Angola which prevents the Angolan people from freely adopting the type of government and the course of development of their choice.

We hope that the cessation of foreign military involvement in Angola would provide an opportunity for the political leaders of the country to renew their search for a peaceful resolution of the problems arising from ideological and other differences, in the interest of all the Angolan people.

165

3. The possible escalation of the conflict in Angola has to be viewed particularly against the background of developments in southern Africa. The rapid acceleration of the militarization of South Africa and current efforts to integrate its military system with the Western defence network have already increased tensions in the region. They have also been the subject of international concern and debate. South Africa's intervention in Angola has seriously reduced prospects of a peaceful solution to the problem of the area.

4. The WCC calls upon the governments involved to respect the independence and territorial integrity of Angola and to withdraw all military units and to stop the supply of arms. The Council reiterates the appeal of the General Secretary to all churches and Christians to challenge those foreign powers which are exacerbating this explosive situation by supplying arms to the different groups, and instead to contribute to the resolving of the present conflict through existing international channels, especially the Organization for African Unity and the United Nations.

Appendix

Statement by the General Secretary of the World Council of Churches, dated 10 November, 1975

POTTER URGES IMMEDIATE END OF ANGOLA
CONFLICT ON INDEPENDENCE EVE

Geneva, 10 November (EPS)—on the eve of Angolan independence which falls tomorrow (11 November), Dr Philip A. Potter, general secretary of the World Council of Churches, called for an end to the strife in that country and expressed solidarity with the Angolan people and churches in their aspirations for a peaceful and united nation.

Dr Potter's full statement follows:

1. The Angolan people have been looking forward to November 11, 1975, as the end of 493 years of Portuguese colonial rule and as the day which would herald an era of independence and unity for the whole country. What was to have been a day of joy and celebration for all is now likely to become one of disappointment and disillusionment. Instead of unity and peace, the country is divided and plunged into civil war.

2. The origins of this situation go far back in the history of Angola. But more recently they are to be found in the very struggle of the Angolan people against Portuguese colonialism. The three liberation movements— MPLA, FLNA, and UNITA—have come into being in the last twenty years. Their very existence reflects differing regional, social, and ideological patterns which are to be found elsewhere in Africa and in today's pluralistic world. Unfortunately, this complex situation has not yet been handled responsibly by the liberation movements and has been exploited by

outside powers which support particular movements in order to further their own political and economic interests.

3. The World Council of Churches, in addition to ministering to the many Angolan refugees, has had contacts with all the three liberation movements and assisted them to meet their social, medical, and educational needs. We had hoped that, with the change of the Portuguese regime in April 1974, and the installation in Angola in January 1975 of the coalition transitional government, the country would be led to independence in an orderly way. It is a tragedy that the transitional coalition government was not even given a chance to function, because of conflicts among the liberation movements. The World Council of Churches has expressed its concern about the serious consequences of this conflict which has already resulted in the killing of thousands of largely civilian people.

4. The World Council of Churches recently sent a team of two persons to express to the churches and people of Angola the solidarity of the world Christian community and to assess the needs of the people. The team visited the areas controlled by the three liberation movements and at present a programme of humanitarian relief to all parts of Angola is under way. However, further attempts of the World Council and of the All Africa Conference of Churches to send a team of mediation to the areas controlled by the three movements have so far been unsuccessful.

5. On the eve of independence, we express our solidarity with the Angolan people and the churches in their aspirations for a nation united in seeking to build a just and peaceful society.

We appeal to the political leaders of Angola to bring an immediate end to the armed conflict; urge them to discern and correct their mistakes, and to mobilize their energies to serve their people in realizing their aspirations.

We further call upon all churches and Christians to challenge those foreign powers which are exacerbating this explosive situation by supplying arms to the different factions to cease doing so and instead to contribute to the resolving of the present conflict through existing international channels, especially the Organization for African Unity and the United Nations. The text follows.

The Reverend Dr U. Lochmann (United, Federal Republic of Germany) presented a report on *Nuclear Collaboration with South Africa* which was *adopted* after the acceptance of three minor amendments.

Nuclear Collaboration with South Africa

1. The WCC Fifth Assembly expresses its deep concern that certain governments and multi-national companies are becoming involved in the

financing and construction of nuclear power generating plants in South Africa. Those countries and companies known to us to be taking part are:

(1) a. General Electric, *USA*;

b. Rijn-Schelde-Verolme Machinefabrieken en Scheepswerven N.V. (R.S.V.); Verenigde Bedrijven Bredero N.V. (V.B.B.); Ingenieursbureau Comprimo N.V., *Netherlands;*

c. Brown-Boveri International Corporation, *Switzerland.*

(2) Kraftwerk Union (K.W.U.), *Federal Republic of Germany* (Participants: Siemens and A.E.G.).

(3) Framatome, *France* (Participants: Creusot-Loire group and Westinghouse—USA).

2. The technical expertise and commercial benefits rest with the companies, but the normal official and financial requirements covering export licences and credit guarantees are the responsibility of the national governments concerned. Acceptance of one or two of the tenders now under preparation with endorsement by the relevant governments will result in a further economic and financial undergirding of apartheid. Furthermore, Western technological expertise is assisting South Africa in the development of a nuclear enrichment plant which will make South Africa self-sufficient in nuclear fuel for civil and military use. Economic and industrial resources in the West will thus be still more intimately committed to the expansion of a system which denies to the majority of the inhabitants the prospect or right of personal, social, and political freedom.

3. The Assembly is further concerned at the military implications of these nuclear developments, especially since South Africa is not a signatory power to the Non-Proliferation Treaty. South Africa's military expenditure has increased from R255m (US \$300m) in 1965/6 to over R1000m (US \$1200m) in 1975/6; nuclear power plants and nuclear enrichment plants will facilitate development of nuclear weapons. Already there are grave fears of South African military activity beyond its borders, previously in Zimbabwe and now in Angola as well as Namibia. Any implied condoning of this military capability by any governments or company will precipitate serious anxiety and strong objections on the part of the people throughout Africa.

4. The WCC calls on its member churches in those countries involved to:

(a) ascertain the extent of their own country's commercial and governmental commitment to South Africa's nuclear programme;

(b) make public the political and military implications and consequences of pursuing a policy of collaboration with the South African authorities;

(c) challenge those companies and governments involved to revise their policies in the light of considerations which are broader than the commercial and economic criteria involved.

DISARMAMENT—THE HELSINKI AGREEMENT—RELIGIOUS LIBERTY

The Report on *Disarmament—The Helsinki Agreement* was presented by Dr E. Wildbolz (Swiss Protestant Church Federation). Dr J. Rossel (Swiss Protestant Church Federation) proposed an amendment to the end of the final paragraph: "The WCC is concerned about restrictions to religious liberty, particularly in the USSR. The Assembly respectfully requests the Government of the USSR to implement effectively principle No. 7 of the Helsinki Agreement."

The amendment was seconded by the Reverend Richard Holloway (Episcopal Church in Scotland). Metropolitan Juvenaly and Metropolitan Nikodim both spoke against the amendment. Mr V.H. Devadas (Church of North India) proposed the closure, which requires a two-thirds majority. There was uncertainty in the minds of some delegates as to whether the vote was for closure of the debate or for the amendment proposed by Dr Jacques Rossel. In response to a question from the floor, the Moderator made it clear that the vote was for closure and not for the amendment. A vote was taken, and with 279 for and 181 against the motion was lost.

Archbishop E.W. Scott (Anglican Church of Canada) moved an amendment to Dr Rossel's amendment as follows, "The WCC is concerned about the restriction to religious liberty in many parts of the world, including the USSR. It is grateful for the leadership the government of the USSR gave in the development of the Helsinki Agreement and calls upon it and all governments to give full implementation to section 7 of that Agreement."

Dr Payne urged that Archbishop Scott's amendment be referred back to the Committee with a view to securing a wider and more carefully considered consensus. After further debate, the motion to refer back to the Committee was passed by 259 to 190.

An open hearing of the Committee was held later in the evening and was attended by a large number of participants.

The Assembly returned to the subject on Tuesday, 9 December, when Dr T. B. Simatupang, Moderator, presented the draft of a further statement which had been prepared in the small hours in the "light of the moving experience" of the open hearing, by a small group of General Simatupang, Mr A. Buevsky (Russian Orthodox Church), and Dr W.P. Thompson (Presbyterian, USA) with staff, and unanimously approved by the Policy Reference Committee. Dr Thompson read the document, which was designed to follow on to the document already presented about the Helsinki agreement. Mr Buevsky spoke briefly in support of the draft.

Dr. J. Rossel (Swiss Protestant Church Federation) said that though the draft "did not correspond to our expectations" he and Mr Holloway were prepared to withdraw their amendment on condition that an additional recommendation be included as follows:

The Assembly requests the General Secretary to see to it that the question of religious liberty be the subject of intensive consultations with the member churches of the signatory states of the Helsinki agreement and that a first report be presented at the next Central Committee meeting in August 1976.

General Simatupang accepted this amendment on behalf of the Committee. A. van den Heuvel (Netherlands Reformed Church) supported this motion.

At the open hearing, I had the opportunity of learning a number of things. I learned that we help our Russian brethren and ourselves when we distinguish between a general problem and specific problems. Secondly, I learned again that we cannot speak about human rights in eastern Europe unless we put it squarely in a common struggle for détente in Europe and for common involvement in peace work; that we cannot work for human rights in eastern Europe if we do not put it in the context of fraternal relationships, and if we do not devise a language of respect and sympathy for all those churches who witness in another social system. I have also learned that we cannot speak about individual cases without making known more of the research work which is little known in western and eastern countries. Finally, I learned that we have no way of having a fraternal debate together if we do not recognize our frailty. In this paper there is a stress on four points: the differences between the situations in the different countries; the acknowledgement that churches dare not be silent, which I hold to be the great breakthrough of this debate; an emphasis on the need for consultation; and instructions to the General Secretary that we can go to work. I hope we will accept Rossel's amendment in order to make sure that this work will start.

Canon P. H. Boulton (Church of England, UK) moved that there should be added as an appendix to the document the following:

This Assembly recognizes that all the signatory nations appended below have equal responsibility to observe and carry out all the principles of this solemn agreement. The full list of the signatories to the Helsinki Agreement is as follows.

Dr Joseph Jackson (National Baptist Convention, USA) said, "With much prayer, I was moved this morning to move the following amendment:

We commend the nations who drew up the noble principles of the Helsinki Agreement and signed them. We hope and pray that these nations will do all in their power to implement these principles; and we urge other nations to join them in this worthwhile venture."

Both these amendments were accepted by General Simatupang for the Committee.

Bishop Kirill (Russian Orthodox Church) moved to delete from Dr Rossel's amendments the reference to August 1976 on the ground that little worth while could be achieved in so short a time. This motion was defeated.

Dr David Russell (Baptist, UK) proposed that the Moderator should read out the names of those who had submitted amendments, and the content of their amendments, and then ask someone to move the closure. The Moderator agreed, but since he had already called on Professor Roger Mehl to speak, asked him first to do so.

Professor Roger Mehl (Reformed, France) said that he was sensitive to the considerable effort that had been made by the drafting committee. However, he could not accept the motion now before the Assembly. Other motions concerning other countries had been voted and they were perfectly clear. This one was not. He could not forget that a different text had been voted the previous day, and while he realized that that vote was no longer considered valid, it had been taken publicly in the presence of the press and if a different text were now to be voted, what would happen to the credibility of the WCC? He personally did not run the slightest risk when he returned to his country, nor did the churches of his country run any risk. He understood the position of the brothers in the countries of eastern Europe and they could not vote on a text in which their country was called into question. He would have understood and respected that but emphasized that the credibility of the WCC was being called into question. He therefore called on his brothers from the East not to question this basic credibility and the freedom of the Assembly. He then moved that the list of speakers be read and that the debate then be closed.

Dr Thomas then read the list of names and amendments.

The motion to close the debate was seconded, put, and carried by a very large majority. The Reverend G. J. Stalsett (Church of Norway) said that his delegation would not be able to vote because of the short and inadequate debate.

The paper as amended was then put to the vote and approved by a large majority.

Professor Vitaly Borovoy (Russian Orthodox Church) asked permission to explain why his delegation had abstained from voting. (He spoke in

Russian: the following English text was prepared by the Russian Orthodox delegation.)

On behalf of the Russian Orthodox Church delegation I should like to declare that we abstained not because we do not wish to collaborate with our Christian brethren in an endeavour to study, to deepen our understanding of, and to apply, human rights, including religious freedom, in all places wherever these rights may be infringed or misinterpreted. We were always ready, and at this present moment declare our readiness to participate in open, brotherly, and equitable discussion of these problems which are of prime importance for us all. We are prepared for frankness, for dialogue and for co-operation. But we were unpleasantly disappointed by the prevailing atmosphere which surrounded the discussion of these questions at the Assembly, an atmosphere compounded of haste, nerves, emotion, and divisiveness. Although we believe and affirm that Jesus Christ frees and unites us, in this matter we have permitted sinful passions and divisions to sway us. We deeply regret this and it is in order to indicate our disapproval of this atmosphere that we have abstained. However, as concerns the substance of this matter, we are prepared for both co-operation and dialogue, though in an equitable and fraternal atmosphere. We ask your prayers and we pray for you.

The entire document was then put to the Assembly and adopted by the Assembly by an overwhelming majority with four contrary votes and a number of abstentions. The text follows.

Disarmament—The Helsinki Agreement—Religious Liberty

1. Ecumenical bodies (WCC, CEC, LWF) and several churches of Europe have played an active part in the efforts which led to the signing of the Helsinki Agreement on Security and Co-operation in Europe in 1975. They regard this Agreement as a sign of hope in a world torn apart by opposing ideologies and divided by conflicting interests.

2. The Fifth Assembly of the World Council of Churches appeals to the signatory governments to implement the Helsinki Agreement without delay and in all its parts. A climate of mutual trust will be created by respecting the Ten Principles governing relations between nations.

3. These principles are:

(1) Sovereign equality for the rights inherent in sovereignty.
(2) Refraining from the threat or use of force.
(3) Inviolability of frontiers.
(4) Territorial integrity of states.
(5) Peaceful settlement of disputes.

(6) Non-intervention in internal affairs.

(7) Respect for human rights and fundamental freedoms, including the freedom of thought, conscience, religion, or belief.

(8) Equal rights and self-determination of peoples.

(9) Co-operation among states.

(10) Fulfilment in good faith of obligations under international law.

4. We emphasize the clause referring to fundamental human rights as proclaimed by the United Nations' Declaration of Human Rights. The churches have the responsibility to be involved whenever it is necessary to make clear that security and the development of genuinely human relationships across frontiers go together. The churches should be especially concerned with the need for rules of behaviour, the purpose of which is to avert the danger of violent action in the attempt to establish new conditions securing respect for the dignity of men and women in Europe. Non-violent structures are also needed for the settlement of disputes between nations (e.g. "Draft Convention on a European System for the Peaceful Settlement of Disputes").

5. The churches appeal to the good will of all in every nation who are entrusted with authority to make decisions. They are nevertheless realistic, and recognize the power of evil (individual and collective egotism, distrust, search for power, etc.). Their contribution will be effective as individuals and nations begin to learn that peace demands the willingness to admit one's own faults. Peace demands also the preparedness to give up one's own position. The churches will show forth the implications of reconciliation for the relationships of nations.

6. Concrete proposals on all the many aspects of security and co-operation in Europe will be needed for the forthcoming bilateral and multilateral negotiations over the implementation of the Helsinki Agreement. The churches can contribute much from their experience of contacts across frontiers and of humanitarian work.

7. The individual churches of Europe, the Conference of European Churches (CEC), and the Churches' Commission on International Affairs (CCIA) need to be prepared for this task. They must also be ready to speak of their experiences in the implementation of the Helsinki Agreement at the evaluation meeting of the CSCE to be held in Belgrade in 1977.

8. The churches will also be concerned with those clauses in the Helsinki Agreement which deal directly with their own position and functions (religious freedom, freedom of belief and worship, contacts between the churches, exchange of information, etc.). They will make clear to the governments their own understanding of these sections and how they could be implemented.

* * * * *

9. We commend the nations who drew up the noble principles of the Helsinki Agreement and signed them. We hope and pray that the nations will do all in their power to implement these principles; and we urge other nations to join them in this worthwhile venture.

*   *   *   *   *

10. The Assembly has devoted a substantial period to the discussion of the alleged denials of religious liberty in the USSR.

11. The Assembly recognizes that churches in different parts of Europe are living and working under very different conditions and traditions. Political systems, constitutions, and administrative practices vary from nation to nation. In most western European countries the churches have the opportunity to seek to reach people through many different public media and to organize special groups for young people and others. In the absence of such possibilities in many eastern countries, the churches reach people including youth through religious education of children in the family, catechizing in the Church of interested persons, and vital public worship.

12. In spite of these differences, Christians in both parts of Europe, and indeed throughout the whole world, are one in Christ. The solidarity which results from faith in our common Lord permits the mutual sharing of joys and sufferings and requires mutual correction. Christians dare not remain silent when other members of the Body of Christ face problems in any part of the world. But whatever is said and done must be preceded by consultation and must be an expression of Christian love.

13. When a problem relates to fundamental freedoms, including freedom of thought, conscience, religion, or belief, the Helsinki Declaration provides a new opportunity for solutions. The spirit of Helsinki clearly reflects the commitment of the signatories to prevent a new era of "cold war".

14. Therefore the Assembly urges the Central Committee and the General Secretariat to take such situations seriously and to undertake appropriate actions.

15. The Assembly requests the General Secretary to see to it that the question of religious liberty be the subject of intensive consultations with the member churches of the signatory states of the Helsinki Agreement and that a first report be presented at the next Central Committee meeting in August 1976.

16. This Assembly recognizes that all the signatory nations appended below have equal responsibility to observe and carry out all the principles of this solemn agreement.

Appendix: Signatories to the "Final Act" of the Conference on Security and Co-operation in Europe, Helsinki, August 1975

The Federal Republic of Germany
The German Democratic Republic
The United States of America
The Republic of Austria
The Kingdom of Belgium
The People's Republic of Bulgaria
Canada
The Republic of Cyprus
Denmark
Spain
The Republic of Finland
The French Republic
The United Kingdom of Great Britain and Northern Ireland
The Hellenic Republic
The Hungarian People's Republic
Ireland
Iceland
The Italian Republic
The Principality of Liechtenstein
The Grand Duchy of Luxembourg
The Republic of Malta
The Principality of Monaco
Norway
The Kingdom of the Netherlands
The Polish People's Republic
Portugal
The Socialist Republic of Romania
San Marino
The Holy See
Sweden
The Swiss Confederation
The Czechoslovak Socialist Republic
The Republic of Turkey
The Union of Soviet Socialist Republics
The Socialist Federal Republic of Yugoslavia

EAST TIMOR

The Report of Policy Reference Committee III was presented at the request of the Moderator by Dr George Koshy (Church of South India) who had chaired a work group of two Australians and two Indonesians.

Dr Koshy outlined the events in East Timor since the process of decolonization had started which had caused this issue to be raised at the Assembly.

The Reverend Russell Gilmore (Church of Christ in Australia) moved an amendment as follows:

"The Assembly makes urgent request to the Australian government to facilitate the evacuation of refugees from East Timor and to offer sanctuary and resettlement for those refugees who may desire to settle within Australia,"

which should, if adopted, be placed between clauses 5 and 6.

Professor Koshy agreed that refugees needed help but said the amendment was not acceptable to the Committee. However, when it was put to the Assembly it was passed by a very substantial majority.

Ms Amelia Rokotuivuna (Methodist, Fiji) said that the three parties in East Timor would never come to negotiate if Indonesia were a party and that clause 5 was meaningless since there was Indonesian military intervention. She urged that the UN be requested to help Portugal arrange peace negotiations. The Reverend John Brown (Presbyterian, Australia) said that all governments had failed in their duty. The situation had now changed and the proposed text was irrelevant. He therefore moved that clause 5 be amended to read as follows:

We appeal to all foreign powers to refrain from any action in East Timor which will prevent the people of East Timor from freely deciding their own future, and specifically we call on the government of Indonesia to withdraw its armed forces to enable self-determination to occur.

This was seconded.

Dr Sutarno (Christian Churches of Java, Indonesia) reminded the Assembly of the events which had led to this situation in East Timor, which was surrounded by Indonesian territory.

Professor Koshy said that the Committee hoped that the amendment would not be accepted. The amendment was put to the Assembly with the following result: for the amendment 277; against 37; abstentions 123.

The document as amended was put to the Assembly and passed by an overwhelming majority. The text follows.

East Timor

1. The Fifth Assembly of the World Council of Churches expresses deep concern over the deterioration of the situation in East Timor. The Assembly wishes to reaffirm, in this context, the principles of the rights of all peoples for self-determination.

2. We welcome the Rome agreement between Portugal and Indonesia according to which a solution to the problem can be found only by the speedy and orderly implementation of the act of self-determination by the people concerned.

3. We deplore all the developments in East Timor since the Rome agreement, and we consider the present situation to be tragic to the people of East Timor.

4. The Assembly calls upon Portugal and Indonesia as co-signatories to the Rome agreement together with the neighbouring country of Australia as well as the parties in East Timor to co-operate in the implementation of the Rome Agreement so as to end armed strife and bring about a peaceful and orderly transfer of power.

5. We appeal to all foreign powers to refrain from any action in East Timor which will prevent the people of East Timor from freely deciding their own future, and specifically we call on the government of Indonesia to withdraw its armed forces to enable self-determination to occur.

6. The Assembly makes urgent request to the Australian government to facilitate the evacuation of refugees from East Timor and to offer sanctuary and resettlement for those refugees who may desire to settle within Australia.

7. The Assembly commends the efforts of the Indonesian and Australian Councils of Churches and CICARWS to provide relief to the refugees from East Timor and calls upon the member churches and Councils to come forward to help those who suffer as a result of the conflict.

HUMAN RIGHTS IN LATIN AMERICA

At the request of General Simatupang, the Report was presented by Ms I. Kirkcaldy (United Church of Jamaica and Grand Cayman). Most speeches in the discussion, and the amendments proposed, were intended to make the draft more specific and pointed. A delegate from Latin America said that most of the governments in Latin America are tyrannical. The Church must be concerned with human rights; the right to be human comes from God, and in defending human rights we are defending the will of God. It was also clear that delegates to the Assembly had to return to their countries and very specific references might well lead to serious repercussions. After further discussion of the activities of the USA in Latin America and of the language of the document, it was agreed to refer it back to the Committee for revision.

Later, General Simatupang said that the Officers of the Committee had consulted with a number of people, and had decided that they wished the present draft to stand.

The Reverend Oscar McCloud (United Presbyterian, USA) moved "that Policy Reference Committee III be requested to revise its report to include specific reference to denial of human rights by the government of Brazil, and the Assembly's opposition to the support of the US Government for oppressive regimes in Latin America."

Archbishop Kratz (Episcopal Church, Brazil) said that the churches in Brazil were very much involved both in protest against bad things and in trying to be constructive with the government, and were becoming more united in their efforts toward Christian and human solutions. Specific mention of Brazil would cause problems for churches and individuals. Pastor N. Sepulveda (Pentecostal, Chile) understood the document as an appeal to that majority of Latin American countries where human rights are not respected. The Reverend A. Kunert (Lutheran, Brazil) said that if we want to stand for peace we must be prepared to suffer, but that his delegation desired the name of Brazil to be omitted on the ground that its inclusion would not help the credibility of the WCC among those with whom they had to deal.

Mr McCloud withdrew his amendment and the Report was accepted by the Assembly. The text follows.

Human Rights in Latin America

1. Having approved the document of Section V on human rights, and wishing to place special emphasis on the Latin American situation, the Assembly affirms that:

Despite the fact that the majority of the countries in the Latin American community have subscribed to the Universal Declaration of Human Rights, the fundamental rights to health, education, work, and a living wage have been either ignored completely or not sufficiently implemented by the majority of the governments.

We protest the systematic increase of human rights violations on that continent especially, for political reasons, of individual rights like:

arbitrary and/or unjustified detention, without proper warrants from competent courts;
imprisonment without proper trial;
denial of the right to habeas corpus;
physical violence and torture;
harassment or intimidation of relatives of prisoners;
alleged disappearance of persons and unexplained deaths;
violation of the freedom of expression;
limitation of the right to legal defence;
restriction of the Christian vocation to aid persons whose rights have been violated;
ineffectiveness of the right to asylum and of the rights accorded to refugees by international conventions.

2. Having considered this anguishing reality, we respectfully but ener-

getically exhort the governments of Latin America to comply with the provisions of the Universal Declaration of Human Rights.

3. We exhort as well governments of all countries of the world to open their doors to the thousands of political refugees who have been unable to find a place to reconstitute their lives in peace.

4. We call upon the government of the Republic of Argentina, for humanitarian reasons, to normalize speedily the situations of political refugees and exiles now present in its territory, and urge it to react immediately to the appeal of the UNHCR in connection with Argentina.

5. We call upon the government of the Republic of Chile to reconsider its determination to cancel the permission to reside in the country for Bishop Helmut Frenz of the Evangelical Lutheran Church in Chile, and allow him to continue his pastoral work in the mission of his church. We make this appeal, accepting the assurance of those who know him that all his activities in the Committee of Co-operation for Peace in Chile have been governed by a profound sense of Christian love and service.

6. We also call upon the government of Chile to release the personnel and members of the Committee for Peace now in prison.

7. We express our appreciation for the important work done by the WCC through the CCIA and the Human Rights Resources Office for Latin America, and we urge it to continue to support churches and other bodies in Latin America who work for the defence of human rights, and to inform the churches on a regular basis about the human rights situation on that continent.

8. We call upon the churches in Latin America to:

educate and conscienticize their members in order that they be led to comprehend their responsibility as a community of faith in Christ with respect to the Universal Declaration of Human Rights. This should lead to the implementation of concrete programmes in defence of those rights by the churches and their members;

create ecumenical commissions of churches to promote respect for human rights in their countries, starting with the member churches of the WCC.

9. We appeal to the Christian churches in Chile, especially to members of the WCC, to continue and strengthen the Christian and humanitarian ministry they carry out in the Committee of Co-operation for Peace in Chile.

THE WORLD ARMAMENTS SITUATION

The Report was introduced by Professor K. Skjelsbaek (Church of Norway). Dr H. de Lange (Remonstrant Brotherhood, Netherlands) moved an amendment calling upon the Central Committee to prepare "a programme to combat militarism". Mr David Johnson (Episcopal, USA) and Archbishop Sarkissian proposed drafting amendments which were accepted. Dr Roy Neehall (Presbyterian, Trinidad) moved an additional clause towards the end of the document: "The need for retraining and re-employment of those who now make their living through the arms production industry." This was seconded, resisted by Professor Skjelsbaek, but when put to the vote carried by 179 to 170 votes.

The Report as amended was carried by a considerable majority. The text follows.

The World Armaments Situation

1. Three decades after World War II, humankind is again armed to levels unequalled in history. According to reliable calculations (from Stockholm International Peace Research Institute) world expenditure on arms in 1974 totalled more than 220 billion US dollars. Thus, actual world military spending is about equal to the national income of more than a billion people in the developing countries of South Asia, the Far East, and Africa. The bulk of this expenditure—82 per cent in 1973—is shared by NATO and Warsaw Pact nations. China accounts for about 5 per cent. In addition to the monetary expenditures, the figures represent a tremendous waste of the world's natural resources.

2. The increased expenditure on arms is surpassed only by advances in military technology. Modern nuclear warheads have an explosive power of several *millions* of tons of TNT. Of equal importance are the improvements in speed and accuracy of delivery vehicles of nuclear weapons. In addition to the strategic nuclear weapons designed for intercontinental exchanges, the superpowers have developed a large arsenal of tactical nuclear weapons, thus reducing the potential importance of a threshold between conventional and nuclear warfare.

3. The cancerous growth of military research and development in the post-World War II period reflects the shift in the arms race from competition in quantity to a race for "quality" in both conventional and nuclear weapons. In the conventional field, out of the testing grounds of Indo-China and the Middle East has come a "quiet revolution" in modern warfare, new generations of planes, helicopters, gunships, and bombs. The modern arsenals include among other things electronic tools, guided projectiles, sensors, and a diverse assortment of anti-personnel fragmentation bombs.

4. There is an increasing danger in the proliferation of military bases. The presence of foreign military bases represents a threat to the independence and integrity of many nations. In one zone which so far has been

relatively free from conflict and confrontation, the Indian Ocean, a massive build-up of bases has lately taken place.

5. Another alarming development is the increasing militarization of the Third World. The Third World, China excluded, accounts for 7-9 per cent of world military expenditure, nearly three times the level of official foreign development assistance. In general, the military expenditure of developing countries increases relatively faster than the equivalent expenditure of industrialized nations. Most of the Third World weapons come from developed countries. However, some Third World countries have plans for an armament industry of their own. Armaments and militarization have in many cases contributed to shifting development priorities, to weaken and stifle economic growth and to check socio-political strength.

6. The relationship between the world's two main military blocs is based on the idea of mutual deterrence. However, the dynamics of deterrence tends to accelerate rather than to restrain the arms race. Peace and stability, naturally, cannot be attained by a policy based on threats. The calculation in terms of the worst possible case, and the propensity to over-perception, over-reaction, and over-design escalate the arms race.

7. However, the armament dynamics seems to be rooted not only in external, but also internal forces nowadays. The growing military-industrial-bureaucratic complexes play an important role in speeding up the arms race. In addition, the arms dynamic is propelled by the race in technology, each side trying to maximize its capabilities. Military research and development, as a rule, do not wait for reactions from the other side, but react rather in continuous process to their own achievements.

8. In the past 25-30 years, several attempts to reduce the arms race have been made. Multiple UN resolutions calling for disarmament notwithstanding, only bacteriological weapons have been destroyed as a result of disarmament negotiations.

9. The interest for disarmament has been replaced by a concentration around the notion of arms control, i.e. controlling the advance in armaments. The Antarctic Treaty, the Outer Space Treaty, and the Seabed Treaty, as well as the Partial Test Ban Treaty, could be mentioned in this connection. Most notable is the five-year-old nuclear Non-Proliferation Treaty to prevent the spreading of nuclear weapons. This Treaty also provides for the control of peaceful use of nuclear energy. Regrettably, several important nations have not signed or ratified the Treaty.

10. The SALT negotiations and agreements between the Soviet Union and the United States represent an effort of the two superpowers to accommodate each other in questions of quantities in lines of upward parity. The negotiations may have contributed to a better political atmo-

sphere between the two countries, but have also channelled the strategic arms race primarily in the direction of improved qualities.

11. Although there has been no direct military confrontation between the superpowers, since World War II some hundred wars have been fought, causing the deaths of more than ten million people in about sixty countries. There are limits to how far the great powers, in accordance with the Helsinki Declaration, can develop relationships of partnership and co-operation, under conditions where weapons of massive destruction could be used.

An Appeal to the Churches

1. The above analysis is recommended to the churches for study.

2. Christians must resist the temptation to resign themselves to a false sense of impotence or security. The churches should emphasize their readiness to live without the protection of armaments, and take a significant initiative in pressing for effective disarmament. Churches, individual Christians, and members of the public in all countries should press their governments to ensure national security without resorting to the use of weapons of mass destruction.

3. We call upon the new Central Committee to initiate steps to organize a consultation on disarmament. This consultation should investigate and compare available material on the factors producing the present arms race and the technological, economic, environmental, and military implications. The consultation should aim at proposing a strategy, at national and international levels, to prevent further increased military expenditure. This strategy should include, among others, the following points:

(a) Prepare educational programmes for the use of the churches.
(b) Stimulate public discussion on the matter.
(c) Study the questions of war and peace in a theological perspective.
(d) Share the experience of the historic Peace Churches.
(e) Investigate the involvement of the churches in arms production and trade.
(f) Call for a World Disarmament Conference under UN auspices.
(g) Stress the need for retraining and re-employment of those who now make their living through the arms production industry.

4. The Central Committee should ensure that disarmament is a major concern of the WCC.

5. We appeal to all Christians to think, work, and pray for a disarmed world.

REPRESENTATIVES FROM KOREA

Dr Potter presented on behalf of the Assembly Business Committee a resolution on the refusal of exit permits to four intending participants in the Assembly—Messrs Ahn Byung Moo, Moon Dong Whan, Kuir Kwan Suk, and Kang Noon Kyu—and outlined the recent actions of the WCC in connection with Korea. Dr W.P. Thompson (United Presbyterian, USA) noted the inclusion of Korea in the Human Rights part of the Report of Section V and the shortness of time available. Miss L. Miller (Methodist, USA) thought that the Assembly should act to show its solidarity with Christians of South Korea.

(There are no member churches in North Korea.)

Dr M.M. Thomas, presiding, put a motion to refer the matter to the Central Committee and there voted in favour 234 and against 148.

UNITED NATIONS ENVIRONMENT PROGRAMME

On Monday, 8 December, the Assembly welcomed Mr Maurice Strong, Director of the United Nations Environment Programme whose offices are in the Kenyatta Conference Centre Tower Block, and invited him to address the Assembly.

Mr Strong traced the history of the relationship of the WCC to the UN and its agencies. "I must say with all the strength that is in me that the churches, who were so crucial in the creation of the United Nations, must not slacken in their commitment to the only world body in which humankind has at least a chance to co-operate on the complex and in some cases terrifying international economic, social, and humanitarian problems."

After describing briefly the UN Environment Programme's role as "catalyst, initiator, and co-ordinator", Mr Strong spoke of the hopes and tasks of the future.

1. We must reduce demand on natural resources and environment—a new commitment to conservation.

2. We must increase world food supply without destroying the ecological basis for sustaining production.

3. We must stabilize world population.

4. We must create a new approach to societal decision-making.

5. We must redirect the urban revolution.

6. We must reorganize and reorient science and technology.

7. We must take a new approach to growth.

8. We must manage and care for the oceans.

9. We must create a new international economic order.

10. We must have a revolution in values and behaviour. It must be evident that all the foregoing proposals will require significant changes in our present system of values and patterns of behaviour. Most of these changes must be made in the industrialized world which today commands such a disproportionate share of the wealth and power that the technological society has made possible. In effect, the western world needs its own "cultural revolution"—and it needs it urgently.

Such a strategy will require "a sustained act of collective will"; and he appealed finally as a Christian to his fellow-Christians to help lead in making "the transition to a sustainable global society".

Thanking Mr Strong on behalf of the Assembly, Dr M.M. Thomas wished him well in the new tasks he would take up in 1976 as Director of the Energy Commission of Canada.

3. THE MESSAGE COMMITTEE

The Message Committee had met at intervals throughout the Assembly. It had had on 1 December a meeting with conveners of the Work Groups, and in this and many other ways attempted to discern what the spirit was saying to the churches and what the churches were hearing. As Dr van den Heuvel (Reformed, Netherlands) explained in presenting the proposed Message on behalf of the Committee on 9 December, the Committee had studied the Messages of the four previous Assemblies, and had come early to the conclusion that the Message of this Assembly should be in the form of prayer which should use both contemporary and ancient forms. At one stage it had tried to find a way of making use of the Assembly emblem or logo which had (if the wall-newspaper was to be trusted) stirred the imaginations of participants. Consideration of problems in the constituencies of member churches had, however, led to the reluctant abandonment of this idea. (For inescapable practical reasons the Message reflected the mind of the Assembly as the Committee had apprehended it at the point it had reached on Monday, 8 December, rather than its mind and mood when it ended two and a half days later, after several critical debates.)

A number of amendments were suggested, most of which the Committee was able to take account of in the final text printed earlier in this volume. The Committee found, however, that it was unable without unduly lengthening the Message to meet the desire expressed by Bishop Hempel (Lutheran, German Democratic Republic), but queried by Dr Potter and Metropolitan Osthathios (Syrian Orthodox, India) for a mention of eucharistic fellowship.

The Message was adopted unanimously. It is printed on page xi.

4. THE FUTURE OF THE WORLD COUNCIL OF CHURCHES

In this section are collected those debates and actions of the Assembly which concerned the future leadership, programmes, and relationships of the World Council of Churches. Most of the matter is grouped under one or other of the following Committees:

The Nominations Committee
Policy Reference Committee I
    (concerned with the constitution, rules, etc.)
Policy Reference Committee II
    (concerned with relationships with world confessional bodies, regional and national councils, the Roman Catholic Church, etc.)
The Finance Committee
The Programme Guidelines Committee

Many of these matters came before the Assembly more than once, but the arrangement here is not chronological but by subject.

THE NOMINATIONS COMMITTEE

The Nominations Committee appointed on 24 November presented its first and preliminary Report to the Assembly on Tuesday, 2 December, consisting of a statement of the principles by which the Committee had been guided and of the procedure for amendment and election that it recommended, together with a list of proposed names for the Presidents and the members of the Central Committee. Dr Robert Marshall (Lutheran, USA), the Moderator of the Committee, stated that though the proposed revision of the Constitution and Rules would allow for a Central Committee of up to 145 members, the Executive Committee had advised in April that in view of financial stringency the number should not exceed 125. A Central Committee of this size represented approximately one Central Committee member for each five Assembly delegates. The Nominations Committee had also been bound by the due regard to be paid to geographical and confessional balance, due proportions of laity, women, and young people, and adequate representation of the major interests of the World Council (these are set out in full in the Constitution and Rules in the Appendix). The provisional list presented by the Committee contained a total of 128 names. Dr M.M. Thomas, Moderator, pointed out that there would be no discussion of names at this session. The early presentation of the Report was to give time for churches to register any unacceptability of nominees and for delegates to propose changes.

A discussion followed in order to clarify matters of procedure. Mr David Johnson (Episcopal, USA) moved that the nominees for President not be counted in the proportional quota for his or her church, confessional family, and geographical area, and that the number in the Central Committee be raised to 140. He was supported by Metropolitan Juvenaly (Russian Orthodox), who thought the number of Orthodox too low. He was resisted by Dr E.A. Payne (Baptist, UK) on financial grounds; moreover, the increase of member churches meant that some churches which had had larger representation on the Central Committee in the past would have to accept reductions. The motion was defeated.

The Assembly approved in general the principles adopted by the Nominations Committee with regard to the size and proportions of representation for the Central Committee.

The Assembly approved the recommendations:

1. that the Nominations Committee present its final Report in Business Session on Friday, 5 December;

2. that the Report contain no further recommendations but only the list of nominees for Presidents and members of the Central Committee;

3. that no action be taken with regard to the Report at this time;

4. that any additional nominations by delegates be submitted in writing during the period between presentation of the final Report on Friday, 5 December and the beginning of the Business Session on Saturday, 6 December;

5. that the votes on these nominations be taken individually by ballot at the Business Session on 6 December;

6. that the vote on the nominations submitted by the Nominations Committee together with any amendments resulting from the vote on nominations made by delegates be taken at the same Business Session on 6 December in a single action on the complete list by a show of hands.

The final Report was presented to the Assembly on Friday, 5 December. Over twenty changes had been proposed by delegates which had been carefully considered by the Committee. The final list of six Presidents and 130 members of the Central Committee included twelve changes from the first Report.

Action was taken in a Business Session on Saturday, 6 December, Dr E. A. Payne presiding.

Dr W. P. Thompson (United Presbyterian, USA) moved that the vote on nominees for President be taken by a written ballot permitting a separate vote for or against each nominee. Dr Payne ruled that, in the light of the 2 December decision that the vote be taken on 6 December in a single action on a complete list by a show of hands, Dr Thompson's motion was out of order. Dr Thompson challenged this ruling. The Assembly sustained Dr Payne's ruling by 456 votes to 128.

A counter-nomination as President of Dr M. M. Thomas in place of Metropolitan Nikodim (Russian Orthodox) had been received; but Dr Thomas was not prepared to stand.

For the Central Committee

Professor Dr Gerhard Grohs (EKD, United, German Federal Republic) had been nominated in place of Dr Brandes (EKD, Lutheran, German Federal Republic), who had withdrawn, and on a show of hands Dr Grohs was elected.

Fr Vitaly Borovoy (Russian Orthodox) had been nominated in place of Mr A. Osipov (Russian Orthodox), who withdrew. This substitution was also approved.

Metropolitan John of Finland (Russian Orthodox) had been nominated in place of Metropolitan Paul of Sweden (Ecumenical Patriarchate).

After brief speeches by Dr Nikolainen (Lutheran, Finland), Metropolitan Meliton (Ecumenical Patriarchate), and Dr Robert Marshall (Moderator of the Nominations Committee), the issue was put to the ballot, with the result

Metropolitan Paul of Sweden	437
Metropolitan John of Finland	144
Blank papers	13

The substitution was therefore *not* approved.

The Nominations Committee recommended that Dr W. A. Visser 't Hooft should be continued as *Honorary President*. Dr Clinton Hoggard (African Methodist Episcopal Zion Church, USA) and twenty-six other delegates had given notice of a motion not on the agenda that the Assembly authorize the election of an additional Honorary President. Dr M. M. Thomas outlined the advice of the Nominations and Business Committees, and stated that accordingly the Officers ruled that this motion should not be put on the agenda. After further discussion, the resolution to include this motion on the agenda was lost.

Dr W.P. Thompson (United Presbyterian, USA) had given notice of a motion to amend the Rules to provide for the election of one or more Honorary Presidents. Dr Payne outlined the history of the Presidency and the Honorary Presidency in the World Council of Churches and said that this motion could be passed to Policy Reference Committee I for later action in the Assembly.

The list presented by the Nominations Committee as amended was put to the vote on a show of hands and carried by an overwhelming majority with three negative votes. It is printed as Appendix 7. Dr Payne thanked the Nominations Committee for their work. Dr Thompson later withdrew his motion.

Presbyterian Church in Mozambique

At the conclusion of the debate on the Nominations Committee Dr Potter read part of a letter of greeting from the Presbyterian Church of Mozambique which looked forward to the help of the WCC and the member churches in facing the tasks of a new period. The church's application for membership would be dealt with in due course by the newly-elected Central Committee, but its delegated observer, Mr I. Funzamo, was present. He was welcomed amidst applause by Dr Payne and Dr M. M. Thomas.

POLICY REFERENCE COMMITTEE I
CONSTITUTIONAL MATTERS

Ms Theressa Hoover (Methodist, USA), Moderator, presented the Reports of the Committee.

The Report of the Moderator

The following resolution from the Committee was carried unanimously.

1. That the Assembly receive with gratitude the Report of the Moderator (Appendix 3) and express appreciation for the depth and width of his Report and for the central emphasis on evangelism. Many of the issues he has raised require further discussion and clarification, notably the adequacy and meaning of his phrase "Christ-centred syncretism", the question of Christ at work outside the Church, the relation of dialogue and evangelism, and of evangelism and social involvement. The Assembly expresses gratefulness for his contribution to this discussion.

2. That the Assembly express deep gratitude to Dr M. M. Thomas for the leadership he has given to the World Council of Churches since Uppsala, for his theological and social insights, and for his friendly and forthright style of moderatorship.

The General Secretary's Report

The following resolution from the Committee was carried unanimously.

That the Assembly receive with gratitude the Report of the General Secretary (Appendix 4) and express appreciation for the interrelationship and complementary nature of this Report with that of the Moderator of the Central Committee. The Assembly notes particularly that the Moderator's emphasis on evangelism should be placed side by side with the General Secretary's masterly analysis of the global situation and the human predicament. It notes that much more attention must be given to listening to the churches as well as communicating to them. It agrees with his statement that human rights are violated everywhere but feels that these violations occur in differing

188

degrees in different places. It welcomes his emphasis on the need for repentance (*metanoia*) and conversion and his challenge that it should bear fruit in concrete situations.

The Constitution

The Proposed Revised Constitution of the World Council of Churches had been sent to member churches six months before the Assembly and had also been published in the Assembly Work Book alongside the existing Constitution.

Policy Reference Committee I proposed the Proposed Revised Constitution as printed to be adopted by the Assembly with two slight changes:

1. Article III of the Proposed Revised Constitution shall be adopted as replacing Article III of the Present Constitution with the exception of Article III (v) of the present Constitution which shall become Article III (iii) of the Proposed Revised Constitution, and subsequent clauses shall be renumbered (iv), (v), (vi), and (vii).

(The Article in question in the present Constitution reads: "(v) to support the churches in their worldwide missionary and evangelistic task".)

2. Article V 2 (c) (viii) of the Proposed Revised Constitution, "the desired distribution among church officials, parish ministers, lay-persons—men, women, and young people; and participation by persons whose special knowledge and experience will be needed" should be amended in order to clarify the intent: "The desired distribution among church officials, parish ministers, and lay persons; among men, women, and young people; and participation by persons whose special knowledge and experience will be needed".

Policy Reference Committee I had also stated the following interpretation with respect to Article V 2 (c) (viii) and Rule III 1 (a) (ii) which concern selection of delegates to an Assembly:

The Central Committee can determine the number of delegates to the Assembly and their allocation among the member churches, giving due regard to geographical and cultural balance. This does not limit the right of the churches to determine who their delegates shall be. In reference to the distribution among church officials, parish ministers, lay persons, men, women, and young people, the Central Committee can only give recommendations. The definition of the terms: church officials, parish ministers, and lay persons is left to the churches.

On 9 December, the Assembly acted as follows on the Proposed Revised Constitution, in every case by the necessary two-thirds majority.

Article I Basis was adopted.
Article II Membership was adopted.

On *Article III Functions and Purposes* there was some debate on the phrases "visible unity" and "eucharistic fellowship" in Article III (i) "to call the churches to the goal of visible unity in one faith and in one eucharistic fellowship. . .".

Bishop Nikolainen said on behalf of his Church: "The Lutheran Church of Finland has officially discussed the proposed new constitution and is willing to accept it, because it holds that the goal of visible unity does not necessarily mean unity of jurisdiction or church government. I request that this statement be included in the Minutes."

Commissioner Williams (Salvation Army) said that the inclusion of the phrase "eucharistic fellowship" acted against such denominations as the Salvation Army and the Society of Friends.

The General Secretary said the functions are not binding upon the member churches but are what the WCC is expected to promote.

There was extended debate on whether the insertion of Article III (v) from the old Constitution into the Proposed Revised Constitution constituted an amendment of which six months' notice should be given and which therefore could not now be acted upon by the Assembly. Mr J.W. Bullimore (Church of England) said the Assembly was dealing with a matter which was well known to the member churches; there was not any overlapping; and Article III (v) from the old Constitution clearly reflected a concern of delegates to the Assembly. After further discussion, a vote was taken on the motion that the insertion of Article III (v) of the old Constitution into the Proposed Revised Constitution as Article III (iii) did not constitute an amendment, with the following result. For the motion 382; against 46; abstentions 29.

On a point of order Bishop J. Mathews (Methodist, USA) asked that the Assembly vote on the Sub-Sections of Article III separately.

Article III (i) was carried by 461 to 31, with 13 abstentions.
Article III (ii) was carried.
Article III (iii) was carried.
Article III (iv) was carried.
Article III (v) was carried.
Article III (vi) was carried.
Article III (vii) was carried.
Article III as a whole was carried.
Article IV was carried.

On *Article V Organization* it was noted that the change was not an amendment but a clarification.

Article V was carried.
Article VI was carried.
Article VII was carried.

The Proposed Revised Constitution was carried as a whole by an overwhelming majority and was adopted as The Constitution of the World Council of Churches. It is printed in Appendix 11.

The Rules

Notice had been given by Policy Reference Committee I of the following proposed amendments to the Rules:

Rule I.4 Associate Membership. To insert after the first sentence the following additional sentence: "A church applying for associate membership must ordinarily have at least 10,000 members."

(The Committee also suggested that the Central Committee examine further the criteria of membership.)

This amendment was carried.

Rule III 1 (a) (ii) Composition of the Assembly: Delegates. The penultimate sentence to run: "The Central Committee shall recommend the distributions within delegations among church officials, parish ministers, and lay persons; and among men, women, and young people."

There was considerable debate on the change from "determine" to "recommend" between those who felt that the final decision should lie with the churches and those like Archbishop Scott (Anglican Church of Canada) that "in a period of transition" churches need more than mere recommendations. When the recommendation was put to the vote 335 voted for, 199 against, and there were four abstentions. The Committee's recommended change was adopted.

Rule IV 1 (c) Central Committee Membership. To insert at the end of the paragraph: "If a member, or his or her substitute, is absent without excuse for two consecutive meetings, the position shall be declared vacant and the Central Committee shall fill the vacancy according to the provisions of Article V 2 (b) (iii) of the Constitution."

This was carried.

Rule IV 3 (a) (v) Nominations Committee of the Central Committee. To add to the present text: "Nominate members of Committees and Boards" the words "and where appropriate their moderators".

This was carried.

Rules I and IV as printed in the Work Book were carried by a two-thirds majority, these being rules which can only be amended by the Assembly.

A further eleven recommended changes in the Rules of a kind which do not require action by the Assembly were referred to the Central Committee. The text of the Rules printed in Appendix 11 was finally adopted after action by the Central Committee on 11 December, 1975.

French and German Texts of the Constitution and Rules

The following were requested by the Assembly to verify the corrections of the translations of the French and German texts of the Constitution and Rules.

French Text

The Reverend Dr André Appel (France), Evangelical Church of the Augsburg Confession of Alsace and Lorraine.

Pasteur Jacques Maury (France), Reformed Church of France.

Dr Jacques Rossel (Switzerland), Swiss Protestant Church Federation.

German Text

Pastor Hans Frei (Switzerland), Old Catholic Church of Switzerland.

Professor Dr Gerhard Grohs (West Berlin), Evangelical Church in Germany—United

Oberkirchenrat Hartmut Mitzenheim (GDR), Federation of Evangelical Churches in the GDR.

By-Laws and Constitutions of Commissions

Policy Reference Committee I recommended the Assembly to approve the following By-Laws and Constitution:

1. By-Laws of the Commission of the Churches on International Affairs.

2. By-Laws of the Faith and Order Commission.

3. Constitution of the Commission on World Mission and Evangelism after noting that:

a) the By-Laws of the Faith and Order Commission and the Constitution of the Commission on World Mission and Evangelism have been approved by the Central Committee.

b) the By-Laws of the Faith and Order Commission use the term "chair-person" and suggests that these By-Laws might conform to general World Council terminology.

c) the Commission on World Mission and Evangelism has a constitution and suggests that by due processes this might be brought into conformity with the World Council practice of having By-Laws for Commissions.

The Assembly adopted these recommendations.

Unit Structures

Policy Reference Committee I received a report on the new structure of the Unit on Education and Renewal (III) and noted the proposal to have within this Unit four sub-units on: Education; Women in Church and Society; Renewal Movements; Youth.

It also received a report on proposals to improve the functioning of the Unit on Justice and Service (II).

Policy Reference Committee I noted that none of the Units has thus far prepared By-Laws as requested in Rule VI 1. It *recommends* that each Unit prepare such By-Laws for presentation to the Central Committee.

The report of the Policy Reference Committee was approved by the Assembly; and the Committee thanked for its services by Dr M.M. Thomas.

POLICY REFERENCE COMMITTEE II
RELATIONSHIPS

Common Date for the Celebration of Easter

Bishop H. Harms (EKD, Germany) read the Statement recommended by the Committee which was unanimously received:

In the churches of the Eastern and Western traditions, the resurrection of Jesus Christ is commemorated on different dates. Some years ago, the World Council of Churches conducted an inquiry with all member churches and a number of non-member churches concerning the possibility of a common date for the celebration of Easter. The responses clearly showed that all churches, faithful to the Spirit of the Council of Nicea, desire to find a common date. The churches of the Western tradition in great majority favour a fixed date, e.g., the Sunday after the second Saturday in April.

In preparation for the Fifth Assembly another attempt was made by the World Council of Churches to test the mind of the member churches on this matter. The Assembly notes that the inquiry led to the following results:

a) The great majority of the member churches confirm their readiness to accept a common and even fixed date of Easter, e.g., the Sunday after the second Saturday in April.

b) The Orthodox Member Churches indicate that any change of the present mode of calculating Easter requires an explicit agreement of all Orthodox Churches and that, as long as such an agreement has not been reached, they feel bound to follow the present method of calculating the date.

c) In a resolution adopted by the Second Vatican Council, the Roman Catholic Church stated that it was prepared to accept a common mobile or fixed date for Easter if agreement between the churches could be established. The Holy See has expressed its willingness to collaborate towards reaching an agreement.

The authority to decide on such a matter belongs to the churches. Only if requested by the churches and in order to facilitate their common action could the World Council of Churches make a specific proposal. In the light of the response received, the Assembly

recognizes that, at this stage, a specific proposal would not lead to a date uniting all Christians in the celebration of Easter on the same day;

193

expresses the hope that the urgent desire to find a common date can be fulfilled as soon as possible by a common decision of all churches;

instructs the Central Committee to encourage further developments.

In the absence of Metropolitan Meliton (Ecumenical Patriarchate) Fr Damaskinos (Ecumenical Patriarchate) presented the following Statement on behalf of the Eastern Orthodox delegates, which was read in English by Dr V. Istavridis (Ecumenical Patriarchate):

We, the delegates of the Eastern Orthodox Churches, members of the World Council of Churches, present at its Fifth Assembly, expressing the unanimous decision of our respective churches, and after conferring here in Nairobi on the issue of a fixed date for a common celebration of the Resurrection of the Lord by all Christians, declare:

1. We greet with joy the initiative of the World Council of Churches and of the Secretariat for Promoting Christian Unity of the Vatican to bring this matter before this Assembly and to the attention of all Christian churches.

2. We remind all Christians that the wish to have a common celebration of Easter and a common witness of the resurrection of our Lord at the same day was expressed years ago by the Eastern Orthodox Church, and we are happy that this issue has been a matter of serious consideration by the World Council of Churches and the Vatican.

3. Although we recognize and respect the efforts of the United Nations towards a common Easter by all Christians and we acknowledge the importance of the social and economic considerations behind these efforts, we nevertheless wish to give priority to the sacredness of the celebration of the resurrection of our Lord in accordance with the tradition of the ancient Church.

4. It is on these grounds that our respective churches, after correspondence on this matter, have decided that no individual Orthodox Church may take any position on this issue without a general Pan-Orthodox decision.

5. In accordance with and in consequence of the above-mentioned initiative of the Orthodox Church for the common celebration of Easter, we declare that, since this subject has already been put under examination before the Eastern Orthodox Church in its entirety, it is left to us to suggest to our churches that this subject be examined and decided upon in one of the forthcoming Pan-Orthodox meetings.

6. We are asking the head delegate of the Ecumenical Patriarchate to make this declaration before the Assembly.

*Relationships between the WCC and Regional, National, and Local
Councils of Churches*

Bishop H. Harms presented the following Report which was unanimously
adopted:

The main purpose of the World Council of Churches is to promote the
renewal, the visible unity, and the common witness of the churches. Many
ecumenical structures and efforts, at different levels of the life of the
churches, pursue the same or similar objectives, particularly regional,
national, and local Christian councils and councils of churches. It has
always been recognized that the WCC, in order to fulfil its task, needs to
be in close contact with these structures and efforts. As the ecumenical
movement advances, the relationships need to be reviewed to ensure the
maximum of concerted and complementary action. In the past years many
new developments have taken place. Many councils have now an expanded
membership, e.g., one regional and nineteen national councils have Roman
Catholic membership. Regional councils have acquired new significance in
the life of the churches. Many councils at all levels have developed new
programmes. These and other developments make it imperative to reflect
afresh on the relation between the WCC and other ecumenical bodies.

Therefore the Assembly *recommends* that

The Central Committee encourage further reflection on this matter
and recommend steps to increase co-operation with such councils and
define anew the WCC's relationship with them.

Relationships between the WCC and World Confessional Families

Bishop H. Harms presented the Report.

Professor Kyaw Than (Baptist, Burma) expressed reservations about
paragraph 10 (iii) which it was agreed would be met by the addition of a
footnote; proposed to amend paragraph 11 by the addition at the end of
the sentence of the words "and face together a common calling to Christ
who frees and unites", which was accepted; and proposed to amend
paragraph 13 by the addition at the end of clause (1) of the words "and in
different regional settings with the active participation of relevant ecumenical organizations".

The Report as amended was adopted. The text follows.

1. The relation between the WCC and the World Confessional Families requires new attention. While Councils bring together churches of
different confessional origin, each World Confessional Family gives
expression to the common heritage of a group of churches throughout
the world. The nature of the Councils and World Confessional Families
is understandably different. In the past, this difference has often led to
tensions and conflicts. However, in recent years, changes have taken

195

place which may lead to a new relationship between the WCC and the World Confessional Families.

2. The Secretaries of World Confessional Families meet informally once a year together with Roman Catholic representatives to exchange information and discuss common problems. The Faith and Order Secretariat is a regular participant in these meetings. In December 1974, they produced a "Discussion Paper on the Ecumenical Role of WCFs in the Ecumenical Movement" which has been sent to all Families for their reaction and comment and also to the WCC. These developments seem to indicate that, though the purposes of the WCC and the World Confessional Families are different, a constructive and complementary way of contributing to the advance of the ecumenical movement can be found.

3. The document says:
The following new developments have called forth an intensified ecumenical response from the WCFs.

4. First, within the ecumenical movement the issue of the universal fellowship of the people of God has come to the fore (e.g., Uppsala, 1968).

5. Second, the fact of the official entry of the Roman Catholic Church into the ecumenical movement has brought forth from the WCFs a generally positive response, acting as partners in ecumenical encounter with the RCC.

6. Third, the increase of church union conversations has challenged the WCFs to greater ecumenical involvement. While some of the churches participating in union negotiations have hesitated because of fears of alienation from the fellowship of their historical confessional families, most of the WCFs have come to consider such union negotiations as legitimate forms of ecumenical involvement, and do not inhibit them or withdraw financial support. WCFs should therefore encourage union endeavours in areas where their member churches are moving in this direction.

7. As a result of these developments the WCFs have played an increasingly important role in the ecumenical movement, and face the challenge of an even more important role in the future.

8. The World Confessional Families have initiated bilateral conversations among themselves. They have taken measures to manifest more fully the universality of the Church. In several World Confessional Families the churches of the Third World play a more significant role than before.

9. The critical questions raised by the churches engaged in the ecumenical movement, especially the churches of the Third World, have

not lost their validity. Some of these questions were voiced at the Faith and Order Consultation in Salamanca, 1973. It asked the WCFs to consider seriously whether:

(i) they give sufficient attention to the local situation in the processes of agenda-setting and decision-making;

(ii) they engage in sufficient consultation with each other and the World Council of Churches;

(iii) their structures, policies, and activities in fact encourage and support their member churches as they move towards union, and do not prevent local ecumenical commitment;

(iv) their financial policies, or the policies of the boards or agencies of some of their member churches, lead to domination and a dependence on the part of member churches which restricts ecumenical engagements;

(v) their policies encourage consultation and common planning for mission, service, and development at local and national levels.

(Discussion Paper, § 38)

10. These critical questions are increasingly raised by the WCFs themselves. The discussion paper addresses to the World Confessional Families specific questions:

(i) Should there not be fuller co-operation between the WCFs and the WCC in applying the Lund dictum that the churches "should act together in all matters except those in which deep differences of conviction compel them to act separately"?

(ii) Should not more ongoing vehicles of consultation be created in which the complementary roles of the WCFs and the WCC can be worked out? In some areas the efforts of these bodies overlap—thus could, for example, inter-church aid be rendered more effectively if the WCFs and the WCC pooled their efforts more completely?

(iii) Could the influence of the WCFs in the policy-making agencies of the WCC, or its Unit programmes, be strengthened? Could there also be WCC voices in the decision-making meetings of the WCFs?*

(iv) From the point of view of the WCFs as well as the WCC, would it not be advantageous for the WCFs to utilize the WCC as a forum, or instrument for common action, e.g., in matters relating to international affairs, or to human rights and religious freedom? (Discussion Paper, § 41)

---

*The Fifth Assembly notes that this could be counter-productive and feels that clauses (i), (ii), and (iv) should be given priority consideration.

11. Therefore, they need to be discussed by the WCC on the basis of the recognition that the WCC and the WCFs face together a common calling to Christ who frees and unites.

12. In pursuing these questions, the following considerations and points need to be taken into account:

13. The World Confessional Families differ in nature and organization. They can, therefore, not easily be considered as one group. Some of the member churches of the WCFs are not themselves members of the WCC. While some collaboration may be possible with all the WCFs, other areas of collaboration may need to be discussed and agreed upon with some or even one family, and in different regional settings with the active participation of relevant ecumenical organizations.

14. There is need to pursue with the World Confessional Families the discussion on the unity we seek and witness we present in the world. Concerted action in the service of the ecumenical movement is only possible if mutual understanding can be reached in this respect. The findings of the WCC Assemblies on the "visible unity in one faith and one eucharistic fellowship" should guide these discussions.

15. The growing number of bilateral conversations between World Confessional Families calls for a careful evaluation (cf. Discussion Paper, § 54 (ii)). Significant conclusions both at the theological and the practical level have been reached in these conversations. How can they effectively be related to the work of the WCC?

16. The Assembly *welcomes* the proposal that the World Confessional Families, in close collaboration with the Faith and Order Commission of the WCC, should establish a forum for the regular evaluation of bilateral conversations.

17. Co-operation should be developed in other fields. Closer contacts in the field of CWME, all aspects of Unit II, Theological Education Fund, etc., should be established. The Assembly recognizes the need for closer contacts with the WCFs in these fields and also the general new situation, and asks the Programme Units and Boards to strengthen the already existing co-operation with the WCFs.

18. Special attention needs to be paid to the place of United Churches in the ecumenical movement and especially to new relationships with the WCFs. At a recent meeting (Toronto, June 1975) representatives of all United Churches affirmed their commitment to the ecumenical movement and called for an open discussion about the implications of church union for the future of the ecumenical movement. Therefore, the Assembly *authorizes* the Faith and Order Secretariat to assist the United Churches in the furtherance of this discussion.

Relations with the Roman Catholic Church

Bishop Harms presented a Report based on the Fourth Report of the Joint Working Group (printed as Appendix 6) and referred also to the messages received from His Holiness the Pope and Cardinal Jan Willebrands (printed on pp. 153-155).

Dr Paul Minus (Methodist, USA) proposed an amendment, to add to the end of the penultimate paragraph of Section I of the Report after the words " . . . membership of the Roman Catholic Church" the further sentence, "This Assembly looks forward eagerly to the day when it will be possible for the Roman Catholic Church to become a member of the World Council of Churches".

Bishop Harms said that the Committee had considered this point carefully but had felt that there might be a new sense of frustration if the Roman Catholic Church were not to be in a position to join the WCC. The amendment was put to the vote and carried.

Dr R. McAfee Brown (Presbyterian, USA), who had been a Protestant Adviser at the Second Vatican Council, noted that Sunday, 8 December had been the tenth anniversary of the close of Vatican II, and urged unanimous adoption of the Report.

The Report was unanimously adopted. The text follows.

Relations with the Roman Catholic Church

I. General Considerations

Looking back at the period since Uppsala, this Fifth Assembly feels that there is much reason for gratitude to God. New perspectives of co-operation have been opened. A few may be mentioned:

(a) The theological discussion has led to new and unexpected results. Subjects which could not be taken up a few years ago have now become matters of common investigation. Bilateral conversations between the Roman Catholic Church and various confessional traditions have led to significant convergence which, although they await the judgement of some of the churches involved, provide a basis for advance towards fuller unity.

(b) Co-operation in the field of Bible translation has expanded beyond expectation. In many countries, the churches not only share the same text of translation, but co-operate in the distribution of the Bible.

(c) Increasingly, the Roman Catholic Church participates as a full member in regional, national, and local Councils. Recent publications of the Secretariat for Promoting Christian Unity of the Roman Catholic Church give significant encouragement in this direction.

At the same time, it must be recognized that in other areas the advance has become slower, even though mutual engagement has become irreversible. Nevertheless, a new situation has been created by the pace of advance in the past few years which must be viewed against the previous lack of progress seen in historical perspective. It is this accelerated pace, together with its consequent need for commitment, which presents new problems. The initial stage of encounter is over, and the churches now face the deeper problems of ecumenical fellowship.

Where are the obstacles? The principal difficulty has been to find ways to witness together as a fellowship of churches. The Roman Catholic Church is constituted as a universal community. Its belief that the one Church of Jesus Christ subsists in it does not exclude dialogue and co-operation with other churches, but the emphasis it places on its identity and proper initiative makes it difficult to act with other churches. The international juridical recognition given to the Holy See makes co-operation between it and the World Council of Churches especially difficult in areas like International Affairs (especially representation at the United Nations), and in Relief and Aid, etc. Similarly, the emphasis on identity of member churches of the World Council can create obstacles to further co-operation.

In order to prepare the way into the future, it will be necessary to reach a deeper mutual understanding of the "unity we seek" and provide a more solid basis for the common witness which is required in today's world. The opportunities offered by the full membership of Roman Catholic theologians in the Faith and Order Commission should be even more fully utilized in the years to come. The Fourth Report of the Joint Working Group contains a statement on the *Common Ground* (page 146 of *Workbook*—English edition) which may provide a useful starting point for further and more complete reflections. The forum suggested for the evaluation of bilateral conversations between the various confessional traditions could make an important contribution (page 152 of *Workbook* —English edition). The similarity of themes at recent important conferences of both the World Council of Churches and the Roman Catholic Church provides an encouraging sign for future development.

At the Uppsala Assembly, the issue of Roman Catholic membership in the World Council of Churches was raised. In the meantime, it has become clear that the Roman Catholic Church will not apply for membership in the immediate future. Nevertheless, this Assembly gladly agrees to work with the Roman Catholic Church according to the pattern which was established at the time of the Second Vatican Council and which has developed since. It remains convinced, however, that the unity of the Church can be visibly promoted through the concerted action of all churches embodied in a structural ecumenical fellowship. The World Council of Churches is one model of such a fellowship. This Assembly reiterates, therefore, the conviction stated at the Fourth Assembly concerning the membership of the Roman Catholic Church. This Assembly looks forward eagerly to the day when it will be possible for the Roman Catholic Church to become a member of the World Council of Churches.

Meanwhile, the significant developments which are taking place today at the regional, national, and local levels need to be encouraged and intensified, so that future co-operation may build upon the experience so gained. And, finally, this Assembly expresses the hope that, responsive to the renewing power of the Holy Spirit, both the World Council of Churches and the Roman Catholic Church may dare boldly to proclaim a more effective common witness.

II. Fourth Official Report of the Joint Working Group between the Roman Catholic Church and the World Council of Churches

The Assembly *approves* the Fourth Report.

In particular, it agrees to the setting up of a new Joint Working Group and expresses its agreement with the description of its mandate. It approves the general lines of the programme as described in Part IV; and expresses the hope that:

(i) the Joint Working Group will work out reports on specific aspects of the ecumenical movement, submit them regularly to the Central Committee and through the Central Committee to the member churches;

(ii) efforts be made to associate the member churches to the fullest possible extent in the work of the Joint Working Group and to build future work on the experience of dialogue, common witness, and collaboration at regional, national, and local levels;

(iii) particular attention will be given to the question of the role *and development* of ecumenical structures of collaboration of regional, national, and local levels, and to clarification of the relation of these structures to the concept of conciliar fellowship.

III. SODEPAX *(Committee on Society, Development, and Peace)*

The Assembly commends the activities of SODEPAX and agrees to the recommendation of the Joint Working Group as presented in its Fourth Report that SODEPAX continue for a further period of three years, beginning 1 January, 1976.

(The Policy Reference Committee II recommends that the comments on the Fourth Report of the Joint Working Group, submitted by the Secretariat for Promoting Christian Unity of the Roman Catholic Church, be incorporated in the official report of this Assembly.)

Comments on the Fourth Official Report by the Vatican Secretariat for Unity

1. *Unity* (see **Part I** a) The existing communion; **Part IV** 1) a) the unity of the Church).

The ecumenical movement has become a multi-faceted movement taking within the scope of its concern almost every aspect of church life and of human endeavour, thereby being enabled to make a rich contribution to Christian understanding and to the living of a Christian life in the contemporary world. Yet it loses its meaning unless it has as both its initial impulse and its ultimate goal the unity which is the gift of Christ to his faithful people. In our understanding, therefore, the essential characteristic of the ecumenical movement is a longing "for the one visible Church of God, a Church truly universal and sent forth to the whole world so that the world may be converted to the gospel and so be saved, to the glory of God" (*U.R.* 1).

There is a sense in which the unity of the Church is an end in itself since it is meant to be the living illustration of that mystery of unity which is the life of the Trinity (*U.R.* 2). This truth specifies both the nature and shape of the Church and its essential mission, to sum up all things in Christ. It is in this context that the Roman Catholic Church understands and affirms its service of the unity willed and given by our Lord Jesus Christ.

It is one of the important insights of the ecumenical movement that there is an already existing communion among Christians and that an urgent task for Christ's followers is the effort to give this correct and adequate expression (see *U.R.* 3). However, the scope of ecumenical endeavour has another necessary aspect. This communion is as yet incomplete. It is rendered so by important and even fundamental issues which still separate Christians. Thus ecumenism entails also the work of overcoming these separations, the sorting out of the causes of division by patient, careful effort done in full loyalty to the gospel teaching and to right conscience, so that full and perfect communion may eventually be achieved (*U.R.* 4). We believe that the Roman Catholic understanding of ecclesial communion, presented with openness of spirit, can be a positive contribution.

We believe that in stating this clearly we are giving a realistic orientation for the common research to be fostered by the Joint Working Group. It does mean that the promising insights offered by an understanding of conciliarity as a feature of the Church and its life ought to be developed in relation to, and without devaluation of, the notion of organic unity. It is in this context too that the possibilities and limits of a legitimate diversity within the life and expression of the Church may be understood.

Given such a context we can envisage the role of the Joint Working Group as one of encouragement for ecumenical efforts at the local level, stimulating awareness of the original ecumenical contribution which is to be expected from the diverse situations but always within the bonds which link the local community to the universal fellowship.

It is in this context too that we are able to welcome the idea that, with the approval and co-operation of the churches involved, there be established a forum for the exchange of information about the existing bilateral confessional dialogues, including those in which the Roman Catholic Church is engaged. This forum could also assist in the process of evaluating the emerging trends in the bilaterals and therefore be of benefit to the theological work of the Faith and Order Commission of the World Council of Churches and of ecumenical research generally. However, we do not see such a forum as a means of co-ordination of bilateral dialogues which remain the direct responsibility of the two partners, nor, except in a very general sense, as an advisory board.

2. *Common Witness* (see Part I b) Common witness; Part IV 1) b) common Christian witness).

The studies already undertaken by the Joint Working Group on this subject have been given a new actuality by the exhortation of the 1974 Synod of Bishops to "broader common witness to Christ". This common witness is central to the ecumenical task, but in attempting to carry it out we touch upon crucial ecumenical problems. The promise of the ecumenical movement is that there are convergences; its problem is that the convergences have not yet reached full maturity. These convergences are taking place on the level of our understanding of the fundamental Christian faith and on the level of our understanding of the nature and demands of ecclesial communion. The oneness we already share on both these levels warrants and impels us to a certain common witness. Where differences still exist on either of these levels so that we have not yet achieved a convergence in the perfect unity of the one Church of Christ, theological and pastoral reasons will require the establishment of certain limits to the common witness we are able to give. These limits are not to be determined *a priori*. They will be determined in specific cases according to the concrete objectives of common witness.

In this context the Joint Working Group will make its further inquiries into the question of common witness recommended in the Report. It will direct our attention again to the issues of unity, of fellowship, and of authentic doctrine, made more urgent than ever by the extent and the depth of those things we hold in common and which are drawing us closer together, as well as by the need of human beings for the faith and love of Christ.

3. *Development and Peace* (see Part IV 1) c)).

We believe the existence and work of SODEPAX are symbolic, in manifesting a common Christian response to an imperative which is an essential consequence of the gospel, and an effective means of enabling the World Council of Churches and the Roman Catholic Church to communicate and act together in the fields of justice and peace and to stimulate regional and local action.

Of its nature the scope of SODEPAX is limited. It cannot in any conceivable way cover the entire field of its particular subject. However, we believe its influence has been and can again be great as in its current programme it will seek to give to poor countries and poor Christian communities a voice in the search for a more just and sustainable world society.

4. *Ongoing Collaboration* (see Part IV 3) c)).

It seems to us the contacts and collaboration already taking place between the Roman Catholic Church and the World Council of Churches are greater than this section might indicate. Certainly we are convinced that matters listed under this head are important and that persevering and patient effort needs to be given to continuing and, wherever appropriate, expanding this kind of collaboration. In most cases it will take place in a step-by-step process, but we are sure it is necessary to continue wholeheartedly with this solid if unspectacular part of our relationship.

5. *The Joint Working Group* (see Part III).

The importance of the Joint Working Group lies in the visibility which it gives to the RCC/WCC relationship, the manifestation it affords of the mutual ecumenical commitment, and equally in the way in which it enables this relationship to be given practical expression. The reality of the relationship and its seriousness are expressed in the Report. Given that the Roman Catholic Church will not in the immediate future give expression to it by seeking membership in the Council, the role of the Joint Working Group becomes crucial.

We see the Joint Working Group as a point of co-ordination and reflection. It is to be an instrument by which the two separate bodies may co-ordinate both studies and activities. It is a kind of vantage point from which the ecumenical collaboration of the Roman Catholic Church and the World Council of Churches and its member churches can be surveyed, assessed, and promoted. It is a highly useful means of assessing what can be done in terms of resources and in terms of our respective theological understandings.

With the proposed re-structuring of the Joint Working Group we will be rendered more flexible and more effective. We intend as far as possible to organize our participation in it so that it will encourage and serve both ecumenical efforts on the international level and those that take place regionally and locally.

Monsignor Charles Moeller, General Secretary of the Secretariat for Promoting Christian Unity at the Vatican, was welcomed amidst applause to the platform and spoke as follows:

It has been of real importance for the Roman Catholic Church, although not a member of the World Council of Churches, to be associated with you on the occasion of this Fifth Assembly. Treating the theme: "Jesus Christ frees and unites", we have tried here in Nairobi to grapple with the truth that faith, its celebration and its practice, have their expression in a community of culture, history, and destiny. With you, we in the Roman Catholic Church are challenged radically at present by the pressing need to go beyond the admirable set of expressions of the Faith created in past times in a no longer dominant Western-Catholic culture. This means we have to ensure that expressions of these spiritual realities be specified, adapted, and, as it were, completed in the local churches on the basis of a full recognition of cultural circumstances.

In facing this enormous task, the Roman Catholic Church associates itself with the World Council of Churches and its member churches. Faithfulness to this task requires that the relationship between the Roman Catholic Church and the World Council of Churches should continue to become stronger and more effective. Pope Paul VI indicated this in his message of greeting to the Assembly as he told you of "the fraternal solidarity" of the Catholic Church with you on this occasion. The presence of a notable number of Roman Catholic observers appointed by the Holy See has in a certain way brought the Roman Catholic voice to the Assembly and as well affords a means of communication with our Church. And the Fourth Report of the Joint Working Group which you have now approved and which is officially and wholeheartedly accepted by the Roman Catholic Church marks out the path of our collaboration for the next few years.

In this Fourth Report we have together reflected on the deep sources of that communion between us, already begun but yet to be perfected. We have sought out possible areas for study and action in the years ahead; we have considered the work to be done by SODEPAX under its renewed mandate, and we have made proposals for reshaping the Joint Working Group so that it may be an effective instrument to promote the collaboration.

Struck by the challenge which the modern world offers to the Church and by the fear and anxiety with which countless people seek a meaning for life, we are convinced that what still divides us is ultimately less important than the gifts we hold in common, and that the witness we can even now give together to the content of the gospel is deeper and more impelling than those factors which still necessarily limit it. With you we want to engage in an ecumenism which is wholehearted and joyous and which tries faithfully to come to grips with the urgent task of expressing the gospel of Jesus Christ in the flesh of a specific, concrete humanity.

THE PROGRAMME GUIDELINES COMMITTEE AND THE FINANCE COMMITTEE

On 9 December, with Ms Pauline Webb as Moderator, the Report of the Programme Guidelines Committee was presented by Archbishop Sarkissian (Armenian Orthodox). The Assembly accepted with acclaim the recommendations concerning the report *Uppsala to Nairobi*.

Archbishop E.W. Scott (Anglican, Canada) spoke to the Report of the Finance Committee.

In response to a question, the General Secretary stated that the summary Report of the Hearings was an appendix to the Programme Guidelines Committee Report, and debate should concentrate on the Report itself. The full Reports of the Hearings would be sent to the Central Committee.

The Reverend Murray Rogers (Anglican, Jerusalem) and the Reverend Aram Keshishian (Armenian Orthodox) pleaded for more spirituality. Professor V. Istavridis (Ecumenical Patriarchate) objected on theological grounds to unacceptable details in the formulation of paragraph 12(b) on p. 6, one of which was accepted and incorporated.

The Report of the Programme Guidelines Committee was accepted.

Dr H.-R. Draeger (EKD, Germany) proposed a motion about the Ecumenical Institute. Archbishop Scott and the Reverend Oscar McCloud (United Presbyterian, USA) both said it would be inconsistent with the terms of the Finance Report to enter into any binding commitment. Bishop J. Matthews (Methodist, USA) asked that the Finance Committee examine the possibility of making a service charge for the large sums of money handled by the WCC. Dr Ernest Payne urged the Assembly to pay attention to the seriousness of the financial situation. Dr W. Keesecker (Presbyterian, USA) and Principal Engstrom (Mission Covenant Church, Sweden) were concerned in different ways about the relation between the Council and member churches.

In summing up, Archbishop Scott said that a vote in favour of the Finance Committee Report was also a personal commitment.

The Recommendations in the Report were voted upon individually and the Report as a whole approved by an overwhelming majority.

5. THE CLOSING CEREMONIES

RECEPTION AT CITY HALL

On Tuesday, 9 December, the participants in the Assembly were graciously entertained in the City Hall by the Mayor of Nairobi, Miss Margaret Kenyatta, and other civic leaders. The Mayor made a speech of welcome to which the General Secretary of the World Council, Dr Philip Potter, and the General Secretary of the National Christian Council of Kenya, Mr John Kamau, made replies.

A GIFT FROM THE KENYA CHURCHES

On Wednesday, 10 December, Bishop Imathiu, Chairman of the Local Arrangements Committee, said that the Committee and the Kenya churches had felt that participants should have a souvenir of the Assembly and were happy to present a pennant to each of them. Ms Pauline Webb, Vice-Moderator, presiding, said that this delightful gift would be a reminder of a happy time in Nairobi.

THE FINAL SESSION

Dr M.M. Thomas, Moderator, called upon Fr Pierre Duprey, a Delegated Observer of the Roman Catholic Church, to give some impressions of the Assembly. Speaking in French, he said that they had not observed the enormous labour of the Assembly from the outside but had shared from within the common search for the Christ whom we proclaim—the Christ who frees and unites us in him. They especially appreciated the effort to express this search for Christ in a prayer which surrounded and inspired our work.

It seemed that the Assembly marked a deepening maturity in the WCC's understanding. The basic attitudes at Uppsala were not called in question, but the Assembly had been forced to see them in a more total dimension—both spiritually and in terms of effective action.

A perception of the wholeness of reality can in fact inspire a more radical involvement. The Spirit draws us to *all* that Jesus said and did, and guides us with all truth. He draws us to a deeper conversion towards him who freed us by his sacrifice on the cross. We must make a choice for the whole, for it is the whole Christ we proclaim to all men.

So to choose the whole may lead those interested principally in partisan positions to the criticism that we have not made a choice, but to choose wholeness is the only possible choice for a Christian. "We detected this desire for integration in the speeches, reports, and Sections of the Assembly; but, of course, it is not yet achieved and we were, to be frank, sometimes taken aback by the speed with which documents were prepared and votes taken."

This attempt at integration is one of the essentials for a real progress towards unity, a unity which will the more respect diversity as it is the more rooted in the gospel.

Fr Duprey ended by expressing "our very lively gratitude".

The Moderator, amidst applause, thanked Fr Duprey for his words; and then called on the General Secretary to speak.

Dr Philip Potter spoke of the feeling of relief that we had reached this stage where we could *see* one another, having passed through times when the Assembly had seemed faceless—a matter of attitudes and structures, alienation and frustration. Yet in spite of all this and the difficulties of language, the gift of love had been among us, and had opened us to giving and to sharing. We began with this note and on this note we shall end.

We have been in conflict with one another, and there has been frustration and disillusionment. It has been painful. At Uppsala the mood was one of Exodus, going out to change the structures of society and the perspective of races. Now we find ourselves in the wilderness. A pilgrim people in conflict and penury, we have discovered a need for spirituality, a spirituality of penitence and hope. We have had to understand the inability of our churches and congregations to face together what it means to believe in Jesus Christ. Before the Assembly many people expected a confirmation between the different cultures. But what happened was exposure to one another in faith and common need. Dr Robert McAfee Brown set an example, which we began to follow and will need to go on pursuing in the WCC as well as in the churches; and we must pay much more attention to the relation between the member churches and the Council.

In a journey towards the Cross, the nearer we are to the Lord the more we stretch out our hands to one another. Only so will we find the true freedom to live in conflict and confusion.

Dr M. M. Thomas recognized and thanked the retired and retiring Presidents—Dr Akanu Ibiam, Dr Martin Niemöller, Bishop Hans Lilje, Ms Takeda Cho, Dr Ernest Payne—and the Honorary President, Dr W. A. Visser 't Hooft, who was not retiring. He mentioned gratefully the three retiring Presidents who were unable to be present, Bishop Alphaeus Zulu, Dr John Coventry Smith, and Patriarch German.

Dr Potter paid tribute to the officers of the retiring Central Committee, and in particular to Dr M. M. Thomas and Ms Pauline Webb, and to Metropolitan Meliton who was unable to be present.

Dr M. M. Thomas recognized the new Presidents of the World Council who were present: Ms Cynthia Wedel, Metropolitan Nikodim, General T. B. Simatupang, and Archbishop Olof Sundby.

He then thanked the WCC member churches in Kenya for the invitation to hold this Assembly here, and the National Christian Council of Kenya, who associated themselves with the invitation, and also the All Africa Conference of Churches. He particularly thanked the Local Arrangements Committee and its chairman. He thanked the Kenyan congregations for their invitation and hospitality; the staff of the Conference Centre; Menno Travel for the transport arrangements; East African Airways for the travel arrangements; members of the WCC staff, and in particular David Gill; the co-opted staff, including interpreters and translators; the stewards, under Mr Bethuel Kiplagat; the bus drivers, and the musicians of the Peter Janssens Song Orchestra. He then thanked Dr John Gatu, Canon Burgess Carr, and Mr John Kamau.

These proceedings were accompanied by happy and continuous applause.

Dr M.M. Thomas then brought the Business Sessions of the Fifth Assembly to a close with a final short personal address.

Dr Thomas said that it would take many days of reflection to make sense of these complex, crowded days. But, looking back, it seemed that we had begun rightly by affirming our solidarity in the personal and corporate confession of sin and divine forgiveness. This unity was sealed in the celebration of love in the prayer of worship service and the discussions of the work groups.

And then fears assailed us. Were we escaping from the tension and conflict of the world into a cheap unity? Would we be able to go on facing the issues of racism and development and at the same time take on issues not primarily central to our life—the liberation of women in church and society; the search for community in dialogue with those of other faiths; the struggle for people's participation and human rights? These are explosive; but there were sufficient spiritual roots to our unity to enable us to struggle together. It was important that there should have come from Pastor Bokaleale a passionate protest against the lack of eucharistic fellowship and a fresh and deeply felt reply from Professor Nissiotis. We look forward not merely to the day when the Roman Catholic Church may become a member of the WCC but to the day when the undivided Church can enable a "pre-conciliar WCC" to disappear.

More personally "M.M." spoke of his gratitude to our African hosts who had contributed so much and so variously, from the chance to meet African students in a small group to the provision by the government of Kenya of a special WCC stamp on our passports at immigration. He ended with a testimony of gratitude and love to the ecumenical movement which had meant so much to him for so long. "I am sure this Assembly has developed and extended that community throughout the world, and will sustain the movement in the years to come."

"With these words, I declare that the Business Session of the Fifth Assembly of the World Council of Churches is concluded."

IV
Appendices

Appendix 1
The Assembly Programme

Sunday, 23 November
16.45   Participants gather in the plaza area in front of the Ken-
               yatta Conference Centre
17.00-18.30   OPENING CELEBRATION, beginning in the plaza and
               moving into the Kenyatta Conference Centre

Monday, 24 November
08.30-10.00   OPENING SESSION OF THE FIFTH ASSEMBLY
10.30-12.30   PLENARY PRESENTATION
               "Jesus Christ frees and unites", by the United Bible Soci-
               eties
14.30-16.00   PLENARY
               Report of the Moderator of the Central Committee
16.30-18.00   PLENARY PRESENTATION
               Muntu—a play by Mr J. de Graft

Tuesday, 25 November
07.30-08.45   EUCHARISTIC CELEBRATION (Oriental Orthodox)
09.30-12.30   PLENARY PRESENTATION
               "Who is this Jesus Christ who frees and unites?" Professor
               Robert McAfee Brown and discussion
16.30-18.00   WORK GROUPS

Wednesday, 26 November
08.30-10.15   PLENARY
               Report of the General Secretary and discussion
10.45-12.30   PLENARY
               Finance Report
               Discussion of the Report of the General Secretary and the
               Finance Report
14.30-18.00   WORK GROUPS

Thursday, 27 November
08.30-10.00   PLENARY PRESENTATION
               "That all may be one . . ." Presented by Ms Mercy
               Oduyoye, Professor John Deschner, Rev. Cyril Argenti, Dr
               Manas Buthelezi, Rev. Gordon Gray, Rev. Wesley Ariarajah
10.30-12.30   WORK GROUPS and COMMITTEES
14.30-16.00   WORK GROUPS and COMMITTEES

16.30-18.00	PLENARY PRESENTATIONS
	" . . . That the world may believe"
	Address, Bishop Mortimer Arias
	Responses, Rev. John Stott, Ms R. Andriamanjato, Archbishop Samuel Carter, S.J.

Friday, 28 November
08.30-10.00	PLENARY PRESENTATION
	"Women in a changing world." Presented by Dr Sylvia Talbot, Ms Teny Simonian, Ms Dorothy McMahon, The Hon. Dr Julia Ojiambo, M.P., Dr Una Kroll, Justice Annie Jiagge, Archarn Prakai Nontawassee
10.30-12.30	BUSINESS SESSION
	Greetings and Messages
	Report of Credentials Committee
	Applications for Membership
	Report from Business Committee
14.30-16.00	SECTIONS
16.30-18.00	SECTIONS

Saturday, 29 November
08.30-10.00	PLENARY PRESENTATION
	"From shackles of domination and oppression"
	Address, H.E. The Right Hon. Michael Manley
10.30-12.30	SECTIONS
14.30-18.00	SECTIONS

Sunday, 30 November
| 10.00-12.00 | ADVENT RALLY, at Uhuru Park |
| | Speaker: Bishop Festo Kivengere |

Monday, 1 December
08.30-10.15	PLENARY PRESENTATION
	"Creation, technology and human survival"
	Address, Professor Charles Birch
	Responses, Metropolitan Paulos Gregorios, Professor Kosuke Koyama
10.30-12.30	HEARINGS
14.30-16.00	COMMITTEES
16.30-18.00	SECTIONS

Tuesday, 2 December
08.30-12.30	HEARINGS
14.00-15.10	PLENARY
	Committee Reports
15.15-16.00	WORSHIP (A Service of Anticipation) Dr E.C. Blake
16.30-18.30	RECEPTION (for Delegates only) at State House

Wednesday, 3 December
08.30-09.45	EUCHARISTIC CELEBRATION
	(A United Liturgy for East Africa)
10.30-12.30	HEARINGS
14.30-16.00	SECTIONS
16.30-18.00	WORK GROUPS

Thursday, 4 December
08.30-10.00   WORK GROUPS
10.30-12.30   HEARINGS
14.30-16.00   PLENARY
               Reports from Sections
16.30-18.00   PLENARY
               Reports from Sections

Friday, 5 December
08.30-10.15   PLENARY
               Reports from Sections
10.30-12.30   SECTIONS
14.30-16.00   COMMITTEES
16.30-18.00   COMMITTEES

Saturday, 6 December
08.30-10.00   PLENARY
               Committee Reports
10.30-12.30   SECTIONS
14.30-18.00   COMMITTEES
               (16.00-16.30 break)

Sunday, 7 December
Morning   WORSHIP with local congregations

Monday, 8 December
07.00-08.45   EUCHARISTIC CELEBRATION (Eastern Orthodox)
09.45-12.30   PLENARY
14.30-18.00   PLENARY

Tuesday, 9 December
08.30-12.30   PLENARY
               Reports
               (10.00-10.30 break)
14.30-17.30   PLENARY
               Reports
17.30-19.30   RECEPTION by the Mayor of Nairobi, Miss Margaret
               Kenyatta, at the City Hall
19.30-21.00   PLENARY
               Reports

Wednesday, 10 December
08.30-12.30   PLENARY
               Reports
14.30-16.30   PLENARY
               Reports
16.45-18.00   CLOSING ACTIONS
18.15-20.00   CLOSING WORSHIP

Appendix 2
The Assembly Officers and Committees and their Members

SECTION 1:
Moderator	Dr William LAZARETH (USA, Lutheran)
Vice-Moderators	Rev. Edwin TAYLOR (Bahamas, Methodist)
	Ms ANDRIAMANJATO (Madagascar, Reformed)
Secretary	Dr Nikos NISSIOTIS (Greece, Orthodox)

SECTION 2:
Moderator	Bp K. WOOLLCOMBE (UK, Anglican)
Vice-Moderators	Met. PARTHENIOS-ARIS (Ecumenical Patriarchate, Libya, Orthodox)
	Ms Jeanne Audrey POWERS (USA, Methodist)
Secretary	Rev. John THORNE (South Africa, Congregational)

SECTION 3:
Moderator	Met. Paulos GREGORIOS (India, Orthodox)
Vice-Moderators	Ms Mercy ODUYOYE (Ghana/Nigeria, Methodist)
	Dr Karoly TOTH (Hungary, Reformed)
Secretary	Principal Olle ENGSTROM (Sweden, Congregational)

SECTION 4:
Moderator	Mr Harry ASHMALL (UK, Reformed)
Vice-Moderators	Ms Constance TARASAR (USA, Orthodox)
	Mr BENA-SILU (Zaïre, Kimbanguist)
Secretary	Rev. Ron O'GRADY (New Zealand, Churches of Christ)

SECTION 5:
Moderator	Rev. John GATU (Kenya, Reformed)
Vice-Moderators	Bp ANTHONY of Romania (Romania, Orthodox)
	Ms Jean FAIRFAX (USA, United)
Secretary	Ms Dorothy McMAHON (Australia, Methodist)

SECTION 6:
Moderator	Ms Birgitta HAMBRAEUS (Sweden, Lutheran)
Vice-Moderators	Ms T. O. IHROMI (Indonesia, Reformed)
	Professor Nicolas ZABALOTSKY (USSR, Orthodox)
Secretary	Dr H. de LANGE (Netherlands, Congregational)

HEARING ON:

General Secretariat:
Moderator	Ms Marion KELLERAN (USA, Anglican)
Vice-Moderators	Met. NIKODIM (USSR, Orthodox)
	Ms C. LATUIHAMALLO (Indonesia, Reformed)
Secretary	Dr André APPEL (France, Lutheran)

Unit I:
Moderator	Met. I. HAZIM (Syria, Orthodox)
Vice-Moderators	Dr von STIEGLITZ (FRG, United)
	Ms Janet HENDERSON (UK, Anglican)
Secretary	Dr Emerito NACPIL (Philippines, Methodist)

Unit II:
Moderator	Ms Annie JIAGGE (Ghana, Reformed)
Vice-Moderators	Professor Todor SABEV (Bulgaria, Orthodox)
	Bp John ADAMS (USA, Methodist/AME)
Secretary	Ms Teny SIMONIAN (Lebanon, Orthodox)

Unit III:
Moderator	Dr Paul CROW (USA, Disciples)
Vice-Moderators	Ms Michiko OKUDA (Japan, United)
	Mr Hans-Rolf DRAEGER (FRG, Lutheran)
Secretary	Rev. A. H. MacLEOD (New Zealand, Baptist)

WORKSHOP ON:

Spirituality:
Moderator	Abp F.D. COGGAN (UK, Anglican)
Secretary	Rev. Oka FAU'OLO (Western Samoa, Congregational)

Youth:
Moderator	Professor Samuel AMIRTHAM (India, CSI)
Secretary	Ms Jan LOVE (USA, Methodist)

COMMITTEE ON:

Nominations:
Moderator	Dr Robert MARSHALL (USA, Lutheran)
Secretary	Professor Anwar BARKAT (Pakistan, United)

Programme Guidelines:
Moderator	Abp SARKISSIAN (Lebanon, Orthodox)
Vice-Moderator	Dr Koson SRISANG (Thailand, Reformed)
Secretary	Ms Jean SKUSE (Australia, Methodist)

Credentials:
Moderator	Dr Won Yong KANG (Korea, Reformed)
Secretary	Ms Jean WOOLFOLK (USA, Disciples)

Worship:
Moderator	Mr David JOHNSON (USA, Anglican)
Vice-Moderator	Met. FILARET (USSR, Orthodox)

Press and Broadcasting:
Moderator	Bp Henry OKULLU (Kenya, Anglican)
Vice-Moderator	Mr Penry JONES (UK, Reformed)—Adviser

Finance:
Moderator	Abp E.W. SCOTT (Canada, Anglican)
Vice-Moderator	Dr R. PAYNE (Liberia, Lutheran)
Secretary	Dr Heinz-Joachim HELD (FRG, United)

Work Groups and Message:
Moderator	Dr Albert v.d. HEUVEL (Netherlands, Reformed)
Vice-Moderator	Met. JUVENALY (USSR, Orthodox)
Secretary	Ms Constance PARVEY (USA, Lutheran)

Policy Reference Committee I
(Reports of Chairman and General Secretary; Constitutional matters, etc.)
Moderator	Ms Theressa HOOVER (USA, Methodist)
Vice-Moderator	Mr Albert LAHAM (Lebanon, Orthodox)
Secretary	Ms Helena LASSEUR (Netherlands, Reformed)

Policy Reference Committee II
(Applications for membership, Report of Joint Working Group including SODEPAX, Relations with World Confessional Families, etc.)
Moderator	Bp H.H. HARMS (FRG, Lutheran)
Vice-Moderator	Bp SAMUEL (Egypt, Orthodox)
Secretary	Ms Margaret YOUNGQUIST (USA, Reformed)

Policy Reference Committee III
(Public Affairs)
Moderator	General T.B. SIMATUPANG (Indonesia, Reformed)
Vice-Moderator	Mr William THOMPSON (USA, Reformed)
Secretary	Ms Kerstin ANER (Sweden, Lutheran)

ASSEMBLY BUSINESS COMMITTEE

The Business Committee consisted of:

The Presidents of the WCC;
Members of the retiring Executive Committee;
Moderators of
 the Policy Reference Committees,
 the Nominations Committee,
 the Finance Committee,
 the Programme Guidelines Committee,
 the Worship Committee,
 the Press and Broadcasting Committee,
 and the Work Groups and Message Committee;
Moderators of the six Sections;
Moderators of the four Hearings;
Chairman of the Local Arrangements Committee;
Moderators of the two Workshops;
A representative under the age of 30 of the Youth Workshop;
Dr M.M. Thomas (Moderator);
Dr Philip Potter (Secretary).

NOMINATIONS COMMITTEE

Dr Robert MARSHALL	Lutheran (USA, *Moderator*)
Met. VLADIMIR	Orthodox (USSR)

218

Ms Joan Marian ANDERSON — Presbyterian (New Zealand)
Ms Carmen LUSAN — Methodist (Caribbean)
Dr Jean KOTTO — Evangelical (Cameroon)
Prof. Anwar M. BARKAT — United (Pakistan, *Secretary*)

Dr Helmut HILD — Evangelical (FRG)
Rt Rev. Alexander Mar THEOPHILUS — Mar Thoma (India)
Rev. Jona H. WIAKOTAN — Reformed (Indonesia)
Dr Won Yong KANG — Reformed (Korea)
Ms Bodil SØLLING — Lutheran (Denmark)
Rev. Jacques MAURY — Reformed (France)
Abp I. HARKIANAKIS — Orthodox (Ec. Patr.)
Dr George BEBAWI — Orthodox (Egypt)
Rev. Ewen D. CAMERON — Anglican (Australia)
Mr Kifle MELAKU — Orthodox (Ethiopia)
Dr Josiah KIBIRA — Lutheran (Tanzania)
Met. Parthenios COINIDES — Orthodox (Libya)
Dr Robert WALLACE — United (Canada)
Mr Enilson ROCHA SOUZA — Pentecostal (Brazil)
Ms Jean FAIRFAX — United (USA)
Mr Johannes CIESLAK — Lutheran (DDR)
Ms Kathy JOHNSON — Baptist (USA)
Ms Nancy DENNIS — Methodist (Ghana)
Rev. W. B. JOHNSTON — Reformed (UK)
Bishop LAVRENTIJE — Orthodox (Yugoslavia)
Bishop Frederick JORDAN — AME (USA)

PROGRAMME GUIDELINES COMMITTEE

Mother Natalia NITA — Orthodox (Romania)
Prof. Vitaly BOROVOY — Orthodox (USSR)
Rev. Christoph HINZ — United (DDR)
Mr Jan ANCHIMIUK — Orthodox (Poland)
Prof. Joseph SMOLIK — Reformed (CSSR)
Bp Zoltan KALDY — Lutheran (Hungary)
Bp DOMINITIAN — Orthodox (Bulgaria)
Abp F. Donald COGGAN — Anglican (UK)
Dr André APPEL — Lutheran (France)
Dr W.M.S. WEST — Baptist (UK)
Ms Marja van der VEEN — Reformed (Netherlands)
Rev. Henrik SVENUNGSSON — Lutheran (Sweden)
Bp Yannoulatos ANASTASIOS — Orthodox (Greece)
Dr Hans Otto WOLBER — Lutheran (FRG)
Rev. Johannes LANGHOFF — Lutheran (Denmark)
Ms Julia RODUNER-LAEDRACH — Reformed (Switzerland)
Met. Paul MENEVISOGLOU — Orthodox (Ec. Patr.)
Dr Koson SRISANG — Reformed (Thailand, *Vice-Moderator*)

Prof. Samuel AMIRTHAM — United (India)
Dr Emerito NACPIL — Methodist (Philippines)
Ms Chitra FERNANDO — Anglican (Sri Lanka)

Dr Chung-Hyun RO	Reformed (Korea)
Rt Rev. John SAMUEL	United (Pakistan)
Prof. Franz SIANIPAR	Lutheran (Indonesia)
Rev. Tetsuro NISHIMURA	Anglican (Japan)
Ms Annie JIAGGE	Reformed (Ghana)
His Grace ATHANASIOS	Or. Orthodox (Egypt)
Mr Joel OBIANG-ONDO	Reformed (Gabon)
Mr Julien AYITE	Methodist (Dahomey)
Mrs Marie MOMO	United (Cameroon)
Rev. August HABELGAARN	Moravian (South Africa)
Ms Clara MEADOWS	Ch. Lord Aladura (Nigeria)
Dr Marion KELLERAN	Anglican (USA)
Ms Janice LOVE	Methodist (USA)
Prof. Warren QUANBECK	Lutheran (USA)
Prof. John DESCHNER	Methodist (USA)
Mr David JOHNSON	Anglican (USA)
Dr John ROBINSON	United (USA)
Ms Letty RUSSELL	Reformed (USA)
Dr Paul CROW	Disciples (USA)
Ms Lois MILLER	Methodist (USA)
Ms Marlyne MYLES	United (Canada)
Mr Arturo BLATESKY	United (Argentina)
Rt Rev. Neville de SOUZA	Anglican (Jamaica)
Abp Karekin SARKISSIAN	Or. Orthodox (USA/ Lebanon, *Moderator*)
Ms Teny SIMONIAN	Or. Orthodox (Lebanon)
Met. Ignatios HAZIM	Orthodox (Syria)
Ms Jean SKUSE	Methodist (Australia, *Secretary*)
Rev. Angus MacLEOD	Baptist (New Zealand)
Rev. Leslie BOSETO	United (Papua-New Guinea)

FINANCE COMMITTEE

Rt Rev. Jeremiah KANGSEN	Reformed (Cameroon)
Dr R.J. PAYNE	Lutheran (Liberia, *Vice-Moderator*)
Ms Janet WESONGA	Anglican (Uganda)
Mr Victor KUNDYA	Lutheran (Tanzania)
Dr Peter WONG	United (Hong Kong)
Mr Padinjarekara ABRAHAM	Oriental Orthodox (India)
Mr Renato MALVAR	Independent (Philippines)
Bp G.D. LEONARD	Anglican (UK)
Dr Heinz-Joachim HELD	United (FRG)
Ms Hildegard ZUMACH	United (FRG)
Dr Govaert KOK	Old Catholic (Netherlands)
Rt Rev. Antonie PLAMADEALA	Orthodox (Romania)
Most Rev. Olof SUNDBY	Lutheran (Sweden)
Met. D. PAPANDREOU	Orthodox (Ec. Patr.)

Dr David PREUS	Lutheran (USA)
Ms A. Jean WOOLFOLK	Disciples (USA)
Mr John Thomas FISHER	Episcopalian (USA)
Rev. James E. ANDREWS	Reformed (USA)
Rev. J. Oscar McCLOUD	Reformed (USA)
Rev. Dr Robert V. MOSS	United (USA)
Bp Ralph Taylor ALTON	Methodist (USA)
Rev. Dr Tracey K. JONES	Methodist (USA)
Most Rev. Edward Walter SCOTT	Anglican (Canada, *Moderator*)
Rev. Donald G. RAY	United (Canada)
Ms Dorinda SAMPATH	United (Trinidad)
Rev. Russell Neil GILMORE	Disciples (Australia)
Rev. Dr Ernest Alexander PAYNE	Baptist (UK, WCC *President*)
Rev. Hans Otto HAHN	Lutheran (FRG, *Adviser*)
Dr Paul Frederick McCLEARY	Methodist (USA, *Adviser*)
Rev. John Masaaki NAKAJIMA	United (Japan, *Fraternal Delegate*)
Rev. Dr Kenneth SLACK	Reformed (UK, *Fraternal Delegate*)

WORSHIP COMMITTEE

Ms Pauline Mary WEBB	Methodist (UK)
Ms Sylvia Lee WRIGHT	Pentecostal (Brazil)
Mr David Enderton JOHNSON	Anglican (USA, *Moderator*)
Rev. Kondothra Mathew GEORGE	Syrian Orthodox (India)
Bp Inkomo BOYAKA	Disciples (Zaïre)
His Eminence FILARET	Orthodox (USSR, *Vice-Moderator*)
Abp F. OLANG'	Anglican (Kenya, *Guest*)
Prof. Masao TAKENAKA	United (Japan, *Adviser*)
Fr Charles Murray ROGERS	Anglican (Jerusalem, *Adviser*)
Rev. Frederik Herman KAAN	Reformed (UK, *Adviser*)
Ms Doreen Ethel Olive POTTER	Methodist (Jamaica, *Adviser*)

CREDENTIALS COMMITTEE

Rev. Dr Won-Yong KANG	Reformed (Korea, *Moderator*)
Ms A. Jean WOOLFOLK	Disciples (USA, *Secretary*)
Ms Betty Campbell GRAHAM	Anglican (Canada)
Abp Donald ARDEN	Anglican (Malawi)
Mr Heinz-Hermann NORDHOLT	Reformed (FRG)
Very Rev. Ioann ORLOV	Orthodox (USSR)

Rev. Dr David Syme RUSSELL	Baptist (UK)
Rt Rev. Jeremiah Chi KANGSEN	Presbyterian (Cameroon)
Ms Anaseini QIONIBARAVI	Methodist (Fiji)
Dr Andreas MITSIDES	Orthodox (Cyprus)

PRESS AND BROADCASTING COMMITTEE

Bp Henry OKULLU	Anglican (Kenya, *Moderator*)
Mr Penry JONES	Reformed (UK, *Vice-Moderator*)
Ms Benita JOHANSON	Lutheran (Finland)
Ms Olivia Pearl STOKES	Baptist (USA)
Mr DHAMARAJ	United (India)

WORKGROUPS AND MESSAGE COMMITTEE

Rev. Dr Albert VAN DEN HEUVEL	Reformed (Netherlands, *Moderator*)
Rev. Constance F. PARVEY	Lutheran (USA, *Secretary*)
Rev. Dr Kenneth GREET	Methodist (UK)
Met. JUVENALY	Orthodox (USSR, *Vice-Moderator*)
Rev. Doyce Mwelwa MUSUNSA	United (Zambia)
Mr John Elliott KITAGAWA	Anglican (USA)
Prof. Basil ANAGNOSTOPOULOS	Orthodox (Ec. Patr.)
Rev. Chris A. KITING	Reformed (Indonesia)
Dr Johannes Wilhelm HEMPEL	United (DDR)
Ms Ana Beatriz FERRARI	Methodist (Argentina)

ex officio

Moderator of Press and Broadcasting Committee (Rt Rev. Dr Henry OKULLU, Anglican)
Editor of Assembly Report (Canon David M. PATON, Anglican)

POLICY REFERENCE COMMITTEE I

Ms Theressa HOOVER	Methodist (USA, *Moderator*)
Mr Albert LAHAM	Orthodox (Lebanon, *Vice-Moderator*)
Rev. Goro TOKUNAGA	United (Japan)
Rev. Paul Hein ROMPAS	Reformed (Indonesia)
Bp Estanilao ABAINZA	Reformed (Philippines)
Ms Shanti Rajeshwari SOLOMON	United (India)
Pastor Albert Theodore NYEMB	Reformed (Cameroon)
Bp PAULOS	Orthodox (Ethiopia)
Rt Rev. Gottfried Kwadwo SINTIM-MISA	Reformed (Ghana)
Rev. Dr Sione Amanaki HAVEA	Methodist (Tonga)

Abp Allen Howard JOHNSTON	Anglican (New Zealand)
Rev. John Percival BROWN	Presbyterian (Australia)
Mr Oscar Milburn BIRD	Anglican (Caribbean)
Prof. Dr Gerhard GROHS	United (FRG)
Ms Olga DYSTHE	Lutheran (Norway)
Ms Helena LASSEUR	Reformed (Netherlands, *Secretary*)
Ms Eileen Margaret STEEL	Reformed (UK)
Mr John Wallace BULLIMORE	Anglican (UK)
Mr Kriton CHRYSSOCHOIDIS	Orthodox (Greece)
Mr Ivan GELEV (Dimitrou)	Orthodox (Bulgaria)
Prof. Dr Stojan GOSEVIC	Orthodox (Yugoslavia)
Rt Rev. Dr Petros Arsen BERBERIAN	Armenian (USSR)
Rev. Mother Lucia J. DUMBRAVA	Orthodox (Romania)
Rev. Prof. Gerassimos Chrysostomos ZAPHIRIS	Orthodox (Jerusalem)
Rev. Dr Donald Cantlay SMITH	Reformed (Canada)
Dr Thomas KILGORE, Jr.	Baptist (USA)
Dr Arnold R. MICKELSON	Lutheran (USA)
Rev. Dr Marion de VELDER	Reformed (USA)
Rt Rev. Dr Aimo Tauno NIKOLAINEN	Lutheran (Finland)
Rt Rev. Leonid Svistoun MAKARY	Orthodox (USSR)
Rt Rev. Per LØNNING	Lutheran (Norway)

POLICY REFERENCE COMMITTEE II

(Certain Delegated Observers and Fraternal Delegates were invited to attend certain of the sessions of this Committee.)

Bp Hans Heinrich HARMS	Lutheran (FRG, *Moderator*)
His Grace Bp Cairo-Abbaseya SAMUEL	Orthodox (Egypt, *Vice-Moderator*)
Bp L. Easter RAJ	Lutheran (India)
Ms Margaret Ann YOUNGQUIST	Lutheran (USA, *Secretary*)
Rt Rev. Tuhwan Mark PAE	Anglican (Korea)
Ms Daisy GOPAL RATNAM	United (India)
Rev. Ms Augustina LUMENTUT	Reformed (Indonesia)
Rev. Zablon John NTHAMBURI	Methodist (Kenya)
Pastor Raymond BUANA KIBANGI	Reformed (Congo-Brazzaville)
Bp Timothy Omotayo OLUFOSOYE	Anglican (Nigeria)
Prof. Josias Ibinyane MOHAPELOA	Reformed (Lesotho)
Rev. Geoffrey Leon BARNES	Reformed (Australia)
Mr Isaac MULUNGU	United (Papua-New Guinea)
Abp Arthur Rolopho KRATZ	Anglican (Brazil)
Rev. Prof. Martin Hawley CRESSEY	Reformed (UK)
Ms Mary Kenning BOYD	Reformed (Ireland)
Ms Fernanda COMBA	Waldensian (Italy)
Dr André Julien PIETERS	United (Belgium)
Prof. Dr Roger MEHL	Reformed (France)
Rev. Thomas HOPKO	Orthodox (USA)
Dr Ursula BUSCHLUTER	Old Catholic (DDR)

Prof. Dr Dumitru POPESCU	Orthodox (Romania)
Ms Annette HUTCHINS-FELDER	Methodist (USA)
Dr Jorge LARA-BRAUD	Reformed (USA)
Rev. Dr David M. STOWE	United (USA)
Bp Anastasios YANNOULATOS	Orthodox (Greece)
Very Rev. Arch. KIRILL GOUNDIAEV	Orthodox (USSR)
Bp N.D. Anandarao SAMUEL	United (India)
Rev. Prof. Norman James YOUNG	Methodist (Australia)
Dr. Robert CAMPBELL	Baptist (USA)
Dr Jacques ROSSEL	Reformed (Switzerland)
Dr Carlos CARRASCO	Methodist (Peru, *Fraternal Delegate*)
Rev. Manuel SILVA DE MELLO	Pentecostal (Brazil)

POLICY REFERENCE COMMITTEE III

Dr Tahi B. SIMATUPANG	Reformed (Indonesia, *Moderator*)
Mr William P. THOMPSON	Reformed (USA, *Vice-Moderator*)
Ms Kerstin ANER	Lutheran (Sweden, *Secretary*)
Prof. George KOSHY	United (India)
Mr Somchai OBBOON	Reformed (Thailand)
Commissioner Gladys M. CALLISS	Salvation Army (Sri Lanka)
Rev. Abel E. HENDRICKS	Methodist (South Africa)
Pastor Harry Y. HENRY	Methodist (Dahomey)
Rev. Wilson T. LWANGA-MUGERWA	Anglican (Uganda)
Ms Julienne MAKANY	Reformed (Congo-Brazzaville)
Rev. Fred Karlo TIMAKATA	Reformed (New Hebrides)
Mr Geoffrey BRENNAN	Anglican (Australia)
Bp Helmut FRENZ	Lutheran (Chile)
Ms Ivy D. KIRKCALDY	United (Jamaica)
Prof. Kjell SKJELSBAEK	Lutheran (Norway)
Dr Ullrich LOCHMANN	United (FRG)
Rev. John E. RICHARDSON	Methodist (UK)
Rev. Jaakko M. RUSAMA	Lutheran (Finland)
Rev. Dr Eduard WILDBOLZ	Reformed (Switzerland)
Mr Alexey S. BUEVSKY	Orthodox (USSR)
Rev. Alexei BICHKOV	Baptist (USSR)
Bp Albert KLEIN	Reformed (Romania)
Bp Dr Tibor BARTHA	Reformed (Hungary)
Rev. Albert ISTEERO	Reformed (Lebanon)
Congressman John BRADEMAS	Methodist (USA)
Ms Julia ESTRELLA	United (USA)
Rev. Robert LELAND	Disciples (Canada)
Archimandrite Cornelios E. RODOUSSAKIS	Orthodox (Israel)
Bp Janusz NARZYNSKI	Lutheran (Poland)
Met. Georges KHODRE	Orthodox (Lebanon)
Vizepräsident Hans-Philipp MEYER	Lutheran (FRG)

Rev. Pedro MAYOR-MONTES	Methodist (Cuba, *Fraternal Delegate*)
Mr José M. LEITE	Reformed (Portugal, *Fraternal Delegate*)
Ambassador Olle DAHLEN	Reformed (Sweden, *Adviser*)

Note: WCC Presidents and members of the Central Committee not already assigned above were free to sit in on any of the three policy reference committees.

Appendix 3
The Report of the Moderator of the Central Committee

1. As Moderator of the Central Committee of the World Council of Churches, it is my privilege and pleasure to welcome you all to the Fifth Assembly of the Council.

2. As we meet today, we remember the many leaders of the World Council of Churches who were with us at the time of the last Assembly but are no longer with us today. I must make special mention of those who were members of our Presidium—J. H. Oldham, Archbishop Fisher, D. G. Moses, and D. T. Niles. Joe Oldham was closely associated with the ecumenical movement from its first organized beginnings in Edinburgh 1910; largely to his vision we owe many aspects of the movement—as, for instance, dialogue between theologians and lay experts on the witness of the Church in the secular world, the recognition of racism in Africa and elsewhere as a crucial Christian issue, and the acceptance of study as a primary responsibility. It was under Fisher's chairmanship that the World Council of Churches was formally constituted at Amsterdam in 1948, and he supported its work through the years. I recollect his intervention at the Chichester meeting of the Central Committee to amend the Statement on Totalitarianism by adding the crucial sentence: "Religious freedom is the foundation and guardian of all other freedoms." D. G. Moses was associated with the International Missionary Council for many years; after its integration with the WCC, he became a President of the WCC in 1961. A philosopher in the tradition of A. G. Hogg, he was from the days of the meeting of the International Missionary Council at Tambaram engaged in working out an approach to the relation between Christianity and other religions—an approach which goes beyond that of Hocking, Radhakrishnan, and Kraemer. D. T. Niles was the ecumenical preacher from Tambaram 1937, through Amsterdam 1948, to Uppsala 1968. He promoted dialogue between churches and missions on the implications of the emerging selfhood of the churches in the Two Thirds world, helped give regional expression to the ecumenical movement in Asia, and was fully involved in the movement for church union in Ceylon which is soon to be realized. Let us thank God for these and other founding fathers of the World Council of Churches, and for all those who have brought us to where we are now, and pray that we may be worthy of the heritage they have left us.

THE FIFTH ASSEMBLY IN PERSPECTIVE

3. WCC Assemblies have always had an element of the unpredictable about them. The present one is not likely to be an exception—not only because of the greater geographical, cultural, and confessional diversity it represents, but also because of the larger proportion in its voting membership of pastors of local congregations, lay men and women, and youth, and the very large percentage of delegates attending the Assembly for the first time.[1] Furthermore, meeting as we are for the first time on the African continent, the Assembly is bound to feel more strongly than other such meetings the impact of the human and the Christian climate of renascent Africa on its corporate thought, emotion, and will. All these urge us to be expectant, to be prayerfully sensitive to the Spirit of God who blows where he wills, and to hear the voice of God speaking a new word to us, amidst the noise and in the silences of our gatherings.

4. For the last seven years, the work of the Council has been carried on within the mandate given by the last Assembly. It has been in the hands of the Secretariat under the direction of the Central Committee elected at Uppsala. Not that they were left on their own. In fact, during these years, the member churches have been involved in a continual dialogue with one another and with the Secretariat and the Central Committee, and they in their turn have sought not only to keep the churches and the public informed of what they were thinking and doing, but also to respond to what they heard the churches and the public saying to them. And this is as it should be. We have had a very competent Secretariat which is increasingly becoming representative of the world-wide fellowship. Under the able guidance of the General Secretary (Eugene Carson Blake till 1972, and Philip Potter since then) it has done a magnificent job of implementing, in consultation with the Central Committee, the policies it had laid down. I want to take this opportunity to express our appreciation to the staff on behalf of us all. Over the years, the Central Committee has been able to keep within a fellowship of mutual trust centred in Jesus Christ the inevitable tensions and conflicts of a world body involved in the diversities and divisions of the world. The Presidium elected by the Uppsala Assembly, consisting of Hon. President W. A. Visser 't Hooft and Presidents Patriarch German, Bishop Zulu, Bishop Lilje, Ernest Payne, John Coventry Smith, D. T. Niles (till 1970), and Mrs Takeda Cho (since 1971), has brought to those meetings of the Central and Executive Committees which they attended the richness of their mature experience and wisdom; and for this we are grateful. Metropolitan Meliton, Pauline Webb, and I consider it a privilege to have chaired the Central and Executive Committee meetings. Every three months we have met as officers with the General Secretary (and sometimes also with the chairman of the Finance Committee, the Earl of March) to review the day-to-day work of the Council.

5. When I think of this Assembly and what it may mean for the future, of the seven years since we last met, and of the years before them, my dominant feeling is one of deep thankfulness to God for the World Council of Churches and the larger ecumenical movement of which it is the privileged instrument. Through the World Council, the churches throughout the world have expressed their commitment to fellowship—not a fellowship of human good will but of common celebration of the Christ-event and common exploration into the truth and meaning of that

event for us all and for all humanity and of common action. Celebration and exploration have always been held together in the ecumenical movement—the joyful celebration of the Communion which God has given us in the Church as the basis for our continuing exploration of ways by which we may heal the wounds of division; the exaltation of the resurrection-power of the crucified Jesus present in the world as the ground of our common striving to share his suffering in the world and to know him and the power of his resurrection; our joyous expectation of the coming of his Kingdom at the End as the foundation of our search together for ways in which we may give an account of the hope that is in us to the many who question us. Indeed, we press on to make this hope our own, because Christ Jesus has made us his own (Phil. 3.12). This gracious divine initiative is our starting point—for our understanding of the ecumenical movement as well as for our approach to the celebrations and the deliberations of this Assembly. As Archbishop Temple once said, no human agency has planned this—it is the work of God. No doubt we have our share of disappointments and regrets. The Roman Catholic Church is not yet a full member of our fellowship as we hoped at Uppsala that it might be; we do not have here representatives of the Church from the People's Republic of China; the goal of eucharistic fellowship still eludes us. And there are many who have begun to speak of the crisis of the ecumenical movement; in some quarters there is a weariness in the ecumenical spirit and a great deal of disillusion with the institutional expressions of ecumenism. But our expectations for this Assembly are based on our faith that the God who has begun the good work of uniting us to be a witness to himself is faithful and able to accomplish his purpose. We are a generation privileged to experience and participate in a happening which God himself has brought about. If only we allow ourselves to be caught up by the movement of the Holy Spirit, we shall receive the power of spiritual discernment and see the glory of the transfigured Jesus, the glory of God, in our midst.

FOR THE SAKE OF THE WORLD

6. The book *Uppsala to Nairobi* is the Central Committee's report and self-evaluation of its stewardship in the last seven years. I presume all of you have read it. You, as the Assembly of the Council, will have an opportunity to evaluate its work in the Hearings. In my report, I do not wish to repeat anything that has already been set out in detail in the book. It seems to me that it will be more useful if I, as one who has been part insider and part outsider in the day-to-day work of the Council during the period, share with you a few of my personal reflections on that work and on the task of this Assembly. I shall look at these from one particular perspective—namely, our new theological understanding of the relation between the Church and the world. It is not my primary intention to be either defensive or critical; I merely wish to start an open dialogue on the theological basis or bases of the ecumenism of the late '70s, a dialogue which, I hope, will go on throughout the Assembly.

7. I recall what David L. Edwards, then Dean of King's College, Cambridge, said, commenting on Uppsala—that "for the sake of the world the next Assembly should be more theological".[2] It is indeed for the sake of the world that God became man in Jesus Christ. The heart of the gospel is that God loved the *world* so much that he gave his only begotten Son to be its salvation (John 3.16), that God was in Christ, reconciling the *world* unto himself (2 Cor. 5.19). Therefore, if at any time we have done theology for any purpose other than the world, we were not being Christian. Looking at the main themes of the Assemblies of the WCC— *Man's Disorder and God's Design;*[3] *Jesus Christ, the Hope of the World;*[4] *Jesus Christ, the Light of the World;*[5] and *Behold, I Make All Things New*[6]—we can affirm with justice that "God's Purpose for the World in Jesus Christ" has indeed been our basic theme throughout. The Christ-centredness of the Council makes the world central to its theological orientation. Theology is alive only at the cutting edge between the Word and the world.

8. Since New Delhi 1961 and Uppsala 1968, ecumenism has been marked by two thrusts which have made it theologically distinct from the position during the earlier period of the WCC. First, the theological impact of the integration of the Faith and Order, Life and Work, and missionary movements. The three separate streams have coalesced into one mighty flow, and this has produced an interaction at theological and spiritual depth between the ecumenical concerns for unity, mission, and service. While each concern is distinct and should remain so in order to retain its identity, each has been forced to define itself more explicitly in the context of the other two. This has brought the problems and tasks of formulating a new theological redefinition of the three concerns.

9. Secondly, a deeper awareness of the contemporary realities of the world has made its own theological impact on ecumenism. This has been experienced through three channels. The large number of churches of eastern Europe, Africa, Asia, and the Pacific, the Caribbean, and Latin America have brought with them into the Council the hopes, aspirations, and struggles of their peoples, races, and nations. For the first time, they have ceased to be external objects for observation and become internal subjective realities of the Council's fellowship. The Council has also listened to the poor, the marginalized, and the oppressed people with a new sensitivity. Further, the lay experts with whom the Council has consulted constantly on social questions, especially in the 1966 World Conference on Church and Society, and, more recently, the technologists, the natural and social scientists, and the politicians, who have come together with theologians to consider their own Christian vocation or the Church's mission in the secular world of international affairs, of world development, and of the struggle for racial and social justice, have brought to the Council a new awareness of the problems and tasks facing the contemporary world. The world has come alive in a new way: the world of rapid social change, diverse cultures, different religions, and conflicting ideologies; the world of poverty and the awakening poor; the world of national and racial revolts, and of movements for social liberation; the world, in short, in which mankind is seeking unity in and through a variety of forces. As D. T. Niles commented, Uppsala placed Christians and churches "in and with the world rather than over against it".[7] As a result, most of our traditional understandings of and responses to the world lie

shattered, and this demands of us fresh theological exploration at many levels. The Council has come to realize that the life and mission of the Church must be rethought in the context of, and in challenging relevance to, the human issues agitating mankind in our present historical situation. And, conversely, it has also realized that the contemporary world is prepared to listen to the Church's interpretation of the human issues of our time only if this interpretation is set within the context of the Church's faith in and witness to the renewal of all things in Jesus Christ.

10. Let me illustrate this interrelational approach of "contemporary ecumenism" from the developments and debates in the World Council of Churches on church unity and world evangelism, on the one hand, and on the quality of life, world service and development, and human liberation on the other.

UNITY OF THE CHURCH AND HUMAN ISSUES

11. In the history of the ecumenical movement, it has always been recognized that ecumenism was not merely a matter of inter-ecclesiastical relations, but was closely related to the Church's task in and for the world; but in recent years it has become increasingly clear that, as the Uppsala statement on Catholicity said, the secular pressure of an increasingly interdependent world makes it "more imperative to make visible the bonds which unite Christians in universal fellowship", and a new dimension emerged when it spoke of the Church's understanding of itself as "the sign of the coming unity of mankind".[8] We recall also the Vatican II definition of the Church as the sacrament of the unity of mankind. At Louvain '71, the Faith and Order Commission took as its theme "The Unity of the Church and the Unity of Mankind". Its aim was, in John Deschner's words, "to recognize two contexts, the Church and the world, in such a way that the pressure for church unity is taken seriously in both". It affirmed the need "to confront church unity with the problem of human unity, and human disunity with the promise of church unity".[9] As a result of discussing church unity in the secular contexts of "political struggles, racism, cultural differences, interreligious dialogue, and discrimination against the handicapped", the traditional problems of life and work were seen as directly relevant and integral to the search for church unity, and *vice versa*.[10] The relation and interaction between Christian identity, conferred in baptism and expressed in the eucharistic fellowship, and the particular identities given by race, caste, class, nation, or movements engaged in the struggle for freedom or justice has become a Faith and Order issue. For instance, questions like the following have become central:

> What could it mean in a southern American town to have in its midst a congregation disciplined in its opposition to the sin of racism, teaching and practising the import of baptism for the sense of Black identity, reconciling black and white in its practice of eucharistic fellowship, making room for the indispensable ministry of black to white in a situation of racial oppression?[11]

230

What is implied in the claim that "the uniting power of the sacraments is inseparable from the principle of social justice"?[12]

How can we develop a church order which recognizes the "possibility of contest and tension within the Church"?[13]

The presence within the Church of people with different cultures, ideologies, and religious backgrounds, all of whom are becoming aware of their unique identity, is beginning to produce different understandings of Jesus Christ and of the form of the Church. James Cone's Black theology and Gustavo Gutierrez's Latin American theology oriented to social liberation, Seth Nomenyo's African theology, and Kosuke Koyama's Asian theology oriented to renascent indigenous cultures, the new expressions of Christ in traditional and modern artistic forms being produced in all cultures and reflecting new experiences of him—these, to take a few examples, are all attempts on the part of Christians to emancipate themselves from the Latin or Hellenistic captivity of the Church. What kind of church growth and church unity will support this necessary diversity, while at the same time preventing harmful division and making for the transformation of all ideologies and cultures in Christ? And what is the relevance of our concept of unity in diversity for the struggle of new nations to build a community transcending divisions of tribe, language, caste, and class, and the struggle of mankind for world community? These are the kind of issues with which the 1974 Accra meeting of the Faith and Order Commission was concerned in its study of "Giving Account of the Hope that is within us". The increasing collaboration of Faith and Order in its theological work with the Programme to Combat Racism, and Dialogue with People of Living Faiths and Ideologies, is an inevitable development of such thinking on church unity.

THE CONCEPT OF EVANGELISM IN THE MODERN WORLD

12.   No less remarkable is the radical change which has come about in the concept and form of world evangelism as a result of our taking seriously as its context the conviction that the Church and the world exist for each other in the gospel. In 1970, Bishop Lesslie Newbigin wrote that the urgent questions for Christian world mission were "the substance of the gospel itself" and the relation of its proclamation to "the action of God in the secular world, to the service rendered by Christians to their fellow men, and to the life of the Church".[14] This became clear not only at the 1973 Bangkok Assembly of the Commission on World Mission and Evangelism on "Salvation Today", but also at the 1974 International Congress on World Evangelization, Lausanne, and at the 1974 Bishops' Synod in Rome on Evangelism in the Modern World. The Orthodox churches have clarified their understanding of salvation both before and after Bangkok '73 and more especially in the Orthodox Consultation on "Confessing Christ Today" at Bucharest 1974, chaired by Nikos Nissiotis. All these are to be considered as conversations and encounters within the ecumenical movement. Their theological convergence is very striking. It is evident at three points. *Firstly*, in their emphasis on the whole gospel for

231

the whole man in the whole world; *secondly*, in their effort to relate evangelism to the identity of the Church and to its growth, renewal, and unity; and *thirdly*, in their affirmation of the realities of the contemporary world, especially the renascence of cultures and religions, and the dynamics of service, development, and justice in society. Precisely because of this convergence, it is worth looking at the remaining divergences in our concept of evangelism, so that our dialogue at this Assembly may be more ecumenical.

13. Bangkok '73 speaks of the salvation which is offered in the crucified and risen Jesus Christ, and in which we participate, as "a comprehensive wholeness in this divided life". It is the salvation of soul and body, persons and structures, humankind and creation. Just as sin has both individual and corporate dimensions, so too has salvation. "Therefore we see the struggles for economic justice, political freedom, and cultural renewal as elements in the total liberation of the world through the mission of God", and this liberation is a present reality finding final fulfilment only when death is swallowed up in victory. It demands of the churches "a matching comprehensive approach to their participation in salvation".[15] Lausanne '74 defines the gospel in terms of "God's cosmic purpose" and speaks of world evangelization as requiring "the whole Church to take the whole gospel to the whole world".[16] It defines salvation as involving the transformation of humanity "in the totality of our personal and social responsibilities" and affirms "socio-political involvement" as an essential part of Christianity. It does, however, make a clear distinction between evangelism and social action, and would prefer a definition of the former which limited it to "the proclamation of the historical biblical Christ as Saviour and Lord, with a view to persuading people to come to him personally and to be reconciled to God"[17] and, as a consequence, also to be incorporated into the Church and become engaged in responsible service to the world. Also, in the light of the Christian hope in the return of Christ "personally and visibly in power and glory to consummate his salvation and judgement", Lausanne rejects "as a proud self-confident dream, the notion that man can ever build a utopia on earth".[18] Fr Amalorpavadass defines the Vatican Bishops' Synod approach to "the integral salvation towards which the work of evangelization is directed" as embracing "the whole of man and the whole of human society, body and spirit, time and history as well as the fullest achievement of the Kingdom of God". Though salvation cannot be "reduced to" or be "wholly identified with" any "intra-historical human (economic, political, cultural) liberation", salvation "includes it, demands it, and leads it to its fulfilment and true purpose".[19]

14. It seems to me that the consensus of Bangkok, Lausanne, and Rome with regard to salvation comes at three points—the affirmation of its comprehensive nature, the recognition of the eschatological basis for historical action, and the understanding of the Church as the sign and bearer of salvation in the world. The remaining differences centre around these same issues: *What* is—no longer *whether* there is any—the *relation* between the personal, social, and cosmic dimensions of salvation offered in Jesus Christ? *What* is the *nature* of Christian action within history which expresses the eschatological hope; and, in the light of the promise of the Kingdom, now and at the end, *what future* may faith realistically expect and work for in history through world evangelization, dialogue among religions and cultures, and the struggle for human community, justice, and

232

freedom in the nations and the world? *What* is the *locus of identity* of the Church as the bearer of salvation? These are old theological issues, but they have to be taken up afresh in this Assembly, and elsewhere, in relation to our theme "Jesus Christ frees and unites", for the sake both of greater theological unity and common Christian witness in the contemporary world. Let me make a few brief comments on these theological issues.

15. The gospel is essentially the message of divine reconciliation in Jesus Christ addressed to the world of people. Only people can be addressed and only people can respond. But people are not isolated individuals; they are social beings, inextricably related to the structures of nature, history, and cosmos through which they express the creativity of their freedom as well as the sin of self-love and self-righteousness. Persons, society, and cosmos interpenetrate one another in the unity of human existence. Therefore, if salvation from sin through divine forgiveness is to be truly and fully personal, it must express itself in the renewal of these relations and structures. Such renewal is not merely a consequence but an essential element of the conversion of whole human beings. In the words of Bishop Yannoulatos, the goal is "an organic communion of persons in love, not a mere co-existence of individuals".[20] This is why the Church with its corporate and sacramental life is a constitutive aspect of the gospel of salvation. As the Orthodox Consultation puts it: "We personally encounter Christ in the eucharistic communion, but his creative presence extends to the whole cosmos and leads all of history towards fulfilment in Him."[21]

16. Human culture is both created and fallen. As the Lausanne document puts it: "Because man is God's creature, some of his culture is rich in beauty and goodness. Because he has fallen, all of it is tainted with sin and some of it is demonic."[22] Principalities and powers do enslave persons in the modern world, as they did in the ancient. Under their domination, technology, politics, and revolution devour their own children.[23] Oppressive structures of corporate life are the result of the accumulated sins of generations, and they develop an anonymity and a momentum almost independent of persons now living. The gospel is that, through the cross and the resurrection, Jesus Christ has triumphed over the demonic powers which dehumanize our culture, technology, politics, and social structures, and that in him we can resist these powers and renew these realms of life.

17. Indeed, the positive relation between evangelism and Christian social responsibility has been recognized by all the ecumenically concerned churches and groups we are considering. There is agreement that because of this relation Christians must share the concern of God for "justice and reconciliation throughout human society and for the liberation of man from every kind of oppression";[24] that God's justice manifests itself in salvation "both in the justification of the sinner and in social and political justice".[25] The Bishops' Synod speaks of the Church's participation in human liberation in society as opening up a new dimension and imparting a new meaning to the task of human liberation by linking it to the redemptive plan of God for mankind in Jesus Christ and by interpreting it as a realization in the world of the "total human redemption which has been wrought already in Christ's paschal mystery (and yet in some true sense remains to be completed by us in Him)"; it believes that "this ecclesial participation in human liberation motivated by a truly evangelical vision of history" opens the liberation movements to "the light, the

233

energies, the dynamism which spring from the gospel".[26] Bangkok and Rome quote Jesus' Nazareth Manifesto in Luke 4.18 to indicate the scope of Christ's and the Church's mission to the poor and the oppressed.

18. The question is often raised as to whether in this emphasis on social and political justice there is not present a social utopianism which denies the fact of sin and affirms a self-redemptive humanism. Yes, the danger is always present. So is the opposite danger that we may not take seriously enough the fact of divine grace and the power of righteousness it releases to a daring faith in the realm of social and political action. It is the task of ecumenical theology to warn us against both these dangers. For instance, in the Accra 1974 discussions on "Giving Account of the Hope that is within us", it is clearly affirmed that "the future of perfected humanity lies in the fullness of the Godhead" beyond this side of history where sin and death prevail. But our hope in the coming Kingdom of God in Jesus Christ "takes on the character of a concrete utopia, that is, an idea of our aim and a critical point of reference for our action in society. This provides us with an incentive to participate in efforts to build a more human social order in the perspective of the Kingdom of God." The statement then goes on to point out how every social order is limited by "the continuing sinfulness of man" which corrupts the very institutions which are meant to protect human beings in society. Given this limitation, "concrete social utopias can correspond to the eschatological reality of the Kingdom of God".[27] Here, then, is no utopianism of the kind which we must reject on theological grounds; we have rather the picture of a penultimate hope for the effective realization of the ultimate hope within the limits of a sinful history. In this sense, as Paulo Freire says, the Church "can never cease being utopian".[28] And often anti-utopianism lays itself open to the suspicion that it is not an expression of faith but an ideology of the *status quo* and an excuse for non-participation in human liberation in history.

19. The Orthodox critique of and the inter-Orthodox debate on the World Council of Churches' stance on the relation between salvation and society are a mark of increasing Orthodox participation in the life of the Council. The Holy Synod of the Russian Orthodox Church has felt that sometimes the WCC has not placed its thinking on the social content of salvation solidly within the perspective of "the ultimate goal of salvation . . . the eternal life in God", with the result that appropriation of eternal life is made to depend on social conditions rather than social conditions on the appropriation of eternal life;[29] and the Ecumenical Patriarchate has warned us that in "turning towards the anguish of the man of today", the WCC "must not forget the basic truth that man sees himself as hungering for an answer to a basic question over and beyond his acute interest in the most vital socio-political problems of the day. This question is: what is the reason for man's existence on earth, as a living person, as an ethical personality, as an entity stretching out towards something beyond this present life and finally embracing the eschaton." [30] These comments and warnings must be heeded. For the historical and ethical dimensions of life will be handled superficially if we lack awareness of their ontological and eschatological roots. But here again the point has been made by the Orthodox themselves that the hunger for meaning and eternal life is not merely "over and beyond" but also "within and through" the anguished longing for fuller humanity. As Uppsala 1968 said,

it is in the cry arising out of the conditions of contemporary existence that the Church can discern that the "deepest cry, albeit often unrecognized, is for the Triune God".[31] According to the Bucharest Orthodox Consultation on "Confessing Christ Today", the Church's mission is "ultimately concerned with pointing to a quality of existence which reflects that of the Trinity"; at this point, the anthropological, sociological, and ecclesiological concerns of the Church overlap; they all point towards "the event of communion which God offers to the world as the Body of Christ, the Church".[32]

20. The presence of God and his Spirit outside the Church, his self-disclosure and the saving work of Christ outside the Church, and the discernment of and response to these by the Church are theological issues of great importance. They have been raised in relation to the Christian theology of dialogue with people of living faiths and secular ideologies. It is perhaps here that we have the deepest theological cleavage demanding fuller exploration. In fact, it is my impression that on the whole no group has formulated a theology of dialogue. Some are convinced that in the pluralistic communities in which we live a dialogical existence, "dialogue needs no defence"; and they hope that in the very process of dialogue a Christian theology will evolve. Others are reluctant to enter into dialogue without clear theological presuppositions. Many are taking the first course—they are engaging in interfaith dialogue on the basis of our common humanity, with, as immediate objectives, an understanding of each other's faith and co-operation in developing a human community which recognizes but transcends religious differences. In this process, the relation of the immediate objectives to the ultimate goals of each faith must inevitably be faced. As the Working Group of the WCC Sub-unit on Dialogue has put it: "A fresh theological framework where the imperative of love clearly demands a two-way openness on the part of Christians needs to be worked out".[33] We are only at the very beginning of our reflection; it is not yet time to crystallize a theology of dialogue. Nevertheless, conversations with this aim in view must be continued.

21. The Lausanne document rightly rejects as "derogatory to Christ and the gospel every kind of syncretism and dialogue which implies that Christ speaks equally through all religions and ideologies", but it advocates "that kind of dialogue whose purpose is to listen sensitively in order to understand".[34] Lausanne recognizes that "all men have some knowledge of God through his general revelation in nature", but since this knowledge is corrupted by sin, it cannot save. It denies that the universality of Christ's saving work means that all men are "either automatically or ultimately saved" without the response of personal repentance and faith, or that "all religions offer salvation in Christ".[35] Lausanne speaks of the Holy Spirit as being present within the Church and in its proclamation of Jesus Christ, to effect faith, new birth, and Christian growth. The Declaration of the Synodal Fathers speaks of "the Spirit of Christ who is always at work in the life of the Church itself and in all human history so that every one may have the fullness of a better life"; it further speaks of the Church "acquiring the ability to discern the signs of the times and to recognize and respect" the action of the Spirit of Christ thus at work. With regard to the basis and objectives of dialogue, it says: "Confident in the Holy Spirit's action which overflows the bounds of the Christian community, we wish to further dialogue with other religions which are not

235

Christian, thus to achieve a deeper understanding of the Gospel's newness and of the fullness of revelation, and to be able to show them thereby the salvific truth of God's love which fulfils itself in Christ."[36]

22. Bangkok, while confessing belief in the presence of God in his whole Creation, refuses to "make this belief an operative principle for pointing out exactly where he is at work, lest we say: here is the Messiah, or there is the Messiah, when he is not there". Therefore, while recognizing that "the Spirit translates the groaning of all mankind into prayers acceptable to God", that insight is seen more as a reason to worship his freedom than as an invitation to theologize, or to "pinpoint the details of his presence", or to claim for Christ the Christ-like action of groups which do not acknowledge him. The Church's preoccupation is with "the revealed Christ and with the proclamation of him". Christians must take as their starting point for dialogue faithfulness to the centrality of the crucified and risen Jesus Christ, just as they expect adherents of other living religions to start from their own faith-commitment. But "conscious of God's movement towards men both as Creator and Saviour", Christians will be "keenly open to discover what he is doing among people of other faiths". We will rejoice in "the common ground we discover and be equally eager to discover our differences". Dialogue involves sharing of common human aspirations and responsibilities and co-operation in meeting human need and in the search for world community.[37]

23. Is there the possibility of going beyond these tentative approaches? Any Christian theology of dialogue has to be Christ-centred, for, as Visser 't Hooft said at New Delhi, we know of no unity broader or more inclusive than that of the New Humanity created by God in Jesus Christ. But since we believe, as the Zürich Consultation of theologians pointed out,[38] that in spite of man's idolatrous rebellion against God, Christ holds all things together *now* (Col. 1) and will sum up all things in himself in the *end* (Eph. 1), should we not make greater efforts to discern how Christ is at work in other faiths, generally in their traditional patterns and more particularly in their renewal movements which have felt the impact of Jesus Christ? Can we not, at a time when all religions are in the ferment of change, speak of the cross of Christ as in some measure breaking down the walls of partition between peoples of all religions and ideologies as it did the wall of partition between Jew and Gentile? Is it not legitimate to welcome a Christ-centred process of interreligious and intercultural penetration through dialogue? If you will permit the use of the word "syncretism" to denote all processes of interpenetration between cultures and religions, the only answer to a wrong syncretism which means the uncritical, superficial, normless mixing of basically incompatible religious conceptions and cultural attitudes is a Christ-centred syncretism which grapples with and evaluates all concepts and attitudes critically in the light of Jesus Christ and converts them into vehicles for communicating the truth of the gospel and for expressing its meaning for life. Acknowledging the common humanity given in Christ, can we not work with men of all religions and no religion for a secular human culture and community, and even for a secular humanism open to insights from all religions and ideologies, evaluated in the light of and informed by the true manhood of Jesus Christ?

THEOLOGY AND SPIRITUALITY FOR COMBAT

24. So far I have tried to illustrate the development of the theology of contemporary ecumenism in relation to the unity and evangelistic mission of the Church. Let us now look at the theological ferment which has developed within our various programmes aimed at relieving human suffering and combating the dehumanizing forces of poverty, oppression, and injustice. Theology and spirituality provide the essential framework and anchor for the Christian and the Church as they engage in responsible action to transform the world. Though I have not been able to go along with the enthusiasts who make absolute distinctions between "doing theology" and "rethinking theology", I believe that there can be no authentic theology except within responsible encounter with the contemporary world in the name of the dignity of humanity. That is why I welcome the intercontextual method of theologizing which has come into being in Faith and Order, and the action-reflection method which has come to dominate WCC's programme of justice and service. The WCC, since the time of the 1937 Oxford Conference on Church, Community, and State, has brought together lay men and women involved in the secular world to reflect theologically. It has also, through the Commission of the Churches on International Affairs, and the Commission on Inter-Church Aid, Refugees, and World Service, involved itself in action in the world. To these we have now added programmes like those to combat racism and sexism, and those to promote the Church's participation in world development, in movements of social liberation, in urban and rural people's organizations, in community health and medicine, and in education in self-awareness.

25. This more intense preoccupation with the world on the part of the WCC has been regretted by some on the ground that it makes for less concern with theological reflection, or that it may lead the Council to seek justification by some ideology of works rather than by faith. In our programmes we must surely guard against that danger, but when we consider the quantity and quality of the theological output, through which the gospel of Christ has been communicated to unbelievers and ex-believers, we see that such fears have been belied. Richard Dickinson, in his book *To Set at Liberty the Oppressed*, dealing with the dynamics of the WCC development/liberation programme, surveys the theological reflections related to it. The participation of minority and oppressed groups in this reflection has produced patterns of theologizing which have, undoubtedly, challenged the assumptions of some traditional western ways of articulating the faith. Because they are more praxis-oriented and emerge in concrete historical situations, they are, says Dickinson, "more biblically centred, less inclined to systematics, and more predisposed to an apologetic and advocacy stance". He comments that "Fresh theological movements within the churches have always had this character".[39] And he concludes: "At present we have experienced the shattering of traditional formulations. We are in the stage of creating new articulations of the meaning of the gospel for a new world situation and perspective; but the new synthesis is not yet apparent."[40] The "new articulations", or even old articulations given new depth, provide a relevant and challenging context for the unity and evangelism concerns of contemporary ecumenism. Let me briefly touch on a few issues which could be crucial in the search for such articulations and hence crucial for the future of ecumenism as well.

26. Firstly, the search for a theological anthropology for today which speaks of the New Humanity in Jesus Christ in terms of the totality of the human family and is challengingly relevant to modern life. This has been our emphasis in our Humanum Studies. As urged by Brigalia Bam and the Berlin Conference on Sexism, we require a theology of human wholeness which incorporates the experience and insights, the understanding of what it means to be human, which come from women and from other sections of humanity who have thus far been wholly or partially excluded from effective participation in the decision-making processes of church and society. The wholeness of both church and society is at stake here. A contemporary theological anthropology should also be able to speak of God and Christ in terms of the self-understanding of modern men and women and their search for a better quality of life and for social justice within a limited natural environment and an interdependent world. Technology and politics do have their positive roles to play in bringing human wholeness, but where the sense of mystery and transcendence of the personal being is lacking, they themselves become forces of dehumanization. It is significant that many scientists and historians as well as theologians[41] are today becoming increasingly conscious of the need to redefine the categories of Creation, Fall, and Redemption in order to understand and grapple with the modern human situation. The publication of the *Common Catechism* (1975), edited by Johannes Feiner and Lukas Vischer, is an important joint move in this direction by the Protestant and Catholic theologians of Europe.

27. Secondly, the ultimate hope of the fulfilment of history in the coming of Christ and his Kingdom is the enduring basis of the human responsibility to mould the future of the world. This is the one dominant note in all the theological reflections of Christian action groups in the Council. For instance, scientists, technologists, and theologians considering "The Future of Humanity in a World of Science-based Technology" hold that the eschatological perspective liberates history from bondage to necessity or fatalism and keeps it open-ended. "The temptation of much futurology", says one report, "is to place hope in the capacity of man to control and mould his own destiny. The hope then falls into fatalism when it is disappointed. The contribution Christians can make is to lift this fatalism from the souls of people with a promise which is not deduced from the analysis of the trend of past events, but from the God whose Kingdom is coming, even understanding physical death itself as an act of God's blessing within his promise." This perspective provides history with new beginnings and gives men and women "freedom to make history in partnership with him".[42]

28. The fundamental captivity of the modern world, according to Fr Paul Verghese (Metropolitan Paulos Gregorios) is that of "a closed secular world, deprived of any valid symbols of hope or transcendence".[43] As Metropolitan Anthony Bloom has pointed out, what distinguishes the Church from the world is the eschatological perspective of seeing history not only as darkened by sin, but also as "transfigured, (a history) in which the resurrection and eternal life are already present".[44] This perspective provides the basis for the joy, gratitude, and enduring hope of the Christian in the most hopeless situations, of which there are indeed many—including the world food situation which has been rightly described as a threat to human survival. In the face of such realities, many people of good will have given up their faith in the unity of mankind and have taken

238

to a "life-boat ethics" which would allow those in heavily populated poor countries to perish for the sake of the selective survival of the rich and those for whom help would bring about readily discernible improvement. In this kind of situation, the idealist's endless talk of "what we ought to do" is silenced, leaving only the realist's talk of "what is". But the news "Christ is risen" is part of this dimension of realism, of even the most doomed situation; it brings hope, and literally breaks open new historical possibilities. In the near future, as in the past, perhaps more than in the past, the unity of mankind, the universality of human rights, and the hope-full engagement in historical action can be defended only by a confessing Church. As Jan Lochman has often stated, it is only the humanism of the gospel that can remain universal and unconditioned.

29. Thirdly, the rediscovery of the Christ of the poor and the oppressed is the basis of the solidarity and identification of the Church with those struggling for liberation. C.I. Itty speaks of "faith in Christ who came to liberate the poor and the oppressed" as the power sustaining Christians committed to the struggle for liberation in times of hopelessness.[45] Miguez Bonino points to the question this raises for the meaning of the Church and evangelism when he says that "the Church is there where the Gospel of the Kingdom is announced to and demonstrated in the liberation of the poor". And he adds that, in this context, "socio-analytical and ideological political criteria now become an integral part of ecclesiology".[46] A Joint CCPD/CICARWS Statement pursues this line further:

> The Lord's words in the synagogue at Nazareth that he has been anointed to bring good news to the poor and to proclaim liberty to the captives ring true with new meaning today. The righteousness of God in the Old Testament has shown itself in the deliverance of the poor from their oppressors, in the vindication of the defenceless, in the protection of the orphan and the widow, in a definite taking of sides with the victims of injustice. Jesus Christ reveals the righteousness of God also in this partisanship with the poor, and we need to ask the ecclesiological question whether the Church can be the Church if it is not identified with the poor . . . . Has a Church the right even to assist the poor when it is allied with the oppressor? How can its proclamation then be good news to the poor?[47]

This does not mean that the Church is not the Church for all men; it means that "it is on the side of all men in terms of the justice and truth of God".[48]

30. Fourthly, the need to struggle for justice with an awareness of human solidarity in sin and acknowledgement of divine forgiveness. In moving from the concept of charity to that of justice, we have come to recognize the need for changing existing power structures. How can the struggles and conflicts to bring human dignity to the poor and the oppressed, even the power politics which oppose institutionalized violence with counter-violence, be kept within the spiritual framework of the ultimate power of the crucified Christ and the ultimate goal of reconciliation of all people in Christ? This requires recognition that "our conflicts, even those which are most real and serious, can only be seen as penultimate. None of our battles is the final battle. None of our enemies facing us is the final enemy, the ultimate evil. Our contrasts are never black and white, always grey. Today's enemy must tomorrow be accepted at another

level as a brother. Similarly, it prevents us from seeing our achievements in absolute terms."[49] It is in this context that the exploration of non-violent techniques of struggle for social justice acquires great significance.[50] As Nicolas Berdyaev has said, Christians know that social justice will not solve all human problems, that when the struggle for human survival and dignity at the material and social level is over, the deeper and the more tragic spiritual dimensions of the human self and the alienation of human existence will be better exposed and confronted by the gospel of the crucified and risen Christ. But the question is, how can the Church be the visible expression of this double awareness, that of the significance and urgency of all politics of justice, on the one hand, and that of the ultimately tragic character and the inescapable relativity of all historical achievements, on the other? How can the Church participate in political ideologies, structures, and processes in our nations in a manner which will communicate this awareness? We need a theology of political engagement that will help Christians and churches in such participation, a theology that will clarify the dialectical relation between faith and ideology in the light of the cross and the resurrection.

31. All these issues bring us to the need for a "spirituality for combat"—an expression that comes from David Jenkins. In his address on the theological inquiry on human rights he says: "Perhaps what Christians are particularly called to work out . . . is what might be called a spirituality for combat. Can our very struggles become part of our celebration of man as we understand him, in the image of God and died for by the Son of God? How might we help one another to so conduct our struggles that they become part of our worship?"[51] Hans-Ruedi Weber has described the spiritual vocation of the laity in the secular world as "holy worldliness". The contribution of Taizé to the search for a holiness in action combining struggle with contemplation has been remarkable. The rediscovery of the Bible and the Liturgy is basic here. In this context, the Orthodox concept and practice of *theosis*, and the centrality of the Eucharist as the celebration of a humanity in community with transfigured nature, society, and cosmos, need to be redefined and reaffirmed in relation to the spirituality of contemporary struggles for the defence of the *humanum* and the unity of mankind. Let us not forget that our struggle is not merely against others but also against ourselves, not against flesh and blood, but against the false spiritualities of the idolatry of race, nation, and class, and of the self-righteousness of ideals which reinforce collective structures of inhumanity and oppression. Any spirituality of righteousness must start with a turning in repentance from idols to the living God and justification by faith.

JESUS CHRIST FREES AND UNITES

32. A word about our theme: "Jesus Christ Frees and Unites". In the Bible, there are many motifs and patterns of freedom and unity. First, there is the liberation of Abraham from a settled community, under the divine promise of a future. Then in Exodus Israel is liberated from slavery in Egypt to serve a living God in the wilderness *en route* to the promised land. There they are liberated from lawlessness to become a people

disciplined in righteousness under the Divine Law. In Canaan they are liberated from nomadism for settled communal life with land, temple, and king. In the Exile they are liberated from the idolatry of land, temple, and kingdom to know a God who is present with them as a people under the covenant promise. Through the prophets they are liberated from the national messianism of conquest for the universal messianism of the suffering servant. Through the death and resurrection of Jesus the Messiah, they are liberated from bondage to law for the community of the Spirit through faith and are brought into unity with the Gentiles. Jesus, God incarnate, crucified by all that was best in church, community, and state of his time, reveals the idolatrous spirit of human bondage which works in every unity we realize; the risen Jesus is the guarantee of a total liberation from sin and death for a new humanity that awaits us in the end and which already works in history as the instrument of the permanent liberation. The history of the Church and mankind is evidence that Jesus Christ and the ferment he creates continue all the motifs of liberation present in the Old and New Testaments. He shatters every unity which turns into bondage, whether it be social, moral, cultural, or religious; he makes men and women free to establish a more mature unity, only to break it when it too turns into bondage. He works in the same way in relation to the integration of persons; he disturbs personal integration at one level to reintegrate it at another, only to disturb it again. The divine promise in Jesus Christ of humanity's ultimate maturity is the ever-present dynamic within the dialectic between freedom and unity which we call history. In the light of the continuing work of Christ to liberate people from premature unities for more mature unities, we have to see every unity and every freedom which beckon us in personal, social, or church life as *en route*—as helping us in our pilgrimage of faith, under the guidance of the Holy Spirit, to "a city which hath foundations, whose builder and maker is God" (Heb. 11.10).

33. Let me conclude with some words of adoration and expectation from the Theological Reflections adopted by the CCPD/CICARWS Consultation:

> God be praised, not all is darkness. The light shines in the darkness and the darkness shall never be able to quench it. There are witnesses to the light. The power of Jesus Christ is at work and the Holy Spirit will bring to perfection that which God has begun. The new age is not a myth or a symbol, but a powerful reality which overthrows the mighty from their thrones and fills the hungry with good things. . . . The Church, called to be Herald, Sign, Sacrament, and Agent of the Kingdom, waits for her own liberation by the power of the New Age.[52]

NOTES

[1] I have appended to this Report some rough figures to show how far the staff represents geographical regions, confessions, women, laity and youth in its composition, relative to the representation of voting delegates nominated to this Assembly (based on figures available in the first week of October, 1975).

[2] *The Uppsala Report 1968* (WCC, Geneva, 1968), p. 85.
[3] Amsterdam 1948.
[4] Evanston 1954.
[5] New Delhi 1961.
[6] Uppsala 1968.
[7] *Uppsala 1968*, op. cit., p. 38.
[8] Ibid., p. 17.
[9] John Deschner, "The Unity of the Church and the Unity of Mankind", in *Uniting in Hope, Accra 1974*, Faith and Order Paper 72 (WCC, Geneva, 1975), p. 85.
[10] *Minutes of the Commission and Working Committee, Louvain, 1971*, Faith and Order Paper 60 (WCC, Geneva, 1971), quoted by Deschner in *Uniting in Hope*, op. cit., p. 86.
[11] John Deschner, op. cit., p. 87.
[12] *Louvain 1971; Study Reports and Documents*, Faith and Order Paper 59 (WCC, Geneva, 1971), p. 191.
[13] Ibid., p. 192.
[14] *The Ecumenical Advance*, ed. Harold E. Fey (London, SPCK, 1970), p. 197.
[15] *Bangkok Assembly 1973*, Minutes and Report of the Assembly of the Commission on World Mission and Evangelism (WCC, Geneva, 1973).
[16] "The Lausanne Covenant", in *Let the Earth Hear His Voice* (Minneapolis, World Wide Publications, 1975), para. 6, p. 5.
[17] Ibid., para. 4, p. 4.
[18] Ibid., para. 15, p. 8.
[19] Fr D.S. Amalorpavadass, "Pastoral Recommendations for Evangelization", in *Word and Worship*, Vol. VIII, No. 1 (January-February 1975), p. 51.
[20] *Towards World Community: The Colombo Papers*, ed. S. Samartha (WCC, Geneva, 1975), p. 48.
[21] Papers on Confessing Christ, p. 55.
[22] "The Lausanne Covenant", op. cit., para. 10.
[23] Cf. William Stringfellow, *An Ethic for Christian and Other Aliens*, quoted in papers on Confessing Christ Today; also Engelbert Mveng in *Anticipation* (August 1974), pp. 9f.
[24] "The Lausanne Covenant", op. cit., para. 5, p. 4.
[25] *Bangkok '73*, p. 88.
[26] *Word and Worship*, op. cit., p. 52.
[27] *Uniting in Hope*, op. cit., p. 31.
[28] "Witness of Liberation", in *Seeing Education Whole* (WCC Office of Education, Geneva, 1971), p. 70.
[29] Letter to the Chairman of the Central Committee, 7 August, 1973.
[30] Declaration of the Ecumenical Patriarchate on the occasion of the 25th Anniversary of the WCC, 16 August, 1973.
[31] *Uppsala 1968*, op. cit., p. 28.
[32] Assembly papers on "Confessing Christ", Section I, p. 58. It should be noted that when this report was prepared the Report of the "Orthodox Consultation on Confessing Christ Today through the Liturgy", held in Etchmiadzin, 16-21 September, 1975, was not available.
[33] *The Ecumenical Review* (January 1975), p. 74.
[34] "The Lausanne Covenant", op. cit., paras. 3, 4.
[35] Ibid., para 3.
[36] *Word and Worship*, Vol. VIII, No. 1 (January-February 1975), pp. 97 and 99.

[37] *Bangkok 73*, pp. 77 ff.

[38] See "Christians in Dialogue with Men of other Faiths", *International Review of Mission*, Vol. LIX, No. 236 (October 1970).

[39] R. Dickinson, *To Set at Liberty the Oppressed* (WCC, Geneva, 1975), p. 54.

[40] Ibid., p. 60.

[41] See duplicated papers by Charles Birch, Mary Hesse, Arthur Peacocke, and W.S. Pollard written in preparation for the Mexico Consultation on Christian Faith and the Changing Face of Science and Technology, and articles by André Dumas and Charles West in *The Ecumenical Review* (January 1975).

[42] *Anticipation*, No. 15 (December 1973), p. 15.

[43] "Does Jesus Christ Free and Unite?" *The Ecumenical Review* (July 1974), p. 370.

[44] A. Bloom and G. Lefebvre, *Courage to Pray* (London, Darton, Longman & Todd, 1973), p. 58.

[45] Dickinson, op. cit., p. 55.

[46] "The Struggle of the Poor and the Church", *The Ecumenical Review* (January 1975), p. 42.

[47] "Structures of Captivity and Lines of Liberation", *The Ecumenical Review* (January 1975), p. 45.

[48] *To Break the Chains of Oppression* (WCC, Geneva, 1975), p. 64.

[49] J. Miguez Bonino, *Study Encounter* (1973), No. 1, SE/36, quoted in *To Break the Chains of Oppression*, op. cit., p. 65.

[50] See the WCC report on Violence, Non-violence, and the Struggle for Social Justice (1973).

[51] "Some questions, hypotheses and theses for a theological inquiry concerning human rights", in *Human Rights and Christian Responsibility* (WCC, CCIA, Geneva, 1974), p. 34.

[52] "Structures of Captivity and Lines of Liberation", op. cit., pp. 45 and 46.

APPENDIX

Percentages of Staff in Grade I-V and VI-X and corresponding percentages of delegates in Nairobi Assembly (rough calculation on the basis of figures obtained in the first week of October, corrected to whole numbers)

Total no. of delegates nominated   698—100%
Grade I-V staff   176—100%
Grade VI-X staff   119—100%

	Assembly %	Grade I-V staff %	Grade VI-X staff %
Men	78	10	74
Women	22	90	26
Laity	42	100	66
Youth (b. 1945 or after)	10	39	4
Africa	16	3	5
Asia	14	3	9
Australia & Pacific	6	0	4
Caribbean	1	1	1
Eastern Europe	14	1	1
Western Europe	22	88	60
North America	20	3	14
Latin America	3	1	6
Middle East	4	1	0
Anglicans	10	11	11
Lutherans	15	15	17
Methodists	11	3	12
Orthodox-Eastern	13	2	4
Orthodox-Oriental	5	0	1
Reformed/Presbyterian	18	25	32
United	12	2	7
Roman Catholic	0	34	11
Others	15	10	6

(Confessions below 5% in the
Assembly clubbed together)

Appendix 4
The Report of the General Secretary

Dear Brothers and Sisters in Christ,

It is a joy to see you all gathered here for this Fifth Assembly of the World Council of Churches. We have all been looking forward eagerly to this event. The churches in Indonesia had been preparing for us to come to Jakarta when circumstances beyond their control made it inadvisable for us to meet there. For the past fifteen months the churches of Kenya, the National Christian Council of Kenya, and the All Africa Conference of Churches have laboured hard and willingly to receive us in Nairobi. Churches and delegations all over the world have also been preparing themselves for this Assembly by their prayers, their study, and their support. And now we meet for the first time in Africa and, more than at any other Assembly, as a truly *World* Council of Churches.

The Moderator has already drawn attention to the representative character of this Fifth Assembly. What does it mean for us that we are gathered here representing in varying ways all the Christian confessions? What does it mean that we are here as a fellowship of churches which confess the Lord Jesus Christ as God and Saviour? What does it mean for us to come from all the corners of the globe to confess together that this Jesus Christ frees and unites and is the source and goal of all true liberation and community? Fellowship or communion, community, communication—these words are basic to the nature and task of our meeting here, and indeed of the ecumenical movement and of the World Council of Churches.

Actually, the word "community" and its cognates "communion" (fellowship), "communication" come from a Latin word whose origin probably goes back to the Sanskrit word *mu*, "to bind". There is also a similar Latin word *munus* meaning "service, obligation, duty". This belongingness, this bond, this mutual obligation and service is central to our confession of Jesus Christ. This is precisely what St Paul refers to when he speaks in 1 Corinthians 12 of the Church as a charismatic fellowship. The Spirit makes available to each of us—individuals, races, sexes, cultures—his gift of grace (*charisma*), i.e. his self-giving love, for the common good. But these are gifts which only become operative as we are baptized into the body of the crucified and risen Christ whatever our race or condition may be. Therefore, every part of the body has its own identity, its own integrity, and can never be assimilated or dominated by the other parts. But every part of the body is at the same time responsible for the others in suffering and joy. As the Zulu proverb puts it: "When a thorn gets into the toe, the whole body stoops to pick it out." Jesus Christ frees us to be ourselves as part of his Body and to be united to each other in the one Body in love and service.

245

That is what the ecumenical movement, as also the World Council, is about, and that is what we are about in this Assembly.

This understanding of our life together as Christians and as churches is nothing new in the ecumenical movement. In fact, we celebrate this year the fiftieth anniversary of the first international ecumenical conference of officially appointed representatives of the Orthodox, Protestant, and Anglican churches at Stockholm. This pioneering conference was the fruit of the indefatigable labours of Archbishop Nathan Söderblom of Sweden who early had the vision of an ecumenical council of churches which could speak for the whole of Christendom on the religious, moral, and social concerns of humanity. The Ecumenical Patriarchate of Constantinople had also written an encyclical in 1920 calling for the formation of a *koinonia*, a fellowship of churches dedicated to the task of drawing the scattered people of God together to work for the unity of the Church in obedience to our Lord's prayer. The Universal Christian Conference on Life and Work at Stockholm in August 1925 was a beginning of that drawing together of the churches which has borne such rich fruit during these fifty years, in spite of all the obstacles which centuries of division had imposed on the churches.

As we begin our work in this Assembly, it is salutary to recall that the true title of that first inter-confessional ecumenical gathering on Life and Work was *Communio in adorando et serviendo oecumenica*—Ecumenical Fellowship in Worship and Service. For the participants life was worship and work was service, and both became meaningful in ecumenical fellowship. In fact, this title describes very aptly the character of the ecumenical movement. It was in this perspective that the Stockholm participants said in their message to the churches:

The Conference has deepened and purified our devotion to the Captain of our Salvation. Responding to His call 'Follow Me', we have in the presence of the Cross accepted the urgent duty of applying His Gospel in all realms of human life—industrial, social, political and international. . .

Only as we become inwardly one shall we attain real unity of mind and spirit. The nearer we draw to the Crucified, the nearer we come to one another, in however varied colours the Light of the World may be reflected in our faith. Under the Cross of Jesus Christ we reach out hands to one another. The Good Shepherd had to die in order that He might gather together the scattered children of God. In the Crucified and Risen Lord alone lies the world's hope.

We are, indeed, inheritors of a great ecumenical tradition. The spirit in which those pioneers started their long pilgrimage is as relevant for us today as it was in the 1920s. They perceived clearly that fellowship, communion, community is nothing which we can create, but is God's work in Christ. As they affirmed: "The nearer we draw to the Crucified, the nearer we come to one another . . . . Under the Cross of Jesus Christ we reach out hands to one another."

It is in this spirit that we are invited during these crowded days to confess our faith in Jesus Christ who frees and unites. Through Bible study and group discussion we shall share that faith with one another; in our Sections we shall come to grips with some major concerns which this faith raises for us in today's world; and in Hearings and Committees we shall review the activities of the World Council and give direction to its work in the coming years. The Moderator referred to the work of the Council over these past seven years, as reported in the book *Uppsala to Nairobi*. He has himself given a masterly survey of the insights we have gained through his reflections on "our new theological understanding of the relation between the Church and the world". Our predecessors at Stockholm would have been happily astonished to hear this survey which is very much in line with what they envisaged as the calling of the Church in the world. My responsibility is to share with you some reflections on the nature and task of the World Council during these years and in the years to come. Our theological insights were the result of particular studies and activities carried out by this particular body called the World Council of Churches. Of course, the World Council has been deeply sensitive to the challenges posed by the shattering events in our world in this period. If we no longer say, as confidently as some years ago, that the world provides the agenda for the Church, we can at least assert that it is in discerning what God has been doing in his world that we have been given our marching orders to do what we have done. I want, therefore, to situate my reflections in the context of the significant trends in the life of our world which have influenced both the content and style of the work of the World Council.

The most striking fact of our time is that all the major issues, whether political, economic, social, racial, or of sex, are global and interrelated in character. What happens in one place affects all places. What appears to be a political issue tends, on closer examination, to have many other dimensions. As St Paul reminds us about the body, "If one member suffers, all suffer together" (1 Corinthians 12.26). This is as true of the body politic as it is of the Body of Christ.

During these years we have experienced a number of conflict situations, such as Vietnam and the Middle East. These did not and could never remain localized, although the toll of suffering has been largely local. The super-powers and their allies were and are deeply involved and the repercussions of these conflicts have been felt all over the world. In fact, there is ample evidence to show that wherever there are conflicts—and there are many all over the world today, not least on this continent of Africa—the interests of other nations are engaged, bringing about greater suffering to the peoples caught in these conflicts. And they are exacerbated by the arms race. More and more deadly weapons are being produced. We now live under the permanent threat of the ultimate annihilation of the human species. The economy of many industrialized countries is now heavily geared to or dependent on the production and sale of arms. There is no world authority to limit this indiscriminate traffic in arms. Hence conflicts inevitably develop into armed struggle which engulfs more and more people.

In fact, it has become fashionable to speak of the threats to human survival. During these past seven years, some of these threats have been highlighted. The threat to the human environment was brought forcibly to our attention by the UN World Conference at Stockholm in 1972, which created an important new inter-governmental organization with headquarters in this city of Nairobi. The incredible advance of science and technology has provoked an unbridled exploitation of the world's natural resources everywhere and is causing havoc to our environment—water, air, cultivable land, food, vegetable and animal species, primary products, even climatic conditions—all that should contribute towards maintaining in some equilibrium the natural habitat of human beings is threatened.

247

Moreover, our scientific apocalyptists have been informing us that there is nothing unlimited about the natural resources of our globe. A few years ago, a group of savants in a report entitled *Limits to Growth* warned that "if the present growth trends in world population, industrialization, pollution, food production, and resource depletion continue unchanged, the limits to growth on this planet will be reached within the next one hundred years".

Perhaps the most serious threat today is the widening gap between the rich and the poor both within and between nations. The Fourth Assembly in 1968 drew the attention of Christians and the world at large to this fact, and proposed that massive aid be given to the poorer countries to assist them in their development. In this short period of seven years, the situation has greatly deteriorated. It has become abundantly evident that this gap is the direct effect of the prevailing world economic order, which is based on the survival of the fittest, the profit motive, the emphasis on the unlimited increase of the gross national product, a monetary system which is manipulated to the advantage of the affluent and powerful, galloping inflation, the extraordinary imbalance in the handling of economies when nations, and not least poor nations, spend such vast sums on armaments. This widening gap has been dramatically demonstrated by the shortage of food and growing famine, mainly in the poor countries. Over a billion people live below the minimum annual income of $200. Half that number are on the edge of starvation. And yet, there is no world food policy or structure for meeting hunger and famine in a concerted way. The UN World Food Conference a year ago tried with little success to mobilize international concern and action.

Even more significant have been the special sessions of the UN on the world economic order—in April 1974 and September 1975. The earlier meeting proposed "the establishment of a new international economic order based on equity, sovereign equality, interdependence, common interest and co-operation among all States, irrespective of their economic and social systems which shall correct inequalities and redress existing injustices, make it possible to eliminate the widening gap between the developed and the developing countries, and ensure steadily accelerating economic and social development and peace and justice for present and future generations". We face the alternatives of co-operation in finding a new way of relating to each other as nations, or of confrontation leading to mutual destruction.

The proliferation of more lethal weapons of war; increasing world population; hunger, undernourishment, and famine; pollution of the human environment; the limits of natural resources; the gap between rich and poor, and between developed and underdeveloped countries; the energy crisis of the last two years—all these and more are threats to the survival of humanity, and they are interrelated. These are all global in their dimensions and demand global perspectives in dealing with them. We are all called to think, decide, and act globally and not out of national or sectional self-interest.

But we must not forget that these threats to survival are the result of human decisions and actions. The real threat to the survival of the human species is humanity itself. As the Executive Committee of the Commission of the Churches on International Affairs declared last year in a statement on "Economic Threats to Peace", ". . . through indifference, greed, envy, fear, love of power, and short-sighted stupidity, men have created, or allowed to develop, a demonstrably unjust economic order".

Similarly, in these years we have been deeply exercised over the issues of racism. The most frightening aspect of this dreadful human disease is the way in which the sale of arms, economic investments, and bank loans, involving individuals, groups, and governments of many countries, maintain the oppressive racist structures, especially in Southern Africa. Racism must be understood and tackled globally. Again, our investigations have shown that human rights are being violated everywhere, and that we can no longer separate personal from social rights. They belong inextricably together, and their violation is related to these threats to survival.

If, then, the issues of our time—and I realize I have been selective in describing them—are global in character and need global perspectives for action, there is urgent need for mobilizing world Christian forces to meet them. That is precisely what the World Council of Churches has tried to do during these seven years. The Central Committee report before you and the annotated agendas for the Sections tell a vivid story of the ways in which we have sought to face the global challenges of our time with a global outlook. Many have questioned this preoccupation as diverting the ecumenical movement from what they consider to be its proper task of working for the unity of the Church and a true confession of faith in Christ. But when we speak of conflicts between and within nations, threats to human survival, racism, and violations of human rights, we are not talking about abstractions. We are addressing ourselves to human beings who create and operate them. The focus is on the human race itself—men and women, singly and corporately. We are talking about human sin in all its protean forms. And that is what our biblical faith is about. It is, indeed, on the basis of this biblical faith that the churches which confess Jesus Christ, who frees and unites, are called to recognize their inescapable responsibility for humanity.

Fifty years ago, the Stockholm Conference declared: "The world is too strong for a divided Church." At that time those Christian leaders were deeply exercised by the fact that, confronted by the conflicts which brought about the carnage of the First World War, the churches in Christian Europe were helpless to do anything about it and, in fact, reflected the conflicts, divisions, and national parochialism which gripped Europe. They were, nevertheless, not calling for a united front over against the world. What they saw clearly was the need for churches to be renewed together under the Cross of Christ as they reached out hands to one another for the sake of making a common witness to the world. Hence the one important decision they took was to provide for the continuation of their work together—a continuation which, with the movement of Faith and Order and the International Missionary Council, went into the formation of the World Council. As Archbishop Söderblom said at the end of the Stockholm Conference: "When Christendom is gathered together in life and work around the Saviour he will be in the midst of us, irresistible through the almighty power of love." The question for us today is still: Dare we do without a charismatic fellowship of churches, which receive the Spirit's irresistible power of love in order to bring to bear on the global concern of our time the perspectives of the universal gospel? Since the First Assembly of the World Council of 1948 we have learned to say that the evident demand of God upon us is that the whole Church should bring the whole gospel to the whole human being in the whole world. A major task for us, therefore, during these coming days is to discover what God may be calling us to do together for the sake of the world he loved and redeemed in Christ. In doing so we shall have to examine our programmes to see whether they are carried out in a manner which reflects the interrelatedness of the issues which disturb our world today.

While we have been discerning the global and interrelated character of the issues in our world, we are equally conscious of the fact that there is a decided movement in the other direction. There is everywhere a growing regional and national consciousness. Regional military and economic pacts have been proliferating. A noted recent effort was the agreement on European Security and Co-operation. Peoples are seeking to rediscover their national destiny and are asserting their rights to their natural resources and to making their own decisions about their development, etc. Even within nations there are various groups searching for cultural identity, for ways of affirming creatively their existence over against all the alienating forces which are so oppressively present. It is unnecessary to illustrate these tendencies because all of us come from countries where they are pressingly at work.

It is none the less true that global problems and global perspectives have to be given local and particular applications. There is a necessary tension between the global and the local. Our very Christian faith reminds us that the Saviour of the world came as Jesus of Nazareth, and was very conscious of his mission of salvation to the Jews. There is also an understandable reaction to any global domination, as exercised by powerful nations and multi-national enterprises. It is only as nations and peoples are able to develop and assert their own integrity and selfhood that they can meaningfully participate in working for global structures towards a just and peaceful world community.

How has the ecumenical movement and especially the World Council of Churches responded to these challenges during these seven years under review? First, the World Council has throughout its brief life encouraged the formation of regional conferences of which there are now six, with one in process of formation. Over the years there has been a healthy tension between the World Council and these conferences. How can we maintain the global Christian approach to the issues of our time while respecting a regional understanding and response to these issues? A recent first consultation of representatives of regional conferences and of the World Council noted the importance for the world ecumenical movement of a regional understanding and approach to our Christian witness. It also recognized the need for these conferences to be in communication with each other, and where necessary to act together as a world Christian community. In the proposed revised Rules of the World Council there is a section on Regional Conferences, which are considered to be essential partners in the ecumenical enterprise. There is also a charge placed on the World Council, in addition to its communication directly with its member churches, to inform each of the Regional Conferences regarding important ecumenical developments and consult them regarding proposed World Council programmes in their regions. What are the implications of these directives both for the World Council and for the Regional Conferences? I hope that this Assembly will give some guidance on this matter.

Secondly, the World Council has always recognized that however global the character of the issues in our world, Christian obedience must happen "in each place". The ecumenical movement consists in seeing "the local task within a total vision". How can churches manifest their calling together locally? This has been the preoccupation of the national Christian or ecumenical Councils. There are some ninety of these Councils which are in one way or another related to the World Council. A survey carried out through visits and consultations, culminating in a world consultation in 1971, revealed that the major weakness of the Councils was the fact that member churches were seldom really committed to the Councils, let alone to one another. How then can the ecumenical movement respond to the challenges presented by the new trends towards national consciousness and cultural identity? In this connection one issue which is emerging strongly everywhere is the relationship of Church and State. What is the selfhood of the churches *vis-à-vis* State and community and how can the churches confess their faith in Christ and render a prophetic witness to the sovereign will of God in their societies? What is the role of a world ecumenical body such as the World Council of Churches in this regard? I have the impression that we have hardly begun to face these challenges in our various countries.

Thirdly, in its programmes the World Council has sought to come to terms with pluralism and locality. I need mention only a few activities. In the last few years, the thinking about the unity of the Church has been increasingly directed towards the unity which must find expression at different levels of the life of the Church. In the past, we tended to speak about unity in rather general terms. It now becomes clearer that the quest for unity must take into account the characteristics and the particular context of each region or community. The Faith and Order Commission has recently organized a consultation on unity in the context of Africa. The studies on "Salvation Today" and "Giving an Account of the Hope that is in us" brought out the richness and diversity of our ways of expressing the salvation which Christ offers and which is received, and of the hope which is in us. Evangelism can never be carried out as a global campaign or from one centre in the world to other places. As the Bangkok Conference on "Salvation Today" put it:

> Christ has to be responded to in a particular situation. Many people try to give universal validity to their own particular response instead of acknowledging that the diversity of responses to Christ is essential precisely because they are related to particular situations and are thus relevant and complementary.

In order for this to happen, churches in different situations must be given a chance to find their proper style of life and witness without feeling the need to perpetuate and imitate foreign styles. That is what is involved in what is described as the call for a "moratorium", especially by churches in the Third World. The five-year study on what it means to be human has forced us to remember that one cannot come to terms with one's humanity except in living, particular situations. The Church's task is to draw unfailingly on the resources of Christian faith and hope to help men and women to discover for themselves how to live hopefully and creatively with the concrete questions which their life in the world puts to their humanity. The Theological Education Fund, in its current mandate, has been emphasizing theological education in context, as the only means whereby theology can become truly evangelistic—a living encounter of the universal gospel with the realities which human beings face in each place. Ecumenical youth work has increasingly been developed on regional levels, with an emphasis on the involvement of youth in local concerns, especially in the struggle for human dignity and social justice.

We are discovering that, in the words of the Humanum report,

> the search for the truly ecumenical involves attempts to develop a particular quality of concern for the particularities of race, culture,

251

language or situation and for the particularities of women in their distinctiveness from men. This is a concern which involves a readiness to be accountable to one another, to cultivate and receive criticism, challenge and support.

The World Council aims at stimulating this search for the truly ecumenical in flexible, decentralized ways. This Assembly will have to indicate ways in which this can be more effectively done.

There is a third major trend which has become increasingly evident during these years. All over the world people are becoming more determined than ever to participate in decision-making, in efforts towards self-reliance, in movements of various kinds which give them scope to be themselves and to be authentically with others. They no longer accept passive roles, or being treated as objects rather than as subjects. Even the pundits of science and technology now realize that such matters as nuclear energy, genetics, and planning can no more be left to governments and other power elites. The people themselves should be allowed to see the issues and express themselves on options.

In a real sense, this has been a major emphasis of the World Council's activities during these seven years. Development has been seen as people seeking through participation and self-reliance to achieve social justice. Many other programmes are concerned with empowering the powerless to be able to make their own decisions and assert their dignity as human beings, e.g. Inter-Church Aid projects; development counterpart groups; the promotion of community health care; Programme to Combat Racism grants to the racially oppressed groups; people's movements promoted by Urban and Industrial Mission; the programme on Sexism in the 1970s, the determination of women to challenge the age-old discrimination against them in Church and society and to contribute to fullness of life for all. I have the impression, moreover, that these activities have provoked very strong reactions in many of our member churches. Why is this so? It may well be that despite their profession that the Church means the whole people of God, most churches have not yet learned what this may mean in their life and witness. The same hierarchical and non-participatory structures which exist in society are reflected in our church structures and styles of living—preaching, teaching, decision-making, authority. There is, therefore, bound to be resistance to the growing demand for participation and a tendency to accuse those who promote this participation of "left-wing" ideological motivation. It is interesting to note that in countries officially "left-wing" the cry for participation is suppressed for fear of "right-wing" tendencies.

Whatever ideological party slogans are peddled around, there is no doubt that a truly charismatic fellowship is one in which God wills to apportion to each person a particular gift of grace (charisma) for the common good and all share the supreme and indispensable gift of love. Everyone has the privilege and responsibility to develop and share his or her gift in the fellowship of the Spirit. It is, therefore, the task of the ecumenical movement and of the World Council to encourage the churches to further this participation of all who are made in God's image and are empowered by his Spirit to play their part in the life of the congregation and of the community. That is why such a great effort was made to ensure that a larger number of women and youth should be present as delegates at this Assembly as a sign to the churches of what should be normal in their life and decision-making processes.

It must, however, be admitted that the cry for participation all over the world is matched by an increasing trend towards the violent suppression of those who demand a bigger share in the life of their countries. This in turn provokes counter-violence which is called terrorism. During these years under review there has been an increase of military coups and guerilla movements and the steady erosion of private and public liberties in East and West, in North and South. The whole world is caught in a profound conflict between those who yearn and struggle to participate in change for a more humane existence and those who seek to maintain the *status quo* of power relations whether their ideology is capitalist or socialist—between people wanting to share power to shape the future and people holding on to power that shaped the past.

As I have already indicated, the World Council and its member churches have been deeply exercised by this phenomenon of the universal violation of human rights. Matters are not made any easier by the fact that nations caught in different ideological camps hurl accusations and abuses against each other. Even the World Council does not escape these attacks. We are expected to react in an identical way in all situations of the violation of human rights. In fact, one often has the impression that the call for "even-handedness" masks a longing to escape from facing the particular challenges which concern us as churches and nations directly or indirectly in our own situations. Apart from the many activities in which the World Council, through its studies and programmes, is involved with local groups which are seeking to promote participation in the life of the community, we have expended a great deal of energy on general and specific issues of human rights and especially on the matter of "Violence, Non-violence, and the Struggle for Social Justice" (an important study completed in 1973). I hope that this Assembly will give some clear guidance to the Council and to the churches in the coming years on these universal concerns. But in doing so, we must seek to explore what all this means for the relations between Church, State, and community.

Underlying all these trends and threats to human survival is a growing malaise of the human person, the spiritual crisis which is everywhere evident. This takes different forms. People are gripped with fear—fear of losing privileges; fear of accepting responsibility for one another because of the perplexity of problems and the consequences of engagement; fear of difference and of conflict; fear of violence; fear of change; fear of expressions of faith and of church life different from their own. People feel so alienated from themselves and from one another that they are unable to trust each other. They create or hide themselves behind walls of non-communication with other persons and peoples. It was the Jewish thinker, Martin Buber, who, in an essay on "Hope for this Hour", wrote:

> Direct, frank dialogue is becoming ever more difficult and more rare; the abysses between man and man threaten ever more pitilessly to become unbridgeable . . . It is necessary to overcome the massive mistrust in others and also in ourselves . . . The hope for this hour depends upon the renewal of dialogical immediacy between men.

This fear and this mistrust dehumanize persons to the point where they relapse into fatalism, nihilism, or a crude paganism of escape from reality through material self-indulgence, sex, drugs, black magic, and violence to themselves and others. All these are manifestations of a crisis of faith and of faithfulness. We do not experience or attempt enough to dare believe, and we do not believe enough to dare obey and attempt to act.

The theme of this Assembly, "Jesus Christ frees and unites", is a challenge to this crisis of faith. It was not chosen haphazardly, but is the culmination of many efforts by which the World Council, the churches, and various charismatic and renewal groups have been seeking to meet this crisis of faith. The studies on "Salvation Today", "Giving Account of the Hope that is in us", and "Humanum" have endeavoured to explore ways in which people, in the midst of their struggles and the threats to their existence as persons, can find and express their faith in Christ. Our contacts with various charismatic and renewal groups, and also dialogue with people of other faiths, have brought to light the ways in which people are learning through communities of prayer and contemplation, of mutual trust and sharing to find a spirituality for engagement rather than for escape.

In all this we are brought face to face with that revelation of the free, authentic Man Jesus who calls us all to repentance, *metanoia*, the radical change of our thinking and attitudes, indeed, of our whole beings, towards God in Christ and our fellow human beings in faith. It is an act of sharing in the death of Christ, the crucifixion of our selfish existence, and in the resurrection of Christ, the affirmation of the impossible becoming real, of life being wrested from death. Faith in the crucified and risen Lord is, therefore, a radical break from a static understanding of our existence into a dynamic living and daring God's future. It also challenges our corporate existence and calls for the radical transformation of the structures of churches and societies so that they may become more fruitful instruments of God's Kingdom.

It was Thomas Münzer, that Christian radical of the sixteenth century, who said, "Faith gives us the possibility of attempting and accomplishing the things which seem impossible." Charles Wesley put it in song:

Faith, mighty faith, the promise sees,
And looks to that alone;
Laughs at impossibilities,
And cries: It shall be done!

Søren Kierkegaard speaks of one who has faith as having "the passion of the possible". Faith in Christ makes us new men and new women called joyfully to join in God's process of creating a new order in which truth, justice, and fullness of life will prevail. Such a faith is not an opium but rather a ferment operating in concert with God's purpose of transforming his world into his Kingdom of love, joy, and peace. To have faith is to hope and to act in hope. Such faith liberates us to struggle for a shared life in community. This is our vocation as churches and as Christians. This is the meaning of being together in this Assembly as a fellowship of faith, hope, and love.

I have so far tried to situate the activities of the World Council in the context of what is happening in our world and to persons today. In doing so, I want to keep always before our minds the fact that the ecumenical movement is concerned with the *oikoumene*, the whole human race as it struggles to discover what it means to be human in the purpose of God. The Moderator has already indicated how this has been worked out in terms of our theological reflections. My own preoccupation is to draw attention to the ways in which theological reflection becomes possible and results in positions and actions which are relevant for the life of the whole *oikoumene*. The question, however, arises: How can the churches, which are effectively a minority in our strident world, and how can a body like the World Council of Churches, with its severely limited resources and capacities, be obedient to God's call today in a way befitting those who confess the Lord Jesus Christ as God and Saviour according to the Scriptures? What kind of World Council and what kind of churches are envisaged as we face the challenges of the coming decade? What are the indispensable tasks which God imposes on his people today as they seek to fulfil together their common calling?

These are questions with which the Assembly will have to grapple. The last Assembly called for such a reappraisal of the tasks and structures of the World Council. You will be reviewing the new structure which was put into effect from 1971. You will also be asked to vote on the revised Constitution which includes new formulations of the functions and purposes of the World Council. I will only quote here these proposed functions and purposes:

(i) to call the churches to the goal of visible unity in one faith and in one eucharistic fellowship expressed in worship and in common life in Christ, and to advance towards that unity in order that the world may believe;

(ii) to facilitate the common witness of the churches in each place and in all places;

(iii) to express the common concern of the churches in the service of human need, the breaking down of barriers between people, and the promotion of one human family in justice and peace;

(iv) to foster the renewal of the churches in unity, worship, and service;

(v) to establish and maintain relations with national councils and regional conferences of churches, world confessional bodies, and other ecumenical organizations;

(vi) to carry on the work of the world movements for Faith and Order and Life and Work and of the International Missionary Council and the World Council of Christian Education.

(*Workbook*, pp. 113, 115)

While these functions have existed in some form or other in the constitutions of various Commissions of the World Council, the effort is made here to spell them out in one place as a way of expressing what it means for the churches to "seek to fulfil together their common calling". They explicate the basis of the World Council. Thus the goal of this fellowship of churches is "visible unity in one faith and in one eucharistic fellowship expressed in worship and in common life in Christ". The common calling of the churches is to give a common witness in each place and in all places, and that includes the concern for all in need, the breaking down of all human barriers, and the promotion of one human family in justice and peace. This committed fellowship calls for a mutual sharing of the tradition of God's revelation in Christ mediated through the traditions of our various churches in worship and teaching, a mutual exposure to one another as we are challenged by the world in which we are sent to witness and to serve, and the willingness to be renewed in order to become credible and "unitable" churches. And this we must do on all levels—locally, nationally, and internationally, and also with world confessional bodies, non-member churches, and all those engaged in the same quest.

The question for us at this Assembly is whether, in the light of all we have said about the Church in the world today, these functions express adequately and in their interrelationship what is required not only of the World Council of Churches but of the member churches themselves. In fact, I would make bold to say that it is only as these functions constitute the life and mission of the member churches that they have meaning for this fellowship of churches which is called the World Council of Churches. If this is true, then some consequences must be drawn for our life together.

First, there has been, from the beginning of the life of the World Council, too great a gap between the member churches and the World Council. When Dr Visser 't Hooft presented to the First Assembly the report of the provisional committee on its work during ten years of preparation, he mentioned as one of the lessons learned the following:

> We have furthermore learned that the vitality of this Council depends wholly on the vitality of the churches which compose it. It is not merely that we cannot undertake tasks unless the churches support them. It is especially that our common witness in word and deed has no substance and no convincing power unless that witness is rendered locally and nationally in all the churches.

At every Assembly and in every ecumenical meeting it has been said again and again that the credibility of the ecumenical movement depends upon the active engagement of every church and every congregation. The time has come for us to stop talking about it and really to work out ways in which there can be a genuine chain of partnership in obedience between the people of God in each place and in all places. The churches and the World Council are called to be in constant conversation with each other, to be exposed and therefore disclosed to each other, to be free with each other in a community of learning and sharing under the guidance and in the fellowship of the Holy Spirit and for the sake of God's mission in the world. This is a very costly task, because it challenges all our traditional assumptions and attitudes. It is what I have called costly ecumenism. But it is the only way in which we can be liberated for community, for a truly charismatic fellowship. This Assembly will have failed in its purpose if we do not advance to a new covenant relationship between the member churches at all levels of their life and the World Council at all levels of its activities.

Secondly, however prophetic the World Council may seek and be encouraged to be *vis-à-vis* the world and also the churches, it must never be allowed to forget that its *raison d'être* is to be God's instrument for supporting and enabling the churches, in communication with each other, to be the Church in each place and in all places. It is precisely for this reason that the World Council is often called upon by the member churches to act as a channel for mutual support by sharing resources of finance, personnel, experiences, and insights, and to be a means of manifesting ecumenical solidarity in the particular struggles of the churches in their local situations. Our present resources are inadequate to meet such varied needs and pressing demands. Therefore we shall have to establish guidelines for priorities. These priorities must be seen in global perspective, but as being worked out in given situations where the people of God struggle to witness to the world-embracing grace of God in the particularities of their existence.

Thirdly, if the churches and the World Council have common functions and purposes on the basis of a common confession of faith in the Lord Jesus Christ, then their financial resources ought to be seen in an interrelated way. Later this morning you will be hearing a very sombre report on the financial situation of the World Council. You have received a letter telling of some drastic economies which will have to be made in 1976, and the gloomy prospects for 1977. This is nothing new to you. Probably all the churches represented here are going through similar financial agonies. And the present world monetary crisis looks like being with us for many more years. We are, perhaps, confronted with what might well be a breakdown of the economic system far worse than the world depression of 1929. We are therefore facing the possibilities of becoming a fellowship of penury. But how do we deal with this financial crisis in the churches and in the Council? Do we see it as a challenge to all of us to consider afresh what God's calling is upon us, what our priorities are, and how we can pool our resources in meeting these priorities in each place and in all places? If we did, then the programme and budget of the World Council would become the intimate concern of every member church and vice versa. Then we would all be asking urgent questions as to whether the global and interrelated character of our tasks is expressed in to mission, service, and unity. Moreover, we would have to consider whether the global and interrelated character of our tasks are expressed in the very divided way in which the churches and the World Council raise and administer their funds. We shall have further to see how the dynamic relationship of global and local approaches to our tasks can be expressed in a non-competitive way of funding between world, regional, and national councils.

What I have indicated here is in the realm of what has been described as "practical ecclesiology", i.e. the nature, shape, and methods which will enable Christian communities, in an ecumenical communion of worship and service, to live openly with the questions, problems, and struggles of our time in the certainty of God's future for his children in Christ.

Such an understanding of practical ecclesiology or of charismatic fellowship has become apparent in the relations between the World Council and its member churches and the Roman Catholic Church. You will be considering the Fourth Report of the Joint Working Group which was set up in 1965 "to explore the possibilities of dialogue and collaboration". This report speaks of the power of the communion which has been experienced by the churches during these ten years. It says in particular:

Christians have been gathered together. They have been enriched in their experience and have been given new strength. They have been seized by the vision of unity in Christ, a unity which is not necessarily free from tensions and conflicts, but a fellowship in which Christians are committed together to proclaim the Gospel, not in uniformity, but so rooted in Christ that they are able to bear the diversities which arise between them as they seek to fulfil the will of Christ for his Church.

(*Workbook*, p. 147)

The progress in the relations between the Roman Catholic Church and the World Council and its member churches has been varied in different places and at different times. Nevertheless, there can be no doubt about the reality of the fellowship which now exists between them. The challenge posed to us in the World Council and to the Roman Catholic Church is that we shall dare to allow ourselves to be led to more effective common witness through the renewing power of the Holy Spirit. I hope that this Assembly will take up the challenge not only for the World Council itself, but for the member churches locally and across the globe.

At this Assembly we shall be attempting to state afresh the unity we seek and which is God's will for his people and what it requires. During these years since the last Assembly, much has been done to promote a fuller understanding of the unity we seek. All the member churches have received the agreed statements on "Baptism, Eucharist, and a Mutually Recognized Ministry", and have been asked to express their judgement on them. But we have been discovering that there is need to redefine the unity of the church in the highly complex situation in which our churches find themselves today in relation to each other and to society. The description of the unity we seek must do justice to the many and varied efforts undertaken today, e.g. bilateral and multilateral conversations, union negotiations, collaboration in action groups, renewal groups which cut across confessional loyalties, etc. In this regard, the description of the goal of unity produced by the Faith and Order Commission, at its meeting at Salamanca, Spain, in 1973, is significant:

> The one Church is to be envisioned as a conciliar fellowship of local churches which are themselves truly united. In this conciliar fellowship, each local church possesses, in communion with others, the fullness of catholicity, witnesses to the same apostolic faith and, therefore, recognizes the others as belonging to the same Church of Christ and guided by the same spirit. As the New Delhi Assembly pointed out, they are bound together because they have received the same baptism and share in the same Eucharist; they recognize each other's members and ministries. They are one in their common commitment to confess the Gospel of Christ by proclamation and service to the world. To this end each church aims at maintaining sustained and sustaining relationships with her sister churches, expressed in conciliar gatherings whenever required for the fulfilment of their common calling.

The World Council exists to assist the churches to move forward into the fullness of conciliar fellowship—that unity of a fully committed, charismatic fellowship of all churches in each place and in all places. Our task at this Assembly will be to see how the World Council can be the privileged instrument of God to further this goal in the coming years.

And so we end these reflections where we began, with the vision of a charismatic fellowship, sharing the varied gifts of the Spirit in suffering and joy, and through love being drawn by the power of the Cross to a fully committed and eucharistic fellowship. That was the hope of the pioneers of the ecumenical movement, especially at the Stockholm Conference fifty years ago. It was in that spirit that, on my appointment as General Secretary three years ago, I expressed the conviction "that we will not only stay together, but grow together, go forward together, and suffer together under the sign of the Cross and in the power of the risen Lord". It is my hope and prayer that at this Assembly we shall be guided and empowered by the Holy Spirit to receive afresh that liberation in Christ which will bind us closer together and send us forth to be messengers in word and deed of the freedom and unity which Christ gives and wills to give to the whole human family.

Appendix 5
The Finance Report
Presented by Dr. E. A. Payne

INTRODUCTION

1. It is much to be regretted that the Earl of March is unable to be here to present this report. Since the lamented death of Bishop Reed of Canada, he has been the Chairman of the Finance Committee and has given to the financial affairs of the World Council the benefit of his professional skill as an accountant, his wide contacts, and his deep commitment to the ecumenical cause. The WCC has been fortunate in those who have chaired the Finance Committee—Bishop Bromley Oxnam, Dr Eugene Carson Blake, Dr Martin Niemöller, Bishop Reed, and Charles March, the last by no means the least. I am here this morning as a stop-gap, but as one who was drafted to the Finance Committee in 1954 and has failed on successive occasions to secure the release I would have welcomed, I felt I had no right to refuse the request of the Executive to present this Report. But I am happy to say that yesterday I received a cable from the Earl of March, which reads: "Please assure Assembly I am in agreement with the Finance Report. Regret absence owing to other commitments. Regards to all."

2. Since the World Council was formed, the interdependence of world economies has become ever clearer and in the years since the last Assembly international monetary and exchange problems have greatly complicated affairs. But we come to the Fifth Assembly without the threat of an unmanageable deficit on the accounts for 1975 and with the costs of the Assembly covered, we hope. For this we have every reason to be grateful to the member churches, to individuals and foundations, and to the care exercised by the Department of Finance in Geneva—in particular that of the Director of Finance, Frank Northam, who was appointed, I believe, on the eve of the Amsterdam Assembly. His is a remarkable record of able, faithful, and conscientious service.

3. However, the further prospects, to which we must now give attention, are serious. They will involve actions and changes which were not foreseen even a few months ago, and which none of us is likely to welcome. Looking at bills, examining resources, deciding what can or should be afforded is never a pleasant process, whether at the personal, the denominational, the national, or the international level; but deciding on priorities may be salutary.

4. I have now to lay before you the facts as seen by the Finance Committee and the Executive and some suggestions. They will no doubt be referred to the Finance Committee of the Assembly for close scrutiny.

259

But they must be kept in mind throughout the discussions in every Section, Hearing, and Committee in the hope that at the beginning of next month we come to a common mind as to what the World Council and the member churches we represent should do.

THE FINANCIAL OPERATIONS OF THE WCC AND THE PRESENT POSITION

5. The main activities of the WCC are presently financed under no fewer than seven separate budgets: the General Budget; Commission on Inter-Church Aid, Refugee and World Service; Commission on World Mission and Evangelism; Theological Education Fund; Christian Medical Commission; Commission on the Churches' Participation in Development; and Office of Education. The World Council has faced constant and growing difficulties in the financing of the work in the years since the Uppsala Assembly. Problems and difficulties in different degrees now arise in respect of each of those budgets but the most critical is that of financing operations under the General Budget. The problems and difficulties in most other parts of the work are not of the same magnitude and urgency.

6. There are two reasons for the seven separate budgets. One is historical. After the Amsterdam Assembly in 1948, there were two budgets—the General Budget and Inter-Church Aid—a budget for an activity which developed from the needs following World War II and which initially was essentially concerned with assistance to the churches in war-ravaged Europe and the needs of refugees after the war. After the integration of the World Council and the IMC at the New Delhi Assembly in 1961, a third budget came into being—the budget of CWME. After the Uppsala Assembly in 1968, two new activities were started—each with its own budget: the Commission on the Churches' Participation in Development; and the Office of Education, which received further importance following the merger of the WCCE with the WCC in 1971. Finally, there are the sponsored agencies, each with its own separate budget, operating under CWME: the Theological Education Fund was established by the IMC in 1959; and the Christian Medical Commission was established in 1967.

7. The second reason for the seven separate budgets and for the complex financial structure of the WCC is the need to match the varied structures of the member churches. The specialized agencies of the member churches need the assurance that the support which they give is used for work in specialized fields of activities—service monies for service, development monies for development, mission monies for mission, etc. The total resources needed in 1975 to finance the activities of the WCC are budgeted at about Frs. 25,000,000. As stated earlier, the most critical problem is that of financing operations under the General Budget—the budget which is supported by the central treasuries of the churches. The amount of that budget for 1975 is Frs. 6,950,000—that is little more than a quarter of the total. And the operations financed under that budget are the General Secretariat, the main meetings of governing bodies, Faith and Order, Church and Society, Renewal, Laity, the Ecumenical Institute and

the New York Office, and also varying proportions of the operations of Dialogue, PCR, CCIA, Communication and Finance, and Central Services.

8. In addition to the activities under its own budgets, the WCC is an instrument by which the churches respond together to a multiplicity of church and human needs. These needs are of many kinds: natural and man-made disasters, church service and mission projects, development operations, grants to organizations combating racism, medical and theological work, education, refugee programmes, urban industrial mission, family ministries, and so on. The WCC handles approximately Frs. 75,000,000 annually for such needs. The purposes for which they are to be used are designated before the monies reach the WCC and no charge whatsoever is made by the WCC for the considerable task of negotiation and administration. It has been felt by the WCC from the outset that it should provide these services without charge for the agencies which wish to handle these operations through WCC channels and procedures. The expense is covered through the budgets of the responsible commissions—primarily by the budget of CICARWS financed by the service agencies of the member churches. While it is tempting to feel that this activity should be a source of income for the WCC itself, it has always been assumed that any such charges would be open to misunderstanding and could only result in a diminution of the willingness of the contributors to work together through the WCC. The funds do not in any sense belong to the WCC. They are simply church funds handled ecumenically.

9. Turning back to the problems of financing the activities of the WCC, it should be recalled that the difficulty in respect of financing General Budget operations is not new. The Finance Committee at the Uppsala Assembly in 1968 noted that the proposed model General Budget of $1,320,000—limited in size because more resources were not foreseeable—was probably an underestimate of needs and reported that a sounder estimate of true needs for the coming period was probably $1,500,000, which at that time was equivalent to Frs. 6,420,000. The Finance Committee further reported that resources adequate for the financing of the work under the General Budget would not be available unless there was a considerable increase in total member church contributions.

10. The member churches have demonstrated their commitment by increasing their contributions, even though they too face financial difficulties in most countries. The increases between 1968 and 1974 were as follows: the member churches in the USA, though experiencing particular problems themselves, increased their contributions by 16%; the Evangelical Church in Germany made an increase of 155% and now gives almost as much as the total contributions of the US member churches; and the member churches in other countries increased their giving by 67%. But in recent years—particularly since 1971—the increased support of the member churches was eaten up by declining exchange rates and inflation. The member church contributions to the General Budget in 1974 produced Frs. 5,211,132. If exchange rates had remained as they were in 1968, those contributions would have produced Frs. 6,567,500—about Frs. 1,350,000 or 26% more. As a second example, the total contributions of the US member churches show a 16% increase in dollar amount between 1968 and 1974, but the Swiss franc value dropped by 32% because of exchange rates. Furthermore, a 37.6% increase in income in Swiss francs was needed in 1974 by comparison with 1968 merely to finance the same work by reason of increased costs caused by inflation.

11. For the first two years after the Uppsala Assembly, it was hoped that the financial difficulties were temporary and they were overcome by *ad hoc* solutions—by securing special contributions of a non-recurring nature by appeals to member churches, individuals, etc. In 1970 and 1971, a series of measures was adopted—partly reducing expenditure, partly seeking extra income, and partly seeking contributions from other separate budgets towards the financing of activities which had been carried by the General Budget, but which were of concern to the Commissions, etc. responsible for those separate budgets. In 1972, it appeared that reasonable financial equilibrium had been restored, but there then arose a series of further problems—mostly as a consequence of world monetary and economic difficulties and thus entirely beyond the control of the World Council. It was recognized in 1973 that in the period following this Assembly it might be necessary to restructure the World Council at a lower level of expense on the General Budget, but it was felt that if an adequate job of preparation for the Assembly was to be done, further cuts in staff could not be envisaged without crippling the whole operation. It was therefore decided to make a determined effort to finance operations until the Assembly, so that the Assembly and the 1976 Central Committee, acting in the light of guidelines given by the Assembly, might establish priorities and decide policy for the following period.

12. When the Executive Committee met last April, it could already be seen that it might prove impossible to reach that objective. The Executive Committee therefore asked the Officers together with the Chairman of the Finance Committee to review the position in September. They were empowered to take such action as might seem necessary in the light of the estimated position at that date. When they met at the end of September, they were faced with estimates which can be summarized as follows: a deficit of Frs. 965,000 is foreseen on General Budget operations for 1975. This can be met perhaps in full or at least almost fully from the Special Reserve—a balance which has been built up by economies and special contributions in recent years. It is when we turn to 1976 and the period for which this Assembly has to plan and will be appointing a new Central Committee that the seriousness of the situation is evident. Total expenditure for 1976 on present activities is estimated at Frs. 8,200,000 and income presently foreseeable amounts to only Frs. 5,600,000. Member churches are reporting that their own problems are such that they cannot make the full increases in contribution requested of them by the Central Committee in 1974—a one-third increase from Germany and the USA and a 50% increase by all other member churches. These figures imply a deficit on General Budget operations in 1976 of Frs. 2,600,000. There are still some special resources which can be used next year; about Frs. 1,150,000 towards covering the deficit could be provided from the profit on the sale of the property adjoining the Ecumenical Centre—a profit which it had been hoped might be held for future capital needs—together with a foundation grant which it is hoped will be received next year. But there would still remain an uncovered deficit of about Frs. 1,500,000. And the General Reserve of the World Council amounts to only about Frs. 1,000,000 or about six weeks' expenditure under the General Budget. This General Reserve has been built up by annual allocations from current income in accordance with the decision of the Amsterdam Assembly in 1948, reaffirmed by each subsequent Assembly, in order to provide some resource to be called on only in the event of a major emergency. One

must, of course, try to look further ahead into 1977, though here one enters the realm of crystal gazing rather than estimation. But an operation requiring a budget of Frs. 8,200,000 in 1976 would surely involve more expense in 1977, if only because of inflation. And there are no present indications that any significant increase in income can be expected. Thus, with all special funds exhausted, it might be necessary to face a deficit of more than Frs. 2,600,000.

13. When they met in September, the Officers and the Chairman of the Finance Committee therefore concluded that the need to reduce expenditure under the General Budget was inescapable and agreed on a number of measures. Information about these decisions was sent in mid-October to the member churches and to all registered delegates. It was decided that there must be a reduction of Frs. 300,000 in the planned expenditures of the Communication Department; that vacant posts in the Secretariat for Faith and Order and the CCIA New York office be left unfilled; and that salary increases foreseen in but not automatic under the Staff Regulations be withheld. A case could be made against every one of those decisions. None of them is welcome. But together they will result in savings estimated at Frs. 740,000.

14. The Officers also submitted to the Executive Committee, which has been meeting in Nairobi, proposals involving the Ecumenical Institute, Bossey, and the WCC involvement in the support of the North American Office maintained in New York by the WCC and the US Conference for the WCC. The Executive Committee, recognizing the critical financial situation of the General Budget and strongly aware of the importance of the Ecumenical Institute and of the widespread interest in its work expressed by the member churches, urged that an alternative way of financing the Institute in the future be actively pursued, and examined proposals for such a plan. Meanwhile, the Executive Committee declared that the WCC dare not run the risk of incurring a deficit in General Budget operations. It therefore assured up to Frs. 750,000—a reduction of Frs. 500,000 in the planned 1976 General Budget provision—for the support of the Ecumenical Institute, Bossey, in 1976 and the situation will have to be reviewed by the new Executive and Central Committees. Further details of the action of the Executive Committee will be communicated to the relevant hearing. As to the New York Office, the Executive Committee agreed that the WCC's share in the maintenance of that office be reduced in 1976 by $53,055 (approximately Frs. 132,000). The Executive Committee recognized that a continuation of the New York Office, if possible, was desirable. Further details of the action of the Executive Committee, regarding continuing discussions between the General Secretariat and the US Conference, the American member churches, and other appropriate organs, to find alternative means of supporting the joint office will be communicated to the relevant Hearing.

15. These measures, together with some planned economies on expense for meetings in 1976 (about Frs. 50,000), should result in a saving on the General Budget of about Frs. 1,400,000 and should go a long way to wipe out the threatened 1976 deficit. They should thus save the WCC from financial disaster, but it still remains necessary for the Assembly to review all activities of the WCC and the way in which they can be financed.

16. Unfortunately, it must be reported that further dangers have

appeared since the estimates were prepared on the basis of which the measures reported in the last few paragraphs were developed as proposals. It now appears that the financial difficulties of CWME may become acute earlier than expected and call for a revision of the CWME support for some activities financed jointly by CWME and the General Budget. The amount of the reduction could be significant. Proposals regarding the financing of the Office of Education and the Portfolio for Biblical Studies could also result in increased expense on the General Budget. These matters will need the attention of the Finance Committee of this Assembly.

17. This factual part of this Report can, however, end on a more positive note. It is, of course, too early to expect accurate estimates regarding the outcome of the accounts for the Assembly. If, however, expenditure is held within the limits of the authorized budget, income is available to cover the expense. Appreciation must be expressed to member churches which by their special contribution have made possible this encouraging note in this Report and to the member churches which have made special efforts to cover or make substantial contributions to the travel expenses of their delegations attending the Assembly.

QUESTIONS AND SUGGESTIONS FOR CONSIDERATION BY THE ASSEMBLY

18. What can the Assembly do to advance solutions to the financial problems outlined in the first part of this Report? The suggestions which follow are grouped under three headings: the establishment of priorities and the reduction of expense; the seeking of new and increased income and the shape of support; and the seeking of improved budget procedures and presentation.

THE ESTABLISHMENT OF PRIORITIES AND THE REDUCTION OF EXPENSE

19. It is clear from the information already given that there will be need, at least in the next few years, to exercise economy and reduce expenditure. The financial difficulties which the WCC is experiencing are a reflection of the world economic and monetary problems and of the difficulties which are being experienced by the member churches themselves. Indeed, it may well be that the WCC and the member churches should join in study of what the many changes in the financial situation of the churches imply for the ongoing life of the churches themselves and of the WCC. The question of priorities—the selection of those programmes and operations which are essential to the effective continuance of the World Council—will be examined by the Programme Guidelines Committee, in close consultation with the Finance Committee, and their report will be presented to the Assembly.

THE SEEKING OF NEW AND INCREASED INCOME AND THE SHAPE OF SUPPORT

20. The most agreeable solution to the present problems would, of course, be to find ways of securing increased support sufficient to solve the financial problems. It is, unfortunately, unlikely that this can be achieved, but it may well be that the Assembly can take action to open the way to securing additional resources and reducing the problems.

21. A fundamental question concerns the past assumption that while much support comes from specialized church and other agencies (clearly designated), the "basic" church support comes mainly from central treasuries. Such central contribution is a clear implication of membership. But does it sufficiently express the ecumenical commitment of the local congregations and members of the churches? Is their apparent inability to get involved caused by their substantial ignorance of, and indifference to, the WCC? Are the churches themselves not changing in many places in such a way that central treasuries do not any longer represent the giving capacity of those churches? Are the central treasury contributions any longer an adequate expression of the involvement of the whole people of God?

22. Because of the urgency of these questions, the Executive Committee submits a number of proposals for consideration by the Assembly. They require careful consideration. Even if approved, they will be of only modest immediate financial consequence. What is sought at this time is the guidance of the Assembly as to the types of procedures which should be strenuously promoted by the churches themselves as well as by the staff. If the proposals win approval, they will prove effective only in so far as they are actually followed and promoted in the member churches. That means that any vote taken later in the Assembly should imply a serious commitment to action by the delegates in their respective churches.

The proposals are five:

(a) There has been strong support from many parts of the world and from WCC Executive in April 1975 for the idea of churches having a special "ecumenical Sunday". It would be an occasion when, with help from the WCC staff, ecumenical information could be provided for congregations and an offering could be received for the WCC—either generally, or for some agreed aspect of its work. There are many different ways of organizing it. It is quite clear that for some churches this would not be practicable for one reason or another, but there is evidence that for many it could be almost the only way by which they could increase support. Would the Assembly commend the proposal to each church for consideration, and instruct staff to enter into the appropriate negotiations with the churches concerned?

(b) It has been suggested that the WCC should urge upon all member churches a minimal level of financial support. This has never been done before. It is almost impossible to define. One proposal is that every church with from, say, 50 to 400 pastors be asked to consider as a minimum contribution the equivalent of what is paid to one pastor as an annual salary. This would clearly be better than any fixed financial amount. Many churches of this size have rated their financial support far lower than the

265

total amount it costs them to support one pastor. Clearly this suggestion is irrelevant to the larger and more affluent churches, and also to churches which do not provide regular monetary salaries to their clergy. Twenty-three churches have not ever paid anything to the General Budget (excluding a few churches in countries where it is legally impossible for them to do so).

(c) Another question is whether the WCC should assist those churches which are finding it difficult to secure support, by providing them certain options of contributing to the support of a specific item in the WCC programme. This is of course a highly risky procedure in that there is clearly need for support for some items which are not for many contributors very interesting! But would it help certain churches to become involved?

(d) Some member churches—notably those in the socialist countries of eastern Europe—have difficulty in securing authorization to transfer contributions to Geneva. Can ways be found by consultation between the WCC and the churches in question by which they can none the less provide greater material support for the activities of the WCC?

(e) In a few countries there are schemes for individuals to contribute directly to the WCC, although this has never been proposed internationally or promoted vigorously. The fact remains that the highest per capita giving to the WCC from any group of churches is equivalent to about 20 Swiss centimes; a few other churches average above 5 centimes, and the great majority of even the affluent churches give between 0.01 and 1.5 centimes per person per year. It is fully recognized that these figures depend on a great variety of church statistics that are not comparable, but the overall implication is nevertheless clear. Surely there are vast numbers of people who would want to make a more substantial and more personal contribution if a method were available. Are there groups of delegates in the Assembly who could promote some such schemes in their country, with the good will of the central church authorities there?

23. It is recognized that the danger involved in increasing designated giving in any form, even in non-financial forms, is that it may impose a certain inflexibility upon the Council. There would remain the need for the central church contributions to be general and of increasing size. But these suggestions are offered in the hope that they would enable some of the churches to increase not only their financial support but also their real involvement in the Council in other ways. If such suggestions are in fact followed up, it may be necessary to establish staff responsibilities for major follow-up work in relation to the churches. It is our hope and prayer that from the life of this Assembly other patterns of support may emerge which will indicate our common will to survive the present financial storm and build strong foundations for the future.

THE SEEKING OF IMPROVED BUDGET PROCEDURES AND PRESENTATION

24. The present style and structures of the financial operations of the WCC have been inherited from the past. Are there changes and improvements which could be adopted and which could be helpful in the coming period?

25. The number and nature of the various separate budgets has already been explained, as well as the historical processes by which they came into being. The complexity of the situation, however, is greatly increased (even if the financial situation is somewhat eased) by the interrelatedness of most of those "separate budgets". They are interrelated in two main ways. First, each sub-unit with its separate budget helps to pay for some of the services it receives from other sub-units, e.g. Finance, Communication, Building Maintenance, Personnel Office, etc. Some of these payments are for specific services rendered, some are a proportionate share of the costs involved in another department. But, secondly, such sub-units have frequently felt that, while their separate budget was for their own area of concern, it was possible within that concern responsibly to share in financing part or all of the work of another sub-unit. For example, CICARWS in Unit II provides for the cost of the Scholarships operation and World Youth Projects in Unit III. CWME provides almost all the funds for Dialogue. CWME in Unit I and CCPD and CICARWS in Unit II all provide part of the budget of CCIA. But there are many other examples. Many of those responsible for these separate budgets have handled them with a wide and generous concern for the whole, with the agreement of the donors who relate to their respective Commissions.

26. The negative consequences of the complex presentation of the finances of the WCC are, however, becoming more evident. The member churches find difficulty in understanding the position and become unclear about just which parts of the WCC their gifts do support. The General Budget, originally designed to cover the whole work of the WCC, except inter-church aid, is now often assumed to cover what can vaguely be called "central administration", whereas, as already explained, it does in fact cover the General Secretariat, the main meetings of the governing bodies, Faith and Order, Church and Society, Renewal, Laity, the Ecumenical Institute, and the New York Office and also varying proportions of the operations of Dialogue, PCR, CCIA, Communication and Finance, and Central Services. In other words, it covers those elements of the work which do not have an identifiable, separate supporting constituency. It is this complex of operations which is under the most immediate financial strain. Some of the other budgets are also facing major problems in the near or relatively near future, but yet others are not in immediate danger. This leads to a Council structure in which different parts are under different degrees of financial threat. In addition, while responsible and representative Commissions administer the different budgets, the Central Committee does not have effective control of the whole.

27. While it is clear that the determining factor in the shape of WCC budgeting is the designation of monies at source in the churches, the question is raised whether, even within these limitations, a clearer method of budgeting could not be devised to become operative at the beginning of 1977. It seems that what many of the churches want can be summed up as follows:

(a) A single WCC budget presentation indicating the total cost of each part of the WCC, whatever the source of support each part has. This would of course be supplemented with the detailed breakdown of each separate item. A first attempt has been made along these lines with the "Composite Statement of Needs".

A copy of the Composite Statement of Needs 1975/76 has been made available to each delegate with the text of this Report. It indicates the expenditure forecast, the number of staff, and the sources of financing foreseen for each sub-section of WCC activities. Those who are willing to study it may find it a useful "tool" for their participation in the hearing on finance. The expenditure figures have validity as a general indication of projected costs but it should be noted that the statement was prepared nine or ten months ago, that some modifications have since been made, and that the 1976 needs may be somewhat over-stated, since they include provision for inflation at 12%—a rate which at the time did not seem unreasonable but which fortunately now appears unnecessarily high. Copies of the printed Financial Report for 1974 have also been distributed.

(b) The possibility of making their church contribution share in the whole of the WCC operation. Many churches in fact believe that their annual contribution helps with WCC concerns in evangelism, for example, but at present, in most cases, that work is entirely supported from other sources. Some method would have to be agreed whereby a section of the budget that was fully or over-subscribed would contribute at least part of its "surplus" to other sections.

(c) The possibility of a church, or church agency, or other organization making a designated contribution to a specific budget item. Clearly this would be necessary. But equally clearly such designated items would have on some agreed basis to be charged a percentage for the support of the whole. There is considerable evidence that many, if not all, of those giving designated support would willingly accept such a clearly defined arrange-ment. Obviously the matter is of concern to the whole of the Assembly. One specific suggestion is that interest accumulated on all WCC funds (including perhaps even "transferred money" on short-term stopover in Geneva) might be accepted as undesignated support to the whole budget by agreement with major donors.

(d) The total budget in the interrelatedness of its parts would be effectively under the overall policy control of the Central Committee, and not be merely a composite of budgets under effective control in a multi-plicity of other committees. This of course would not in fact deny the considerable responsibility of the unit and sub-unit committees for de-tailed operations.

DECENTRALIZATION OR REMOVAL FROM GENEVA

28. As participants of the Assembly have listened to the problems arising for the WCC from the very high value of the Swiss franc in relation to other currencies, many will undoubtedly ask: Then why not move part or all of the Council to another place? Naturally such a solution has been considered many times, and should never be forgotten. But there are many factors which must be remembered, such as the fact of the existence of an adequate debt-free headquarters building in Geneva, the presence of a host of related international organizations, and the convenience for inter-national travel. While there have recently been increasing difficulties, it has

been generally possible to get staff from any country into Switzerland. Visas can be secured for participants from all countries for meetings in Geneva. Whatever might be the long-term consequences (and they are impossible to foretell), any such major move would clearly add to the short-term financial problems of the Council. Furthermore, Switzerland is a country where the fight against inflation at the present time is producing positive results.

SUMMING UP

29. Decisions on some or all of these and other suggestions are sought from the Assembly. None of them would bring immediate solutions. But hopefully over a period of time some changed procedures might not only bring increased support, but also involve the churches much more effectively in their renewed covenant together in the work and witness of the WCC. We hope and pray that at this Assembly ways may be found not only to deal with the immediate and serious financial problems facing it, but also to release the strength of the peoples working together in a growing and more effective obedience to our common Lord.

30. The situation may be summed up as follows:

We must face the fact that, despite increasing support from the member churches and substantial economies by the staff, the financial situation of the WCC—caused primarily by economic factors over which it has no control—has come to the point where, in the interests of its whole future, major action must be taken. We have seen this situation coming for many years, and now action is unavoidable. Nothing proposed in this Report can relieve the Council of the need to make major cuts in its 1976 expenditure (particularly but not exclusively under the General Budget) of at least the dimensions decided upon by the Executive Committee. It is equally clear that, whatever steps may be planned by this Assembly for increased long-term support, further major cuts in 1977 expenditure will have to be planned in 1976 to enable us to cope with the problems of that year.

Secondly, we must face the fact that the WCC today has inherited a budgeting structure which reflects on the one hand the organizational history from which it has been built up, and on the other the member church structures through which the churches want to channel designated support to various specific purposes within and primarily beyond the WCC itself. While no easy administrative decision can be made to simplify this situation, there is an urgent need to consider what ways there are to achieve a more visible unity within the financing of the life and programme of the WCC, while at the same time preserving the right of the churches and their agencies to support (or refrain from supporting) specific aspects and activities.

CONCLUSION

31.   This has been a lengthy and complex Report. Permit me a final word.

32.   A newly elected Synod of the Church of England met a fortnight ago and one of the members objected to a report on "The Churches' Needs and Resources" appearing on the agenda the first day "as if", it was said, "finance was our master, not our servant". It was alleged by the speaker that that particular report revealed no spiritual aspect; it could have been the report of any business organization. I am not a member of the Church of England and have no knowledge of what was in the report in question. But I know that this kind of comment is heard in many churches. Some of you may be thinking along these lines this morning.

33.   There are, I believe, most important spiritual implications in the Report I have presented. Our churches came together in 1948 under strong spiritual impulses. They have remained together out of loyalty to their understanding of what Christian witness and discipleship demand in the twentieth century. They are convinced of the need to act together in their witness and service. All this, and the organization to make it possible, requires money. It is possible only if there is regular, generous giving that is, as far as possible, shared fairly. And the administration must be strictly businesslike, if our wide-ranging operations are to be carried out and if confidence is to be maintained. Most of the member churches, in spite of current difficulties, have large resources. In some they are more readily accessible than in others. In some they are largely untapped. The difficulties we face are not insuperable. In the end their solution depends less on wise administration, business acumen, and an understanding of the international monetary system than on knowledge, vision, continued good will, and mutual trust. And these are spiritual qualities.

34.   "The silver and the gold are mine, saith the Lord of Hosts", according to the prophet Haggai in a passage well worth our attention. But I remind you also of our Lord's parable about those to whom a man entrusted his property. All, whether they had much or little, were expected to act responsibly.

Appendix 6
The Fourth Official Report of the Joint Working Group between the Roman Catholic Church and the World Council of Churches

PREFACE

In the course of the last three decades, the relations among the churches have changed profoundly. Though continuing to live in a state of division, they have discovered anew, through the ecumenical movement, the bond which holds them together despite their differences. They have entered into dialogue. They have begun to witness and to work together. They have begun to experience a common spiritual joy. Attitudes of mutual exclusion have been replaced by a common search for that true unity the disciples are called to show forth in the world.

In this development, the World Council of Churches has played a significant role. It has been an instrument helping the churches to engage in encounter and exchange and calling them to bear witness together to Jesus Christ and to the salvation he has brought to the world.

The Second Vatican Council gave a decisive further impulse to the ecumenical movement. In the documents of the Council, in particular in the constitution *Lumen Gentium* and the decree on Ecumenism, the Roman Catholic Church has given new expression to its understanding of the unity of the Church and committed itself to participation in the ecumenical movement. This decision opened the doors for mutual discovery and made possible, in some measure, common witness and collaboration.

Inevitably, the question arose as to how the Roman Catholic Church would relate to the World Council of Churches. In 1965, after many preliminary contacts and conversations, it was decided to set up the body known as the Joint Working Group, a commission with the mandate to explore the possibilities of dialogue and collaboration. More than ten years have passed since the decree on Ecumenism was promulgated and the Joint Working Group brought into existence. Therefore it has to be asked: Where have we been led during these years? What has been achieved? What should and can be our goal in the years to come?

The Joint Working Group has served to strengthen the links between the Roman Catholic Church and the World Council of Churches. In a number of fields, joint study and collaboration have been initiated. On the other hand, the regular contacts and the common reflection have also made the two partners more fully aware of the implications of their collaboration. They have come to see more clearly the obstacles which need to be overcome if fellowship and collaboration among the churches are to grow.

Both the Roman Catholic Church and the World Council of Churches are determined to continue their collaboration and to seek together ways to serve the ecumenical cause. Therefore, after ten years of common experience, it is appropriate to ask anew the question how they can, together, best further the ecumenical movement. How should the Roman Catholic Church and the World Council of Churches be related to one another? What areas require primary attention? What kind of common structure should be adopted?

The present Report attempts to answer these questions and submits to the parent bodies a number of recommendations as to the next steps to be taken.

THE COMMON GROUND

Before turning to any specific considerations, it is essential to recall the common ground shared by the Roman Catholic Church and the World Council of Churches. In the course of the last ten years, three perspectives have gained increasing importance. They should guide the planning for the future.

THE EXISTING COMMUNION

Despite all divisions which have occurred in the course of the centuries, there is a real though imperfect communion which continues to exist between those who believe in Christ and are baptized in his name. They confess that Christ, true God and true Man, is Lord and that it is through him and in him alone that we are saved. Through the Spirit, they offer praise and thanksgiving to the Father who, in his Son, reconciles the world to himself. They proclaim the love of God, revealed by the Son who was sent by the Father bringing new life to the human race, and who through the promise and gift of the Holy Spirit gathers together the people of the New Covenant as a communion of unity in faith, hope, and love.

Through the development of the ecumenical movement that communion has been experienced anew. This is not to claim that it has been created anew. Since it is beyond human power and initiative, it precedes all ecumenical effort for the restoration of the unity of all Christians. The gift of communion God has bestowed in Jesus Christ remains a reality, even where Christians may obscure or damage it by their lack of understanding, their disobedience and mutual estrangement. The ecumenical movement is therefore the common rediscovery of that existing reality and equally the common effort to overcome the obstacles standing in the way

272

of perfect ecclesial communion. It is at the same time a return and a new departure. It is a return to the original gift in many ways distorted by human failures in the course of history and an attempt to understand and accept the way in which God wants to lead us to his Kingdom. The ecumenical movement is a constant invocation of the Spirit, that he may lead us into new awareness of the original revelation and guide us to the future God is preparing for us.

The joy of the ecumenical movement lies in the fact that the power of this communion has become more evident among the churches. Christians have been gathered together. They have been enriched in their experience and have been given new strength. They have been seized by the vision of unity in Christ, a unity which is not necessarily free from tensions and conflicts, but a fellowship in which Christians are committed together to proclaim the gospel, not in uniformity, but so rooted in Christ that they are able to bear the diversities which arise between them as they seek to fulfil the will of Christ for his Church. Though this vision of perfect unity is far from being fulfilled, and even its concrete shape cannot yet be fully described, it has already become part of the life of the churches. They can no longer move back from it nor hold to the former separation. Thus work for the unity of the Church is a vital and inescapable necessity. It is not a luxury which can be left aside, nor a task which can be handed to specialists but rather a constitutive dimension of the life of the Church at all levels and of the life of Christians themselves.

The nature of the communion by which we are held together cannot yet be described together in concrete terms. The language we use is marked by the divisions of history. Each church has its own approach and its own ecclesiological terminology. But since the churches meet in Christ's name and share in his gift, their fellowship must have ecclesial reality. As they move forward together, both the nature of the present communion they already have and the future unity they seek may become clearer and their divisions may be healed.

THE NEED FOR COMMON WITNESS

The gift of communion calls for common witness in the world. The ecumenical movement does not only aim at healing the divisions among Christians. It seeks at the same time to enhance the credibility of the churches' witness in the world.

Ecclesial unity is a sign destined for all people, a sign testifying that God has reconciled them in Jesus Christ, a living invitation to believe in him as their Saviour. The churches' search for the restoration of unity among all those who are baptized and believe in Christ as Lord and Saviour will be genuine only if they live in the constant expectation that this sign will become manifest through them to the world. They will, therefore, not only engage in dialogue about unity, but will bear witness to Christ wherever the partial communion in faith and life, as it exists among them, makes it possible (see *Ad Gentes*, 15; *Common Witness and Proselytism*, 9-13, 17, 19). As they seize these possibilities of common witness, their search for unity will in turn advance. In the perspective of witness many of the problems which still divide them will appear in a new light.

For some churches, the scandal of division came to be felt first as they faced the missionary task and they were led into the search for unity by this experience. It is significant that it was the World Missionary Confer-

273

ence in Edinburgh (1910) which gave the impulse for the movement on issues of Faith and Order. For other churches the starting point was the consideration of the essential oneness of the body of Christ. They asked how the one Church founded by Jesus Christ in history could ever be divided. Thus their first interest was in the restoration of unity between Christians, and common witness in the world was not their primary motive for ecumenical involvement. The two approaches had to learn that mission without unity lacks the perspective of the body of Christ and that unity without mission is not a living reality. In recent years the Roman Catholic Church and the World Council of Churches have come to see more clearly the implications of the intimate relationship between unity and common witness.

THE CALL TO RENEWAL

Christians in their relation to Christ need to be constantly renewed by the power of the Holy Spirit. So also do the churches. This is particularly true in today's world where change seems to have become a permanent factor. New problems and new tasks arise, and if the churches are to respond to them in obedience they need to be prepared for renewal.

There is a growing awareness that the churches need to engage themselves in the struggle for justice, freedom, and community. Sin is manifesting itself not only in personal failure but in injustice, oppression, and dehumanization. Salvation is spiritual liberation and new life for each individual person, enabling him to offer himself as a living sacrifice through prayer, praise, and new obedience. But salvation is also a liberating force pointing to a more human society. Christian faith calls for the commitment to struggle for that society and by this very commitment to proclaim Christ and the good news of salvation.

The Spirit speaks to the churches in the actual event of history, calling into question the outlook they have come to be accustomed to. In all churches, historical, political, and cultural factors, sometimes of many centuries' standing, obscure the true meaning of the gospel. The spirit urges Christians to discern and interpret together the signs of the times. He is the power of renewal.

The changes in today's world are so great that they fill many Christians with a feeling of uncertainty. There is a widespread crisis of faith. Can the inherited faith be maintained in the transformations the present generation is experiencing? Many respond with timidity to this challenge; many regard the maintenance of the *status quo* as the only expression of tradition and identity. But should it not be seen as a challenge of the Holy Spirit to fresh obedience of mind and soul? Is it not our task to go forward together? Are Christians not called to interpret together signs of the times and to discern the will of Christ for the present generation? Unity is required to face the challenge, and as the churches respond they will in turn be led into fuller unity.

Already very similar concerns occupy the churches. To give only a few examples, the theme of the World Missionary Conference in Bangkok, "Salvation today", is very close to that of the Roman Catholic Synod of Bishops in 1974, "Evangelization in the contemporary world". The biblical concepts and realities of "liberation" and "communion" which are at the heart of the Fifth Assembly of the World Council of Churches with its theme, "Jesus Christ frees and unites", are analogous to the theme of "Renewal and reconciliation" which is central for the Holy Year, 1975.

Does this not indicate that the churches are offered the *kairos*, the propitious time, to commit themselves together to the task of renewal?

THE COLLABORATION 1965-1975

Since the Joint Working Group was formed in 1965, co-operation and collaboration between the Roman Catholic Church and the World Council of Churches have developed progressively. There have been the jointly sponsored studies on "Common witness and proselytism" and "Catholicity and apostolicity". Roman Catholic membership in the Faith and Order Commission has come about, and the Roman Catholic Church has set up consultative relations with the Commission on World Mission and Evangelism and the Christian Medical Commission. The preparation of material for use in the annual Prayer for Christian Unity is done jointly. The concern for development and peace was taken up in partnership by the formation of the joint Committee on Society, Development, and Peace (SODEPAX).

It was this growth of collaboration that created the atmosphere in which the Joint Working Group was led to consider the possibility of membership by the Roman Catholic Church in the World Council of Churches.

At its meeting in Gwatt, Switzerland, in 1969, the Joint Working Group decided that the "advantage of . . . a closer and more permanent association of the Roman Catholic Church with the World Council of Churches" should be studied. Thus a study got under way and the consideration given to this question occupied on both sides a great amount of time and energy. The results of the study were published in 1972,[1] but by this time it had been made clear that an application by the Roman Catholic Church for World Council membership would not be made in the near future.

Why did it not prove possible to give this form of visible expression to the relations between the Roman Catholic Church and the World Council of Churches? There is no doubt that the Roman Catholic Church could accept the basis of the World Council of Churches, but there are factors, some theologically based, which at present militate against membership as the visible expression of the relationship between the Roman Catholic Church and the World Council of Churches. To a much greater degree than other churches, the Roman Catholic Church sees its constitution as a universal fellowship with a universal mission and structure as an essential element of its identity. Membership could present real pastoral problems to many Roman Catholics because the decision to belong to a world-wide fellowship of churches could easily be misunderstood. Then there is the way in which authority is considered in the Roman Catholic Church and the processes through which it is exercised. There are also practical differences in the mode of operation, including the style and impact of public statements.

The decision at present not to apply for membership was not intended to weaken or downgrade the need for close collaboration. Cardinal Willebrands and Dr Eugene C. Blake, in their preface to the report on possible Roman Catholic membership, stated this quite clearly: "Co-operation . . . must not only continue, it must be intensified".[2] The same

275

conviction was reiterated and confirmed in the message sent by Pope Paul VI to the Central Committee on the occasion of the silver jubilee celebrations of the World Council of Churches, on 26 August, 1973, when he said: "It is our sincere desire that this collaboration may be pursued and intensified in accordance with the spirit of the Second Vatican Council".[3] The decision also does not mean that the question of membership has been closed. At its meeting in Windsor, in 1973, the Joint Working Group explicitly stated that it could be "reopened at a later date". But for the immediate future another question has to be asked: How can the Roman Catholic Church and the World Council of Churches, without forming one structured fellowship, intensify their joint activities and thereby strengthen the unity, the common witness, and the renewal of the churches?

At Windsor, the Joint Working Group had an extensive discussion on this question and came to the conclusion that for the planning of the future collaboration, a careful analysis of the actual ecumenical experience in different national and local situations was required. It was recognized that the progress of the ecumenical movement largely depends on the commitment of Christians in their actual life situations, and thus interaction of ecumenism at the local level and the international level is of fundamental importance. Joint activities at the international level must therefore be intimately related to the experience of the churches and seek to serve their needs. For this reason, the Joint Working Group decided to undertake a survey on the present state of the ecumenical movement. What are the problems the churches face as they carry out their mission? What are their consequences for the ecumenical movement? This survey formed the basis of discussion at the following meeting of the Joint Working Group in Venice, 1974, as it sought to discern appropriate programmes and patterns of collaboration for the future.[4]

The debate resulted in the recommendations which follow.

GUIDELINES FOR THE FUTURE OF THE JOINT WORKING GROUP

CONTINUATION OF THE JOINT WORKING GROUP

There continues to be the need for a forum enabling the Roman Catholic Church and the World Council of Churches to evaluate together the development of the ecumenical movement. Therefore, a joint group with continuity of membership and sufficient breadth of representation from both sides should be appointed. As an instrument of the parent bodies, it will be in close contact with them and accountable to them.

THE FUNCTIONS OF THE JOINT WORKING GROUP

The Joint Working Group will primarily aim at discovering and assessing promising new possibilities for ecumenical development. It has the task of stimulating the discussion on the ecumenical movement in being a challenge to the parent bodies by proposing new steps and programmes.

The Joint Working Group will endeavour to interpret the major streams of ecumenical thought and action in the Roman Catholic Church and in the member churches of the World Council of Churches. It will facilitate the exchange of information about the progress of the ecumenical movement, especially at the local level.

The Joint Working Group will seek to establish the collaboration between the various organs and programmes of the Roman Catholic Church and the World Council of Churches. In accordance with the principles and procedures of the parent bodies it should encourage the genuine development of any ecumenical collaboration. It should draw upon the insights gained from local experience to foster such collaboration. As in the past, it will remain a consultative group, not an operative agency. It may be empowered by the parent bodies to develop and administer programmes it has proposed when this is called for.

As the Joint Working Group seems to initiate and help keep alive the discussion on the implications of the ecumenical movement in the Roman Catholic Church and in member churches of the World Council of Churches, it will seek the best means of communicating its findings and recommendations.

An essential aspect of its task is to share its findings with parent bodies.

EXPANDED RELATIONSHIP

The Joint Working Group will be in contact with a large number and range of ecumenical organizations and programmes, especially on the local level. It may call upon various offices and programmes of the parent bodies for assistance when special help is needed in certain areas in the process of collaboration. It will also seek information and advice from individuals and organizations which have particular ecumenical experience and competence.

FLEXIBLE STYLE

As the Joint Working Group seeks to meet the needs of the churches, the style of collaboration must be kept flexible. It must be adaptable to the various and changing needs. Therefore, it will seek to keep new structures to a minimum, while concentrating on *ad hoc* initiatives, as they are required by the actual developments within the ecumenical movement. On occasion, of course, particular projects may call for some structural organization which will be set up after due authorization. Flexibility of style does not mean unplanned activity or lack of accountability. It rather means more careful attention to the setting of priorities and to the use of resources.

SUGGESTED STRUCTURES

On the basis of these general considerations the following is proposed:

1. The Joint Working Group shall be a group of approximately sixteen members, some of whom shall be chosen from the staff of the

World Council of Churches and the Secretariat for Promoting Christian Unity (and other organs of the Curia).

2. The Joint Working Group will normally meet once a year. Further, enlarged meetings could be held on occasion to deal with specific issues. Such meetings may be arranged to coincide with some important regional event when this is judged useful.

3. A small Executive Group of six members shall be responsible for the ongoing work between meetings and for preparing the meetings of the Joint Working Group.

THE WAY AHEAD

What are the priorities for the joint activities in the coming years? The following section attempts a first answer. Obviously, further developments may bring to the fore new tasks. At this stage, the Joint Working Group submits to the parent bodies the following programme for approval and authorization.

JOINT PROGRAMMES

Joint programmes are proposed in the three areas of the unity of the Church, common Christian witness, and development and peace.

The Unity of the Church

The progress achieved in mutual understanding in recent years is considerable. Bilateral confessional dialogues and multilateral ecumenical conversations are leading to doctrinal convergences. Although these findings still have to be submitted to the judgement of the churches involved, they have decisively contributed to a new climate. There is a new readiness to recognize a plurality of expression in confessing the same faith. There is also the considerable growth of local ecumenism which constitutes an important factor in the growth towards unity.

Only a small beginning has so far been made in the evaluation of the relationship of bilateral confessional dialogues to one another and to multilateral conversations. An attempt needs to be made to bring together and share widely the various insights gained in the course of these discussions so that it may be seen more clearly how they interact.

Roman Catholic membership in the Faith and Order Commission offers a promising opportunity for collaboration. The instrument of the Faith and Order Commission should be made use of to the fullest possible extent. Certain studies of the Commission deserve special attention, e.g. its studies on Baptism, Eucharist, and Ministry, and on "The teaching office in the Church".

The Joint Working Group should explore ways of facilitating the exchange of information and initiating joint reflection on all of these activities with a view to preparing a report on this.

Finally, the question needs to be examined as to the role of ecumenical structures of collaboration, such as regional, national, and local councils. In many places Roman Catholic dioceses or parishes are full members in councils, and in other places membership is proposed. The Secretariat for Promoting Christian Unity has recently worked out a document on ecumenical collaboration at regional, national, and local levels. The World Council of Churches, through its desk for relations with National Councils of Churches, is engaged in a fresh evaluation of present structures of collaboration. It has also been agreed that a survey be made jointly of these councils of churches where there is Roman Catholic membership and an informal paper prepared.

Common Christian Witness

Both sides agree that their ecumenical commitment should find expression also in common witness. In October 1974, the Bishops' Synod in Rome stated this need in the following terms:

> In carrying out these things we intend to collaborate more diligently with those of our Christian brothers with whom we are not yet in the union of a perfect communion, basing ourselves on the foundation of baptism and on the patrimony which we hold in common. Thus we can henceforth render to the world a much broader common witness of Christ, while at the same time working to obtain full union in the Lord. Christ's command impels us to do so: the work of preaching and rendering witness to the Gospel demands it.[5]

The Joint Working Group has already undertaken a study and produced a document on "Common witness and proselytism"[6] which spoke of the conditions for common witness. It now seems appropriate to take up the study again in terms of the possibilities and limits of such common witness with regard to both its intent and method. It is proposed that the Joint Working Group arrange such a study. It should draw on the documents of the Second Vatican Council and subsequent official documents of the Roman Catholic Church, the reports of the Assemblies of the World Council of Churches, the results of the World Missionary Conference on "Salvation today", the Faith and Order study on "Giving account of the hope that is within us", the section on "Confessing Christ today" of the Fifth Assembly of the World Council of Churches, and on the findings of the Roman Synod of Bishops, "The evangelization of the contemporary world".

Consideration should also be given to the renewal in catechetics in the churches. The issue has already been considered in documents such as the Roman Catholic Directory on Catechetics[7] and the Ecumenical Directory, Part II, on Ecumenism in Higher Education.[8] It is suggested that organized common reflection should determine what possibilities there are for a common basis for religious instruction.

All of these developments point to another area for discussion and mutual stimulation. It is proposed that the Joint Working Group consider how new common insights from this relationship may best be used, and report its findings to the parent bodies.

Development and Peace

For six years, the Committee on Society, Development, and Peace (SODEPAX) has been in existence, and has enabled the Roman Catholic

Church and the World Council of Churches to face together vital issues of international social justice and to bear common witness in this field. The experience of these years suggests that the co-operation should be continued in the future. Efforts should concentrate on the role of the Church in the search for a new, more just and viable world order.

Both sides have given approval in principle for the continuation of the Committee on Society, Development, and Peace for a new term of three years, beginning on 1 January, 1976, under the sponsorship of the Roman Catholic Church (Pontifical Commission on Justice and Peace) and the World Council of Churches (Unit on Justice and Service).

(i) A joint secretariat with at least two full-time staff members will be maintained.

(ii) It is agreed that the main purpose of the Committee on Society, Development, and Peace be education and motivation of Christians in these fields; it should also draw the attention of the parent bodies to the important aspects of the joint research and suggest steps to be taken either separately or together by them, or also through SODEPAX.

(iii) It is agreed that the Committee, while continuing its present work, shall initiate a study on Christian community and the search for a new world order. This study should be carried out in close co-operation with regional bodies already in existence on both sides. It may be concluded with a joint international conference on the theme.

(iv) The Committee and the Secretariat shall be entrusted with the responsibility for carrying this programme and shall report annually to the parent bodies on the progress made; SODEPAX shall be invited to give an account to the Joint Working Group between the Roman Catholic Church and the World Council of Churches of the aspects of its work which are relevant for the promotion of the ecumenical movement in general.

(v) It is understood that the parent bodies commit themselves to seek the funds required for the administration and programme budget of SODEPAX.

(vi) The parent bodies will instruct the present SODEPAX Steering Committee to work out the detailed proposals for the future joint programme.

MUTUAL EXCHANGE AND STAFF CONTACT

There are areas in which collaboration has been at the level of the mutual exchange of information and staff contact. Such areas include dialogue with people of living faiths and ideologies, the role of women, the family, human rights, international issues, and laity concerns. These contacts have served to discover further subjects for study and to indicate collaboration which might be undertaken together. There are, for instance, the whole range of important issues such as spirituality, the mystical life and worship, pluralism, and cultural diversity. There are other subjects too which do not require continual study but which need to be considered from time to time, such as mixed marriages.

The present level of mutual exchange and staff contacts ought to continue and collaboration be intensified wherever possible. The consultation on laity formation, held in Assisi in late 1974, under the sponsorship of the Roman Catholic Laity Council and the WCC Unit of Education and Renewal, has been a particularly promising example of encounter and exchange.

OTHER ONGOING COLLABORATION

There is an amount of ongoing collaboration which should continue and develop. Notable are the following:

Week of Prayer for Christian Unity

For several years, a joint Roman Catholic Church and World Council of Churches' Group has been responsible for preparing the material to be used as a help in this annual observance. Since 1972, a small consultation of Roman Catholics and WCC staff has edited the material for international use from initial material prepared by a local committee. A group in Melbourne, Australia, prepared the initial material for the Week of Prayer 1975, and the Caribbean Conference of Churches is preparing the material for 1976.

Christian Medical Commission

The WCC Christian Medical Commission seeks to develop an understanding of the nature of the Christian ministry of healing and the role of the Church in health and medical work. The Roman Catholic Church has had observers at several of the meetings of the Commission and has for the past three years appointed a staff consultant to the Commission. A new mandate for the Commission is at present under discussion. It is desirable that Roman Catholic collaboration be continued in the future.

These examples of collaboration, given under the above headings, are not exhaustive. Further forms will need to be developed as Christians in various local situations are informed of what is happening in other places and themselves proceed with appropriate initiatives.

Relations with CWME

There are also noteworthy developments in the field of mission. A number of Roman Catholic missionary orders which work with the Congregation for the Evangelization of Peoples have developed links with the Commission on World Mission and Evangelism of the World Council of Churches. They have accepted a consultative relation with the Conference on World Mission and Evangelism and have named observer consultants to the Commission for a fixed term.

CONCLUSION

The Roman Catholic Church and the World Council of Churches remain open to unexpected possibilities, ready to undertake new tasks which will be demanded by the developing dialogue and co-operation. Thus the Joint

Working Group looks to the future with a renewed commitment to the one ecumenical movement. It will go on trying faithfully to discern the impulses of the Holy Spirit, given by God as guide on the way ahead.

NOTES

[1] *The Ecumenical Review*, vol. XXIV, no. 3 (1972), pp. 247-88.

[2] Ibid., p. 249.

[3] Cf. *Minutes and Reports* of the 26th Meeting of the World Council of Churches Central Committee, Geneva 1973, p. 77.

[4] *One in Christ*, 1975/1; *Il Regno-Documenti*, 1975/1; *Unité des chrétiens*, 1975/1; *Dialogo Ecuménico*, 1974, nn. 35-36; *Una Sancta*, 3 (1975), pp. 156-169.

[5] "Declaration of the Synodical Fathers", in *L'Osservatore Romano* (English edition, 7 November, 1974).

[6] *"Common Witness and Proselytism"*, a study document. *The Ecumenical Review* (January 1971), pp. 9-20; also SPCU *Information Service* (1971/II, no. 14), pp. 18-23.

[7] *Sacred Congregation for the Clergy, General Catechetical Directory* (London, Catholic Truth Society, 1972).

[8] Ecumenical Directory, Part II, in *Information Service* (no. 10, 1970/II).

Appendix 7
The Presidents and Members of the Central Committee

Honorary President: Rev. Dr W.A. Visser 't Hooft
Presidium:
Ms Annie Jiagge
Dr J. Miguez-Bonino
His Eminence Nikodim, Metropolitan of Leningrad and Novgorod
Dr T.B. Simatupang
Most Rev. Olof Sundby
Dr Cynthia Wedel

MEMBERS OF THE CENTRAL COMMITTEE

Most Rev. S.J. Ajamian, Armenian Apostolic Church
Rt Rev. John M. Allin, Episcopal Church, USA
Bishop Ralph T. Alton, United Methodist Church, USA
Mr Jan Anchimiuk, Autocephalic Orthodox Church in Poland
Mrs Joan Anderson, Presbyterian Church of New Zealand
Dr Rakoto-Andriajarimaona, Malagasy Lutheran Church
*Rev. Dr André Appel, Evangelical Church of the Augsburg Confession of
    Alsace and Lorraine
Mr Harry A. Ashmall, Church of Scotland
*Prof. Dr Anwar M. Barkat, Church of Pakistan
Bishop Dr Tibor Bartha, Reformed Church in Hungary
*Mr Bena-Silu, Church of Christ on Earth, Zaïre
Rt Rev. Dr P.A. Berberian, Armenian Apostolic Church

---

*Members also of the Executive Committee elected by the Central Committee

283

Rev. Alexei Bichkov, Union of Evangelical Christian Baptists of USSR
†Rev. Jacques Blanc, Protestant Church of Algeria
Rev. Prof. Vitaly Borovoy, Russian Orthodox Church
Rev. Leslie Boseto, United Church in Papua-New Guinea and the Solomon Islands
Hon. Mr John Brademas, United Methodist Church, USA
Rev. John P. Brown, Presbyterian Church of Australia
Rt Rev. J.L. Bryce, Church of the Province of New Zealand
Mr Alexey Buevsky, Russian Orthodox Church
Dr Robert Campbell, American Baptist Churches in the USA
Rev. Chan Chor Choi, Anglican Church of China including Hong Kong
*His Eminence Konstantinidis Chrysostomos, Ecumenical Patriarchate
Most Rev. Kriton Chryssochoidis, Church of Greece
Metropolitan Pathenios-Aris Coinidis, Greek Orthodox Patriarchate of Alexandria
Mrs Fernanda Comba, Waldensian Church, Italy
Rev. Dr Paul Crow, Jr, Christian Church (Disciples of Christ), USA
Rev. E.A. Dahunsi, Nigerian Baptist Convention
Rev. Meirion Lloyd Davies, Presbyterian Church of Wales
Mr John Doom, Evangelical Church of French Polynesia
Rev. Canon E.P.M. Elliott, Church of Ireland
Principal Olle Engstrom, Mission Covenant Church of Sweden
Prof. Dr Hans Helmut Esser, Evangelical Church in Germany (Reformed)
Miss Ana B. Ferrari, Evangelical Methodist Church of Argentina
Mr Ludwig Franke, Evangelical Lutheran Church of Thuringia, GDR
Dr Hans Alfred Frei, Old Catholic Church of Switzerland
*Rev. John G. Gatu, Presbyterian Church of East Africa
Mrs Daisy Gopal Ratnam, Church of South India
Rev. David X.J. Gqweta, Moravian Church in South Africa
*Metropolitan Paulos Gregorios, Orthodox Syrian Church, Catholicate of the East
Rev. Dr John S. Groenfeldt, Moravian Church in America (Northern Province)
Prof. Dr Gerhard Grohs, Evangelical Church in Germany, United
*Bishop Hans Heinrich Harms, Evangelical Church in Germany, Lutheran
Metropolitan Ignatios Hazim, Greek Orthodox Patriarchate of Antioch and All the East
Dr Heinz Joachim Held, Evangelical Church in Germany, Lutheran
*Bishop Dr Johannes Wilhelm Hempel, Evangelical Church of Saxony, GDR
Rev. Harry Henry, Protestant Methodist Church in Dahomey and Togo
Rev. Dr Albert van den Heuvel, Netherlands Reformed Church
Bishop Dr Friedrich Huebner, Evangelical Church in Germany, Lutheran
Rev. Albert Isteero, Evangelical Church, the Synod of the Nile
His Grace Zakka Iwas, Syrian Orthodox Patriarchate of Antioch and All the East
Dr Joseph H. Jackson, National Baptist Convention USA Inc.
Dr Emil A. Jeevaratnam, Methodist Church, Sri Lanka
Mrs Heather Johnston, Presbyterian Church in Canada
Bishop Frederick D. Jordan, African Methodist Episcopal Church, USA
His Eminence Justin (Moisescu), Metropolitan of Moldavia, Romanian Orthodox Church

†Co-opted by the Central Committee

His Eminence Juvenaly of Tula and Belev, Russian Orthodox Church
*Rev. Dr Won Yong Kang, Presbyterian Church in the Republic of Korea
Rt Rev. Dr Josiah M. Kibira, Evangelical Lutheran Church in Tanzania
*Very Rev. Kirill (Gundyayev), Russian Orthodox Church
Bishop Chester A. Kirkendoll, Christian Methodist Episcopal Church,
    USA
Bishop Albert Klein, Evangelical Church of the Augsburg Confession,
    Roumania
Most Rev. Arthur Kratz, Episcopal Church of Brazil
Rev. Johannes Langhoff, Church of Denmark
Miss Cynthia Latuihamallo, Protestant Church in Indonesia
Rev. Samuel Lehtonen, Evangelical-Lutheran Church of Finland
†Mr José Leite, Evangelical Presbyterian Church of Portugal
Rt Rev. Per Lønning, Church of Norway
Ms Janice Love, United Methodist Church, USA
Rev. Augustina Lumentut, Christian Church in Mid-Sulawesi
Rev. Wilson T. Lwanga-Mugerwa, Church of Uganda, Rwanda, Burundi
    and Boga Zaire
Miss Evelyn Mahlatsi, Church of the Province of South Africa
Mr Renato Z. Malvar, Philippine Independent Church
†Rev. Roberto Mariano, Evangelical Methodist Church in Uruguay
*Rev. Dr Robert J. Marshall, Lutheran Church in America
Bishop James K. Mathews, United Methodist Church, USA
Miss Teli Matthew, Federation of Evangelical Lutheran Churches in India
Archbishop Janis Matulis, Evangelical Lutheran Church of Latvia
Mrs Jean Mayland, Church of England
*Rev. J. Oscar McCloud, United Presbyterian Church in the USA
Rev. Prof. Jean Meyendorff, Orthodox Church in America
Mrs Marie Momo Kingue, Evangelical Church of Cameroon
Rev. Dr Robert V. Moss, United Church of Christ, USA
Rev. Armencius Munthe, Simalungun Protestant Christian Church
Rt Rev. Gerald B. Muston, Church of England in Australia
Dr Emerito P. Nacpil, United Methodist Church
Prof. Dr Nikos A. Nissiotis, Church of Greece
†Rev. Francisco Norniella, Presbyterian Reformed Church in Cuba
Pastor Lukombo-Kitete Ntontolo, Evangelical Church of Zaïre
Dr Maurice Nyembezi, Methodist Church of South Africa
Ms Mercy Oduyoye, Methodist Church, Nigeria
Mrs Michiko Okuda, United Church of Christ in Japan
Rt Rev. Dr Henry Okullu, Church of the Province of Kenya
Metropolitan Pankratiy, Bulgarian Orthodox Church
Metropolitan Paul (Menevisoglou) of Sweden, Ecumenical Patriarchate of
    Constantinople
Bishop Paulos, Ethiopian Orthodox Church
Rev. Margaret Barnes Perry, Presbyterian Church in the United States
Miss Waltraut Peper, Evangelical Church of Anhalt, GDR
*Rt Rev. Antonie Plamadeala, Romanian Orthodox Church
Mr Albert J. Price, United Church of Christ, USA
Prof. Warren Quanbeck, American Lutheran Church
Deacon Radomir Rakic, Serbian Orthodox Church
Most Rev. Panteleimon Rodopoulos, Church of Greece
Mrs Julia Roduner Laedrach, Swiss Protestant Church Federation
*Dr Jacques Rossel, Swiss Protestant Church Federation
Rev. Dr David S. Russell, Baptist Union of Great Britain and Ireland

*Mrs Dorinda Sampath, Presbyterian Church in Trinidad and Grenada
His Grace Bishop Samuel, Coptic Orthodox Church
*Most Rev. Karekin Sarkissian, Armenian Apostolic Church (*Vice-Moderator*)
*Most Rev. Edward W. Scott, Anglican Church of Canada (*Moderator*)
Pastor Manuel de Mello Silva, Evangelical Pentecostal Church "Brazil for Christ"
Rt Rev. Gurbachan Singh, Church of North India
*Ms Jean Skuse, Methodist Church in Australia (*Vice-Moderator*)
Prof. Josef Smolik, Evangelical Church of Czech Brethren
Rt Rev. Neville W. de Souza, Church in the Province of the West Indies
Dr Koson Srisang, Church of Christ in Thailand
Rev. Dr Sutarno, Christian Churches of Java
Mr Nikolay Teteryatnikov, Russian Orthodox Church
Prof. Kyaw Than, Burma Baptist Convention
Dr M.M. Thomas, Mar Thoma Syrian Church of Malabar
Ms Barbara R. Thompson, United Methodist Church, USA
Mr William P. Thompson, United Presbyterian Church in the USA
Mr Habte Tsegaye, Ethiopian Orthodox Church
Mrs Marja van der Veen-Schenkeveld, Reformed Churches in the Netherlands
Rev. Dr Marion de Velder, Reformed Church in America
Rev. Dr Robert A. Wallace, United Church of Canada
*Miss Pauline M. Webb, Methodist Church, UK
Commissioner Harry W. Williams, Salvation Army
Ms A. Jean Woolfolk, Christian Church (Disciples of Christ), USA
Rt Rev. Kenneth Woollcombe, Church of England
Ms Margaret A. Youngquist, American Lutheran Church
Mrs Jean Zaru, Friends United Meeting
Prof. John Zizioulas, Ecumenical Patriarchate
Mrs Hildegard Zumach, Evangelical Church in Germany, United

Appendix 8
The Report of the Finance Committee Adopted by the Assembly

INTRODUCTION

1. The Finance Committee would associate itself with the affirmation made in the Finance Report presented by Dr E.A. Payne that it is dealing with concerns that have deep spiritual implications. The financial decisions that are made constitute one of the ways in which we give living expression to the beliefs we proclaim. It is by these decisions that we, in fact, indicate our real priorities. This makes them extremely important.

2. The Finance Committee would reiterate the position set out in the Finance Report presented by Dr Payne that the financial outlook for 1976 is very serious and that its seriousness will greatly increase in 1977 and subsequent years (see Appendix) unless action—carefully planned action— is authorized by this Assembly. The Finance Committee therefore recommends:

(*a*) that the Assembly commend the Officers and the Executive Committee for responsibly reacting to the now apparent financial shortfall for 1976 by making difficult but necessary decisions to curtail programme and reduce expenditure;

(*b*) that the Assembly instruct the Central Committee to adopt a balanced budget for 1977 on the basis of realistic estimates of income. The Finance Committee reluctantly recognizes that this will, in all probability, require a curtailment of programme and staff; and

(*c*) that the Assembly instruct the Central Committee to establish a Review Committee to report to the Executive Committee and Central Committee and to carry out the necessary preparatory work to enable decisions regarding 1977 programme and budget to be taken in August 1976.

The seriousness of the financial situation led the Finance Committee to request that the Programme Guidelines Committee present its report in the form of guidelines, rather than as priority directives to the Central Committee. This procedure would enable the Central Committee to assess the total programme and to take account of the guidelines as given by the Assembly in a responsible manner. The Finance Committee is confident that the Assembly will agree with the wisdom of not seeking to make binding decisions in the limited time available in Nairobi.

ACTIONS TO BE TAKEN BY THE CENTRAL COMMITTEE, EXECUTIVE COMMITTEE, PROGRAMME UNITS AND SUB-UNITS, AND THE STAFF OF THE WORLD COUNCIL

3. The Finance Committee recommends that the Assembly:

A. Instruct the Central Committee to take the initiative in, and request the programme units, sub-units, commissions, committees, and staff to co-operate in developing clearer and simpler budgeting procedures designed to lead to a greater co-ordination of the total programme, while maintaining the integrity of the various specialized sub-units. A start in this process has been made at the level both of commissions and committees and of staff, and the Finance Committee would recommend the combining of elements of two proposals being studied by staff:

(i) one global budget, expressing the oneness of the World Council, divided into a minimum balanced budget and a "goal budget" for supplementary support; and

(ii) flexibility for support designated for particular elements of the budget, within criteria established by the Central Committee.

The Finance Committee believes that this combination would both make possible more adequate support for the central work of the World Council, much of which is at present financed under the General Budget, and also retain the necessary and valuable right of churches and agencies to designate giving to specialized areas of concern within the total programme of the WCC; and develop a simplified, more popular report of the work of the Council designed to assist the member churches in interpreting the *total programme* of the World Council both to church members and also to the general public.

B. In further elaboration of the recommendation in paragraph 2(c), instruct the Central Committee to establish a Review Committee, responsible to Central Committee, whose functions would be to keep the total programme under continuous review, in such a manner as to monitor and assist the commissions and committees of sub-units to fulfil the priorities determined by the Assembly. Such a committee could well facilitate the necessary "pruning" of some programmes, the initiating of new ones and, when called for, the closing out of those which have accomplished their purposes or proved incapable of so doing. The Finance Committee believes that this responsibility is too important to be left to a committee whose primary concern, of necessity, is with the financial implications. The establishing of a Review Committee would call for clarification of the terms of reference of such a committee and of the Finance Committee, so that the relationships between the two Committees and the Central Committee would be creative. The Finance Committee believes that this procedure would help to bring about:

(i) greater co-ordination of all aspects of the Council's work;

(ii) more adequate support of programme units and sub-units within the total programme; and

(iii) a greater sense of confidence on the part of the member churches and agencies in the work of the Council.

C. Direct the Central Committee and staff to assess ways and means by which the Council can establish better rapport with its member churches and church-related agencies so that we may "advance to a new covenant relationship between the member churches at all levels of their life and the World Council of Churches at all levels of its activities" (General Secretary's report, p. 245).

D. Direct the Central Committee and appropriate staff to arrange for consultations (perhaps initially on a country or regional basis) with the appropriate finance, programme, communication, and ecumenical officers of the member churches and their agencies so as better to understand each other's policies, programmes, and financial situations and possibilities and also the particular mandate restrictions which condition the life and work of each. Such consultations should seek to:

(a) identify the office or the person to whom particular communications of the WCC should be addressed in addition to the designated person in each particular member church;

(b) determine ways and means whereby the officers of a member church and World Council officers could mutually support one another in the task of interpretation and communication of the whole gospel to the whole world;

(c) determine the type and form of information which member churches require from the World Council to enable them to fulfil their responsibility of interpreting the life and work of the WCC to their constituency in the most effective way;

(d) explore the extent to which staff of the member churches might be able to undertake particular responsibilities for the WCC; and

(e) explore the extent to which women may participate more fully in the task of communication and interpretation and also in gaining additional financial support for the WCC.

E. Direct the Central Committee and staff members to devise means whereby the work of financial promotion for the WCC as a whole and the General Budget in particular may be better co-ordinated.

REQUESTS TO THE MEMBER CHURCHES AND TO CHURCH-RELATED AGENCIES

4. The Finance Committee recommends that the Assembly should urge:

A. That the member churches recall that the WCC is their council. As the New Delhi report on Programme and Finance put it: "The World Council in its whole life and programme is responsible to the churches which constitute it. Its work must therefore reflect the convictions of the churches concerning their common tasks." Since this is so, member churches should take *greater responsibility* in:

(a) helping to shape the life and work of the Council;

(b) interpreting the life and work of the Council to their own constituencies as an extension of their own work; and (*c*) providing more adequate financial support, primarily to the General Budget and secondly to those programmes which reflect their own priority concerns.

B. That *every* member church make at least a minimum undesignated contribution appropriate to its size of membership and financial resources to the budget of the WCC.

C. If they have not already done so, that all member churches respond positively to the financial requests made to the member churches by the Central Committee in August 1974, namely:

(*a*) that the member churches in the USA be asked to seek to raise by one-third from the level of 1973 contributions the total of the US support for the General Budget for 1976;

(*b*) that the member churches in Germany be asked to seek to raise their contribution for 1976 by one-third from the 1973 level;

(*c*) that all member churches in other countries be asked to raise their contributions for 1976 by at least 50% from the level of the 1973 contribution; and that the member churches keep before them the fourth request:

(*d*) that all member churches be asked in the period following the Fifth Assembly to plan for an annual increase in contributions sufficient to compensate the effects of inflation and maintain the real value of their support.

D. Since the 286 member churches vary greatly in size and administrative structures, it is inevitable that a variety of patterns for relating to, and for financial support of, the World Council must exist. The member churches are therefore asked to examine carefully the following suggested possibilities and to implement those which are appropriate to their particular situation:

(*a*) the possibility of designating an "Ecumenical Sunday" which would provide a focus for communicating information about the WCC and other ecumenical agencies. In some situations, a special offering to support "ecumenical activity" might well be appropriate and productive;

(*b*) where it is difficult to secure increased financial support from members, the focusing of attention on the existing opportunity to designate funds for particular programmes now contained within the General Budget (Biblical Studies, Faith and Order, Church and Society, Renewal, Laity, Ecumenical Institute, etc.) might be helpful;

(*c*) in some parts of the world, it may well be financially helpful for the WCC if it is made more easily possible for individual persons to contribute, preferably through their own church, to the support of the WCC, with particular emphasis on the General Budget;

(*d*) in some churches and countries, in view of the serious financial situation for 1976/77, it might be possible to make a "special appeal" to help in redressing the anticipated deficit;

(*e*) member churches in the Third World might well focus attention on what they can contribute to the development of the policy and programme of the WCC, as well as on its financial needs.

5. The Finance Committee recommends that the Assembly confirm and draw the attention of the member churches to the policy followed since the formation of the WCC that the member churches are responsible for the travel expenses of those of their members who are members of the Central Committee, Executive Committee, and Committees and Commissions of units and sub-units, but that some provision be made in the budget of the World Council for assistance to members from distant and small churches.

REQUESTS DIRECTED TO ALL WHO HAVE PARTICIPATED IN THE FIFTH ASSEMBLY

6. Since the Finance Committee is convinced that the best means of interpreting and communicating—of providing knowledge and understanding, of creating and maintaining good will and trust—is personal contact, it calls on the Assembly to invite the more than 1,500 persons from all parts of the world who have participated in this Assembly to commit themselves to fulfilling their tasks for the World Council. If this commitment is taken up, it will greatly assist in building better rapport between the member churches and the WCC. It will not happen by accident. It will only happen to the degree that you and I:

(a) look upon ourselves as members of the World Council because we are members of a member church and continue to take responsibility for the formation, implementation, and evaluation of the Council's policy and programme;

(b) consciously undertake the task of interpreting this policy and programme to our churches and the community and country in which we live, seeking to widen and deepen the vision of the part the World Council plays and can play in the mission of the Church; and

(c) deliberately seek to secure increased financial support to make possible the implementation of the priority programmes determined by this Assembly.

CONCLUSION

7. In conclusion, the Finance Committee would like to reiterate Dr Potter's words: "a major task before us therefore . . . is to discover what God is calling us to do together for the sake of the world he loved and redeemed in Christ. In so doing, we will have to examine our programmes to see whether they are carried out in a manner which reflects the interrelatedness of the issues which distress our world today." This task poses us with a very direct question: "Are our member churches giving a

high enough financial priority to the things they are calling us to do through the World Council of Churches?"

8. The goal which underlies the Finance Committee's recommendations is to maintain and strengthen the World Council of Churches as a faithful servant of its member churches and of the Lord of the Church. Such strengthening would involve a council which:

(*a*) clearly sees itself as the servant of the living God who in Christ calls us into liberation and unity and which is dependent on him;

(*b*) has a stable basis of financial support;

(*c*) has a sound, comprehensive, co-ordinated, balanced programme; and

(*d*) has developed a new flexibility so that it may:

(i) utilize its human and financial resources more effectively;

(ii) have its programmes and priorities under constant review;

(iii) operate with a deep sense of accountability to the priorities set by this Assembly; and

(iv) carry on its work with increased mutual consultation with the churches which constitute it.

APPENDIX: THE FINANCIAL OUTLOOK FOR 1976/7

1. The Finance Report, presented by Dr E. A. Payne, gave some general forecasts of the outlook, mainly in relation to operations under the General Budget. It was indicated that total General Budget expenditure for 1976 was estimated at SF 8,200,000, and normal income at only SF 5,600,000, implying a deficit of SF 2,600,000. Decisions had been taken by the Officers and by the Executive Committee to reduce expenditure, and those measures, combined with the use in 1976 of special non-recurring resources towards the financing of 1976 operations, were estimated to close the 1976 deficit.

2. The Finance Report also indicated that, after the above estimates had been prepared, further problems had arisen. The financial difficulties foreseen by CWME had become acute earlier than expected and have necessitated revision of the CWME budget plans for 1976. By reason of the interrelationship of budgets, this will worsen the General Budget position for 1976. Proposals regarding the financing of the Office of Education and the portfolio for Biblical Studies will also result in increased expense on the General Budget. There may be some compensating factors, but the estimated shortfall of normal, recurring, annual income for the General Budget in 1976, as compared with the estimated expense of continuing the present level of activities, may well be increased by SF 300-500,000. Further economies may therefore be needed in 1976.

3. Any attempt to look forward to 1977 involves making assumptions regarding developments which are as yet unclear or undecided. The decisions taken by the Officers and the Executive Committee would reduce

expenditure from the present level if those decisions remain operative for 1977. Expenses in 1977 will inevitably be increased by the effects of inflation. The recommendations of the Finance Committee to the Assembly, if adopted and implemented, will undoubtedly have the effect of reducing the gap. The discussions in the Finance Committee and the information received from the representatives of the member churches present in the Assembly, based on the financial position and possibilities of their own churches, would, however, seem to make clear that the approval of a balanced budget for 1977 will be possible only by decision of the Central Committee next August further to curtail programme and staff. The extent to which this may prove necessary depends on the extent to which the implementation of the recommendations of the Finance Committee—notably the action which the member churches take to increase their basic support for the WCC—reduces the gap between foreseeable income and expenditure.

4. It is likewise clear that the financial difficulties of CWME, which now involve curtailment of 1976 activities, will, on present forecasts, become more acute in 1977. Problems must also be foreseen in the financing of other elements of the work of the WCC. The need for increased support for all parts of the work is thus clear.

Appendix 9
The Report of the Programme Guidelines Committee Adopted by the Assembly

FROM UPPSALA TO NAIROBI

1. According to the mandate of the Programme Guidelines Committee (PGC) we reviewed the activities of the WCC in the last seven years as described in the *Uppsala to Nairobi* Report and we make the following observations:

(a) The Report is a most comprehensive presentation of the work of the WCC. It is not prepared in a purely descriptive manner, by giving facts and figures, but indicates the major emphases and the new styles of operation through the programme units and sub-units. The Report portrays the intense activity carried on by the staff and the various committees.

(b) While the Committee appreciates the richness and variety of the WCC programmes, we recognize the fact that the agenda of the WCC has become over-extended. This has made it difficult for staff operations and for a clear understanding by the member churches about the major concerns of the WCC.

(c) We are happy to note that the Report gives an indication of an increasing interrelationship between the various units and sub-units. But there is room for improvement through critical assessment of the interrelationships, in order to avoid overlapping of programmes and duplication of tasks, and in order to secure a greater degree of consolidation.

2. The PGC recommends:

(a) That special thanks be expressed to the officers and members of the Central and Executive Committees, the General Secretary and staff for their work over the last seven years as recorded in the Report.

(b) That the Assembly express its gratitude to the General Editor of the Report, Mr David Johnson, and the editors of the German and French editions, for their tireless efforts in presenting this Report in such an integrated and challenging form.

THE TASK OF THE PROGRAMME GUIDELINES COMMITTEE

3. In addition to proposing formal action on the Report *Uppsala to Nairobi*, the PGC had two further tasks:

(a) "To take careful note of proposals for future programmes that emerge at various points in the Assembly, particularly during the Hearings", and to receive reports from the workshops on Spirituality and Youth, and

(b) "To propose general guidelines for the activities of the World Council of Churches during the period following the Assembly" (*Workbook*, pp. 9, 11).

4. In trying to carry out these tasks we were acutely aware of the limitations of what we could accomplish in the short space of the Assembly meeting. We noted the following limitations:

(a) In the midst of the Assembly process it is still premature to discern the emerging insights in a definitive programmatic way.

(b) Time is needed for further reflection and for clarification and integration of the proposals from the Hearings and Workshops.

(c) Sufficient knowledge of the structural implications of the proposals was not available at this time.

(d) We were working under conditions of uncertainty regarding the ability to make proposals concerning programmatic priorities in the face of the lack of financial solutions.

5. Therefore, we want to stress that we do not understand our task to be the selection and recommendation of specific programme proposals. Rather we have seen our task as formulating and establishing guidelines for the ongoing process of programme planning in the WCC. With this report we hope to open up ways in which a responsible judgement about priorities can be formed.

THE MANDATE OF THE WCC

6. The PGC worked within the overall framework of the Functions and Purposes of the WCC as described in the Proposed Constitution (*Workbook*, pp. 113, 115). These are stated as:

(a) "To call the churches to the goal of visible unity in one faith and in one eucharistic fellowship, expressed in worship and in common life in Christ, and to advance towards that unity in order that the world may believe;

(b) "To facilitate the common witness of the churches in each place and in all places;

(c) "To express the common concern of the churches in the service of human need, the breaking down of barriers between people, and the promotion of one human family in justice and peace;

(d) "To foster the renewal of the churches in unity, worship, mission, and service.

(e) "To establish and maintain relations with national councils and regional conferences of churches, world confessional bodies, and other ecumenical organizations;

(f) "To carry on the work of the world movements for Faith and Order and Life and Work of the International Missionary Council and the World Council on Christian Education."

7. It is significant that with the Proposed Constitution the WCC has been able to state more fully the functions of the council as a whole. In this context we wish to emphasize the following specific points:

(a) As an instrument of the churches and the ecumenical movement, the WCC needs to plan its programmes in constant relationship with activities of the other ecumenical bodies at the world, regional, national, and local levels.

(b) In a world-wide community the WCC is confronted with the global issues facing the churches. There is a need to watch the specific role of the WCC over against other world agencies, both governmental and non-governmental.

(c) The work of the WCC should be seen as a comprehensive whole. Spiritual, prophetic, and enabling dimensions are inseparable parts of the total life and work of the WCC as it acts both with the member churches and for the member churches.

(d) The functions and purposes outlined above clearly indicate that the WCC has a permanent agenda for: unity, witness, service, justice, education, and renewal. This is expressed in the structure of the Programme Units. At the same time there is a changing agenda determined by the circumstances of the churches and the world.

(e) Both the permanent and the changing agenda should be subject to periodic, critical evaluation. Constant attention must be given to the integration of theological reflection and action into all agendas.

CRITERIA FOR ESTABLISHING PRIORITIES

8. We offer the following criteria in order to guide such self-evaluation and conscious planning of programmes in the next seven years. In evaluating programmes the Central Committee should ask itself the following questions:

(a) *Appropriateness.* How appropriate is it for a world ecumenical body such as the WCC to engage in this particular task? Attention should be paid to programmes of others to avoid duplication and to the value of the programme regarding its relevance for ecumenical action and reflection feeding into and receiving from the work of regional bodies and local congregations.

(b) *Feasibility.* How feasible is the proposal in the light of WCC staffing, financing, and constituency involvement? Attention should be given to the correlation of visionary action with the actual potential of the WCC as an organization.

(c) *Urgency.* How urgent is the demand for this programme in the light of the needs of the churches and the world? Particular attention should be paid to the need for prophetic work in response to the challenges of our world and pastoral responsibility for the growth of the ecumenical spirit among member churches.

(d) *Effectiveness.* What is the potential effectiveness of this programme in terms of concrete results? Attention should be paid to the way in which a programme arises out of a broad-based constituency and can become effective in the life and work of that or other constituencies on a short- or long-term basis.

(e) *Integrity.* What is the built-in component for manifesting the integrity of theological reflection and action in this particular programme? In order to avoid the split between faith and action, all programmes should make a conscious effort to integrate these two aspects in their work.

GUIDELINES FOR FUTURE PROGRAMMES

9. In formulating the following three guidelines the PGC wants to offer clear direction to all programmes of the WCC. These guidelines represent examples of the concerns that are regarded as essential for the churches, their fellowship in the WCC, and for the wider ecumenical movement in the years following this Assembly. While the thrusts indicated here have been present in the work of the WCC from the beginning, the PGC is convinced that they should receive central attention in all activities during the coming period. They are mutually interrelated and apply with equal force to the work of all three Programme Units and the General Secretariat of the WCC. Together with the criteria outlined above they are to enable the WCC to assume the conscious responsibility for the continuous process of planning, implementing, and evaluating programmes.

THE QUALITY OF A TRULY ECUMENICAL FELLOWSHIP

10. All programmes of the WCC should be conceived and implemented in a way which enables the member churches to grow towards a truly ecumenical, conciliar fellowship. In this respect, the programmes of the WCC should become living expressions of the covenant relationship among the churches within the WCC and foster growth towards fuller unity. These programmes should challenge the churches beyond the brokenness of our human situation as well as beyond the partial, incomplete character of our ecumenical efforts towards deeper sustained and sustaining relationships. If this is to happen, all member churches must be helped to participate in the process of ecumenical education that is so fundamental to our pilgrimage. The vision of God's will for one fully committed

fellowship in all places and in all ages should continue to be translated into the actual work of the WCC and be incorporated in the witness of the churches.

In particular, this guideline implies:

(a) Dynamic interaction and regular two-way communication between the WCC and the churches. Ways need to be found for more frequent reporting to the churches and receiving their reactions.

(b) Shaping the expectations and programmes of the ecumenical movement so as to reach, engage, and listen to the congregations. This will require a decentralization of programmes in co-operation with regional ecumenical bodies and to give a sense of local identification with the ecumenical agenda, without allowing a new regional parochialism to develop.

(c) Translating our emerging consensus into concrete proposals that can be acted upon by the churches.

(d) Creating a fellowship of mutual intercession whereby the churches regularly pray for each other and have an awareness of each other in their worship life. This is an intensely spiritual matter, far beyond programmes and organizations. It involves deepening the appreciation and respect our churches have for each other.

(e) Accepting a crucial role for Assembly delegates, Central Committee members, and Unit committees, as those who live out the ecumenical fellowship in their meetings and work, and actively assume responsibility as advocates of the ecumenical vision and tasks.

(f) Planning programmes of mutual visitation by special teams and/or individuals.

THE INCARNATION OF OUR FAITH

11. All programmes should be conceived and implemented in a way that engages the churches in the effort to reach a common understanding of the gospel and the tradition and under the guidance of the Holy Spirit to make possible a fuller common witness. At the same time, there is need to search for an authentic incarnation of the Christian faith in the historic circumstances of a given place. They should lead to a fresh exploration of the resources of our faith and bring them to bear on the human struggles and agonies of our time. This means that theological reflection about our faith in Christ must itself become part of and be judged by the way in which our Christian existence manifests the character of the life that we see in Jesus Christ.

In particular, this guideline implies:

(a) The acknowledgement that unity among the churches will grow as they live out more fully their incorporation into Christ and their participation in his mission. All ecumenical strategies and all efforts to formulate consensus should be guided by this basic truth.

(b) The need for a renewal of the dimensions of witness and evangelism in all programmes of the WCC through proclamation of the Word and active engagement.

(c) The courage to be identified and to live with those to whom Christ

298

has addressed his message of liberation (Luke 4.18): the powerless, the poor, those without voice and hope, and serve all people in need.

(d) The willingness to maintain an open dialogue with those who see Christ and the Christian faith through the eyes of a different faith commitment, ideology, or scientific conviction.

(e) The readiness to respect and acknowledge diversity among churches and individual Christians in interpreting the meaning of the faith for their lives today.

THE STRUGGLE FOR TRUE HUMANITY

12. All programmes should be conceived and implemented in a way that expresses the basic Christian imperative to participate in the struggle for human dignity and social justice and, at the same time, maintains the integrity of action and engagement by the churches as rooted in the biblical faith. They should enable the churches to become communities generating hope, reconciliation, liberation, and justice. The Christian community living in Christ cannot but embody the groanings of creation. The programmes therefore will have to acknowledge that in struggling for true humanity we are confronted with the power of sin and evil manifested in human injustice and oppression.

In particular, this guideline implies:

(a) A courageous commitment to press for the fuller understanding and implementation of human rights, including religious freedom, and to struggle against racism, sexism, and any other violations of human dignity wherever they occur.

(b) The readiness to expose instances where the churches themselves are involved in unjust power structures—social, political, and economic—and to call for genuine and active repentance.

(c) The continued search for the foundations of a just and sustainable society, taking into account both the need for a new international economic order and the concern for self-reliant and participatory forms of development which respond to the pressing needs of the people, and particularly programmes that help and encourage self-reliance and self-identity of the member churches.

(d) The need to exercise a ministry of peace and reconciliation and to explore further the significance of non-violent action for social change and the struggle against militarism.

(e) The willingness to confess the limitations of our efforts in achieving these goals while confidently affirming through our actions the power of the resurrection.

IMPLEMENTATION OF GUIDELINES

13. In order to ensure the implementation of the above *Criteria* and *Guidelines*, the PGC recommends that the Assembly resolve the following:

(*a*) These guidelines, if approved by the Assembly, have to be taken into account particularly by the core-groups of future commissions and working groups as they prepare proposals for the programmes of the respective sub-units and units.

(*b*) At its meeting in Nairobi, the Central Committee should appoint a special review committee with the task of making specific recommendations for programme priorities. The committee should include persons with expertise both in programme and finance. It will receive the proposals from the core-groups and should present its report to the next meeting of the Central Committee for consideration and action.

(*c*) For the period following its meeting in 1976, the Central Committee should give serious consideration to the appointment of a standing committee on programme guidelines to continue the work begun by the PGC at this Assembly.

(*d*) The implementation of these guidelines calls for special allocation of staff to work with the General Secretary in keeping the concerns as expressed in this Report alive in the on-going activities of the WCC. In particular, an organic service on the part of staff is required in order to intensify the interaction between the churches and with the WCC.

Appendix 10
A Summary Report of the Hearings

Attached are summaries of the specific programme recommendations submitted by:

the Hearings on the General Secretariat
> the Unit on Faith and Witness
> the Unit on Justice and Service
> the Unit on Education and Renewal,

and the Workshops on Spirituality
> and Youth

They are appended for the information of the members of the Assembly and to make known the directions suggested for the future. The full record of the recommendations of the Hearings, Sub-Hearings, and Workshops will be forwarded to the new Central Committee and recommended for its consideration and action. The proposal made earlier in this Programme Guidelines Committee report for the immediate appointment of a Review Committee would provide a way in which proper preparation can be given for the task of the Central Committee in their meeting in August 1976.

A SUMMARY REPORT OF HEARING I ON THE GENERAL SECRETARIAT

Because of the wide scope of programmes within this Hearing, recommendations largely appear under sub-headings. There were two general findings:

1. The increase in communications and active relations between the WCC and its member churches was given highest priority.

2. Concern was apparent regarding the future of various programmes within the General Budget, but lack of solid information on any new potential financing prevented positive recommendations.

I. *Sub-Hearing A:* General Policy and Administration, including New York Office

1. The strengthening of mutual relationships with member churches should determine activities of the General Secretariat. The WCC should also be the forum for mutual appraisal. Misunderstandings arise from the fact that much information on the WCC reaches churches through the secular press.

2. The widening of the fellowship through new member churches requires study of possibilities of decentralization and the use of other ecumenical groupings (national and regional councils, world confessional families, etc.). Existing duplications could be avoided by WCC co-ordination of such groupings.

3. There should be a balance in communications as between marginal interest groups and official church channels.

4. Staffing of WCC should demonstrate better balance of representation, geographically, among member churches and in categories of men, women, youth, lay, clergy, etc. There should be deepened relations of confidence between staff and with churches. There should be better use of staff travel.

5. There was general recognition of the usefulness of the New York Office and hope for continuation, but no clear views on the financing of the Office.

6. It was proposed that WCC undertake a study of multi-national corporations and resultant problems.

II. *Sub-hearing B:* Communication and the Library

1. There was stress on the communication process and the urgency of proposals to avoid further cuts in the Communications Department. The Committee of Communication is asked to continue explorations of the most effective ways to communicate ecumenical concerns to the world and to the churches. The Committee is asked to:

    (*a*) study the document "Towards a Language Policy"

    (*b*) critically review all WCC publications

    (*c*) study the consequences of the use of mass media and of their pervasive influence upon society and the churches.

2. WCC communications should aim at local congregations, people at the grass-roots level.

3. There could be better balance between the use of the printed word and of other media.

4. It was stressed that early decisions are needed on such matters as language policy, various publications, etc.

III. *Sub-Hearing C:* Ecumenical Institute, Biblical Studies, Humanum Studies

1. There was consensus on the importance of continuing the Ecumenical Institute, and on the value of its Graduate School, although the Hearing could not itself deal with specifics of future plans. There was conviction that links should be kept with the WCC directly and some doubt about establishing a totally independent Foundation for it. Future programmes must depend on the willingness of the churches to gather funds for it, starting here at the Assembly. An immediate transitional budget is required.

2. The portfolio on Biblical Studies is evidence of the WCC's goal of relating its activities to the Scriptures. Hence it should remain in the General Budget. The availability of staff is essential in order to serve the churches and pervade all WCC activities. Orthodox and Roman Catholic participation could be enriching.

IV. *Sub-Hearing D:* Finances

1. Need is urgent for a more comprehensive and unified WCC budget, understandable to those outside the structure. However, the idea of a totally unified budget was rejected as being unrealistic. The proposal, therefore, is for a mixed budget of undesignated contributions by churches to a General Administration budget and special fund-raising for specific

programmes and projects. Improved communication would result in increased support.

2. As means of improving financing:
    (a) churches and local congregations should be approached to fund programmes within their interests;
    (b) an Ecumenical Sunday might be considered;
    (c) expenditures in all departments should be scrutinized for possible reductions;
    (d) attempts to mobilize support should be co-ordinated.

3. A standing Review Committee should be created for constant appraisal of priorities in relation to finances.

A SUMMARY REPORT OF HEARING 2 ON UNIT I:
FAITH AND WITNESS

PROGRAMME DIRECTIONS

1. *Understanding afresh the Apostolic Faith*
This will involve a follow-up of the previous studies on "Salvation Today" and "Giving Account of the Hope that is within us", as well as the Assembly discussion on "Confessing Christ Today". The hearing emphasized the need to undertake this in historical perspective and in relation to specific contemporary issues such as the place of Scripture and the creeds, the authority of the tradition, the role played by worship in confessing Christ.

2. (a) *The Continuing Search for Visible Unity*
The hearing emphasized the task of the Faith and Order Commission in assisting the churches in their search for unity, particularly by co-ordinating their efforts and providing resources such as the document on Baptism, Eucharist, and Ministry.
    (b) *The Pursuit of This Search in Relation to the Unity of Humankind*
It was also concluded that this concern for visible unity should continue to be pursued in relation to contemporary social conflicts and divisions, as this approach opens the way to a close collaboration with other programmes of the WCC and gives a new urgency to the work for unity by setting it in a wider context of concern for the whole of humanity.

3. *The Contribution of Christian Faith, Science, and Technology to the Struggle for a Just and Sustainable Society*
This would involve at least three major programme concerns:
    (a) Science and Faith. The encounter between Science and Faith is mutually challenging at the level of both doctrine and ethics, and the nature of that challenge needs to be carefully explored. The ethical dilemmas arising from the application of modern biology to human problems should be considered here.
    (b) Ethical Problems in the Transition to a Just and Sustainable Society. This would include a careful examination of the concerns of the developing and developed countries in relation to energy and other

natural resources together with strategies for appropriate technologies. Changes in political and economic systems will also need to be investigated.

(c) The Christian Faith and the Vision of a New Society (with special attention to exploring the biblical and theological dimensions of a new social order).

4. *Continuation of Ecumenical Work on the Issues of Violence and Non-Violence in Social Change*

The Hearing urged that the World Council find ways of implementing the recommendations of the 1973 Report regarding training in non-violent action, and stressed the need for further study of the unresolved theological, ethical, and social issues. The issue of Militarism received special attention and the Hearing suggested the possibility of a "Programme to Combat Militarism".

5. *Courage for Dialogue*

Since all human issues increasingly need inter-religious and inter-ideological reflection, co-operation, and participation, the distinctive contribution of the sub-unit for Dialogue with People of Living Faiths and Ideologies should be continued, with participation by men and women at all levels of society, and with emphasis upon programmes in the following areas:

(a) Initiation of and partnership in local, regional, and international dialogues with people of various faiths and ideologies on specific topics of theological and practical concern.

(b) Encouragement of "inner dialogue" among Christians about the cultural heritages or ideological assumptions of individuals, congregations, and churches.

(c) Theological reflection among Christians about the issues raised by the experience of such dialogues, which can function as a "listening post" to enable Christians to see and hear themselves as others see and hear them.

6. *The Proclamation of the Gospel as a Priority of the WCC*

The WCC and the member churches recognize themselves under the imperative and privilege of participating in God's mission sharing the saving knowledge of Jesus Christ with all mankind. The WCC should offer assistance to the churches in the following areas:

(1) A programme of education for mission that will help to awaken in the church the concern for the proclamation of the gospel throughout the world—cross fertilization among congregations—missiological reflection—pilot projects. TEF, UIM, RAM, ESP, Renewal and Education should collaborate together in this endeavour.

(2) The style of the Christian mission is provided by Jesus himself: "As the Father sent me, so I send you" (John 20.21). WCC should help the churches to discover, analyse, and serve with the whole gospel in new frontiers of mission today. They should be assisted to participate in the struggle of the poor, in prophetic ministries, in understanding the evangelistic responsibility in frontiers—the scientific world—the inner city—highly organized religious or ideological systems. UIM, RAM, CMC, TEF, Church and Society, and dialogue could help here.

(3) World mission is a responsibility and privilege of the whole church—unity in mission—relationships developing towards maturity. It is inside this search for a better missionary service and a deeper unity that the debate on moratorium should proceed. Sharing should take place at the

level of suffering, especially in repressive situations. ESP in collaboration with CICARWS and Faith and Order will provide this service.

(4) Communication. Sharing of experiences and theological reflections are essential to the missionary task. The International Review of Mission and the Monthly Letter on Evangelism should be maintained as six continents publications. All efforts should be made to enlarge translations and publications in other languages. Networks of relations among mission action groups should be encouraged.

(5) Two other significant services are rendered through CWME:

(a) The Theological Education Fund, whose work should be expanded to a six continents approach, and,

(b) The Christian Medical Commission which stimulates the responsible participation of churches in community health care. Attempts should be made to develop the local Christian group as a caring community, and to reflect theologically on the meaning of life, health, suffering, and death.

A SUMMARY REPORT OF HEARING 3 ON UNIT II: JUSTICE AND SERVICE

The Hearing reaffirmed the areas covered by the programmes and activities of Unit II as an expression of faith in the purpose of God revealed through the life, teachings, death, and resurrection of Jesus Christ, not merely on humanitarian grounds. Our practical obedience to Christ who frees and unites is to share with him in his liberating and unifying ministries. Therefore, the major thrust for the next seven years should be towards helping member churches to assist and participate in the struggle for liberation of all those who are victims of poverty, oppression, violation of human rights, racial injustice, natural and man-made disasters, and uprootedness. The WCC should be an instrument of sharing the diverse resources (material, human, and spiritual) of the churches for justice, service, and peace.

A. *International Politics and Human Rights*

1. Increase information and communication between CCIA and national churches and regional bodies. Establish contacts with representatives of Christian churches and bodies to which WCC presently has insufficient access. Keep contacts with action groups, liberation movements, dissident groups, women's groups, etc.

2. Consolidate and strengthen relations with international organizations and therefore continue CCIA New York Office.

3. Recognize that in complex conflict areas and where churches and Christians historically may have fixed positions which impede proper analysis of the real issues, purely "diplomatic action" might not do justice to the need for information, sensitization, and education (example: Middle East).

4. Continue to stimulate and enable the activities and potential of those churches and church bodies which might feel hampered in the field of human rights.

5. Give highest possible priority to the question of disarmament and the suicidal absurdity of the arms race, possibly by holding a world-wide Christian consultation.

6. Continue systematically to promote the implementation of the Helsinki Declaration on Security and Co-operation in Europe.

B. *Combating Racism*

1. The Programme to Combat Racism including Special Fund must be strengthened and its scope increased.

2. Racism, whatever its colour, is evil, but PCR should continue to give priority to white racism, because economic, political, and military power is overwhelmingly in white hands and therefore empowers white racism.

3. Similarly, South Africa and Namibia must retain high priority in reaffirmation of policy decisions already taken by Central and Executive Committees 1969-1975. Initiation and activation of non-violent campaigns to halt arms traffic and to discourage tourism should be undertaken.

4. Regional and global issues to be taken up in future:

(*a*) plight of native Americans and other minority groups in USA, aborigines in Australia, Indians in Latin America, Koreans in Japan;

(*b*) racial integration in Malaysia;

(*c*) the implications of racism as sin and the theological dimension of combating racism;

(*d*) the redistribution of power between powerful and powerless (including land rights) as elements in political and spiritual liberation;

(*e*) the linkage between economic and military power with racism.

5. Provision of adequate financial resources for PCR and Special Fund should be sought.

C. *Development and Justice*

1. The Unit, through its appropriate Commissions, should continue to assist churches to participate effectively in the development process by undertaking ecumenical studies, promoting development education, providing technical services, and sharing financial resources.

2. The development challenge is far more serious and urgent today than ever before. Therefore it needs to be considered as high priority in the WCC.

3. In the future programme, emphasis should be given to assisting churches to be a supportive force in the struggle of the poor and the oppressed:

(*a*) by direct support by the WCC to peoples' movements striving for justice and self-reliance; and by assistance in establishing a network relationship among them;

(*b*) by assistance to a few congregations around the world to become a people's organization or part of a people's movement, to struggle against their own poverty and oppression.

4. WCC, through its member churches, action groups, and peoples' movements should strive towards changes in oppressive structures on national and international level. Direct efforts by WCC should include studies and publications and appropriate means of influencing governments and intergovernmental bodies.

5. Special attention should be given to examine and expose the role of transnational corporations.

6. Efforts of Sodepax should be continued and enlarged.

7. Programmes and projects supported by CCPD and CICARWS need to be evaluated periodically.

8. Assistance should be given to aid-giving agencies of the churches to evaluate and improve the quality of their aid.

D. *Ecumenical Sharing of Resources*
1. The WCC and its member churches must work with each other to promote an understanding of resources in the widest possible sense. Resources must be seen as including spiritual experience, theological insights, and basic elements of Christian life, funds, goods, personnel, and cultural heritage.
2. The WCC should continue to take the moratorium concept seriously. There remains a need for serious detailed study and evaluation of the implications. The results of such studies/evaluation to be widely circulated to member churches.
3. We must reach the state of true sharing of resources among equal partners. An emphasis should be given to non-material resources. This sharing too needs to be planned for and organized by WCC. To accomplish this, the WCC should offer a wide variety of instruments:
 (a) the Project System, renewed and improved constantly in the direction of "country programmes";
 (b) ecumenical sharing of personnel, made operational through increased resources;
 (c) interchange of experience, opportunities, and concerns;
 (d) ecumenical scrutiny of partnerships between churches, to co-ordinate and provide objectivity. The WCC should give a special emphasis to enable smaller churches to become *active* partners in the ecumenical sharing process.
4. The WCC should give priority to the development of country programmes and a means of placing the sharing of resources on a basis of mutuality, broader decision-making, and integrity within the national community. The WCC should encourage and facilitate the domestic ecumenical sharing of resources, nationally and regionally.
5. Recognizing that totally ecumenical sharing will not replace bilateralism in the near future, the WCC should stress the development of consortia including giving and receiving churches, acting as facilitator and agent for greater co-ordination and common formulation of objectives, strategies, and criteria.

E. *Service to Human Need*
I. Because of widespread bilateralism and lack of co-ordination among member churches, there is all the more need for ecumenical activity through WCC. Therefore
1. The Project System is affirmed as an essential instrument:
 (a) with expanded service to the larger community;
 (b) with more help to the churches to recognize their own limitations and to perceive the felt needs of the larger community.
2. WCC should continue action on behalf of and with churches in emergencies, disasters, and chronically needy areas.
3. WCC should lead in developing new styles of service, with churches and/or with governments, including community health care, rural development, appropriate technology, etc.
4. WCC should develop consortia in which both giving and receiving churches share perspectives, goals, and decisions on resource allocation.

II. In all ministries to uprooted persons WCC should stress:
1. Pathological and psychological effects of displacement and the spiritual lostness which results, assisting churches in their efforts to deal with these.
2. The special urgency of the churches' enlistment as advocates of migrant workers, political refugees, stranded students—all persons who are refugees by any definition.

3. Assistance to churches to render service to uprooted people:

(*a*) by promoting integration and advocacy of those who wish to remain;

(*b*) by pressing for international and national measures to protect the rights of temporary residents;

(*c*) by assisting in the provision of shelter, livelihood, family life, and dignity to all;

(*d*) by defending the rights of persons of conscience who suffer for their acts;

(*e*) by assisting countries which create refugees and migrants to deal with the root causes of emigration;

(*f*) by providing the churches with information on situations and needs of uprooted people.

III. Service to human need requires changes in life style both by personal resolve for Christian living and by corporate decisions for political action as a means of change.

1. WCC can assist churches in giving witness by self-discipline.

2. WCC can assist churches to be self-critical in the life styles they propose in their projects so they are neither elitist, a betrayal of their own culture's goals, nor thwarting of justice.

SUMMARY REPORT OF HEARING 4 ON UNIT III: EDUCATION AND RENEWAL

INTRODUCTION

Unit III will work along the following lines:

(1) It will be a forum for the exchange of experiences in education from the different regions and churches so that the churches can learn from one another.

(2) It will help the churches by making available mutual information on concrete projects and models such as common catechetical programmes.

(3) It will be encouraged to maintain regionalization in its contacts and programmes, e.g. regional consultations.

(4) On the basis of continuing evaluation it will increase co-operation among its own sub-units where appropriate in order to permit common endeavours.

(5) It will seek closer cooperation with other WCC units.

(6) It will facilitate the education of the laity.

I. EDUCATION

The Education sub-unit will

(1) help to develop programmes and curricula for Christian education within and through congregational life.

(2) help churches to revise their educational programmes in order to promote an education for ecumenism, particularly on the local level.

(3) keep to its commitment to the powerless and voiceless, the dispossessed, disadvantaged, and handicapped persons.

(4) in response to the increasingly dramatic challenge of the growing ecological crisis in the world, including hunger and population, to initiate a task force or a major consultation on the educational consequences of the growing responsibility of Christians and others in all continents.

(5) in the field of general education, to continue to help the churches fulfil their indispensable responsibility in reshaping and humanizing society.

(6) help member churches to re-appraise the role of church-sponsored schools.

(7) develop new styles of leadership and participation patterns which will undergird self-awareness and support of positive images for women and minority groups.

(8) reinforce and expand the WCC Leadership Development and Scholarship Programme.

> (a) All programmes of the WCC agencies dealing with leadership training should be co-ordinated to emphasize the necessity for the development of people and to ensure an integrated approach. In addition, WCC agencies, donor agencies, and member churches should be asked to allocate increased funds to an expanded programme.

> (b) In development projects, member churches should give priority to the development of local leadership for which scholarship programmes can provide support.

> (c) The present scholarship programme aims and functions should be revised to include a greater provision for training opportunities for women and to allow more flexibility regarding candidates' age limit, length of study period, and openness in regard to place of study (own country, continent, or abroad).

II. WOMEN IN CHURCH AND SOCIETY

(1) The sub-unit should collaborate with the Commission on Faith and Order to ensure active continuation of the study "The Community of Women and Men in the Church and Society" over a period of three years (1976-78) in preparation for an ecumenical consultation under the auspices of the WCC in 1979-80.

(2) In co-operation with the Commission on Faith and Order the sub-unit should urge:

> (a) all member churches to encourage fuller participation of women in decision-making bodies.

> (b) those member churches which do not have theological objections to the ordination of women should not be deterred from action by "ecumenical considerations".

> (c) those member churches which do ordain women and those which do not should continue dialogue on the full participation of women in the ordained ministries of the churches according to the measure of their gifts.

(3) Whereas women have traditionally been denied educational opportunities, the sub-unit should give high priority to the development and education of women.

(4) The sub-unit should

> (a) encourage the implementation of or provide programmes for the

recommendations emerging from the conference on "Sexism in the 70's" (Berlin 1974).

(b) examine the feasibility of an exchange system between women theologians.

(5) Through research education and communication with member churches the sub-unit should work for:

(a) the elimination of legal discrimination against women in societies where through tradition and culture women have secondary roles.

(b) a ministry to the family which shall promote equal sharing of family responsibilities.

(c) changes in religious and general education in the textbooks and in mass media which would raise the self-image of women.

III. YOUTH

The "Report of the Youth Workshop" helped us as a basis for our discussions.

There are two main ways in which the participation of youth in the WCC should find expression. The first is to maintain and to strengthen further participation of young people at all levels and in all programmes and units of the WCC. Secondly, we are in full agreement with the report of the Youth Workshop, and would endorse the proposal for a sub-unit and working group on youth work in the WCC.

We would emphasize the following concrete issues for further study and action:

(1) Youth participation in ecumenism on local and international levels.

(2) Youth for social justice.

    (a) Youth and personhood

    (b) Violence and non-violence

    (c) Youth and spirituality

IV. RENEWAL AND RENEWAL MOVEMENTS

A. The *Focus* of the sub-unit will be the laity, the congregation, and the marginalized.

B. The *Style* of the sub-unit will be to work by

(1) seeking to discover signs of renewal and change wherever this is seen to be happening, analysing and evaluating them.

(2) strengthening its work with lay training centres, as servants of local congregations.

C. *Programme Guidelines Proposals*

(1) the WCC's family ministries should be developed, in response to strong pleas from the churches, not least in the Third World, and they should include study, education, and action on, for example, marriage and families of pastors, old people in the family, single families, and population education.

(2) *Risk* should be retained as a much valued means of communication with the people of the churches. It is unique in its style, presentation, and flexibility, allowing in-depth study of particular issues.

(3) the relationship of the Unit with lay training centres, their regional associations, and the World Collaboration Committee should be strengthened.

(4) the Unit should facilitate exchanges of theological insights and experiences between lay training centres, etc.

(5) new means should be explored of promoting education and renewal in congregations through ecumenical programmes.

(6) a survey and theological critique of charismatic renewal movements and their meaning for the church should be undertaken.

(7) theological education for pastors of independent churches should be provided.

(8) local, national, and regional "festivals of celebration" should be held as new means of exploring and expressing renewal and unity.

(9) the results and implications of the "Participation in Change and Leisure Tourism" programmes should be followed through.

REPORT OF THE WORKSHOP ON SPIRITUALITY:
A SUMMARY

I. PREAMBLE

Christian life is a continuous struggle against destructive powers, fears, and despair which bind us in immobility and division (Eph. 6.12), but Jesus Christ frees and unites those who believe in him to participate in the search for a new and hopeful future.

Growing in inner life for Christians means becoming part of God's mission, dying death to one's own desires, and increasing willingness to live and suffer for others for the sake of redemptive liberation and liberated community.

Christians are called to live in the likeness of Jesus Christ. No authentic spirituality serves simply one's own satisfaction. Christian spirituality means repentance, discipline (*ascesis*), sacrifice, and readiness to be humiliated (Phil. 2.7, 8). The cost of discipleship is high. The door to freedom and inner unity in Jesus Christ is narrow (Matt. 7.14), the path of love thorny, and the cross terrible yet glorious. And Christians are sustained by expectation and hope.

The friends of God are the poor, those who mourn, the meek, those who hunger and thirst for righteousness, the merciful, the pure in heart, the makers of peace, those who are persecuted for righteousness' sake (Matt. 5:3-12). We are invited to enter more deeply with God, to be part of the people blessed by God. Invited to renounce ourselves and our privileges, we are called to identify ourselves and our churches *with* God's people rather than to work *for* them.

The continuous struggle against destruction in our lives and communities and the taste of freedom and unity in Jesus Christ are inseparable from the struggle for liberation and humanity in the world. The joy in being reconciled with God in Christ is inseparable from the joy in true reconciliation between people through the establishment of justice. It is the life in Christ in prayer, Bible study, eucharistic communion, singing, and silence that sustains and makes us grow in imagination and love.

Against this background it is clear that the WCC needs no specific "department of spirituality", but that the whole ecumenical community, including the WCC staff, must live freed and united in Christ and thereby be able to assist individuals, congregations, and communities to organize and discipline their life in such a way that they become open to the movements of the Holy Spirit, and for the sake of Christ become more ready to give up their own ways of life for the sake of the freedom and unity of all.

II. PROGRAMME RECOMMENDATIONS

1. *Concerning spiritual resources (1 Cor. 12.1) for Christians involved in daily life*
WHEREAS it is important that the ecumenical fellowship recognize that the spiritual resources which already exist in the churches are insufficiently known about and are not being fully used, therefore:
1.1. IT IS RECOMMENDED that the Programme Unit Faith and Witness should develop a programme to identify men and women in member churches who are exercising influence with regard to spiritual formation and life styles and, in co-operation with member churches, develop the means whereby such people may be available to spend unhurried time with individuals, local congregations, and staff of the WCC, in order to develop ways of encouraging churches to use such resources more effectively.
1.2. IT IS FURTHER RECOMMENDED that steps be taken to explore the many signs of the working of the Holy Spirit today (Mark 16.17-20).

2. *Concerning the life and witness of the local congregation and its involvement in the ecumenical movement*
WHEREAS there is concern for more dynamic interaction between the WCC and the local congregations of member churches,
AND WHEREAS it is deemed important for the integrity of the WCC that a wider level of accountability be inserted into the programme work of the WCC:
2.1. IT IS RECOMMENDED that every study or programme of the WCC should be started with an analysis and description of its specific implications for local congregations (allowing for the variety of situations in which individuals and congregations find themselves).
2.2. IT IS FURTHER RECOMMENDED that future staff travel take into account the congregations so involved, seeking to promote more direct encounters with churches at the local level.
WHEREAS we believe worship to be a distinctive moment in the lives of Christians which transfigures the ordinariness, the exhaustion, and the struggles of daily life,
AND WHEREAS we believe in the transfiguring power of liturgy in its various forms and in the inherent need to transcend the limits of daily life in celebration, therefore:
2.3. IT IS RECOMMENDED that the Assembly *affirm* the recommendations of the Faith and Order Commission meeting at Accra relating to a study on worship. Further, that the sub-unit on Faith and Order together with the sub-unit on Renewal promote a "search and discover" programme, aimed at finding where and how the liturgical life of local congregations as well as the liturgical events of groups and communities displays the sustaining power mentioned above, and that such findings be widely shared.
WHEREAS we affirm the deep significance of Bible study for the people of God and wish to see a wider use of the Bible in ecumenical work and study, therefore:

2.4. IT IS RECOMMENDED that a higher priority be given to the portfolio of biblical studies. Particular attention should be given to developing liaison with Bible Fellowships, Societies, and Movements. We request that a distinctive effort be made to collect studies from various sources in diverse cultural and social contexts which should then be widely shared with the churches aiming to achieve an inter-cultural awareness of how the Bible is understood, reckoning that such a cross-fertilization may facilitate a better ecumenical understanding among Christians.

WHEREAS it is known that many Christians as well as people of other faiths and ideologies engaged in situations of conflicts, combat, and struggle to bring about change find themselves isolated, alienated from the institutional church, and either unable to find spiritual resources in their struggle or to develop their own spiritual resources in community, therefore:

2.5. IT IS RECOMMENDED that the WCC offer opportunities for those able to come out of their situations of conflict from time to time to meet each other in order to meditate together, to share their pain and experiences, to reflect on what sustains them, and to build, for however short or long a time, a sense of community.

3. *Concerning the Quality of Life*
WHEREAS this Assembly has heard with concern that the threats to survival are of growing magnitude and believes that Christian men and women have an obligation to "replenish the earth", recognizing that the WCC has launched a study in this area and is developing a programme through the sub-unit Churches' Commission on Participation in Development and the sub-unit Church and Society, therefore:

3.1. IT IS RECOMMENDED that these programmes be affirmed.

WHEREAS questions concerning the quality of life are reflected by those who are committed to non-violence as a way of life,

AND WHEREAS the study on "Violence, Non-violence, and the Struggle for Social Justice" (1973) has yet to be fully implemented, therefore:

3.2. IT IS RECOMMENDED that the next Central Committee seriously consider what steps should be taken to involve the WCC more visibly in support of those committed to non-violence and to bring to the churches' attention this continuing concern about non-violence.

4. *Concerning the spirituality of the WCC's life in meetings and conferences and in patterns of work of the staff*
WHEREAS there is sufficient reason to reckon that the present situation of the WCC staff in Geneva, their relationship to the vastly different elements of the constituency and the difficulties in presenting an example to the churches of a community style of living better suited to the predicament of our time, severally and together, tend to hinder the building up (*oikodome*) of the charismatic fellowship we yearn for and, at the same time, foster contradictions between the ideals which this Assembly has heard and applauded and the way in which the WCC is seen to be established through its headquarters in Geneva,

AND WHEREAS it is nevertheless recognized that utopian dreams have to be balanced by hard realities, now therefore:

4.1. IT IS RECOMMENDED that the Assembly/Central Committee appoint a Special Commission whose terms of reference will be: (1) To examine ways and means to disperse the staff in groups or teams which do not lose the international and intercultural character now achieved, yet will lessen the natural preponderance of Western European concerns for the WCC headquarters; at the same time, such a dispersal must not jeopardize functions believed necessary in Geneva. (2) To consider the practicability of fostering a community style of life for WCC staff willing to so commit themselves. In this regard, the Commission is asked to consider whether or not the Chateau de Bossey can be a focus for such a development, while not jeopardizing its function as an Ecumenical Institute. (3) The Commission should report its findings and a plan for implementing these recommendations to the Central Committee in August 1976. (4) The Commission should seek written submissions relating to these recommendations from as many sources as possible. (5) The Commission will consist of the Moderator of Central Committee and the General Secretary together with at least three other members of Central Committee.

WHEREAS there is concern expressed at the amount of work committed to the staff of the WCC headquarters and the degree to which this impairs the effectiveness of the staff, and, therefore, the WCC in its pastoral and representative work,

AND WHEREAS this Assembly has set up a Programme Guidelines Committee:

4.2. IT IS RECOMMENDED that the new Central Committee constitutes such a Committee, but clearly empowers it to establish cut-off dates for programmes and the reassignment of staff in a way which effectively lessens the growth of the WCC at this time and which encourages member churches to support and share at a national base in some ecumenical and international programmes.

WHEREAS there is concern over the life style of this Assembly, a concern which has been expressed from time to time in previous Central Committees,

AND WHEREAS the credibility of the WCC suffers if greater care is not taken to match words with deeds, affirmations with actions, therefore:

4.3. IT IS URGED that the staff of the WCC give greater attention to this question in planning all future meetings, conferences, and assemblies of the Council.

REPORT OF THE WORKSHOP ON YOUTH: A SUMMARY

I. PREAMBLE

Young people share the hopes and concerns of the whole of society. However, being a youth is a special phase in the growth of personhood and community: certain concerns, insights, and attitudes are peculiar to them.

Young people are also a vital and integral part of the whole people of God and the ecumenical movement. In spite of the variety of their cultural conditionings, political persuasions, theological convictions, personal life-styles, and changing life-situations, youth discover common world-wide interests and concerns which call for mutual encouragement and concerted action.

The following are three overriding concerns of youth: youth and theology, youth and education, and youth and social justice.

(1) Not yet closed in or conditioned by the culture in which they live,

youth should be given opportunity to come together to explore their understanding of the meaning of the Christian faith and also to share their insights and to explore their theological questionings.

(2) Educational systems often limit and inhibit conscientization among youth about global issues, as well as issues within their own societies.

(3) Youth are often prohibited from participation in the full development of their community and its realization of self-reliance and human dignity of all people, especially in the areas of employment, participation in structures of the societies, and the realization of quality of life.

II. AIM OF YOUTH WORK

Youth work in the World Council of Churches should be organized so as to enable youth together to discover for themselves the freedom and unity in Christ, to voice their concerns and insights effectively, and to participate at all levels of the ecumenical movement, particularly in the WCC. The focus should seek to bring the challenges and concerns of youth into the central life of the WCC in all aspects of its work.

III. FUNCTIONS AND PROGRAMME EMPHASES

1. To develop means of *contact* with youth in churches, ecumenical organizations, and movements at the national, regional, and international levels through visitation, correspondence, etc. Relationships should be developed and maintained with other international youth organizations as well as marginal groups engaged in seeking new forms of expressing their Christian faith and commitment.

2. To develop a *network of communication* among youth, facilitating a flow of information into the WCC and from the WCC to the regional and national levels by means of regular newsletters, occasional publications, etc.

3. To assist the churches on a national and regional level in discerning their *own priorities in youth work and to enable them to initiate appropriate programmes by making resources available* to youth and youth organizations.

4. To *create opportunities* where youth can meet across national, regional, and confessional boundaries to share *common insights* in their struggle for understanding and living the Christian faith, to evolve effective strategies, and to provide mutual encouragement by organizing ecumenical youth encounters, workshops, work camps, service projects, consultations, etc.

5. In collaboration with all programmes and sub-units of the WCC, to develop programmes for ecumenical leadership by constantly advocating the concern of youth within the WCC, so as to achieve *adequate representation* in all committees, commissions, programmes, and staff of the WCC, as well as for the life and work of the ecumenical movement as a whole.

6. To promote and initiate programmes for awareness-building and leadership training among *rural youth* in *support of their concerns* for liberation and development while constantly challenging the churches to take this matter more seriously.

7. To organize and co-ordinate research and information on youth concerns so as to interpret to youth all over the world the vital *need for ecumenical encounter and collaboration*.

315

IV. STRUCTURE

1. Youth work must have a somewhat *autonomous character*, structurally located in one particular Programme Unit, but relating to all units so as to bring the presence and concerns of youth fully into the life of the ecumenical movement. Therefore, it is proposed that a sub-unit on youth with a working group for youth work be created, related to Programme Unit III where there exists a natural link, having priorities for Education and Renewal. The working group should be composed of 15 persons; it is proposed that its membership would include all Regional Youth Secretaries, as well as one other representative coming from each region, preferably under the age of 30.

2. Immediately following the Nairobi Assembly, provision should be made for at least *two full-time staff to implement the programme of youth work as set forth in this document.* It is anticipated that a third programme staff member may be required, especially to concentrate on rural youth work, soon after the meeting of the Central Committee in 1976 reviews and acts upon the Assembly guidelines (at least one of the programme staff of the future sub-unit on youth should be from the Third World; and at least one should be under thirty).

3. The programmes of *World Youth Projects* and *Ecumenical Youth Service* should be continued. It is proposed that the SFr 300,000. now earmarked in the CICARWS Service Programmes Budget for 1976 for "Post-Assembly Programmes (Youth, etc.)" be allocated for the administration of these two programmes.

V. FURTHER RECOMMENDATION

In as much as there is no Regional Youth Secretary for North America at present, it is recommended that the churches in North America facilitate such an appointment.

316

Appendix 11
The Constitution of the World Council of Churches

I. BASIS

The World Council of Churches is a fellowship of churches which confess the Lord Jesus Christ as God and Saviour according to the Scriptures and therefore seek to fulfil together their common calling to the glory of the one God, Father, Son, and Holy Spirit.

II. MEMBERSHIP

Those churches shall be eligible for membership in the World Council of Churches which express their agreement with the Basis upon which the Council is founded and satisfy such criteria as the Assembly or the Central Committee may prescribe. Election to membership shall be by a two-thirds vote of the member churches represented at the Assembly, each member church having one vote. Any application for membership between meetings of the Assembly may be considered by the Central Committee; if the application is supported by a two-thirds vote of the members of the Committee present and voting, this action shall be communicated to the churches that are members of the World Council of Churches, and unless objection is received from more than one-third of the member churches within six months the applicant shall be declared elected.

III. FUNCTIONS AND PURPOSES

The World Council of Churches is constituted for the following functions and purposes:

(i) to call the churches to the goal of visible unity in ore faith and in one eucharistic fellowship expressed in worship and in common life in

Christ, and to advance towards that unity in order that the world may believe;

(ii) to facilitate the common witness of the churches in each place and in all places;

(iii) to support the churches in their world-wide missionary and evangelistic task;

(iv) to express the common concern of the churches in the service of human need, the breaking down of barriers between people, and the promotion of one human family in justice and peace;

(v) to foster the renewal of the churches in unity, worship, mission, and service;

(vi) to establish and maintain relations with national councils and regional conferences of churches, world confessional bodies, and other ecumenical organizations;

(vii) to carry on the work of the world movements for Faith and Order and Life and Work and of the International Missionary Council and the World Council on Christian Education.

IV. AUTHORITY

The World Council shall offer counsel and provide opportunity for united action in matters of common interest.

It may take action on behalf of constituent churches only in such matters as one or more of them may commit to it and only on behalf of such churches.

The World Council shall not legislate for the churches; nor shall it act for them in any manner except as indicated above or as may hereafter be specified by the constituent churches.

V. ORGANIZATION

The World Council shall discharge its functions through: an Assembly, a Central Committee, an Executive Committee, and other subordinate bodies as may be established.

1. THE ASSEMBLY

(a) The Assembly shall be the supreme legislative body governing the World Council and shall ordinarily meet at seven-year intervals.

(b) The Assembly shall be composed of official representatives of the member churches, known as delegates, elected by the member churches.

(c) The Assembly shall have the following functions:

(i) to elect the President or Presidents of the World Council;

(ii) to elect not more than 145 members of the Central Committee from among the delegates which the member churches have elected to the Assembly;

(iii) to determine the policies of the World Council and to review programmes undertaken to implement policies previously adopted;

(iv) to delegate to the Central Committee specific functions, except to amend this Constitution and to allocate the membership of the Central Committee granted by this Constitution to the Assembly exclusively.

2. THE CENTRAL COMMITTEE

(a) The Central Committee shall be responsible for implementing the policies adopted by the Assembly and shall exercise the functions of the Assembly itself delegated to it by the Assembly between its meetings, except its power to amend this Constitution and to allocate or alter the allocation of the membership of the Central Committee.

(b) The Central Committee shall be composed of the President or Presidents of the World Council and not more than 150 members.

(i) Not more than 145 members shall be elected by the Assembly from among the delegates which the member churches have elected to the Assembly. Such members shall be distributed among the member churches by the Assembly giving due regard to the size of the churches and confessions represented in the Council, the number of churches of each confession which are members of the Council, reasonable geographical and cultural balance, and adequate representation of the major interests of the Council.

(ii) Not more than five members shall be co-opted by the Central Committee at its first meeting from among the representatives which the Associate member churches have elected to the Assembly.

(iii) A vacancy in the membership of the Central Committee, occurring between meetings of the Assembly, shall be filled by the Central Committee itself after consultation with the church of which the person previously occupying the position was a member.

(c) The Central Committee shall have, in addition to the general powers set out in (a) above, the following powers:

(i) to co-opt not more than five members of the Central Committee from among the representatives which the Associate member churches have elected to the Assembly;

(ii) to elect its Moderator and Vice-Moderator or Vice-Moderators from among the members of the Central Committee;

(iii) to elect the Executive Committee from among the members of the Central Committee;

(iv) to elect Committees and Boards and to approve the election or appointment of Working Groups and Commissions;

(v) within the policies adopted by the Assembly, to approve programmes and determine priorities among them and to review and supervise their execution;

(vi) to adopt the budget of the World Council and secure its financial support;

(vii) to elect the General Secretary and to elect or appoint or to make provision for the election or appointment of all members of the staff of the World Council;

(viii) to plan for the meetings of the Assembly, making provision for the conduct of its business, for worship and study, and for common Christian commitment. The Central Committee shall determine the number of delegates to the Assembly and allocate them among the member churches giving due regard to the size of the churches and confessions represented in the Council; the number of churches of each confession which are members of the Council; reasonable geographical and cultural balance; the desired distribution among church officials, parish ministers, and laypersons; among men, women, and young people; and participation by persons whose special knowledge and experience will be needed;

(ix) to delegate specific functions to the Executive Committee or to other bodies or persons.

3. RULES

The Assembly or the Central Committee may adopt and amend Rules not inconsistent with this Constitution for the conduct of the business of the World Council.

4. BY-LAWS

The Assembly or the Central Committee may adopt and amend By-Laws not inconsistent with this Constitution for the functioning of its Committees, Boards, Working Groups, and Commissions.

5. QUORUM

A quorum for the conduct of any business by the Assembly or the Central Committee shall be one-half of its membership.

VI. OTHER ECUMENICAL CHRISTIAN ORGANIZATIONS

1. Such world confessional bodies and such world ecumenical organizations as may be designated by the Central Committee may be invited to send non-voting representatives to the Assembly and to the Central Committee, in such numbers as the Central Committee shall determine.

2. Such national councils and regional conferences of churches, other Christian councils and missionary councils as may be designated by the Central Committee may be invited to send non-voting representatives to the Assembly and to the Central Committee, in such numbers as the Central Committee shall determine.

VII. AMENDMENTS

The Constitution may be amended by a two-thirds vote of the delegates to the Assembly present and voting, provided that the proposed amendment shall have been reviewed by the Central Committee, and notice of it sent to the member churches not less than six months before the meeting of the Assembly. The Central Committee itself, as well as the member churches, shall have the right to propose such amendment.

The Rules of the
World Council of Churches

I. MEMBERSHIP OF THE COUNCIL

Members of the Council are those churches which having constituted the Council or having been admitted to membership, continue in membership. The term "church" as used in this article includes an association, convention, or federation of autonomous churches. A group of churches within a country or region may determine to participate in the World Council of Churches as one church. The General Secretary shall maintain the official list of member churches noting any special arrangement accepted by the Assembly or Central Committee.

The following rules shall pertain to membership.

1. APPLICATION

A church which wishes to become a member of the World Council of Churches shall apply in writing to the General Secretary.

2. PROCESSING

The General Secretary shall submit all such applications to the Central Committee (see Art. II of the Constitution) together with such information as he or she considers necessary to enable the Assembly or the Central Committee to make a decision on the application.

3. CRITERIA

In addition to expressing agreement with the Basis upon which the Council is founded (Art. I of the Constitution), an applicant must satisfy the following criteria to be eligible for membership;

(a) A church must be able to take the decision to apply for membership without obtaining the permission of any other body or person.

(b) A church must produce evidence of sustained independent life and organization.

(c) A church must recognize the essential interdependence of the

322

churches, particularly those of the same confession, and must practise constructive ecumenical relations with other churches within its country or region.

(d) A church must ordinarily have at least 25,000 members.

4. ASSOCIATE MEMBERSHIP

A church otherwise eligible, which would be denied membership solely under Rule I.3.(d), may be elected to associate membership in the same manner as member churches are elected. A church applying for associate membership must ordinarily have at least 10,000 members. An Associate member church may participate in all activities of the Council; its representatives to the Assembly shall have the right to speak but not to vote. Associate member churches shall be listed separately on the official list maintained by the General Secretary.

5. CONSULTATION

Before admitting a church to membership or associate membership, the appropriate world confessional body or bodies and national council or regional conference of churches shall be consulted.

6. RESIGNATION

A church which desires to resign its membership in the Council can do so at any time. A church which has resigned but desires to rejoin the Council must again apply for membership.

II. PRAESIDIUM

1. The Assembly shall elect one or more Presidents but the number of Presidents shall not exceed six.

2. The term of office of a President shall end at the adjournment of the next Assembly following his or her election.

3. A President who has been elected by the Assembly shall be ineligible for immediate re-election when his or her term of office ends.

4. The President or Presidents shall be *ex officio* members of the Central Committee and of the Executive Committee.

5. Should a vacancy occur in the Praesidium between assemblies, the Central Committee may elect a President to fill the unexpired term.

III. THE ASSEMBLY

1. COMPOSITION OF THE ASSEMBLY

(a) Delegates

The Assembly shall be composed of official representatives of the member churches, known as delegates, elected by the member churches with the right to speak and to vote.

(i) The Central Committee shall determine the number of delegates to the Assembly well in advance of its meeting.

(ii) The Central Committee shall determine the percentage of the delegates, not less than 85 per cent, who shall be both nominated and elected by the member churches. Each member church shall be entitled to a minimum of one delegate. The Central Committee shall allocate the other delegates in this part among the member churches giving due regard to the size of the churches and confessions represented in the Council, and the number of churches of each confession which are members of the Council, and reasonable geographical and cultural balance. The Central Committee shall recommend the proper distribution within delegations among church officials, parish ministers, and laypersons; and among men, women, and young people. The Central Committee may make provision for the election by the member churches of alternate delegates who shall serve only in place of such delegates who are unable to attend meetings of the Assembly.

(iii) The remaining delegates, not more than 15 per cent, shall be elected by certain member churches upon nomination of the Central Committee as follows:

1. The Central Committee shall determine the categories of additional delegates necessary to achieve balance in respect of:

(a) the varied sizes of churches and confessions;

(b) the historical significance, future potential or geographical location, and cultural background of particular churches, as well as the special importance of united churches;

(c) the presence of persons whose special knowledge and experience will be necessary to the Assembly;

(d) proportions of laypersons—men, women, and young people.

2. The Central Committee shall invite the member churches to propose the names of persons in the categories so determined whom the churches would be willing to elect, if nominated by the Central Committee.

3. The Central Committee shall nominate particular individuals from the list so compiled to the member church of which each individual is a member.

4. If that member church elects the said nominee, he or she shall become an additional delegate of that member church.

5. The member churches shall not elect alternate delegates for such delegates.

Member churches are encouraged to consult regionally in the selection of the delegates described in paragraphs (ii) and (iii) above, provided that every delegate must be elected by the church of which he or she is a member in accordance with its own procedures.

(b) Persons with the Right to Speak but not to Vote

In addition to the delegates, who alone have the right to vote, the following categories of persons may attend meetings of the Assembly with the right to speak, but not to vote:

(i) *Presidents and Officers.* Any President or Presidents of the Council or Moderator or Vice-Moderator or Vice-Moderators of the Central Committee who have not been elected delegates by their churches.

(ii) *Members of the Retiring Central Committee.* Any members of the retiring Central Committee who have not been elected delegates by their churches.

(iii) *Representatives of Associate Member Churches.* Each Associate member church may elect one representative.

(iv) *Advisers.* The Central Committee may invite a small number of persons who have a special contribution to make to the deliberations of the Assembly or who have participated in the activities of the World Council. Before an invitation is extended to an adviser who is a member of a member church, that church shall be consulted.

(v) *Fraternal Delegates.* The Central Committee may invite persons officially designated as Fraternal Delegates by organizations with which the World Council maintains relationship.

(vi) *Delegated Observers.* The Central Committee may invite persons officially designated as Delegated Observers by non-member churches.

(c) Persons without the Right to Speak or to Vote

The Central Committee may invite to attend the meetings of the Assembly without the right to speak or to vote:

(i) *Observers.* Persons identified with organizations with which the World Council maintains relationship which are not represented by Fraternal Delegates or with non-member churches which are not represented by Delegated Observers.

(ii) *Guests.* Persons named individually.

2. PRESIDING OFFICERS AND BUSINESS COMMITTEE

(a) At the first business session of the Assembly the Central Committee shall present its proposals for the moderatorship of the Assembly and for the membership of the Business Committee of the Assembly.

(*b*) At the first or second business session, additional nominations may be made in writing by any six concurring delegates.

(*c*) Election shall be by ballot unless the Assembly shall otherwise determine.

3. AGENDA

The agenda of the Assembly shall be proposed by the Central Committee to the first business session of the Assembly. Any member may move to have included in the Agenda such items of business as he or she may have previously proposed to the Central or Business Committee.

4. NOMINATIONS COMMITTEE OF THE ASSEMBLY

(*a*) At an early session of the Assembly, the Assembly shall elect a Nominations Committee, on which there shall be appropriate confessional, cultural, and geographical representation of the membership of the Assembly and representation of the major interests of the World Council.

(*b*) The Nominations Committee in consultation with the officers of the World Council and the Executive Committee shall make nominations for the following:

(i) the President or Presidents of the World Council of Churches;

(ii) not more than 145 members of the Central Committee from among the delegates which the member churches have elected to the Assembly.

(*c*) In making nominations, the Nominations Committee shall have regard to the following principles:

(i) the personal qualifications of the individual for the task for which he or she is to be nominated;

(ii) fair and adequate confessional representation;

(iii) fair and adequate geographical and cultural representation;

(iv) fair and adequate representation of the major interests of the World Council.

The Nominations Committee shall satisfy itself as to the general acceptability of the nominations to the churches to which the nominees belong.

Not more than seven persons from any one member church shall be nominated as members of the Central Committee.

The Nominations Committee shall secure adequate representation of laypersons—men, women, and young people—so far as the composition of the Assembly makes this possible.

(*d*) The Nominations Committee shall present its nominations to the Assembly. Additional nominations may be made by any six delegates concurring in writing, provided that each such nominee shall be proposed in opposition to a particular nominee of the Nominations Committee.

(e) Election shall be by ballot unless the Assembly shall otherwise determine.

IV. CENTRAL COMMITTEE

1. MEMBERSHIP

(a) The Central Committee shall consist of the President or Presidents of the World Council together with not more than 145 members elected by the Assembly and not more than five members co-opted by the Central Committee (see Constitution, Art. V.2.(b)).

(b) Any member church not already represented may send one representative to the meetings of the Central Committee. Such a representative shall have the right to speak but not to vote.

(c) If a regularly elected member of the Central Committee is unable to attend a meeting, the church to which the absent member belongs shall have the right to send a substitute, provided that the substitute is ordinarily resident in the country where the absent member resides. Such a substitute shall have the right to speak and to vote. If a member, or his or her substitute, is absent without excuse for two consecutive meetings, the position shall be declared vacant, and the Central Committee shall fill the vacancy according to the provisions of Article V.2.(b)(iii) of the Constitution.

(d) Moderators and Vice-Moderators of Committees and Boards who are not members of the Central Committee may attend meetings of the Central Committee and shall have the right to speak but not to vote.

(e) Advisers for the Central Committee may be appointed by the Executive Committee, after consultation with the churches of which they are members. They shall have the right to speak but not to vote.

(f) Members of the staff of the World Council appointed by the Central Committee as specified under Rule VIII.3. shall have the right to attend the sessions of the Central Committee unless on any occasion the Central Committee shall otherwise determine. When present they shall have the right to speak but not to vote.

(g) The newly elected Central Committee shall be convened by the General Secretary during or immediately after the meeting of the Assembly.

2. OFFICERS

(a) The Central Committee shall elect from among its members a Moderator and a Vice-Moderator or Vice-Moderators to serve for such periods as it shall determine.

(b) The General Secretary of the World Council of Churches shall be *ex officio* secretary of the Central Committee.

3. NOMINATIONS COMMITTEE OF THE CENTRAL COMMITTEE

(*a*) The Central Committee shall elect a Nominations Committee which shall:

(i) nominate for possible co-option as members of the Central Committee not more than five persons from among the representatives which the Associate member churches have elected to the Assembly;

(ii) nominate persons from among the members of the Central Committee for the offices of Moderator and Vice-Moderator or Vice-Moderators of the Central Committee;

(iii) nominate a person for the office of President to fill the unexpired term should a vacancy occur in the Praesidium between assemblies;

(iv) nominate members of the Executive Committee of the Central Committee;

(v) nominate members of Committees and Boards and where appropriate their Moderators;

(vi) make recommendations regarding the approval of the election of members of Commissions and Working Groups;

(vii) make recommendations regarding the election of persons proposed for staff positions under Rule VIII.3.

In making nominations as provided for by (i) to (v) above the Nominations Committee of the Central Committee shall have regard to principles set out in Rule III.4.(*c*), and in applying principles (ii), (iii), and (iv) to the nomination of members of Committees and Boards, shall consider the representative character of the combined membership of all such committees. Any member of the Central Committee may make additional nominations, provided that each such nominee shall be proposed in opposition to a particular nominee of the Nominations Committee.

(*b*) Election shall be by ballot unless the Committee shall otherwise determine.

4. MEETINGS

(*a*) The Central Committee shall ordinarily meet once every year. The Executive Committee may call an extraordinary meeting of the Central Committee whenever it deems such a meeting desirable and shall do so upon the request in writing of one-third or more of the members of the Central Committee.

(*b*) The General Secretary shall take all possible steps to ensure that there be adequate representation present from each of the main confessions and from the main geographical areas of the membership of the World Council of Churches and of the major interests of the World Council.

(*c*) The Central Committee shall determine the date and place of its own meetings and of the meetings of the Assembly.

5. FUNCTIONS

In exercising the powers set forth in the Constitution the Central Committee shall have the following specific functions:

(a) In the conduct of its business, the Central Committee shall elect the following committees:

(i) Finance Committee (a standing committee);

(ii) Nominations Committee (appointed at each meeting);

(iii) Reference Committee or Committees (appointed as needed at each meeting to advise the Central Committee on any other questions arising which call for special consideration or action by the Central Committee, except that recommendations from Committees of the Programme Units may be considered by the Central Committee without prior consideration by a Reference Committee).

(b) It shall adopt the Budget of the Council.

(c) It shall deal with matters referred to it by member churches.

(d) It shall organize Programme Units and Specialized Units and regional offices or representations as may be necessary to carry out the work of the World Council of Churches. It shall elect a Committee for each Programme Unit, a Board for each Specialized Unit, and approve the election or appointment of a Commission or a Working Group for each sub-unit of the Programme Units and receive reports from them at each of its meetings. It shall determine the general policy to be followed in the work of each Programme Unit, each Specialized Unit, and the Departments of Finance and Central Services, and of Communication.

(e) It shall report to the Assembly the actions it has taken during its period of office and shall not be discharged until its report has been received.

V. EXECUTIVE COMMITTEE

1. MEMBERSHIP

(a) The Executive Committee shall consist of the President or Presidents of the World Council *ex officio* and the Moderator and Vice-Moderator or Vice-Moderators of the Central Committee *ex officio* and of not less than fourteen nor more than sixteen other members of the Central Committee. Substitutes shall not be permitted to attend in place of elected members.

(b) The Central Committee shall elect an Executive Committee at each of its meetings. Elected members of the Executive Committee shall hold office until the next meeting of the Central Committee and shall be eligible for re-election.

(c) The Moderator of the Central Committee shall also be the Moderator of the Executive Committee.

(*d*) The General Secretary of the World Council of Churches shall be *ex officio* the secretary of the Executive Committee.

(*e*) The officers may invite other persons to attend a meeting of the Executive Committee for consultation, always having in mind the need of preserving a due balance of the confessions and of the geographical areas and cultural backgrounds, and of the major interests of the World Council.

2. FUNCTIONS

(*a*) The Executive Committee shall be accountable to the Central Committee.

(*b*) Between meetings of the Central Committee, the Executive Committee shall carry out decisions of the Central Committee and implement policies adopted by it. The Executive Committee shall not make decisions on policy except in those matters specifically delegated to the Executive Committee by the Central Committee and in circumstances of special emergency when it may take provisional decisions. The Executive Committee's power to make public statements is limited and defined in Rule IX.5.

(*c*) The Executive Committee may make provisional appointments to those staff positions specified in Rule VIII.3. subject to confirmation by the Central Committee.

(*d*) The Executive Committee shall supervise the operation of the budget and may, if necessary, impose limitations on expenditures.

VI. PROGRAMME UNITS, SPECIALIZED UNITS, AND DEPARTMENTS

1. There shall be three Programme Units:

Programme Unit I: Faith and Witness

Programme Unit II: Justice and Service

Programme Unit III: Education and Renewal

The Central Committee shall determine the size and composition of the Committee for each Programme Unit (so that at least two-thirds of the members of each Programme Unit Committee are also members of the Central Committee) and elect the members of each Committee, and its Moderator. Each Committee shall propose, for consideration by the Central Committee, By-laws for the conduct of the work of the Programme Unit, including a statement of the aim and functions of the unit, a description of the sub-units into which the unit will be divided, if any, and the allocation of functions among them, provision for a Working Group or Commission related to each sub-unit, and such other materials as it deems desirable.

2. There shall be two Specialized Units:

(a) Library

(b) Ecumenical Institute, including its Graduate School.

The Central Committee shall determine the size and composition of the Board for each Specialized Unit and elect the members of each Board. Each Board may propose for consideration by the Central Committee By-laws for the conduct of the work of the Specialized Unit.

3. There shall be a Department of Finance and Central Services and a Department of Communication. The Central Committee shall determine the size and composition of the Committee for the Department of Communication and shall elect the members of it.

VII. FINANCE COMMITTEE OF CENTRAL COMMITTEE

1. The Finance Committee of the Central Committee shall consist of not less than nine members, including:

(a) a Moderator, who shall be a member of the Executive Committee;

(b) five members, who shall be members of the Central Committee, two of whom shall also be members of the Executive Committee;

(c) three members, one of whom shall be designated by each Programme Unit Committee from the membership of said Committee. Each Programme Unit Committee may designate an alternate who may attend if his or her principal is unable to be present.

2. The Committee shall have the following responsibilities and duties:

(a) To present to the Central Committee:

(i) in respect of the expired calendar year, an account of income and expenditure of all operations of the World Council of Churches and the balance sheet of the World Council of Churches at the end of that year and its recommendation, based on review of the report of the auditors, regarding approval and granting of discharge in respect of the accounts of the World Council of Churches for the completed period;

(ii) in respect of the current year, a review of all financial operations;

(iii) in respect of the succeeding calendar year, a budget covering all activities of the World Council of Churches and its recommendations regarding the approval of that budget in the light of its judgement as to the adequacy of the provisions made for the expenditure involved in the proposed programme of activities and the adequacy of reasonably foreseeable income to finance the budget; and

(iv) in respect of the year next following the succeeding calendar year a provisional budget prepared on a similar basis together with recommendations thereon as in (iii) above.

(*b*) To consider and make recommendations to the Central Committee on all financial questions concerning the affairs of the World Council of Churches, such as:

(i) the appointment of the auditor or auditors who shall be appointed annually by the Central Committee and shall be eligible for reappointment;

(ii) accounting procedures;

(iii) investment policy and procedures;

(iv) the basis of calculation of contributions from member churches;

(v) procedures and methods of raising funds.

VIII. STAFF

1. The Central Committee shall elect or appoint or provide for the election or appointment of persons of special competence to conduct the continuing operations of the World Council. These persons collectively constitute the staff.

2. The General Secretary shall be elected by the Central Committee. He or she is the chief executive officer of the World Council. As such he or she is the head of the staff. When the position of General Secretary becomes vacant, the Executive Committee shall appoint an acting General Secretary.

3. In addition to the General Secretary, the Central Committee shall itself elect one or two Deputy General Secretaries, one or more Assistant General Secretaries, and the Directors of the Programme Units, the Specialized Units, and the Departments.

4. The Staff Executive Group shall consist of the Deputy General Secretary or Secretaries, the Director or Moderator of the staff of each Programme Unit, the Directors of the Departments and of the Ecumenical Institute, the Assistant General Secretary or Secretaries; and two or three additional executive staff members from each Programme Unit chosen by that Unit. Care shall be taken that there is confessional, cultural, and geographical balance in this group and that women and junior staff members are adequately represented. Additional places shall be available if needed to achieve balance. The possible need for rotation of the members who do not serve *ex officio* shall be examined at least annually, and in any event following each meeting of the Central Committee. The General Secretary shall be Moderator of the Staff Executive Group; in his or her absence a Deputy General Secretary shall act as Moderator. The Staff Executive Group shall advise the General Secretary on the implementation of policy established by the Central and Executive Committees and may, with his or her approval, establish regular and *ad hoc* co-ordinating groups for particular programme activities under the moderatorship of the General Secretary or of a person appointed by him or her.

332

5. The normal terms of appointment for the General Secretary and for a Deputy General Secretary shall be five years and for a Director of a Programme Unit, of a Specialized Unit, or of a Department, three years. Unless some other period is stated in the resolution making the appointment, the term of office of other members of the staff of the World Council shall be three years from the date of the appointment. All appointments made for a term exceeding one year shall be reviewed one year before expiring.

Retirement shall be at sixty-five for both men and women or not later than the end of the year in which a staff member reaches the age of sixty-eight.

IX. PUBLIC STATEMENTS

1. In the performance of its functions, the Council through its Assembly or through its Central Committee may publish statements upon any situation or issue with which the Council or its constituent churches may be confronted.

2. While such statements may have great significance and influence as the expression of the judgement or concern of so widely representative a Christian body, yet their authority will consist only in the weight which they carry by their own truth and wisdom, and the publishing of such statements shall not be held to imply that the World Council as such has, or can have, any constitutional authority over the constituent churches or right to speak for them.

3. Any Programme Unit or Sub-unit may recommend statements to the Assembly or to the Central Committee for its consideration and action.

4. A Programme Unit or Sub-unit may publish any statement which has been approved by the Assembly or the Central Committee. When, in the judgement of a Programme Unit or Sub-unit, a statement should be issued before such approval can be obtained, it may do so provided the statement relates to matters within its own field of concern and action, has received the approval of the Moderator of the Central Committee and the General Secretary, and the Programme Unit or Sub-unit makes clear that neither the World Council of Churches nor any of its member churches is committed by the statement.

5. Between meetings of the Central Committee, when in their judgement the situation requires, a statement may be issued, provided that such statements are not contrary to the established policy of the Council, by:

(i) the Executive Committee when meeting apart from the sessions of the Central Committee; or

(ii) the Moderator and Vice-Moderator or Vice-Moderators of the Central Committee and the General Secretary acting together; or

(iii) the Moderator of the Central Committee or the General Secretary on his or her own authority respectively.

X. ASSOCIATE COUNCILS

1. Any national Christian council, national council of churches, or national ecumenical council, established for purposes of ecumenical fellowship and activity, may be recognized by the Central Committee as an associate council, provided:

(a) the applicant council, knowing the Basis upon which the World Council is founded, expresses its desire to co-operate with the World Council towards the achievement of one or more of the functions and purposes of this Council; and

(b) the member churches of the World Council in the area have been consulted prior to the action.

2. Each associate council:

(a) shall be invited to send a fraternal delegate to the Assembly;

(b) may, at the discretion of the Central Committee, be invited to send an adviser to meetings of the Central Committee; and

(c) shall be provided with copies of all general communications sent to all member churches of the World Council of Churches.

3. In addition to communicating directly with its member churches, the World Council shall inform each associate council regarding important ecumenical developments and consult it regarding proposed World Council programmes in its country.

XI. REGIONAL CONFERENCES

1. The World Council recognizes Regional Conferences of Churches as essential partners in the ecumenical enterprise.

2. Such Regional Conferences as may be designated by the Central Committee:

(a) shall be invited to send a fraternal delegate to the Assembly;

(b) shall be invited to send an adviser to meetings of the Central Committee; and

(c) shall be provided with copies of all general communications sent to all member churches of the World Council of Churches.

3. In addition to communicating directly with its member churches, the World Council shall inform each of these regional conferences regarding important ecumenical developments and consult it regarding proposed World Council programmes in its region.

XII. WORLD CONFESSIONAL BODIES

Such World Confessional bodies as may be designated by the Central Committee shall be invited to send fraternal delegates to the Assembly and advisers to meetings of the Central Committee and the World Council will take steps to develop co-operative working relationships with them.

XIII. LEGAL PROVISIONS

1. The duration of the Council is unlimited.

2. The legal headquarters of the Council shall be at Grand Saconnex, Geneva, Switzerland. Regional offices may be organized in different parts of the world by decision of the Central Committee.

3. The World Council of Churches is legally represented by its Executive Committee or by such persons as may be empowered by the Executive Committee to represent it.

4. The World Council shall be legally bound by the joint signatures of two of the following persons: the President or Presidents, the Moderator and Vice-Moderator or Vice-Moderators of the Central Committee, and the General Secretary. Any two of the above-named persons shall have power to authorize other persons, chosen by them, to act jointly or singly on behalf of the World Council of Churches in fields circumscribed in the power of attorney.

5. The Council shall obtain the means necessary for the pursuance of its work from the contributions of its member churches and from donations or bequests.

6. The Council shall not pursue commercial functions but it shall have the right to act as an agency of inter-church aid and to publish literature in connection with its aims. It is not entitled to distribute any surplus income by way of profit or bonus among its members.

7. Members of the governing bodies of the Council or of the Assembly shall have no personal liability with regard to the obligations or commitments of the Council. The commitments entered upon by the Council are guaranteed solely by its own assets.

XIV. RULES OF DEBATE

1. CATEGORIES OF SESSION

The Assembly shall sit either in general session, in business session, or in deliberative session.

2. PRESIDING OFFICERS

(a) The Moderator of the Assembly in general session shall be one of the Presidents or the Moderator of the Central Committee, as appointed by the Executive Committee.

(b) The Moderator of the Assembly in business session shall be the Moderator or a Vice-Moderator of the Central Committee, or some other member of the Central Committee appointed by the Executive Committee or by the Business Committee of the Assembly.

(c) The Moderator of the Assembly in deliberative session shall be a member of the Praesidium, an Officer of the Central Committee, or a delegate appointed by the Executive Committee or the Business Committee of the Assembly.

3. RESPONSIBILITIES OF THE MODERATOR

The responsibilities of the Moderator shall be to announce the opening, suspension, and adjournment of the meeting. His or her first action shall be to announce clearly that the Assembly is in general session, or in business session, or in deliberative session; he or she shall ensure the observance of the applicable Rules of Debate. He or she shall grant the right to speak and declare the debate closed; he or she shall put questions to the vote and announce the result of the voting. He or she shall seek to understand the sense of the meeting on specific issues under consideration and may announce it without taking votes. He or she shall not make a motion. His or her decision is final in all matters except as to the result of voting or his or her announcement as to the sense of the meeting on an issue. If the Moderator's decision on the result of voting is challenged, he or she shall, without further debate, call for a vote on the motion: "that the Moderator's decision be reconsidered" (reconsideration will be permitted if a majority of the members present and voting approve). If the Moderator's decision on the sense of the meeting is challenged, he or she may allow further discussion or call for a vote as above.

4. GENERAL SESSIONS

When the Assembly is in general session (for ceremonial occasions, public acts of witness, formal addresses, etc.) the only business that shall be in order, except with consent, is that which is proposed by the Moderator or Secretary of the Executive or Business Committee.

5. BUSINESS SESSIONS

The Assembly shall sit in business session when any of the following types of business are on the agenda: adoption of agenda presented by the Business Committee, nominations, elections, proposals with reference to the structure, organization, budget, or programme of the World Council of Churches, or any other business requiring action by the Assembly, except as provided in paragraphs 4 and 6 of this Rule.

The Special Rules of Debate for the Assembly in business session:

(a) If any member desires to propose a motion not on the agenda, he or she shall inform the Moderator beforehand in writing regarding the same; and the Officers shall consider its inclusion. If it is not so included, he or she shall be permitted to have his or her motion read and the reason of the Officers for its exclusion explained. A vote shall be immediately taken as to whether or not his or her motion shall be included in the agenda.

(b) All motions and amendments must be proposed and seconded, handed to the Moderator in writing, and read before a vote is taken. The Moderator has the power to rule an amendment out of order as being substantially a negative of the motion.

(c) Any motion or amendment may be withdrawn by leave of the Assembly.

(d) Subject to the provisions of Rule XIV.5.(j) no member shall speak until the Moderator recognizes him or her and calls him or her to speak. All speeches must be addressed to the Chair.

(e) No member shall speak more than once on the same motion or amendment, except that the mover shall have the right to speak last before the vote is taken. However, the representative of a committee presenting a report may speak more than once for purposes of clarification, as the Moderator decides.

(f) When an amendment has been proposed and seconded the Moderator shall allow discussion on the amendment only. An amendment to an amendment is in order, but an amendment to an amendment to an amendment shall be out of order. Discussion and voting shall be in reverse order of the motions made. When the Assembly has voted to approve or disapprove the amendments which have been proposed and seconded, and the original motion is before the Assembly (amended or not as the case may be), additional amendments are in order except those which are judged by the Chair to be substantially the same as proposals already discussed and decided. A motion to refer a resolution back to the responsible committee, with or without pending amendments, is always in order. Debate on such a motion shall be limited to three minutes by the maker of the motion, and three minutes by a representative of the committee making the original proposal, and comments by the Moderator and Secretary as to the feasibility of handling the matter later in the agenda.

(g) During the discussion, speeches shall be limited to five minutes. A bell shall be rung one minute before a speaker's time is up. A second bell shall be rung one minute later and the speaker shall then sit down, unless the Moderator proposes and receives consent that an additional minute or minutes be allowed the speaker. If translation (other than simultaneous) is required, sufficient additional time shall be allowed by the Moderator.

(h) Those who desire to speak for or against a main proposal before the Assembly must hand to the Secretary, as early as possible, cards with their names, the capacity in which they are attending the Assembly, their church connection, and whether they desire to support or oppose the motion. Those who wish to propose amendments shall follow the same procedure, adding on the card precise information as to the part of the resolution they desire to amend. Those who wish to amend an amendment or to discuss an amendment already proposed shall stand in their places for recognition by the Moderator. The mover of an amendment and a representative of the committee reporting shall be allowed additional final statements in this order before the vote on each amendment is taken.

(*i*) A motion to close the debate in order to proceed immediately to vote on the pending amendments and on the main question shall be in order when admitted by the Moderator. If such a motion is admitted, the Secretary shall be asked to report to the Assembly the names of the delegates still desiring to be heard and the names of delegates whose proposed amendments have not been heard, or the Moderator may ask the meeting for a show of hands of any still desiring to speak; after which the Moderator shall ask the Assembly—"Shall the Assembly now conclude the matter before it?" The Moderator shall put the question to the Assembly, without debate, either when it has been moved and seconded or when he or she judges that the Assembly desires to conclude the matter before it. If two-thirds of the delegates present and voting agree, the vote or votes on the pending amendment and on the main motion shall be taken without further debate.

(*j*) Any member may submit a point of order or procedure to the Moderator and may, if necessary, interrupt a speaker for this purpose. As the Rules do not correspond to those obtaining in any one country, the member raising the point of order shall ensure that it is in the Rules adopted by the World Council of Churches, and indicate the number of the Rule if the Moderator requires it.

(*k*) (i) Voting shall be by show of hands or by standing unless otherwise decided by vote of the Assembly. The Moderator shall read the motion immediately before any vote is taken. He or she shall first ask those in favour of the motion to vote, and then those opposed. The Moderator may, if he or she thinks fit, appoint members or staff to act as tellers, and he or she shall do so in case of doubt as to the result of the vote.

(ii) A majority of those present and voting shall determine the decision except as may be otherwise provided in the Constitution or the Rules.

(iii) When the Assembly is equally divided the motion will be regarded as defeated.

(iv) The Moderator may give the results of the voting without actual count.

(v) The Moderator's decision on the result of the voting may be challenged by any member entitled to vote and the Moderator shall then without further debate follow the procedure set out in Rule XIV.3. above.

(vi) Where a majority of the members present and voting desire that the Moderator's decision be reconsidered, voting shall be by actual count.

(vii) Where a motion for a vote by written ballot is proposed and seconded, the Moderator shall put this motion to the vote without further debate.

(*l*) Those voting with the minority may have their names recorded. Those who abstain from voting may, if they wish, have the fact and number of abstentions recorded.

(*m*) The languages regularly used are English, French, and German. A speech made in any one of these languages shall, if desired, be translated into the other two. It shall be the duty of the Secretary to make arrangements for such translation. A member may speak in a language other than English, French, or German, on condition that he or she arrange for the translation of his or her speech into one of these three languages. If the Moderator shall judge that injustice has been done to a member by the strict application of these Rules of Debate due to the business having been done too quickly for comprehension in a language other than that of the member, the Moderator may suspend the strict application of the rules to allow reconsideration, motions, amendments, or speeches that would otherwise be out of order.

(n) To ensure that the Assembly has a period of general discussion of a resolution or report presented to it from a committee, in order to understand it and develop its mind about it, the Chair may decide that it shall be deliberated by the Assembly for a certain period of time before any amendment, motion, closure, or reference back to the committee is moved.

6. DELIBERATIVE SESSIONS

The Assembly shall sit in deliberative session when resolutions or reports are before it which are of such a theological or general policy nature that in the judgement of the Executive Committee or the Business Committee they ought not to be amended in so large a body as an Assembly. A body reporting shall indicate to the Business Committee its preference regarding procedures. The reports of sections shall be debated in deliberative sessions.

The Special Rules of Debate for the Assembly in deliberative session are the same as those for the Assembly in business session, except that provisions 5(a), (b), (f), and (g) shall not apply, and that the following additional rules shall be in effect:

(a) The only recommendation that shall be in order from committees or sections reporting is that the Assembly approve the substance of the document, and commend it to the churches for study and appropriate action.

(b) The only motions from the floor that are in order are: (i) to refer back to the committee with instructions to consider whether a new or different emphasis or emphases shall be included by the committee in their report, or (ii) to instruct the committee to provide for an open hearing or an additional open hearing on the report before bringing it again to the Assembly.

(c) Those who desire to speak on the resolution or report before the Assembly must hand to the Secretary, as early as possible, cards with their names, the capacity in which they are attending the Assembly, and their church connection, and whether they desire to speak to the report as a whole or to a particular section or sections thereof.

(d) Those who desire to propose either of the motions allowed in (b) above must add this information on their card when sent forward, or else their motion shall be out of order. The Moderator in introducing them shall indicate that a motion is to be moved.

(e) Speeches shall ordinarily be limited to ten minutes. The bell shall be rung at the end of eight minutes and again two minutes later and the speaker shall then sit down unless the Moderator proposes and receives consent that an additional minute or minutes be allowed.

When the number of those desiring to speak is large, the Moderator may ask the Assembly to agree to a shorter time. When translation (other than simultaneous) is required, sufficient additional time shall be allowed by the Moderator.

(*f*) Rule 5(i) shall be followed as far as it applies to close the debate.

7. THE CENTRAL COMMITTEE

The Central Committee shall ordinarily sit in business session and these rules shall be followed except that Rules 5 (*g*) (length of speeches) and (*h*) (handing in name cards) shall only apply when it is so decided by the Central Committee itself. If on recommendation of the Executive Committee the Central Committee shall agree to sit in a general or deliberative session, the rules for these sessions shall be the same as the rules for the Assembly in general session or deliberative session, except that Rules 6 (*c*), (*d*), (*e*), and (*f*) shall not apply.

XV. AMENDMENTS

Amendments to these Rules may be moved at any session of the Assembly or at any session of the Central Committee by any member and may be adopted by a two-thirds majority of those present and voting, except that no alteration in Rules I, IV, and XV shall come into effect until it has been confirmed by the Assembly. Notice of a proposal to make any such amendment shall be given in writing at least twenty-four hours before the session of the Assembly or Central Committee at which it is to be moved.

Appendix 12
List of Member Churches, Associate Member Churches, and Associate Councils

MEMBER CHURCHES

Argentina
Iglesia Evangélica del Río de la Plata
  (Evangelical Church of the River Plata)
Iglesia Evangélica Metodista Argentina
  (Evangelical Methodist Church of Argentina)

Australasia
Methodist Church of Australasia
The United Church in Papua, New Guinea and the Solomon Islands

Australia
Churches of Christ in Australia
The Church of England in Australia
The Congregational Union of Australia
The Presbyterian Church of Australia

Austria
Alt-katholische Kirche Österreichs
  (Old Catholic Church of Austria)
Evangelische Kirche A.B. in Osterreich
  (Evangelical Church of the Augsburg Confession)

Belgium
Eglise Protestante de Belgique
  (Protestant Church of Belgium)
Eglise Réformée de Belgique
  (Reformed Church of Belgium)

Brazil
Igreja Episcopal do Brasil
  (Episcopal Church of Brazil)
Igreja Evangélica de Confissão Lutherana no Brasil
  (Evangelical Church of Lutheran Confession in Brazil)
Igreja Evangélica Pentecostal "O Brasil para Cristo"
  (The Evangelical Pentecostal Church "Brazil for Christ")

Igreja Metodista do Brasil
(Methodist Church of Brazil)
Igreja Reformada Latino Americana
(The Latin American Reformed Church)

Bulgaria
Eglise Orthodoxe Bulgare
(Bulgarian Orthodox Church)

Burma
Burma Baptist Convention
Church of the Province of Burma

Cameroon
Eglise évangélique du Cameroun
(Evangelical Church of Cameroon)
Eglise presbytérienne camérounaise
(Presbyterian Church of Cameroon)
Presbyterian Church in Cameroon
Union des Eglises baptistes du Cameroun
(Union of Baptist Churches of Cameroon)

Canada
The Anglican Church of Canada
Canadian Yearly Meeting of the Society of Friends
Christian Church (Disciples of Christ)
The Evangelical Lutheran Church of Canada
The Presbyterian Church in Canada
The United Church of Canada

Central Africa
Church of the Province of Central Africa

Chile
Iglesia Evangélica Luterana en Chile
(Evangelical Lutheran Church in Chile)
Iglesia Pentecostal de Chile
(Pentecostal Church of Chile)
Misión Iglesia Pentecostal
(Pentecostal Mission Church)

China
China Baptist Council
Chung-Hua Chi-Tu Chiao-Hui
(Church of Christ in China)
Chung Hua Sheng Kung Hui
(Anglican Church in China)
Hua Pei Kung Li Hui
(Congregational Church in North China)

Congo (People's Republic of the)
Eglise Evangélique du Congo
(Evangelical Church of the Congo)

Cook Islands
Cook Islands Christian Church

Cyprus
Church of Cyprus

Czechoslovakia
Ceskobratrská církev evangelická
(Evangelical Church of Czech Brethren)
Ceskoslovenská církev husitská
(Czechoslovak Hussite Church)
Pravoslavná církev v CSSR
(Orthodox Church of Czechoslovakia)
Ref. krest. církev na Slovensku
(Reformed Christian Church in Slovakia)
Slezská církev evangelická a.v.
(Silesian Evangelical Church of the Augsburg Confession)
Slovenská evanjelická církev a.v. v CSSR
(Slovak Evangelical Church of the Augsb. Conf. in the CSSR)

People's Republic of Benin (Dahomey)
Eglise Protestante Methodiste au Dahomey-Togo
(The Protestant Methodist Church in Dahomey and Togo)

Denmark
Det danske Baptistsamfund
(The Baptist Union of Denmark)
Den evangelisk-lutherske Folkekirke i Danmark
(The Church of Denmark)

East Africa
Presbyterian Church of East Africa

Egypt
Coptic Orthodox Church
Evangelical Church—The Synod of the Nile
Greek Orthodox Patriarchate of Alexandria

Ethiopia
Ethiopia Orthodox Church

Finland
Suomen Evankelis-Luterilainen Kirkko
(Evangelical-Lutheran Church of Finland)

France
Eglise de la Confession d'Augsbourg d'Alsace et de Lorraine
(Evangelical Church of the Augsburg Confession of Alsace and Lorraine)
Eglise Evangélique Luthérienne de France
(Evangelical Lutheran Church of France)
Eglise Réformée d'Alsace et de Lorraine
(Reformed Church of Alsace and Lorraine)
Eglise Réformée de France
(Reformed Church of France)

Gabonese Republic
Eglise Evangélique du Gabon
(Evangelical Church of Gabon)

German Churches
Federal Republic of Germany
Katholisches Bistum der Alt-Katholiken in Deutschland
(Catholic Diocese of the Old Catholics in Germany)

Evangelische Brüder-Unität
 (Moravian Church)
Evangelische Kirche in Deutschland
 (Evangelical Church in Germany)
 Evangelische Landeskirche in Baden
 Evangelisch-Lutherische Kirche in Bayern*
 Evangelische Kirche in Berlin-Brandenburg
 Evangelisch-Lutherische Landeskirche in Braunschweig*
 Bremische Evangelische Kirche
 Evangelisch-Lutherische Landeskirche Eutin*
 Evangelisch-Lutherische Kirche im Hamburgischen Staate*
 Evangelisch-Lutherische Landeskirche Hannovers*
 Evangelische Kirche in Hessen und Nassau
 Evangelische Kirche von Kurhessen-Waldeck
 Lippische Landeskirche
 Evangelisch-Lutherische Kirche in Lübeck*
 Evangelisch-reformierte Kirche in Nordwestdeutschland
 Evangelisch-Lutherische Kirche in Oldenburg
 Vereinigte Protestantisch-Evangelisch-Christliche Kirche der Pfalz
 Evangelische Kirche im Rheinland
 Evangelisch-Lutherische Landeskirche Schaumburg-Lippe*
 Evangelisch-Lutherische Landeskirche Schleswig-Holsteins*
 Evangelische Kirche von Westfalen
 Evangelische Landeskirche in Württemberg
Vereinigung der Deutschen Mennonitengemeinden
 (Mennonite Church)

---

*This Church is directly a member of the World Council of Churches in accordance with the resolution of the General Synod of the United Evangelical Lutheran Church of Germany, dated 27 January, 1949, which recommended that the member churches of the United Evangelical Lutheran Church should make the following declaration to the Council of the Evangelical Church in Germany concerning their relation to the World Council of Churches:

"The Evangelical Church in Germany has made it clear through its constitution that it is a federation (Bund) of confessionally determined churches. Moreover, the conditions of membership of the World Council of Churches have been determined at the Assembly at Amsterdam. Therefore, this Evangelical Lutheran Church declares concerning its membership in the World Council of Churches:

i) It is represented in the World Council as a church of the Evangelical Lutheran confession.

ii) Representatives which it sends to the World Council are to be identified as Evangelical Lutherans.

iii) Within the limits of the competence of the Evangelical Church in Germany it is represented in the World Council through the intermediary of the Council of the Evangelical Church in Germany."

German Democratic Republic
Bund der Evangelischen Kirchen in der Deutschen Demokratischen
Republik
(Federation of the Evangelical Churches in the GDR)
Evangelische Landeskirche Anhalts†
Evangelische Kirche in Berlin-Brandenburg†
Evangelische Kirche des Görlitzer Kirchengebietes†
Evangelische Landeskirche Greifswald†
Evangelisch-Lutherische Landeskirche Mecklenburgs†
Evangelische Kirche der Kirchenprovinz Sachsen†
Evangelisch-Lutherische Landeskirche Sachsens†
Evangelisch-Lutherische Kirche in Thüringen†
Evangelische Brüder-Unität (Distrikt Herrnhut)
(Moravian Church)
Gemeindeverband der Alt-Katholischen Kirche in der Deutschen
Demokratischen Republik
(Federation of the Old Catholic Church in the GDR)

Ghana
Evangelical Presbyterian Church
The Methodist Church, Ghana
Presbyterian Church of Ghana

Greece
Ekklesia tes Ellados
(Church of Greece)
Hellenike Evangelike Ekklesia
(Greek Evangelical Church)

Hong Kong
The Church of Christ in China, The Hong Kong Council

Hungary
Magyarországi Baptista Egyház
(Baptist Church in Hungary)
Magyarországi Evangélikus Egyház
(Lutheran Church in Hungary)
Magyarországi Reformatus Egyház
(Reformed Church in Hungary)

Iceland
Evangelical Lutheran Church of Iceland

India
Church of North India
Church of South India
Federation of Evangelical Lutheran Churches in India
Mar Thoma Syrian Church of Malabar
The Orthodox Syrian Church, Catholicate of the East
The Samavesam of Telugu Baptist Churches

Indian Ocean
Church of the Province of the Indian Ocean

---

†United in a fellowship of Christian witness and service in the Federation
of Evangelical Churches in the GDR, these churches are represented in the
Council through agencies of the Federation of Evangelical Churches in the
GDR.

Indonesia
  Banua Niha Keriso Protestan Nias
    (The Church of Nias)
  Gereja Batak Karo Protestan
    (Karo Batak Protestant Church)
  Gereja-Gereja Kristen Java
    (Christian Churches of Java)
  Gereja Kalimantan Evangelis
    (Kalimantan Evangelical Church)
  Gereja Kristen Indonesia
    (Indonesian Christian Church)
  Gereja Kristen Injili di Irian Jaya
    (Evangelical Christian Church in West Irian)
  Gereja Kristen Jawi Wetan
    (Christian Church of East Java)
  Gereja Kristen Pasundan
    (Pasundan Christian Church)
  Gereja Kristen Sulawesi Tengah
    (Christian Church in Mid-Sulawesi)
  Gereja Masehi Injili Minahasa
    (Christian Evangelical Church in Minahasa)
  Gereja Masehi Injili Sangihe Talaud (GMIST)
    (Evangelical Church of Sangir Talaud)
  Gereja Masehi Injili di Timor
    (Protestant Evangelical Church in Timor)
  Gereja Protestan di Indonesia
    (Protestant Church in Indonesia)
  Gereja Protestan Maluku
    (Protestant Church of the Moluccas)
  Gereja Kristen Protestan Simalungun
    (Simalungun Protestant Christian Church)
  Gereja Toraja
    (Toraja Church)
  Huria Kristen Batak Protestan
    (Protestant Christian Batak Church)
  Huria Kristen Indonesia (H.K.I.)
    (The Indonesian Christian Church)
Iran
  Synod of the Evangelical Church of Iran
Italy
  Chiesa Evangelica Internazionale
    (The International Evangelical Church)
  Chiesa Evangelica Metodista d'Italia
    (Evangelical Methodist Church of Italy)
  Chiesa Evangelica Valdese
    (Waldensian Church)
Jamaica
  The Moravian Church in Jamaica
  The United Church of Jamaica and Grand Cayman
Japan
  Japanese Orthodox Church
  Nippon Kirisuto Kyodan
    (The United Church of Christ in Japan)

346

Nippon Sei Ko Kai
  (Anglican-Episcopal Church in Japan)
Jerusalem
  Greek Orthodox Patriarchate of Jerusalem
Kenya
  African Christian Church and Schools
  African Israel Church, Ninevah
  Church of the Province of Kenya
  The Methodist Church in Kenya
Korea
  The Korean Methodist Church
  The Presbyterian Church in the Republic of Korea
  The Presbyterian Church in Korea
Lebanon
  Armenian Apostolic Church
  Union of the Armenian Evangelical Churches in the Near East
Lesotho
  Lesotho Evangelical Church
Liberia
  Lutheran Church in Liberia
Madagascar
  Eglise de Jésus Christ à Madagascar
    (Church of Jesus Christ in Madagascar)
  Eglise Luthérienne Malgache
    (Malagasy Lutheran Church)
Malaysia and Singapore
  The Methodist Church in Malaysia and Singapore
Mexico
  Iglesia Metodista de México
    (Methodist Church of Mexico)
Netherlands
  Algemene Doopsgezinde Sociëteit
    (General Mennonite Society)
  Evangelisch Lutherse Kerk
    (Evangelical Lutheran Church)
  De Gereformeerde Kerken in Nederland
    (The Reformed Churches in the Netherlands)
  Nederlandse Hervormde Kerk
    (Netherlands Reformed Church)
  Oud-Katholieke Kerk van Nederland
    (Old Catholic Church of the Netherlands)
  Remonstrantse Broederschap
    (Remonstrant Brotherhood)
New Caledonia
  Eglise Evangélique en Nouvelle Calédonie et aux Iles Loyauté
    (Evangelical Church in New Caledonia and the Loyalty Isles)
New Hebrides
  Presbyterian Church of the New Hebrides
New Zealand
  Associated Churches of Christ in New Zealand
  The Baptist Union of New Zealand
  Church of the Province of New Zealand
  The Congregational Union of New Zealand

347

The Methodist Church of New Zealand
The Presbyterian Church of New Zealand
Nigeria
Church of the Lord (Aladura)
Methodist Church, Nigeria
Nigerian Baptist Convention
The Presbyterian Church of Nigeria
Norway
Den Norske Kirke
(Church of Norway)
Pakistan
The Church of Pakistan
United Presbyterian Church of Pakistan
Philippines
Iglesia Filipina Independiente
(Philippine Independent Church)
United Church of Christ in the Philippines
Iglesia Evangelica Metodista en las Islas Filipinas
(The Evangelical Methodist Church in the Philippines)
Poland
Autocephalous Orthodox Church in Poland
Kosciola Ewangelicko-Augsburskiego w PRL
(Evangelical Church of the Augsburg Confession in Poland)
Kosciola Polskokatolickiego w PRL
(Polish Catholic Church in Poland)
Staro-Katolickiego Kosciola Mariatowitow w PRL
(Old Catholic Mariavite Church in Poland)
Romania
Biserica Evangelica Dupa Confesiunea Dela Augsburg
(Evangelical Church of the Augsburg Confession)
Biserica Ortodoxa Romane
(Romanian Orthodox Church)
Biserica Reformata Din Romania
(Reformed Church of Romania)
Evangelical Synodal Presbyterial Church of the Augsburg Confession in
the Socialist Republic of Romania
Samoa
The Congregational Christian Church in Samoa
Sierra Leone
The Methodist Church, Sierra Leone
South Africa
The Bantu Presbyterian Church of South Africa
Church of the Province of South Africa
Evangelical Lutheran Church in Southern Africa, South-Eastern Region
Evangelical Lutheran Church in Southern Africa, Transvaal Region
The Methodist Church of South Africa
Moravian Church in South Africa
The Presbyterian Church of Southern Africa
The United Congregational Church of Southern Africa
Spain
Iglesia Evangélica Española
(Spanish Evangelical Church)

Sri Lanka
   The Anglican Church in Sri Lanka
   Methodist Church, Sri Lanka
Sweden
   Svenska Kyrkan
      (Church of Sweden)
   Svenska Missionsförbundet
      (The Mission Covenant Church of Sweden)
Surinam
   Moravian Church
Switzerland
   Christkatholische Kirche der Schweiz
      (Old Catholic Church of Switzerland)
   Schweizerischer Evangelischer Kirchenbund
      (Swiss Protestant Church Federation)
Syria
   The National Evangelical Synod of Syria and Lebanon
   Patriarcat Grec-Orthodoxe d'Antioche et de tout l'Orient
      (Greek Orthodox Patriarchate of Antioch and All the East)
   Syrian Orthodox Patriarchate of Antioch and All the East
Tahiti
   Eglise évangélique de Polynésie francaise
      (Evangelical Church of French Polynesia)
Taiwan
   Tai-Oan Ki-Tok Tiu Lo Kau-Hoe
      (The Presbyterian Church in Taiwan, Republic of China)
Tanzania
   Church of the Province of Tanzania
   Evangelical Lutheran Church in Tanzania
Thailand
   The Church of Christ in Thailand
Togo
   Eglise évangélique de Polynésie francaise
      (Evangelical Church of Togo)
Tonga
   Methodist Church of Tonga
Trinidad
   The Presbyterian Church in Trinidad and Grenada
Turkey
   Ecumenical Patriarchate of Constantinople
Uganda
   The Church of Uganda, Rwanda and Burundi
Union of Soviet Socialist Republics
   Eglise apostolique arménienne
      (Armenian Apostolic Church)
   Eesti Evangeeliumi Luteri usu Kirik
      (Estonian Evangelical Lutheran Church)
   Georgian Orthodox Church
   Latvijas Evangeliska-Luteriska Baznica
      (Evangelical Lutheran Church of Latvia)
   Russian Orthodox Church
   The Union of Evangelical Christian Baptists of USSR

United Kingdom and the Republic of Ireland
   The Baptist Union of Great Britain and Ireland
   Churches of Christ in Great Britain and Ireland
   The Church of England
   The Church of Ireland
   The Church of Scotland
   The Church in Wales
   The Congregational Union of Scotland
   Episcopal Church in Scotland
   The Methodist Church
   The Methodist Church in Ireland
   The Moravian Union
   The Presbyterian Church in Ireland
   The Presbyterian Church of Wales
   The Salvation Army
   Union of Welsh Independents
   United Free Church of Scotland
   The United Reformed Church of England and Wales
United States of America
   African Methodist Episcopal Church
   African Methodist Episcopal Zion Church
   American Baptist Churches in the U.S.A.
   American Lutheran Church
   The Antiochian Orthodox Christian Archdiocese
   Christian Church (Disciples of Christ)
   Christian Methodist Episcopal Church
   Church of the Brethren
   Church of the East (Assyrian)
   The Episcopal Church
   Hungarian Reformed Church in America
   Lutheran Church in America
   Moravian Church in America (Northern Province)
   Moravian Church in America (Southern Province)
   National Baptist Convention of America
   National Baptist Convention, U.S.A., Inc.
   National Council of Community Churches
   The Orthodox Church in America
   Polish National Catholic Church of America
   Presbyterian Church in the United States
   Progressive National Baptist Convention
   Reformed Church in America
   Religious Society of Friends
      Friends General Conference
      Friends United Meeting
   The Romanian Orthodox Episcopate of America
   Seventh Day Baptist General Conference
   United Church of Christ
   The United Methodist Church
   The United Presbyterian Church in the United States of America
West Africa
   The Church of the Province of West Africa

350

West Indies
 The Church in the Province of the West Indies
 The Methodist Church in the Caribbean and the Americas
 Moravian Church, Eastern West Indies Province
Yugoslavia
 Reformatska Crke u SFRJ
  (The Reformed Church in Yugoslavia)
 Serbian Orthodox Church
 Slovenska ev.-kr. a.v. cirkev v. Juhuslavii
  (Slovak Evangelical Church of the Augsburg Confession in Yugo-
  slavia)
Zaïre (Republic of)
 Eglise du Christ au Zaïre (Communauté des Disciples)
  (Church of Christ in Zaïre—Community of Disciples)
 Eglise du Christ au Zaïre (Communauté du Christ Lumière)
  (Church of Christ in Zaïre—Community of Christ the Light)
 Eglise du Christ au Zaïre (Communauté Mennonite au Zaïre)
  (Church of Christ in Zaïre—Mennonite Community in Zaïre)
 Eglise du Christ sur la Terre par le Prophète Simon Kimbangu
  (Church of Christ on Earth by the Prophet Simon Kimbangu)
 Eglise évangélique du Zaïre
  (Evangelical Church of Zaïre)
 Eglise Presbytérienne au Zaïre
  (Presbyterian Church in Zaïre)
Zambia
 United Church of Zambia
Other Churches
 Eesti Evangeeliumi Luteri Usu Kirik
  (Estonian Evangelical Lutheran Church)
 Latvijas Evangeliska Luteriska Baznica
  (Latvian Evangelical Lutheran Church)

ASSOCIATE MEMBER CHURCHES

Algeria
 Eglise Protestante d'Algérie
  (Protestant Church of Algeria)
Argentina
 Junta de los Discípulos de Cristo
  (Disciples of Christ)
 Iglesia Evangélica Luterana Unida
  (United Evangelical Lutheran Church)
Bangladesh
 Church of Bangladesh
Bolivia
 Iglesia Evangélica Metodista en Bolivia
  (Evangelical Methodist Church in Bolivia)

Cameroon
  Eglise Protestante Africaine
    (African Protestant Church)
Chile
  Iglesia Metodista de Chile
    (The Methodist Church of Chile)
Costa Rica
  Iglesia Evangélica Metodista
    (Evangelical Methodist Church)
Cuba
  Iglesia Metodista en Cuba
    (Methodist Church in Cuba)
  Iglesia Presbiteriana-Reformada en Cuba
    (Presbyterian-Reformed Church in Cuba)
India
  Bengal-Orissa-Bihar Baptist Convention
Indonesia
  Punguan Kristen Batak
Japan
  The Korean Christian Church in Japan
Kenya
  African Church of the Holy Spirit
Liberia
  Presbytery of Liberia
Malaysia
  Protestant Church in Sabah
Netherlands Antilles
  Protestantse Kerk van de Nederlandse Antillen
    (Protestant Church of the Netherlands Antilles)
Peru
  Iglesia Metodista del Peru
    (The Methodist Church of Peru)
Portugal
  Igreja Evangélica Presbiteriana de Portugal
    (Evangelical Presbyterian Church of Portugal)
  Igreja Lusitana Catolica Apostolica Evangélica
    (Lusitanian Catholic-Apostolic Evangelical Church)
Samoa
  Methodist Church of Samoa
Spain
  Iglesia Española Reformada Episcopal
    (Spanish Reformed Episcopal Church)
Sudan
  The Presbyterian Church in the Sudan
Uruguay
  Iglesia Evangélica Metodista en el Uruguay
    (The Evangelical Methodist Church in Uruguay)
West Africa
  Iglesia Evangélica de Guinea Ecuatorial
    (Evangelical Church of Equatorial Guinea)
Zaïre
  Eglise du Christ au Zaïre (Communauté Episcopale Baptiste en Afrique
    (C.E.B.A.)
    (Church of Christ in Zaïre)

352

ASSOCIATE COUNCILS

Australian Council of Churches
Ökumenischer Rat der Kirchen in Österreich
Christian Council of Botswana
Burma Council of Churches
Canadian Council of Churches
Ecumenical Council of Churches in the Czech Socialist Republic
Ecumenical Council of Denmark
Ecumenical Council of Finland
Arbeitsgemeinschaft Christlicher Kirchen in der DDR
Arbeitsgemeinschaft Christlicher Kirchen in Deutschland
Hong Kong Christian Council
Ecumenical Council of Hungarian Churches
National Christian Council of India
Council of Churches in Indonesia
The National Christian Council of Japan
Council of Churches of Malaysia
Council of Churches in the Netherlands
National Council of Churches in New Zealand
National Council of Churches in the Philippines
Polish Ecumenical Council
Christian Council of Rhodesia
National Council of Churches, Singapore
The South African Council of Churches
National Christian Council of Sri Lanka
Swedish Ecumenical Council
British Council of Churches
National Council of Churches of Christ in the USA
Ecumenical Council of Churches in Yugoslavia

Appendix 13
List of Participants

SUBDIVISIONS:

1. Presidents
2. Retiring members of the Central Committee
3. Delegates from member churches
4. Fraternal delegates (associate membership)
5. Fraternal delegates (Christian councils)
6. Fraternal delegates (Christian organizations)
7. Fraternal delegates (world confessional families)
8. Advisers
9. Delegated observers (non-member churches)
10. Observers (Christian councils)
11. Observers (international organizations)
12. Guests
13. Host committee
14. WCC staff
15. Co-opted staff
16. Stewards

Key to Abbreviations: M = man; W = woman; O = ordained; L = lay.

1. WCC PRESIDENTS

CHO, Dr. Kiyoko T., WL, The United Church of Christ in Japan
LILJE, D. Dr. Johannes, MO, Evangelical Church in Germany—Lutheran
PAYNE, Rev. Dr. Ernest A., MO, The Baptist Union of Great Britain and Ireland
VISSER 'T HOOFT, Dr. Willem Adolph, MO, Netherlands Reformed Church

2. RETIRING MEMBERS OF THE CENTRAL COMMITTEE

BOKELEALE, Rev. Dr. Itofo, ML, Church of Christ in Zaïre—Community of Disciples
VON BRUCK, Oberlandeskirchenrat Ulrich, MO, Federation of the Evangelical Churches in the GDR

CHANDRAN, Rev. Dr. J. Russell, MO, Church of South India
HAWKINS, Dr. Eoler, MO, The United Presbyterian Church in the USA
KAMAU, Mr. John C., ML, Presbyterian Church of East Africa
LOCHMAN, Rev. Prof. Jan, MO, Swiss Protestant Church Federation
LOCHER, Kirchenrat Benjamin, MO, Evangelical Church in Germany—Reformed/Presbyterian
LUWUM, Most Rev. Janani, MO, Church of Uganda, Rwanda, Burundi and Boga Zaïre
SCHARF, Bishop D. Kurt, MO, Evangelical Church in Germany—United
SCHOLZ, Dr. Gunter, ML, Federation of the Evangelical Churches in the GDR
VON WEIZSAECKER, Dr. Richard, ML, Evangelical Church in Germany—United
WISCHMANN, Dr. Adolf, MO, Evangelical Church in Germany—Lutheran
WOODS, Most Rev. Frank, MO, The Church of England in Australia.

3. DELEGATES FROM MEMBER CHURCHES

ABAINZA, Bishop Estanilão, MO, United Church of Christ in the Philippines
ABOODI, Most Rev. Aphrem, MO, Syrian Orthodox Patriarchate of Antioch and All the East
ABRAHAM, Mrs. P. Anna, WL, The Orthodox Syrian Church, Catholicate of the East
ABRAHAM, Mr. P. Chacko, ML, The Orthodox Syrian Church, Catholicate of the East
ABRUDAN, Rev. Dumitru, MO, Romanian Orthodox Church
ADAMS, Bishop John Hurst, MO, African Methodist Episcopal Church
ADEJOBI, Most Rev. Emmanuel O., MO, Church of the Lord (Aladura)
AFFELD, Mr. Dietrich, ML, Federation of the Evangelical Churches in the GDR
AGUILA, Mr. David, ML, United Church of Christ in the Philippines
AJAMIAN, Most Rev. Shahe, MO, Armenian Apostolic Church
AJAPUHNYA, Pastor Wakapua, MO, Evangelical Church in North Caledonia and Loyalty Isles
ALLIN, Rt. Rev. John M., MO, The Episcopal Church
ALTMANN, Prof. Friedhold, MO, Evangelical Church of the Lutheran Confession in Brazil
ALTON, Bishop Ralph, MO, The United Methodist Church
AMIRTHAM, Prof. Samuel, MO, Church of South India
ANAGNOSTOPOULOS, Prof. Basil, ML, Ecumenical Patriarchate of Constantinople
ANASTASIOS, Bishop Dr. Yannoulatos, MO, Church of Greece
ANCHIMIUK, Mr. Jan, ML, Autocephalic Orthodox Church in Poland
VAN ANDEL, Rev. Dr. Cornelis, MO, Netherlands Reformed Church
ANDERSON, Rev. Boris, MO, The United Reformed Church in England
ANDERSON, Mrs. Joan, WL, The Presbyterian Church of New Zealand
ANDERSON, Rev. Gershon, MO, The Methodist Church, Sierra Leone
ANDERSON, Rev. Dr. Herbert, MO, The United Presbyterian Church in the USA

355

ANDREWS, Rev. James, MO, Presbyterian Church in the United States
ANDRIAMANJATO, Mrs. Rahantavololona, WL, Church of Jesus Christ in Madagascar
ANDRIANARIJAONA, Dr. Rakoto, MO, Malagasy Lutheran Church
ANER, Ms Kerstin, WL, Church of Sweden
ANGGUI, Rev. Andreas, ML, Toraja Church
ANTONIOS, Rev. Ragheb, MO, Coptic Orthodox Church
ANTOUN, Ven. Wadih, MO, The National Evangelical Synod of Syria and Lebanon
APOSTOL, Rev. Janos, MO, The Latin American Reformed Church
APPEL, Rev. Dr. André, MO, Evangelical Church of the Augsburg Confession of Alsace and Lorraine
APPLEBY, Mrs. Elizabeth, WL, The Church of England in Australia
ARDEN, Most Rev. Donald, MO, Church of the Province of Central Africa
ARLINNA, Miss Gunarya, WL, Indonesian Christian Church
ARMSTRONG, Mr. David, ML, The United Church of Canada
ASHMALL, Mr. Harry, MO, The Church of Scotland
ASOR, Rev. McKenzie, MO, The Church of England in Australia
ASSAAD, Sister Nadia, WO, Coptic Orthodox Church
ATHANASIOS, His Grace, MO, Coptic Orthodox Church
AUCHTERLONIE, Dr. Roger, ML, Evangelical Methodist Church of Argentina
AWUME, Pastor Yawo, MO, Evangelical Church of Togo
AZARIAH, Mr. Samuel, ML, The Church of Pakistan
AYITE, Mr. Julien, ML, The Protestant Methodist Church in Dahomey and Togo
BAEREND, Dr. Dietrich, ML, Evangelical Church in Germany—United
BAKHOMIOS, His Grace, MO, Coptic Orthodox Church
BAKHSH, Miss Shunila, WL, The Church of Pakistan
BANKS, Rev. John, MO, United Free Church of Scotland
BARBIER, Pastor Jean-Pierre, MO, Evangelical Lutheran Church of France
BARKAT, Prof. Dr. Anwar M., ML, The Church of Pakistan
BARKER, Rev. James, MO, The Moravian Union
BARNES, Rev. Geoffrey, MO, The Congregational Union of Australia
BARTHA, Bishop Dr. Tibor, MO, Reformed Church in Hungary
BARTHO, Dr. Ondrej, MO, Slovak Evangelical Church of the Augsburg Confession in the CSSR
BAUMAN, Mrs. Margaret K., WL, American Lutheran Church
BAUMFALK, Rev. Johan, MO, The Reformed Churches in the Netherlands
BEBAWI, Rev. Dr. George, MO, Coptic Orthodox Church
BEKY, Bishop Zoltan, MO, Hungarian Reformed Church in America
BENA-SILU, Mr., ML, Church of Christ on Earth by Prophet Simon Kimbangu
BERBERIAN, Rt. Rev. Dr. Petros, MO, Armenian Apostolic Church
BERTELSEN, Rt. Rev. Ole, MO, The Church of Denmark
BERTRAND, Pastor Michel, MO, Reformed Church of France
BICHKOV, Rev. Alexei, MO, Union of Evangelical Christian Baptists of the USSR
BILLINGS, Mr. William T., ML, American Lutheran Church
BINDER, Pastor Heinz-Georg, MO, Evangelical Church in Germany—United
BINGHAM, Rev. Dr. Walter D., MO, Christian Church (Disciples of Christ)

356

BIRD, Mr. Oscar, ML, The Church in the Province of the West Indies
BLATEZKY, Mr. Arturo, ML, Evangelical Church of the River Plata
BOBROVA, Mrs. Nina, WL, Russian Orthodox Church
BOHLER, Mrs. Irmgard, WL, Evangelical Church in Germany—Lutheran
BOKAGNE-BOBIONDO, Pastor Jonas, MO, Presbyterian Church of Cameroon
BONNER-EVANS, Miss Ann, WL, The Methodist Church
BOORMAN, Mrs. Margaret, WL, The United Church of Canada
BOPHELA, Rev. Fritz, MO, Church of the Province of South Africa
BOROVOY, Rev. Prof. Vitaly, MO, Russian Orthodox Church
BOSETO, Rev. Leslie, MO, United Church in Papua-New Guinea and Solomon Islands
BOSSHAMMER, Miss Almuth, WL, Evangelical Church in Germany—United
BOULTON, Rev. Canon Peter, MO, The Church of England
VAN BOVEN, Dr. Theodoor, ML, Netherlands Reformed Church
BOWERS, Miss Pamela, WO, Churches of Christ in Australia
BOWMAN, Dr. S. Loren, MO, Church of the Brethren
BOYAKA, Bishop Inkomo, MO, Church of Christ in Zaïre—Community of Disciples
BOYD, Mrs. Mary, WL, The Presbyterian Church in Ireland
BOZABALIAN, Rt. Rev. Nerses, MO, Armenian Apostolic Church
BRADEMAS, Congressman John, ML, The United Methodist Church
BRANDES, Dr. Barbara, WL, Evangelical Church in Germany—Lutheran
BRENNAN, Mr. Geoffrey, ML, The Church of England in Australia
BRIGGS, Mr. John Henry, ML, The Baptist Union of Great Britain and Ireland
BRINKHUES, Dr. Ilse, WL, Catholic Diocese of the Old Catholics in Germany
BROWN, Rev. John, MO, The Presbyterian Church of Australia
BROWN, Mrs. Mildred, WL, The United Presbyterian Church in the USA
BRYCE, Rt. Rev. Jabez Leslie, MO, Church of the Province of New Zealand
BUANA KIBONGI, Pastor Raymond, MO, Evangelical Church of the Congo
BUEVSKY, Mr. Alexey, ML, Russian Orthodox Church
BUKU, Mr. Joel, ML, Church of the Province of Kenya
BULLIMORE, Mr. John, ML, The Church of England
BURRILL, Rev. William, ML, The Episcopal Church
BUSCHLUTER, Dr. Ursula, WL, Old Catholic Diocese, DDR
BUTTON, Mrs. Wanda, WL, Church of the Brethren
CALLISS, Commissioner Gladys, WO, Salvation Army, Sri Lanka
CAMERON, Rt. Rev. Ewen, MO, The Church of England in Australia
CAMPBELL, Dr. Robert, MO, American Baptist Churches in the United States
CAMPBELL, Mrs. Barbara, WL, Presbyterian Church in the United States
CANNON, Bishop William R., MO, The United Methodist Church
CASTREN, Miss Inga-Brita, WL, Evangelical-Lutheran Church of Finland
CHADWICK, Rev. Claude, MO, Moravian Church in America (Southern Province)
CHAN, Rev. Chor Choi, MO, Anglican Church in China Including Hong Kong
CHANDLER, Mr. Maurice, ML, The Church of England

357

CHAVEZ-CAMPOS, Bishop Enrique, MO, Pentecostal Church of Chile
CHEN, Rev. Peter, MO, The United Methodist Church
CHRYSSOCHOIDIS, Mr. Kriton, ML, Church of Greece
CIESLAK, President Johannes, ML, Federation of the Evangelical Church in the GDR
COENEN, Dr. Lothar, MO, Evangelical Church in Germany—Reformed/ Presbyterian
COGGAN, Most Rev. F. Donald, MO, The Church of England
COINIDIS, Metropolitan Parthenios, MO, Greek Orthodox Patriarchate of Alexandria
COLWELL, Rev. Dr. David G., MO, United Church of Christ
COMBA, Mrs. Fernanda, WL, Waldensian Church
COOK, Rt. Rev. Calvin, MO, The Presbyterian Church of Southern Africa
CORAVU, Prof. Dimitrie, ML, Romanian Orthodox Church
CRADDOCK, Mrs. Fran, WL, Christian Church (Disciples of Christ)
CRESSEY, Rev. Prof. Martin, MO, The United Reformed Church in England and Wales
CROW, Rev. Dr. Paul, Jr., MO, Christian Church (Disciples of Christ)
CUMMINGS, Mrs. C. Clifford, WL, The United Methodist Church
CUTTRISS, Rev. Canon Frank, MO, The Church of England in Australia
DAVIES, Rev. Roy, MO, The Church in Wales
DAVIES, Rev. Meirion, MO, The Presbyterian Church of Wales
VAN DEEMTER-SALOMONS, Mrs. Jannie, WL, Netherlands Reformed Church
DEMAUDE, Pastor Marcel, MO, Reformed Church of Belgium
DENHAM, Colonel Ernest, MO, The Salvation Army
DENNIS, Miss Nancy, WL, The Methodist Church, Ghana
DESCHNER, Prof. John, MO, The United Methodist Church
DE SOUZA, Rt. Rev. Neville, MO, The Church in the Province of the West Indies
DE VELDER, Rev. Dr. Marion, MO, Reformed Church in America
DHARMARAJ, Mr. Alfred, ML, Church of North India
DIEL, Rt. Rev. Camilo C., MO, Philippine Independent Church
DIEL, Ms Crisologa V., WO, Philippine Independent Church
DIETZFELBINGER, Landesbischof Hermann, MO, Evangelical Church in Germany—Lutheran
DLAMINI, Rev. Lindinkosi, MO, Evangelical Lutheran Church in Southern Africa, S.E.
DOMETIAN, Bishop, MO, Bulgarian Orthodox Church
DOOM, Mr. John, ML, Evangelical Church of French Polynesia
DOVLO, Rev. Christian, MO, Evangelical Presbyterian Church
DRAEGER, Mr. Hans-Rolf, ML, Evangelical Church in Germany—Lutheran
DUMBLETON, Miss Anwyn, WL, The Salvation Army
DUMBRAVA, Rev. Mother Lucia J., WL, Rumanian Orthodox Church
DYSTHE, Mrs. Olga, WL, Church of Norway
EASTER RAJ, Bishop Lazerus, MO, Federation of Evangelical Lutheran Churches in India
EGUALE, Dr. Gebre-Yohannes, ML, Ethiopian Orthodox Church
EKLOU, Mrs. Abuwavi, WL, Evangelical Church of Togo
ELLIOTT, Rev. Canon Eric, MO, The Church of Ireland
ENGELEN, Dr. Oscar Eduard, ML, Sangir Talaud Christian Evangelical Church, Indonesia
ENGSTROM, Principal Olle, ML, The Mission Covenant Church of Sweden

ESSER, Prof. Dr. Hans, MO, Evangelical Church in Germany—Reformed/ Presbyterian

ESSIBEN WELLI, Mrs. Sophie, WL, Union of Baptist Churches of Cameroon

ESTRELLA, Ms Julia, WL, United Church of Christ

EWALDS, Mr. Kjell, ML, Evangelical-Lutheran Church of Finland

FAIRFAX, Miss Jean, WL, United Church of Christ

FAISON, Dr. Bernilee, MO, National Baptist Convention, USA, Inc.

FALETOESE, Rev. Kenape, MO, The Presbyterian Church of New Zealand

FANG, Rev. Chung, MO, The Methodist Church in Malaysia and Singapore

FAULK, Mr. I., ML, Christian Methodist Episcopal Church

FAUOLO, Rev. Oka, MO, The Congregational Christian Church in Samoa

FEATHERSTONE, Rev. Rudolph, MO, Lutheran Church in America

FERNANDO, Mrs. Chitra, WL, The Anglican Church in Sri Lanka

FERNANDO, Rev. Kenneth, MO, The Anglican Church in Sri Lanka

FERRARI, Miss Ana, WL, Evangelical Methodist Church of Argentina

FICHTNER, Pastor Hans-Eberhard, MO, Federation of the Evangelical Churches in the GDR

FILARET, His Eminence, MO, Russian Orthodox Church

FISHER, Mr. John, ML, The Episcopal Church

FLOREA, Bishop Simion, MO, Romanian Orthodox Church

FLORES, Rev. Dr. Manuel, MO, Methodist Church of Mexico

FORCK, Dr. Gottfried, MO, Federation of the Evangelical Churches in the GDR

FRANKE, Mr. Ludwig, ML, Federation of the Evangelical Churches in the GDR

FREI, Pastor Hans, MO, Old Catholic Church of Switzerland

FRENZ, Bishop Helmut, MO, Evangelical-Lutheran Church of Chile

FUIMAONO ASUEMU, Mr. Ulufale, ML, The Congregational Christian Church in Samoa

GA, Most Rev. Macario V., MO, Philippine Independent Church

GA, Mrs. Regina N., WL, Philippine Independent Church

GALIATSATOS, Metropolitan Nicodeme, MO, Greek Orthodox Patriarchate of Alexandria

GARBE, Dr. Renate, WL, Federation of the Evangelical Churches in the GDR

GATU, Rev. John Gachango, MO, Presbyterian Church of East Africa

GELEV, Mr. Ivan, ML, Bulgarian Orthodox Church

GEORGE, Rev. A. Raymond, MO, The Methodist Church

GEORGE, Rev. Kondothra, MO, The Orthodox Syrian Church, Catholicate of the East

GERHARDSSON, Prof. Dr. Birger, MO, Church of Sweden

GIFFORD, Rev. Raymond, MO, The Congregational Union of New Zealand

GILMORE, Rev. Russell, MO, Churches of Christ in Australia

GINTING-SUKA, Rev. Anggapen, MO, Karo Batak Protestant Church

GOLDEN, Bishop Charles F., MO, The United Methodist Church

GOPAL RATNAM, Mrs. Daisy, WL, Church of South India

GORLICH, Mr. Joachim, ML, Evangelical Church in Germany—Lutheran

GORODETZKY, Mr. Michel, ML, Russian Orthodox Church

GOSEVIC, Prof. Dr. Stojan, ML, Serbian Orthodox Church

VAN GOUDOEVER, Prof. Jan, MO, Remonstrant Brotherhood

GQWETA, Rev. David Xolile, MO, Moravian Church in South Africa
GRAHAM, Miss Betty, WL, The Anglican Church of Canada
GRAHAM, Rev. Carole, WO, Church of the Province of New Zealand
GRAVES, Rev. Norma, WO, The Methodist Church of New Zealand
GREET, Rev. Dr. Kenneth, MO, The Methodist Church
GREGORIOS, Rev. Prof. Paulos, MO, The Orthodox Syrian Church, Catholicate of the East
GROENFELDT, Rev. Dr. John, MO, Moravian Church in America (Northern Province)
GROHS, Prof. Dr. Gerhard, ML, Evangelical Church in Germany—United
GUDMUNDSSON, Rev. Bernhardur, MO, Evangelical Lutheran Church of Iceland
GUNDYAYEV, Miss Elena, WL, Russian Orthodox Church
HABANDI, Rev., MO, Pasundan Christian Church
HABELGAARN, Rev. August, MO, Moravian Church in South Africa
HABIB, Mr. Gaby, ML, Greek Orthodox Patriarchate of Antioch and All the East
HABIB, Rev. Samuel, MO, Evangelical Church—The Synod of the Nile
HACIS, His Eminence Meliton, MO, Ecumenical Patriarchate of Constantinople
HALL, Mrs. Ina, WL, The Presbyterian Church of Australia
HAMBRAEUS, Mrs. Birgitta, WL, Church of Sweden
HARK, Pastor Edgar, MO, Estonian Evangelical Lutheran Church
HARKIANAKIS, Most Rev. Stylianos, MO, Ecumenical Patriarchate of Constantinople
HARMS, Bishop Hans, MO, Evangelical Church in Germany—Lutheran
HARRIS, Rev. Vivian, MO, The Methodist Church of South Africa
HART, Mrs. Maidie, WL, The Church of Scotland
HART, Dr. Jack, MO, The United Presbyterian Church in the USA
HASTING, Bishop Gunther, MO, Evangelische Brüder-Unität
HASTINGS-SPAINE, Mr. Victor, ML, The Church of the Province of West Africa
HAVEA, Rev. Dr. Sione, MO, Methodist Church in Tonga
HAZIM, Metropolitan Ignatios, MO, Greek Orthodox Patriarchate of Antioch and All the East
HEARN, Dr. J., MO, The United Methodist Church
HELD, Dr. Heinz, MO, Evangelical Church in Germany—Lutheran
HEMPEL, Dr. Johannes, MO, Federation of the Evangelical Churches in the GDR
HENDERSON, Miss Janet, WL, The Church of England
HENDRICKS, Rev. Abel, MO, The Methodist Church of South Africa
HENDRICKSE, Miss Edith Jeanne, WL, The United Congregational Church of Southern Africa
HENDRICKSE, Rev. Helenard, MO, The United Congregational Church of Southern Africa
HENRY, Pastor Harry, MO, The Protestant Methodist Church in Dahomey and Togo
HERMAN (SWAIKO), Bishop, MO, The Orthodox Church in America
HESS, Mr. H. Ober, ML, Lutheran Church in America
VAN DEN HEUVEL, Rev. Dr. Albert, MO, Netherlands Reformed Church
HILD, Rev. Dr. Helmut, MO, Evangelical Church in Germany—United
HILDEBRANDT, Ms Julia, WL, Mennonite Church, GFR

HIMMELBACH, Mrs. Beate, WL, Evangelical Church in Germany—Reformed/Presbyterian

HINZ, Pastor Christoph, MO, Federation of the Evangelical Churches in the GDR

HINZ, Pastor Rudolf, MO, Evangelical Church in Germany—Lutheran

HITE, Mr. James, ML, National Council of Community Churches, USA

HOGGARD, Rev. Dr. J. Clinton, MO, African Methodist Episcopal Zion Church

HOLLOWAY, Rev. Richard, MO, Episcopal Church in Scotland

HOLTER, Prof. Dr. Age, MO, Church of Norway

HOOVER, Ms Theressa, WL, The United Methodist Church

HOPKO, Rev. Thomas, MO, The Orthodox Church in America

HUBANCEV, Mr. Antony, ML, Bulgarian Orthodox Church

HUEBNER, Dr. Friedrich, MO, Evangelical Church in Germany—Lutheran

HULU, Rev. Bazatulo, MO, The Church of Nias

HUSTON, Rev. Dr. Robert, MO, The United Methodist Church

HUTCHINS-FELDER, Ms Annette, WL, The United Methodist Church

IDIKA, Rev. Mba, MO, The Presbyterian Church of Nigeria

IDOWU, Rev. Prof. Emmanuel, MO, Methodist Church, Nigeria

IHROMI, Mrs. Tapi, WL, Pasundan Christian Church

IMATHIU, Most Rev. Lawi, MO, The Methodist Church in Kenya

IONITA, Mr. Viorel, ML, Rumanian Orthodox Church

IOSIF, Very Rev., MO, Russian Orthodox Church

IOSSIF, Archimandrite, MO, Bulgarian Orthodox Church

IRINEY, Most Rev. (Susemihl), MO, Russian Orthodox Church

ISRAELSSON, Bishop Rubin, MO, Federation of Evangelical Lutheran Churches in India

ISTAVRIDIS, Prof. Dr. Vasil T., ML, Ecumenical Patriarchate of Constantinople

ISTEERO, Rev. Albert, MO, Evangelical Church—The Synod of the Nile

IWAS, His Grace Zakka, MO, Syrian Orthodox Patriarchate of Antioch and All the East

IWUAGWU, Mrs. Mabel, WL, The Church of the Province of West Africa

JACKSON, Mrs. Jean C., WL, The Episcopal Church

JACKSON, Dr. Joseph H., MO, National Baptist Convention, USA, Inc.

JACOB, Rev. Max, MO, Protestant Evangelical Church in Timor

JACOBSON, Rev. Dr. Sverre, MO, The Evangelical Lutheran Church of Canada

JEEVARATNAM, Dr. Emil Anthony, ML, Methodist Church, Sri Lanka

JENGIN, Mr. Baling, ML, The Methodist Church in Malaysia and Singapore

JIAGGE, Mrs. Annie, WL, Evangelical Presbyterian Church

JIVI, Mr. Aurel, ML, Romanian Orthodox Church

JOHANNES, Most Rev. (Rinne), MO, Ecumenical Patriarchate of Constantinople

JOHANSON, Miss Benita, WL, Evangelical-Lutheran Church of Finland

JOHN, Rev. M. V., MO, United Presbyterian Church of Pakistan

JOHNSON, Mr. David, ML, The Episcopal Church

JOHNSON, Ms Kathy J., WL, American Baptist Churches in the USA

JOHNSTON, Mrs. Heather, WL, The Presbyterian Church in Canada

JOHNSTON, Rev. William, MO, The Church of Scotland

JOHNSTON, Most Rev. Allen, MO, Church of the Province of New Zealand

JONES, Ms. Blanche, WL, American Baptist Churches in the USA
JONES, Rev. Dr. Tracey K., MO, The United Methodist Church
JONES, Rev. Vivian, MO, Union of Welsh Independents
JORDAN, Bishop Frederick, MO, African Methodist Episcopal Church
JORKEY, Mrs. Eva, WL, Lutheran Church in Liberia
JUMP, Rev. Dr. Chester, MO, American Baptist Churches in the USA
JUVENALY, His Eminence, MO, Russian Orthodox Church
KAFITY, Ven. Samir, MO, Anglican Church, Jerusalem, Extra Provincial
KALDY, Bishop Zoltan, MO, Lutheran Church in Hungary
KALINIK, Metropolitan, MO, Bulgarian Orthodox Church
KALO, Mrs. Gima, WL, United Church in Papua-New Guinea and Solomon
　　Islands
KALOGIROU, Prof. Dr. Johannes, ML, Church of Greece
KANG, Rev. Dr. Won-Yong, MO, The Presbyterian Church in the Republic
　　of Korea
KANGSEN, Rt. Rev. Jeremiah, MO, Presbyterian Church in Cameroon
KASIC, Dr. Dusan, MO, Serbian Orthodox Church
KAUPPINEN, Miss Eila, WL, Evangelical-Lutheran Church of Finland
KAYOKA-LUENDU, Mr., MO, Church of Christ in Zaïre—Community of
　　Christ the Light
KAYUWA-TSHIBUMBU, Patriarch Wa Kahinga, MO, Church of Christ in
　　Zaïre—Community of Christ the Light
KEESECKER, Rev. Dr. William, MO, The United Presbyterian Church in
　　the USA
KELLERAN, Dr. Marion, WL, The Episcopal Church
KERR, Rev. Ian, MO, The Presbyterian Church of Australia
KERR, Deaconess Pamela, WL, The Presbyterian Church of Australia
KESHISHIAN, Rev. Aram, MO, Armenian Apostolic Church
KEUNEN, Rev. Cornie, MO, Reformed Church in America
KIBIRA, Rt. Rev. Dr. Josiah, MO, Evangelical Lutheran Church in Tan-
　　zania
KIEDRON, Rev. Vladislav, MO, Silesian Evangelical Church of the Augs-
　　burg Confession
KILGORE, Dr. Thomas, Jr., MO, American Baptist Churches in the USA
KIM, Rev. Dr. Hyung, MO, The Presbyterian Church of Korea
KIM, Rev. Yoon Shik, MO, The Presbyterian Church of Korea
KIRILL, Very Rev. Gundyayev, MO, Russian Orthodox Church
KIRK, Rev. Prof. John, MO, Anglican South American Diocese
KIRKCALDY, Mrs. Ivy, WL, The United Church of Jamaica and Grand
　　Cayman
KIRKENDOLL, Bishop Chester, MO, Christian Methodist Episcopal
　　Church
KITAGAWA, Mr. John, ML, The Episcopal Church
KITING, Rev. Chris A., MO, Kalimantan Evangelical Church
KJALL, Lt. Colonel Thorsten, MO, Salvation Army, Sweden
VAN KLEEF-HILLESUM, Mrs. Susanna, WL, Polish National Catholic
　　Church of America
KLEIN, Bishop Albert, MO, Evangelical Church of the Augsburg Confes-
　　sion
KLINGER, Rev. Prof. Jerzy, MO, Autocephalic Orthodox Church in
　　Poland
KOK, Dr. Govaert, ML, Old Catholic Church of the Netherlands

KOK-FRIMER LARSEN, Mrs. Grete, WL, Old Catholic Church of Austria
KONIDARIS, Prof. Dr. Gerassimos, MO, Church of Greece
KOSHY, Prof. George, ML, Church of South India
KOSSEN, Prof. Dr. Hendrik, MO, General Mennonite Society
KOTTO, Pastor Jean, MO, Evangelical Church of Cameroon
KOWALSKI, Bishop Stanislaw, MO, Old Catholic Mariavite Church in
Poland
KRATZ, Most Rev. Arthur, MO, Episcopal Church of Brazil
KRUSE, Mr. Max, ML, The Church of Denmark
KULIKOV, Rev. Vitali, ML, Union of Evangelical Christian Baptists of the
USSR
KUNDYA, Mr. Victor, ML, Evangelical Lutheran Church in Tanzania
KUNERT, Rev. Augusto E., MO, Evangelical Church of the Lutheran
Confession in Brazil
KYKKOTIS, Most Rev. Chrysostomos, MO, Church of Cyprus
LABARDAKIS, Bishop Georges, MO, Ecumenical Patriarchate of Constan-
tinople
LACZKOVSZKI, Rev. Janos, MO, Baptist Church in Hungary
LAHAM, Mr. Albert, ML, Greek Orthodox Patriarchate of Antioch and All
the East
LANCASTER, Prof. Abna, WL, African Methodist Episcopal Zion Church
LANEY, Dr. James, MO, The United Methodist Church
DE LANGE, Dr. Harry, ML, Remonstrant Brotherhood
LANGHOFF, Rev. Johannes, MO, The Church of Denmark
LANGI, Rev. William, MO, Christian Evangelical Church in Minahasa
LARA-BRAUD, Dr. Jorge, ML, Presbyterian Church in the United States
LASSEUR, Mrs. Helena, WL, Netherlands Reformed Church
LATUIHAMALLO, Miss Cynthia, WL, Protestant Church in Indonesia
LAVIN, Rev. Ronald, MO, Lutheran Church in America
LAYMAN, Mr. David, ML, The United Presbyterian Church in the USA
LAZARETH, Rev. Prof. William, MO, Lutheran Church in America
LEHTONEN, Rev. Samuel, MO, Evangelical-Lutheran Church of Finland
LELAND, Rev. Robert, MO, Christian Church (Disciples of Christ)
LENGYEL, Prof. Dr. Lorand, MO, Evangelical Synod
LEONARD, Rt. Rev. Dr. Graham, MO, The Church of England
LEVANDOWSKY, Mrs. Liouba, WL, Russian Orthodox Church
LIM, Dr. Eui-Sun, ML, the Korean Methodist Church
LITAAY, Mr. Flip Pieter B., MO, Protestant Church of the Moluccas
LOCHMANN, Dr. Ullrich, MO, Evangelical Church in Germany—United
LODGE, Mrs. Grace C., WL, Salvation Army, USA
LONG, Rev. Robert, MO, American Lutheran Church
LØNNING, Rt. Rev. Per, MO, Church of Norway
LOVE, Ms Janice, WL, The United Methodist Church
LUMENTUT, Rev. Augustina, WO, Christian Church in Mid-Sulawesi
LUNDBY, Mr. Knut, ML, Church of Norway
LUSAN, Miss Carmen, WL, Methodist Church in the Caribbean and the
Church of the Augsburg Confession in Romania
LUSIS, Most Rev. Arnolds, MO, Latvian Evangelical Lutheran Church
LUVANDA, Miss Jilweli, WL, Evangelical Lutheran Church in Tanzania
LWANGA-MUGERWA, Rev. Wilson, MO, Church of Uganda, Rwanda,
Burundi and Boga Zaïre
MACLEOD, Rev. Angus, MO, The Baptist Union of New Zealand

MADUCDOC, Bishop Geronimo P., MO, The Evangelical Methodist Church in the Philippines
MAHLATSI, Miss Evelyn, WL, Church of the Province of South Africa
MAJEWSKI, Bishop Tadeusz, MO, Polish Catholic Church in Poland
MAKAMBWE, Rev. Francis, MO, Church of the Province of Central Africa
MAKANY, Ms Julienne, WL, Evangelical Church of the Congo
MAKARIOS, Bishop, MO, Ethiopian Orthodox Church
MAKARY, Rt. Rev. Leonid, MO, Russian Orthodox Church
MALOALI, Rev. Willem, MO, Evangelical Christian Church in West Irian
MALVAR, Mr. Renato, ML, Philippine Independent Church
MANNING, Miss Claire, WL, The United Presbyterian Church in the USA
MANOOGIAN, Very Rev. Torkom, MO, Armenian Apostolic Church
MARPLE, Dr. Dorothy J., WL, Lutheran Church in America
MARSHALL, Rev. Dr. Arthur, Jr., MO, African Methodist Episcopal Zion Church
MARSHALL, Rev. Dr. Robert, MO, Lutheran Church in America
MATATUMUA, Ms Moana, WL, The Congregational Christian Church in Samoa
MATHEWS, Bishop James K., MO, The United Methodist Church
MATTHEW, Miss Teli, WL, Federation of Evangelical Lutheran Churches in India
MAURY, Pastor Jacques, MO, Reformed Church of France
MAYLAND, Mrs. Jean, WL, The Church of England
MBOMBA, Mrs. Ey'oyaka, ML, Church of Christ in Zaïre—Community of Disciples
MBUNGU, Maitre B. Kadivioki, ML, Church of Christ on Earth by Prophet Simon Kimbangu
MCCLOUD, Rev. J. Oscar, MO, The United Presbyterian Church in the USA
MCDOWELL, Rev. Ian, MO, The Presbyterian Church in Ireland
MCGUINNESS, Mrs. Catherine, WL, The Church of Ireland
MCKNIGHT, Mr. Harold, ML, Lutheran Church in America
MCLEAN, Mr. Alan, ML, The United Church of Canada
MCMAHON, Ms Dorothy, WL, Methodist Church of Australasia
MCMANUS, Mr. Gregg, ML, Christian Church (Disciples of Christ)
MEADOWS, Miss Clara, WL, Church of the Lord (Aladura)
MEHL, Prof. Dr. Roger, MO, Reformed Church of Alsace and Lorraine
MELAKU, Mr. Kifle, ML, Ethiopian Orthodox Church
DE MELLO-SILVA, Pastor Manoel, MO, The Evangelical Pentecostal Church "Brazil for Christ"
MENEVISOGLOU, Metropolitan Paul, MO, Ecumenical Patriarchate of Constantinople
MERCK, Mrs. Ursula, WL, Evangelical Church in Germany—United
MEYER, Vizeprasident Hans Philipp, MO, Evangelical Church in Germany—Lutheran
MICHAEL, Bishop, MO, Russian Orthodox Church
MICHAELIAN, Mr. Tateos, ML, Synod of the Evangelical Church of Iran
MICHALKO, Prof. Dr. Jan, MO, Slovak Evangelical Church of the Augsburg Confession in the CSSR
MICKELSON, Dr. Arnold R., ML, American Lutheran Church
MILLER, Mr. Lawrence, Jr., ML, Friends General Conference
MILLER, Miss Lois C., WL, The United Methodist Church

MILLS-ROBERTSON, Mrs. Efua, WL, The Methodist Church, Ghana
MILOSEVIC, Rev. Mother Teodora, WO, Serbian Orthodox Church
MITSIDES, Dr. Andreas, ML, Church of Cyprus
MITZENHEIM, Oberkirchenrat Hartmut, ML, Federation of the Evangelical Churches in the GDR
MOHAPELOA, Prof. Josias, ML, Lesotho Evangelical Church
MOISESCU, Metropolitan Iustin, MO, Romanian Orthodox Church
MOKOTO, Miss Julia, WL, Evangelical Lutheran Church in Southern Africa, T.R.
MOMO KINGUE, Mrs. Marie, WL, Evangelical Church of Cameroon
MOORE, Rev. Richard, MO, The United Presbyterian Church in the USA
MOOS, Mr. Errol, ML, Moravian Church in South Africa
MORRIS, Bishop Samuel, MO, African Methodist Episcopal Church
MOSHI, Rt. Rev. Dr. Stefano R., MO, Evangelical Lutheran Church in Tanzania
MOSS, Rev. Dr. Robert V., MO, United Church of Christ
MOUROUKA, Mrs. Sophia, WL, Church of Greece
MUGO MWANGI, Rev. Samuel, MO, African Christian Church and Schools, Kenya
MULUNGU, Mr. Isaac, ML, United Church in Papua-New Guinea and Solomon Islands
MUNROE, Mrs. Judy, WL, Methodist Church in the Caribbean and the Americas
MUNTHE, Rev. Armencius, MO, Simalungun Protestant Christian Church
MUNYAMA, Mrs. Lilian, WL, United Church of Zambia
MUSTON, Rt. Rev. Gerald, MO, The Church of England in Australia
MUSUNSA, Rev. Doyce, MO, United Church of Zambia
MYLES, Ms S. Marlyne, WO, The United Church of Canada
NACPIL, Dr. Emerito P., MO, The United Methodist Church
NANG-ESSONO, Pastor Samuel, MO, Evangelical Church of Gabon
NARZYNSKI, Bishop Janusz, MO, Evangelical Church of the Augsburg Confession in Poland
NASIR, Bishop Dr. Eric, MO, Church of North India
NECHAY, Dr. Nikolay, ML, Russian Orthodox Church
NEEHALL, Rev. Dr. Roy, MO, The Presbyterian Church in Trinidad and Grenada
NELSON, Rev. Prof. J. Robert, MO, The United Methodist Church
NGUGI, Colonel Joshua, MO, Salvation Army, Kenya
NICHOLS, Bishop D. Ward, MO, African Methodist Episcopal Church
NICHOLS, Bishop Roy Calvin, MO, The United Methodist Church
NIKODIM, His Eminence, MO, Russian Orthodox Church
NIKOLAINEN, Rt. Rev. Dr. Aimo, MO, Evangelical-Lutheran Church of Finland
NISHIMURA, Rev. Tetsuro, MO, Anglican-Episcopal Church in Japan
NISSIOTIS, Prof. Dr. Nikos A., ML, Church of Greece
NITA, Rev. Mother Nazaria, WL, Romanian Orthodox Church
NIUKULA, Rev. Paula, MO, Methodist Church of Australasia
NORBERG, Rev. Richard C., MO, United Church of Christ
NORDHOLT, Mr. Heinz-Hermann, MO, Evangelical Church in Germany—Reformed/Presbyterian
NORGAARD, Rev. Per, MO, Baptist Union of Denmark
NOVAK, Patriarch Miroslav, MO, Czechoslovak Hussite Church

NSENDA-ILUNGA, Most Rev. Baminyinyi, MO, Presbyterian Church in Zaïre
NTONTOLO, Pastor Lukombo-Kitete, MO, Evangelical Church of Zaïre
NYAMBOLI, Mrs. Elizabeth, WL, Presbyterian Church in Cameroon
NYANGOR, Rev. Albert Boaz, MO, African Israel Church, Ninevah
NYEMB, Pastor Albert, MO, Presbyterian Church of Cameroon
NYEMBEZI, Dr. Maurice, ML, The Methodist Church of South Africa
OBBOON, Mr. Somchai, ML, The Church of Christ in Thailand
OBIANG-ONDO, Mr. Joel, ML, Evangelical Church of Gabon
ODUYOYE, Ms Mercy, WL, Methodist Church, Nigeria
O'GRADY, Mr. Ronald, MO, Associated Church of Christ in New Zealand
OJO, Rev. Dr. William, MO, Nigerian Baptist Convention
OJOK, Miss Filda, WL, Church of Uganda, Rwanda, Burundi and Boga Zaïre
OKUDA, Mrs. Michiko, WL, The United Church of Christ in Japan
OKULLU, Rt. Rev. Dr. Henry, MO, Church of the Province of Kenya
OLIVEIRA, Rev. Prof. Clory, MO, Methodist Church of Brazil
OLSON, Rev. Dr. Otto, MO, Lutheran Church in America
OLUFOSOYE, Bishop Timothy, MO, The Church of the Province of West Africa
ONO, Rev. Ichiro, MO, The United Church of Christ in Japan
ORLOV, Very Rev. Ioann, MO, Russian Orthodox Church
OSIPOV, Prof. Aleksey, ML, Russian Orthodox Church
PAE, Rt. Rev. Tuhwan, MO, Korean Anglican Church, Extra Provincial
PALMA-MANRRIQUEZ, Ms Marta, WL, Pentecostal Mission Church
PANKRATIY, Metropolitan, MO, Bulgarian Orthodox Church
PANTELEIMON, Most Rev., MO, Church of Greece
PAPADOPOULOS, Prof. Stylianos, ML, Greek Orthodox Patriarchate of Alexandria
PAPANDREOU, Metropolitan Damaskinos, MO, Ecumenical Patriarchate of Constantinople
PAPP, Rev. Laszlo, MO, Reformed Church of Romania
PARASKEVAIDES, Most Rev. Christodoulos, MO, Church of Greece
PARVEY, Rev. Constance F., WO, Lutheran Church in America
PASZTOR, Mrs. Judith, WL, Reformed Church in Hungary
PASZTOR, Rev. Janos, MO, Reformed Church in Hungary
PATRA, Mr. Rajeeb Lochan, ML, Federation of Evangelical Lutheran Churches in India
PAULOS, Bishop, MO, Ethiopian Orthodox Church
PAWLEY, Ven. Bernard, MO, The Church of England
PAYNE, Rt. Rev. Dr. Roland, MO, Lutheran Church in Liberia
PECK, Mrs. Dorothy, WL, African Methodist Episcopal Church
PEERY, Rev. Margaret, WO, Presbyterian Church in the United States
PEL, Rev. Cornelis, MO, Evangelical Lutheran Church
PEPER, Miss Waltraut, WL, Federation of the Evangelical Churches in the GDR
PETER, Dr. Hans-Balz, ML, Swiss Protestant Church Federation
PETROS, Rev. G. Silassi, MO, Ethiopian Orthodox Church
PETROVA, Miss Stafanka, WL, Bulgarian Orthodox Church
PHILIP, Mrs. Sarah, WL, The Orthodox Syrian Church, Catholicate of the East
PIETERS, Dr. Andre, MO, Protestant Church of Belgium

PITT-WATSON, Rev. Prof. Ian, MO, The Church of Scotland
PLAMADEALA, Rt. Rev. Antonie, MO, Romanian Orthodox Church
POPESCU, Prof. Dr. Dumitru, MO, Romanian Orthodox Church
POSUMAH, Rev. Junius, MO, Christian Evangelical Church in Minahasa
POWERS, Rev. Jeanne, WO, The United Methodist Church
PREUS, Rev. Dr. David W., MO, American Lutheran Church
PRICE, Mr. Albert, ML, United Church of Christ
PRICE, Dr. Charles, ML, The Church of England in Australia
PRINTZ, Dr. Othon, ML, Evangelical Church of the Augsburg Confession
of Alsace and Lorraine
PULIMOOD, Dr. Benjamin, ML, Mar Thoma Syrian Church of Malabar
PYLEE, Rev. Ampat, MO, Mar Thoma Syrian Church of Malabar
PYO, Rev. Yongeun, MO, The Korean Methodist Church
QIONIBARAVI, Mrs. Anaseini, WL, Methodist Church of Australasia
QUANBECK, Prof. Warren, MO, American Lutheran Church
QUIST, Mrs. Margaret, WL, Presbyterian Church of Ghana
RAIRI, Mr. Nga, ML, Cook Islands Christian Church
RAKENA, Rev. Ruawai, MO, The Methodist Church of New Zealand
RAKIC, Deacon Radomir, MO, Serbian Orthodox Church
RAMAMBASOA, Pastor Joseph, MO, Church of Jesus Christ in Madagas-
car
RANAIVOSON, Mr. Henri, ML, Church of Jesus Christ in Madagascar
RASOLOFOSON, Mr. Alfred, ML, Malagasy Lutheran Church
RAVOLOLOMBOAHANGY, Mrs. Meltine, WO, Church of Jesus Christ in
Madagascar
RAY, Rev. Donald G., MO, The United Church of Canada
RICH, Miss Franziska, WL, Swiss Protestant Church Federation
RICHARDSON, Rev. John, MO, The Methodist Church
RO, Dr. Chung-Hyun, ML, The Presbyterian Church of Korea
ROBINSON, Mr. Mark, ML, United Church of Christ
ROCHA SOUZA, Mr. Enilson, ML, The Evangelical Pentecostal Church
"Brazil for Christ"
RODOPOULOS, Most Rev. Panteleimon, MO, Church of Greece
RODOUSSAKIS, Archimandrite Cornelios, MO, Greek Orthodox Patri-
archate of Jerusalem
RODUNER-LAEDRACH, Mrs. Julia, WL, Swiss Protestant Church Federa-
tion
ROMANIDES, Rev. Dr. John, MO, Church of Greece
ROMPAS, Rev. Paul Hein, MO, Protestant Church in Indonesia
RONNAS, Mr. John, ML, The Mission Covenant Church of Sweden
ROSSEL, Dr. Jacques, MO, Swiss Protestant Church Federation
RUCKERT, Ms Maria, WL, Evangelical Church of the Lutheran Confession
in Brazil
RUDOFSKY, Miss Sheila, WL, The United Reformed Church in England
and Wales
RUHINDI, Rt. Rev. Yustase, MO, Church of Uganda, Rwanda, Burundi
and Boga Zaïre
RUNIA, Prof. Dr. Klaas, MO, The Reformed Churches in the Netherlands
RUSAMA, Rev. Jaakko, MO, Evangelical-Lutheran Church of Finland
RUSSELL, Rev. Dr. Letty M., WO, The United Presbyterian Church in the
USA
RUSSELL, Rt. Rev. Philip, MO, Church of the Province of South Africa

RUSSELL, Rev. Dr. David, MO, The Baptist Union of Great Britain and Ireland
SABEV, Prof. Todor, ML, Bulgarian Orthodox Church
SAMARAJIWA, Mr. Ainsley, ML, Methodist Church, Sri Lanka
SAMPATH, Mrs. Dorinda, WL, The Presbyterian Church in Trinidad and Grenada
SAMUEL, Rt. Rev. John, MO, The Church of Pakistan
SAMUEL, His Grace, MO, Coptic Orthodox Church
SAMUEL, Bishop N. D., MO, Church of South India
SAPINA, Mr. Miroslav, ML, Serbian Orthodox Church
SARKISSIAN, Most Rev. Karekin, MO, Armenian Apostolic Church
SAYAMA, Bishop Dairoku, MO, Russian Orthodox Church
SBAFFI, Rev. Aldo, MO, Waldensian Church
SBAFFI, Rev. Mario, MO, Evangelical Methodist Church of Italy
SCHEFFBUCH, Dekan Rolf P., ML, Evangelical Church in Germany—Lutheran
VON SCHEVEN, Mrs. Ursula, WL, Evangelical Church in Germany—Lutheran
SCOTT, Most Rev. Edward, MO, The Anglican Church of Canada
SEPULVEDA-BARR, Pastor Narciso, MO, Pentecostal Mission Church
SERAFIM, Archimandrite Gregory, MO, Russian Orthodox Church
SEROTE, Rev. Ntwampe, MO, Evangelical Lutheran Church in Southern Africa, T.R.
SHAHBAZIAN, Prof. Parkev, ML, Armenian Apostolic Church
SHAW, Mr. Allan, ML, The Methodist Church
SHAW, Rev. Dr. William, MO, National Baptist Convention, USA, Inc.
SHIOLASHVILI, His Eminence Ilya, MO, Georgian Orthodox Church
SIAHAAN, Rev. Gustaf H. M., MO, Protestant Christian Batak Church
SIANIPAR, Rev. Prof. Frans, MO, Protestant Christian Batak Church
SIDJABAT, Rev. Prof. Walter, MO, Protestant Christian Batak Church
SIMATUPANG, Dr. Tahi, ML, Indonesian Christian Church
SIMEONOV, Rev. Assen, MO, Bulgarian Orthodox Church
SIMONIAN, Miss Teny, WL, Armenian Apostolic Church
SINGH, Bishop Gurbachan, MO, Church of North India
SINSUW-GUNDONG, Dr. Tutty, WL, Christian Evangelical Church in Minahasa
SINTIM-MISA, Rt. Rev. Gottfried, MO, Presbyterian Church of Ghana
SIREGAR PALTI, Mr. Radja, ML, Protestant Christian Batak Church
SITORUS, Rev. T. J., MO, Huria Kristen Indonesia
SKJELSBAEK, Prof. Kjell, ML, Church of Norway
SKOBEI, Mr. Grigori, ML, Russian Orthodox Church
SKUSE, Ms Jean, WL, Methodist Church of Australasia
SLENCZKA, Prof. Reinhard, MO, Evangelical Church in Germany—United
SLOAN, Rev. Harold, MO, The Methodist Church in Ireland
SMALLWOOD, Mr. Wortham, Jr., ML, United Church of Christ
SMELLIE, Rev. Samuel, MO, The United Church of Jamaica and Grand Cayman
SMITH, Rev. Dr. Donald, MO, The Presbyterian Church in Canada
SMITH, Dr. Nelson, MO, Progressive National Baptist Convention/USA
SMOLIK, Prof. Josef, MO, Evangelical Church of Czech Brethren
SMUCK, Mr. Harold V., MO, Friends United Meeting
SNYDER, Mrs. Dorothea, WL, The United Presbyterian Church in the USA

SOARE, Rev. Dumitru, MO, Romanian Orthodox Church
SOEJATNO, Rev. Ardi, MO, Christian Church of East Java
SOFOLAHAN, Mr. Jacob, ML, Church of the Lord (Aladura)
SOLLING, Mrs. Bodil, WL, The Church of Denmark
SOLOMON, Mrs. Shanti, WL, Church of North India
SOLOMON, Mrs. Lorraine, WL, The Methodist Church of South Africa
SONNENDAY, Mrs. Margaret, WL, The United Methodist Church
SORENSEN, Prof. Asger, ML, The Church of Denmark
SORENSON, Rev. Morris, MO, American Lutheran Church
SOUTAPALLI, Mr. Benjamin, ML, The Samavesam of Telugu Baptist
Churches
SPILT, Rev. Gysbert, MO, Netherlands Reformed Church
SRISANG, Dr. Koson, ML, The Church of Christ in Thailand
STADNUK, Very Rev. Matfey, MO, Russian Orthodox Church
STAN, Mr. Alexandru, ML, Romanian Orthodox Church
STEEL, Mrs. Eileen, WL, The United Reformed Church in England and
Wales
VON STIEGLITZ, Dr. Klaus, MO, Evangelical Church in Germany—United
STOIAN, Rev. Alexei, MO, Union of Evangelical Christian Baptists of the
USSR
STOKES, Congressman Louis, ML, African Methodist Episcopal Zion
Church
STOKES, Dr. Olivia, WO, National Baptist Convention, USA, Inc.
STOWE, Rev. Dr. David M., MO, United Church of Christ
SUNDBY, Most Rev. Olof, MO, Church of Sweden
SUPIT, Dr. Bert, ML, Christian Evangelical Church in Minahasa
SUTARNO, Rev. Dr., MO, Christian Churches of Java
SUVARSKY, Archpriest Jaroslav, MO, Orthodox Church of Czecho-
slovakia
SVENUNGSSON, Rev. Henrik, MO, Church of Sweden
TANAMAL, Rev. Pieter, MO, Protestant Church of the Moluccas
TARASAR, Miss Constance, WL, The Orthodox Church in America
TATCHELL, Rev. Canon David, MO, The Anglican Church of Canada
TAYLOR, Rev. Robert H., MO, National Council of Community
Churches, USA
TAYLOR, Rev. Edwin, MO, Methodist Church in the Caribbean and the
Americas
TAYLOR, Dr. David, MO, Presbyterian Church in the United States
TEEGARDEN, Rev. Dr. Kenneth, MO, Christian Church (Disciples of
Christ)
TESFA, Dr. Habte Sellassie, MO, Ethiopian Orthodox Church
TETERYATNIKOV, Mr. Nikolay, ML, Russian Orthodox Church
THAKHOLI, Rev. Salathiel, MO, Lesotho Evangelical Church
THAN, Prof. Kyaw, ML, Burma Baptist Convention
THEODOSIUS, Most Rev. (Nagashima), MO, Japanese Orthodox Church
THEOPHILUS, Rt. Rev. Dr. Alexander, MO, Mar Thoma Syrian Church of
Malabar
THEOPHILUS, Most Rev. Philipos, MO, The Orthodox Syrian Church,
Catholicate of the East
THOMAS, Pastor Gerhard, MO, Federation of the Evangelical Churches in
the GDR
THOMAS, Dr. M.M., ML, Mar Thoma Syrian Church of Malabar
THOMPSON, Ms Barbara R., WL, The United Methodist Church

THOMPSON, Mr. William, ML, The United Presbyterian Church in the USA

THORNE, Rev. John, MO, The United Congregational Church of Southern Africa

TIMAKATA, Pastor Fred, MO, Presbyterian Church of the New Hebrides

TIMIADIS, Rev. Dr. Emilianos, MO, Ecumenical Patriarchate of Constantinople

TOKUNAGA, Rev. Goro, MO, The United Church of Christ in Japan

TOTH, Rev. Dr. Karoly, MO, Reformed Church in Hungary

TRIFUNOVIC, Bishop Lavrentije, MO, Serbian Orthodox Church

TROTT, Mr. William, ML, The Anglican Church of Canada

TROTTER, Rev. Dr. Frederick, MO, The United Methodist Church

TSADALE, Mrs. Yigezo, WL, Ethiopian Orthodox Church

TSEGAYE, Mr. Habte, ML, Ethiopian Orthodox Church

VALENT, Prof. Erno, MO, The Latin American Reformed Church

VAN WYK, Mrs. Julia, WL, Reformed Church in America

VARGA, Dr. Emerich, MO, Reformed Christian Church in Slovakia

VASANTHAKUMAR, Rev. S., MO, Church of South India

VEEM, Rev. Konrad, MO, Estonian Evangelical Lutheran Church

VAN DER VEEN, Mrs. Schenkeveld, WO, The Reformed Churches in the Netherlands

VERGARA, Mr. Wenifredo B., ML, Philippine Independent Church

VIDAL, Prof. Dr. Daniel, MO, Spanish Evangelical Church

VIKA, Rev. Gladwin, MO, The Bantu Presbyterian Church of South Africa

VIKNER, Dr. David, MO, Lutheran Church in America

VLADIMIR, His Eminence, MO, Russian Orthodox Church

WACKER, Rev. Dorothy, WO, The Congregational Union of Australia

WADDELL, Rev. John, MO, The Church of Scotland

WAGNER, Mrs. Elfriede, WL, Federation of the Evangelical Churches in the GDR

WALKER, Rt. Rev. John, MO, The Episcopal Church

WALKER, Dr. Reginald, ML, Methodist Church of Australasia

WALLACE, Rev. Dr. Robert A., MO, The United Church of Canada

WEBB, Miss Pauline, WL, The Methodist Church

WEED, Mrs. Margery, WL, United Church of Christ

WEJRYD, Rev. Anders, MO, Church of Sweden

WESONGA, Mrs. Janet, WL, Church of Uganda, Rwanda, Burundi and Boga Zaïre

WEST, Rev. Dr. William, MO, The Baptist Union of Great Britain and Ireland

WESTPHAL, Miss Marthe, WL, Reformed Church of France

WIDJAJA, Dr. Albert, ML, Protestant Evangelical Church in Timor

WIGGINS, Rt. Rev. Maxwell, MO, Church of the Province of Tanzania

WILDBOLZ, Rev. Dr. Eduard, MO, Swiss Protestant Church Federation

WILHELM, Miss Lya, WL, Evangelical Church of the Lutheran Confession in Brazil

WILLIAMS, Commissioner Harry, MO, The Salvation Army

WIRAKOTAN, Rev. Jona, MO, Indonesian Christian Church

WITTACK, Ms Carolyn, WL, Lutheran Church in America

WOLBER, D. Dr. Hans-Otto, MO, Evangelical Church in Germany—Lutheran

WOLFE, Mrs. Marianne, WL, The United Presbyterian Church in the USA

WONG, Rev. Dr. Peter, MO, Church of Christ in China/Hong Kong Council
WOOD, Rev. Wilfred, MO, The Church of England
WOOLFOLK, Ms A. Jean, WL, Christian Church (Disciples of Christ)
WOOLLCOMBE, Rt. Rev. Kenneth, MO, The Church of England
WRIGHT, Mr. Nicholas, ML, The Church of England
WRIGHT, Miss Silvia, WL, The Evangelical Pentecostal Church "Brazil for Christ"
YAMOAH, Rev. Charles K., MO, The Methodist Church, Ghana
YANNOPOULOS, Mr. Angelos, ML, Church of Greece
YOUNG, Rev. Prof. Norman, MO, Methodist Church of Australasia
YOUNGQUIST, Ms Margaret, WL, American Lutheran Church
YTTERBRINK, Mr. Ingmar, ML, Church of Sweden
ZABOLOTSKY, Prof. Nikolay, ML, Russian Orthodox Church
ZARU, Mrs. Jean, WL, Friends United Meeting
ZAPHIRIS, Rev. Prof. Gerassimos, MO, Greek Orthodox Patriarchate of Jerusalem
ZEYOHANNES, Dr. Tedla, ML, Ethiopian Orthodox Church
ZIZIOULAS, Prof. John, ML, Ecumenical Patriarchate of Constantinople
ZUMACH, Mrs. Hildegard, WL, Evangelical Church in Germany—United

4. FRATERNAL DELEGATES (ASSOCIATE MEMBERSHIP)

BLANC, Pastor Jacques, MO, Protestant Church of Algeria
BRAVO, Rev. Siles, MO, Evangelical Methodist Church in Bolivia
CHOI, Rev. Kyong, MO, Korean Christian Church in Japan
DENUNCIO, Rev. Prof. Raul, MO, United Evangelical Lutheran Church, Argentina
GUIDUCCI, Rev. Angel, ML, Disciples of Christ, Argentina
IHAJI, Mr. Peter, MO, African Church of the Holy Spirit
LEITE, Mr. Jose, MO, Evangelical Presbyterian Church of Portugal
MADALAG, Mr. Manjil, ML, Protestant Church in Sabah/Malaysia
MARIANO, Pastor Roberto, MO, Evangelical Methodist Church in Uruguay
MILO, Rev. Lene, MO, Methodist Church of Samoa
MONDAL, Rt. Rev. Barnabas, MO, Church of Bangladesh
NORNIELLA, Rev. Francisco, MO, Presbyterian-Reformed Church in Cuba
PALOMO, Bishop Luis, MO, Evangelical Methodist Church/Costa Rica
RODRIGUEZ, Bishop Armando, MO, Methodist Church in Cuba
SINAGA, Rev. Linsaner, MO, Punguan Kristen Batak, Indonesia
TAIBO, Rt. Rev. Ramon, MO, Spanish Reformed Episcopal Church, Spain
VOGELMANN, Ms Rose, WL, Church of Christ/Zaïre—Ceba

5. FRATERNAL DELEGATES (CHRISTIAN COUNCILS)

ASSAD, Dr. Maurice, ML, Coptic Orthodox Church
BAXTER, Rev. Alan, MO, Churches of Christ in Australia
BENEDYKTOWICZ, Prof. Dr. Witold, MO, Methodist Church/Poland
BERNER, Dr. Norman, MO, Lutheran Church in America
BERTINAT, Rev. Mario, MO, Waldensian Church
BINTZ, Dr. Helmut, MO, Evangelische Brüder-Unität
BOOTSMA, Mr. Hans, ML, Netherlands Reformed Church
CADOGAN, Rev. Claude, MO, Methodist Church in the Caribbean and the
    Americas
CANTELL, Rev. Risto, MO, Evangelical-Lutheran Church of Finland
CARR, Rev. Canon Burgess, MO, Episcopal Church/Liberia
DATTA, Mr. Dilip, ML, Baptist Union/Bangladesh
DEGENHARDT, Dr. Johannes, MO, Roman Catholic Church
FERNANDEZ CEBALLOS, Rev. Raul, MO, Presbyterian-Reformed
    Church in Cuba
FIOLET, Prof. Dr. H.A.M., MO, Roman Catholic Church
GJERDING, Mr. Uffe, ML, The Church of Denmark
GONZALEZ, Rev. Dr. Nicandro E., MO, The United Presbyterian Church
    in the USA
GRAESHOLT, Rt. Rev. Thorkild, MO, The Church of Denmark
HAARSMA, Prof. Dr. Frans, MO, Roman Catholic Church
HEDBERG, Rev. Dr. Gosta, MO, The Mission Covenant Church of Sweden
HONEY, Rev. Dr. T.E. Floyd, MO, The United Church of Canada
KACHAJE, Rev. Gibiel, MO, Church of the Province of Central Africa
KRUEGER, Dr. Hanfried, MO, Evangelical Church in Germany—Lutheran
MALL, Mr. William, ML, United Presbyterian Church of Pakistan
MANN, Miss Ruth, WL, Church of South India
MERCADO, Rev. La Verne, MO, The United Methodist Church
MICHEL, Dr. Jaime, MO, Lutheran Church, Latin America
MORTON, Rev. Harry, MO, The Methodist Church
MWENDA, Rev. Kingsley, MO, United Church of Zambia
NAKAJIMA, Rev. John, MO, The United Church of Christ in Japan
NDEBELE, Rev. James, MO, Church of the Province of Central Africa
NELSON, Rev. Richmond, MO, Disciples of Christ/Jamaica
NGAKANE, Rev. Moeti, MO, Assemblies of God/South America
PABST, Oberkirchenrat Walter, MO, Federation of the Evangelical
    Churches in the GDR
PATTERSON, Rev. T. Carlisle, MO, The Presbyterian Church in Ireland
PONT, Pastor Maurice, MO, Reformed Church of France
PROHLE, Prof. Dr. Ka'roly, MO, Lutheran Church in Hungary
RAKOTOARIMANANA, Pastor Victor, MO, Church of Jesus Christ in
    Madagascar
RANDALL, Dr. Claire, WL, The United Presbyterian Church in the USA
RATEFY, Rev. Daniel, MO, Church of Jesus Christ in Madagascar
REES, Mr. John, ML, The Methodist Church of South Africa
SEANE, Rev. Samuel, MO, The Methodist Church of South Africa
SLACK, Rev. Dr. Kenneth, MO, The United Reformed Church in England
    and Wales
STALSETT, Rev. Gunnar, MO, Church of Norway
STOCKWELL, Dr. Eugene L., MO, The United Methodist Church
SVOBODA, Rev. Jiri, MO, Czechoslovak Hussite Church

TROEGER, Pastor Berthold, MO, Federation of the Evangelical Churches in the GDR
TUNG, Rev. William C., MO, Methodist Church/Hong Kong
VAN SICHEM, Mr. Paul, ML, The Reformed Churches in the Netherlands
VUKIALAU, Mr. Inia, ML, Methodist Church of Australasia
WAHLEN, Pastor Jakob, MO, Swiss Protestant Church Federation
WALLACE, Rev. Samuel, MO, The Methodist Church, Sierra Leone
WATYOKA, Mr. Cornelius, ML, Methodist Church/Rhodesia
WILLIAMS, Rev. Dr. Glen G., MO, The Baptist Union of Great Britain and Ireland
YAP, Dr. Kim Hao, MO, The Methodist Church in Malaysia and Singapore
ZACHARIAH, Mr. Mathai, ML, Church of North India

6. FRATERNAL DELEGATES (CHRISTIAN ORGANIZATIONS)

ALPHONSE, Rev. Dr. Padinjare, MO, Roman Catholic Church
ARNOLD, Rev. Walter, MO, Evangelical Church in Germany—Lutheran
AYELE, Mr. Tsegaw, ML, Ethiopian Orthodox Church
BUHRIG, Dr. Marga, WL, Swiss Protestant Church Federation
CAMPI, Rev. Emidio, MO, Waldensian Church
CARINO, Dr. Feliciano, ML, United Church of Christ in the Philippines
FICK, Dr. Ulrich, MO, Evangelical Church in Germany—Lutheran
LEONARD, Frere, ML, Taizé Community
MANUEL, Rev. Albert, MO, Church of South India
MUGAVANA, Mr. Karamoja, ML
NTIRO, Mrs. E.S., WL
RAMSAY, Miss Katherine, WL, The Church of Scotland
THAMPY, Mr. Abraham, ML, Mar Thoma Syrian Church of Malabar
THOMAS, Rev. M.A., MO, Mar Thoma Syrian Church of Malabar

7. FRATERNAL DELEGATES (WORLD CONFESSIONAL FAMILIES)

HOWE, Rt. Rev. John, MO, Episcopal Church in Scotland
KINYANJUI KAMAU, Rev. Arthur, MO, Baptist Mission/East Africa
KOK, Most Rev. Marinus, MO, Old Catholic Church of the Netherlands
LEE, Dr. Allan W., MO, Christian Church (Disciples of Christ)
MAU, Dr. Carl, MO, American Lutheran Church
PERRET, Rev. Dr. Edmond, MO, Swiss Protestant Church Federation
SNYDER, Mr. William, ML, Mennonite Church

TUTTLE, Rev. Dr. Lee, MO, The United Methodist Church
WILSON, Mr. Anthony, ML, Society of Friends/UK

8. ADVISERS

ADLER, Mrs. Elisabeth, WL, Federation of the Evangelical Churches in the GDR

VON ALLMEN, Pastor Daniel, MO, Swiss Protestant Church Federation

AMBROSE, Mr. John, ML, The United Church of Canada

ARGENTI, Rev. Cyrille, MO, Ecumenical Patriarchate of Constantinople

ARIARAJAH, Rev. S. Wesley, MO, Methodist Church, Sri Lanka

ARIAS, Bishop Mortimer, MO, Evangelical Methodist Church in Bolivia

ASFOUR, Miss Adeline, WL, Roman Catholic Church

ASHBY, Miss Peggy, WL, Presbyterian Church of Guyana

ASSAAD, Mrs. Maris, WL, Coptic Orthodox Church

BAROT, Dr. Madeleine, WL, Reformed Church of France

BEAUPERE, Father Rene, MO, Roman Catholic Church

BEYER, Rev. Ilse, WO, Evangelical Church A.U.H.B. in Austria

BIRCH, Prof. Charles, ML, Methodist Church of Australasia

BORTNOWSKA, Miss Halina, WL, Roman Catholic Church

BROWN, Rev. Dr. Robert McAfee, MO, The United Presbyterian Church in the USA

BROWN, Ms Margrethe B.J., WL, The United Presbyterian Church in the USA

BUTHELEZI, Rev. Dr. Manas, MO, Evangelical Lutheran Church in Southern Africa, S.E.

CADETTE, Rev. Victor Anthony, MO, Baptist Union/Trinidad and Tobago

CAMPOS, Prof. Julia, WO, Waldensian Church

CARTER, Most Rev. Samuel, MO, Roman Catholic Church

CASSIDY, Mr. Michael, ML, Church of the Province of South Africa

CHATTERJI, Mr. Saral, ML, Church of North India

CHRISTENSON, Rev. Laurence, MO, American Lutheran Church

CONE, Prof. James H., MO, African Methodist Episcopal Church

DAHLEN, Ambassador Olle, ML, The Mission Covenant Church of Sweden

DE SILVA, Rev. Prof. Lynn, MO, Methodist Church, Sri Lanka

DIETRICH, Dr. Gabriele, WL, Evangelical Church in Germany—United

ELONDA, Pastor Efefe, MO, Church of Christ in Zaïre—Community of Disciples

ESCOBAR AGUIRRE, Mr. Samuel, ML

FRANCIS, Dr. John, ML, The Church of England

GAROEB, Mr. M., ML

GIBBES, Miss Emily V., WL, The United Presbyterian Church in the USA

GRAY, Rev. Gordon, MO, The Presbyterian Church in Ireland

GRENGEL, Pastor Christa, WO, Federation of the Evangelical Churches in the GDR

HAHN, Rev. Hans, MO, Evangelical Church in Germany—United

HALLENCREUTZ, Dr. Carl-Fredrik, MO, Church of Sweden

HARVEY, Mrs. Clarie, WL, The United Methodist Church
HOWARD, Miss R. Christian, WL, The Church of England
HOWARD, Rev. M. William, MO, Reformed Church in America
HUBBARD, Dr. David, MO, American Baptist Churches in the USA
IGE, Mr. Bola, ML, The Church of the Province of West Africa
JAMES, Prof. Walter, ML, The Church of England
JANSSENS, Mr. Peter, ML, Roman Catholic Church
JONES, Mr. Penry, ML, The United Reformed Church in England and
    Wales
KAAN, Rev. Frederik, MO, The United Reformed Church in England and
    Wales
KARAGDAG, Ms Carmencita, WL, Philippine Independent Church
KOYAMA, Rev. Dr. Kosuke, MO, The United Church of Christ in Japan
KROLL, Dr. Una, WL, The Church of England
KURIEN, Prof. Dr. Christopher, ML, Church of South India
LIGGETT, Dr. Thomas, MO, Christian Church (Disciples of Christ)
LINN, Rev. Gerhard, MO, Federation of the Evangelical Churches in the
    GDR
LUDWIG, Mr. Joachim, MO, Reformed Church of France
MACTAVISH, Mrs. Shona, WL, The Presbyterian Church of New Zealand
MANLEY, The Hon. Michael, ML, Methodist Church in the Caribbean and
    the Americas
MANUEL, Ms Shanti, WL, Church of South India
MAPANAO, Mrs. Portia, WL, United Church of Christ in the Philippines
MARGULL, Prof. Hans, MO, Evangelical Church in Germany—Lutheran
MCCLEARY, Dr. Paul, MO, The United Methodist Church
MENDEZ, Rev. Hector, MO, Presbyterian-Reformed Church in Cuba
MOLTMANN, Prof. Dr. Juergen, MO, Evangelical Church in Germany—
    United
MULDER, Prof. Dirk, MO, The Reformed Churches in the Netherlands
NABABAN, Rev. Dr. Soritua, MO, Protestant Christian Batak Church
NELLAS, Dr. Panayotis, ML, Ecumenical Patriarchate of Constantinople
NEWBIGIN, Bishop J.E. Lesslie, MO, The United Reformed Church in
    England and Wales
NIPKOW, Prof. Dr. Karl-Ernst, ML, Evangelical Church in Germany—
    Lutheran
NOMENYO, Pastor Seth, MO, Evangelical Church of Togo
NOMURA, Mr. Yushi, ML, The United Church of Christ in Japan
NONTAWASSEE, Mrs. Prakai, WL, The Church of Christ in Thailand
NUGENT, Mr. Randolph, MO, The United Methodist Church
OH, Mr. Jae Shik, ML, The Presbyterian Church in the Republic of Korea
OPOCENSKY, Dr. Milan, MO, Evangelical Church of Czech Brethren
ORTEGA, Rev. Ofelia, WO, Presbyterian-Reformed Church in Cuba
ORTIZ, Rev. Juan, MO, Tab. De La Fe/Argentina
OSEI, Rev. Dr. Joseph, MO, Roman Catholic Church
OSTHATHIOS, His Grace Geevarghese, MO, The Orthodox Syrian Church,
    Catholicate of the East
PARMAR, Dr. Samuel, ML, Church of North India
PAWLICK, Pastor Zdzislaw, MO, Baptist Church/Poland
PEETERS-LE BOULENGE, Ms Denise, WL, Roman Catholic Church
PHILIP, Dr. T., ML, Mar Thoma Syrian Church of Malabar
PIIROINEN, Miss Outi, WL, Ecumenical Patriarchate of Constantinople

POSER, Dr. Klaus, ML, Evangelical Church in Germany—Lutheran
POTTER, Mrs. E. O. Doreen, WL, Methodist Church in the Caribbean and the Americas
POWERS, Rev. Dr. Edward A., MO, United Church of Christ
PRONK, Mr. Johannes, ML, Netherlands Reformed Church
RAVOLOLONARISOA, Miss Micheline, WL, Church of Jesus Christ in Madagascar
RAYAN, Rev. Dr. Samuel, MO, Roman Catholic Church
RENNER, Rev. Eustace, MO, The Methodist Church, Sierra Leone
ROGERS, Father C. Murray, MO, The Church of England
ROKOTUIVUNA, Ms Amelia, WL, Methodist Church of Australasia
SINTADO, Rev. Carlos, MO, Evangelical Methodist Church of Argentina
SOIKO, Rev. Bogdan, MO, Russian Orthodox Church
STENDAHL, Dean Krister, MO, Lutheran Church in America
STOTT, Rev. John, MO, The Church of England
STRANSKY, Rev. Thomas F., C.S.P., MO, Roman Catholic Church
TAKENAKA, Prof. Masao, MO, The United Church of Christ in Japan
TALBOT, Dr. Sylvia, WL, African Methodist Episcopal Church
TERPSTRA, Dr. Lambert, ML, Moravian Church/NL
THIMME, Prases Hans, MO, Evangelical Church in Germany—United
THOMPSON, Ms Betty, WL, The United Methodist Church
TOLEN, Dr. Aaron, ML, Presbyterian Church of Cameroon
TUCCI, Father Roberto, MO, Roman Catholic Church
TUTU, Very Rev. Desmond, MO, Church of the Province of South Africa
UYLENBROECK, Mgr. Marcel, MO, Roman Catholic Church
VAN DER VEEN, Rev. Rein, MO, The Reformed Churches in the Netherlands
WELGE, Pastor Friedrich, MO, Federation of the Evangelical Churches in the GDR
YANNARAS, Dr. Christos, ML, Church of Greece
YAP, Mr. Thiam-Hien, ML, Christian Churches of Java
YODER, Prof. John, MO, Mennonite Church
ZAPATA, Mr. Rolando, ML, Methodist Church of Mexico

9. DELEGATED OBSERVERS (NON-MEMBER CHURCHES)

AMALORPAVADASS, Rev. Dr. Duraisamy, MO, Roman Catholic Church
BEACH, Dr. Bert, MO, 7th Day Adventist Church/GB
CARVALHO, Bishop Emilio De, MO, United Methodist Church/Angola
DANSOKHO, Mr. Samuel, ML, Egl. Prot./Senegal
DIEKE-KOFFI, Pastor Joseph, MO, Egl. Prot. Du Centre
DUPREY, Father Pierre, MO, Roman Catholic Church
ENGEBRETSON, Dr. Milton B., MO, Evangelical Covenant Church of America
EPALANGA, Rev. Ricardo U., MO, Council of Evangelical Churches/Angola
FERREIRA, Prof. Hortensia, WL, Christian Church (Disciples)/Paraguay
FUNZAMO, Pastor Isaias, MO, Presbyterian Church/Mozambique

GAFARINGA, Pastor Edouard, MO, Presbyterian Church/Rwanda
GAKWANDI, Prof. Edouard, MO, Roman Catholic Church
HOTCHKIN, Rev. John F., MO, Roman Catholic Church
JAVIERRE-ORTAS, Prof. Antonio, MO, Roman Catholic Church
KANYONZA, Rev. Vincent, MO, Roman Catholic Church
KLOMPE, Dr. Marga, WL, Roman Catholic Church
KLOPPENBURG, Prof. Dr. Carlos Jose, MO, Roman Catholic Church
KROMMINGA, Dr. John, MO, Christian Reformed Church
LANNE, Dom Emmanuel, MO, Roman Catholic Church
LONG, Rev. John, MO, Roman Catholic Church
MARINI-(BODHO), Rev. Dr. Dirinda, MO, Church of Christ/Zaïre: Evangelical Community
MARTINEZ, Rev. Luis, MO, Pentecostal Church/Cuba
MEEKING, Father Basil, MO, Roman Catholic Church
NAMAGANDA, Miss Elizabeth, WL, Roman Catholic Church
NEFF, Mr. Charles, MO, Church of Jesus Christ of the Latter Day Saints
PREUS, Rev. Jacob, MO, Lutheran Church/Missouri Synod
SAMSON, Rev. Jude, MO, United Church of Christ/Marshall Islands
SARPONG, Most Rev. Peter, MO, Roman Catholic Church
SCHEELE, Prof. Dr. Paul Werner, MO, Roman Catholic Church
SCHOLL, Rev. Fenton, Jr., MO, Southern Baptist Convention
SIMMONS, Sister Gilmary, WL, Roman Catholic Church
SMITH, Prof. John, MO, Church of God/USA
TIDENBERG, Rev. James, MO, Baptist Mission/East Africa
VERONESE, Dr. Vittorino, ML, Roman Catholic Church
YOUNG, Rev. Paul H., Jr., MO, National Association of Congregational Christian Churches/USA
YRI, Dr. Norvald, ML, Evang. Church Mekane Yesus
ZUNGUZE, Bishop E.A., MO, United Methodist Church/Mozambique

10. OBSERVERS (CHRISTIAN COUNCILS)

KHOABANE, Mr. Jubilee, ML
MAHLALELA, Rev. Isaac, MO, Wesleyan Methodist Church/Mozambique
NICOLAS, Pastor Albert, MO, Reformed Church of France
NSUBUGA, Rt. Rev. Dr. Kasi, MO, Church of Uganda, Rwanda, Burundi and Boga Zaïre
SHAURI, Mr. Stanford, ML, Church of the Province of Tanzania

11. OBSERVERS (INTERNATIONAL ORGANIZATIONS)

BERTHOUD, Mr. Paul, ML
BOLIOLI, Rev. Oscar, MO, Evangelical Methodist Church in Uruguay
BURGESS, Mr. David S., ML, United Church of Christ

DOBBELMANN, Dr. Reinerus, ML, Roman Catholic Church
FRANTZ, Mr. Luis M., ML
GRANT, Miss Stephanie, WL
KATO, Rev. Dr. Byang, MO, Evangelical Church/West Africa
MBEKI, Ms Zanele, WL
MOONEYHAM, Dr. W. Stanley, ML
MWANGEMI, Mr. Chrispus, ML
MYERS, Mr. Don, ML, The United Methodist Church
NICHOLLS, Mr. Bruce, ML, The Baptist Union of New Zealand
ROBINSON, Rev. Dr. John, MO
SCHROTENBOER, Rev. Dr. Paul Gerard, MO, Christian Reformed Church
SIKAULU, Mr. Nchimunya, ML, Roman Catholic Church
TIMBO, Mr. Sulaiman, ML
WEGNER, Prof. Dr. Walter, MO, Lutheran Church/Missouri Synod

12. GUESTS

AMRAM, Mr. David, ML
ANKRAH, Mr. Esuman, ML, The Methodist Church, Ghana
BARSOUM, His Excellency Albert, ML, Coptic Orthodox Church
BLAKE, Dr. Eugene C., MO, The United Presbyterian Church in the USA
DAVIES, Mgr. Colin, MO, Roman Catholic Church
DU PLESSIS, Rev. David, MO, Assembly of God
GATHUNA, Rev. George, MO, Greek Orthodox Patriarchate of Alexandria
GATIMU, Bishop, WO, Roman Catholic Church
GUELLY, Mr. Joseph, MO, Episcopal Church/Sudan
HEWAGE, Prof. Lankaputra, ML
IBIAM, Dr. Akanu, ML, The Presbyterian Church of Nigeria
KAHIHIA, Most Rev. Benjamin, MO, African Independent Pentecostal Church
KAUMA, Rt. Rev. Misaeri, MO, Church of Uganda, Rwanda, Burundi and Boga Zaïre
KENYATTA, Miss Margaret, WL
KIVENGERE, Rt. Rev. Festo, MO, Church of Uganda, Rwanda, Burundi and Boga Zaïre
KIZZA, Mr. Martin, ML, Uganda Orthodox Church
LUNGAHO, Mr. Ganira, ML, Friends/East Africa
MARSH, Rev. Dr. Clinton M., MO, The United Presbyterian Church in the USA
MCGEE, Mr. Vincent, ML, Roman Catholic Church
MEAD, Dr. Margaret, WL, The Episcopal Church
MOELLER, Mgr. Charles, MO, Roman Catholic Church
DI MONTEZEMOLO, Mgr. Andrea, MO, Roman Catholic Church
MTANGO, Miss Christine, WL, Evangelical Lutheran Church in Tanzania
NASUTION, Dr. Harun, ML, Muslim
NDINGI MWANA'A NZEKI, Bishop Raphael, MO, Roman Catholic Church
NIEMOLLER, Pastor Martin, MO, Evangelical Church in Germany—United
NTHAMBURI, Rev. Zablon, MO, The Methodist Church in Kenya
OJIAMBO, Drs. Julia Auma, WL, Church of the Province of Kenya

378

OLANG', Most Rev. Festo, MO, Church of the Province of Kenya
OMUSOLO, Rev. Festus, MO, Roman Catholic Church
ONDENG, Mr. Richard, ML, Pentecostal Assembly of God/Kenya
OPIYO, Mrs. Mary Beatrice, WL, Roman Catholic Church
OSEI-MENSAH, Rev. Gottfried, MO, Baptist Convention/Kenya
OTUNGA, Cardinal, MO, Roman Catholic Church
PARKS, Rev. Dr. Robert, MO, The Episcopal Church
RAO, Prof. Seshagiri K.L., ML, Hindu
RIDDELSDELL, Rev. John, MO, Church of the Province of Kenya
SARTORELLI, Most Rev. Pierluigi, MO, Roman Catholic Church
SINGH, Dr. Gopal, ML, Sikh
STRONG, Mr. Maurice F., ML, The United Church of Canada
SWANN, Mr. Donald, ML
TANGEMAN, Mrs. R. Clementine, WL, Christian Church (Disciples of
    Christ)
WASIKYE, Rev. Canon John, MO, Church of Uganda, Rwanda, Burundi
    and Boga Zaïre
WELCH, Mrs. Eileen, WL, Church of the Province of Kenya
WESONGA, Rev. Akisoferi, MO, Church of Uganda, Rwanda, Burundi and
    Boga Zaïre
WOLF, Rabbi Arnold, MO, Jewish

13. HOST COMMITTEE

APPIAH-KUBI, Mr. Kofi, ML, Presbyterian Church of Ghana
CHIURI, Mrs. Nanjiku, WL, Presbyterian Church of East Africa
CRIPPEN, Dr. David, ML, Church of God/USA
GITARI, Rt. Rev. David, MO, Church of the Province of Kenya
GITAU, Rev. Jeremiah, MO, Presbyterian Church of East Africa
JURGENS, Rev. Arnoldus, MO, Roman Catholic Church
KIBICHO, Rev. Dr. Samuel, MO, Presbyterian Church of East Africa
KIPLAGAT, Mrs. Ranivoarimanana, WL, Church of the Province of Kenya
KIRIMANIA, Mr. Erastus, ML, The Methodist Church in Kenya
KISIA, Mr. Joseph, ML, Friends/East Africa
LUKALO, Mrs. Serah-Rose, WL
LUVAI, Mr. Nathan, ML, Friends/East Africa
MAGERIA, Mr. James, ML, Presbyterian Church of East Africa
MAGUA, Ven. Sospeter, MO, Church of the Province of Kenya
MAKOLO, Rev. Luke, MO, Church of the Province of Kenya
MBUGUA, Rev. Canon Leonard, MO, Church of the Province of Kenya
MUGAMBI, Mr. Jesse, ML, Church of the Province of Kenya
MUGO, Mr. Wagichu, ML, Presbyterian Church of East Africa
MUGOFU, Mr. Lizalia, ML, Friends/East Africa
MUYALE, Mr. Akafwale, ML
SERWANGA, Rev. Daniel, MO, Church of the Province of Kenya

14. WCC STAFF

ABRECHT, Rev. Dr. Paul, MO, American Baptist Churches in the USA
ADDISON, Miss Florence, WL, The Methodist Church, Ghana
VAN DEN AKKER, Ms Jaapje, WL, Netherlands Reformed Church
APPIAH, Miss Evelyn, WL, The Methodist Church, Ghana
BAM, Ms Brigalia, WL, Church of the Province of South Africa
BARROW, Miss R. Nita, WL, Methodist Church in the Caribbean and the Americas
BAUSWEIN, Pastor Jean-Jacques, MO, Evangelical Church of the Augsburg Confession of Alsace and Lorraine
VAN DER BENT, Rev. Ans, MO, United Church of Christ
BLANKEN, Mrs. Janny P., WL
BOFFARD, Mrs. Eva, WL, Bund Ev.-Frei. Gem. in Der BRD
BOGLE, Ms Ellen, WL, The Church of Scotland
BONNEWITZ, Miss Siegrid, WL
BOSSY, Mrs. Eliane, WL, Swiss Protestant Church Federation
BOUMAN, Mr. Pieter, ML, Swiss Protestant Church Federation
BRASH, Rev. Dr. Alan, MO, The Presbyterian Church of New Zealand
BREDOW, Miss Susanne, WL
BRIA, Prof. Ion, MO, Rumanian Orthodox Church
BUMA, Rev. Kentaro, MO, The United Church of Christ in Japan
BURROWS, Miss Auriol, WL, The United Reformed Church in England and Wales
BURTON, Mrs. Moya, WL
BYFIELD, Miss Beverley, WL
CARTAGENA, Mr. Richard, MO
CASTRO, Rev. Emilio, MO, Evangelical Methodist Church in Uruguay
CHIPENDA, Rev. Jose Belo, MO
CLAYSON, Ms Zoe, WL
CLEMENTS, Rev. Leslie, MO, The Methodist Church of New Zealand
COATES, Miss Christine, WL, The Church of England
COE, Rev. Dr. Shoki, MO, The United Reformed Church in England and Wales
COURVOISIER, Ms Maryse, WL, Reformed Church of France
CUDRE-MAUROUX, Mr. Gilbert, ML
DAVIS, Rev. Rex, MO, The Church of England in Australia
DAY, Mr. Charles, ML, Swiss Protestant Church Federation
DEFILLON, Miss Jacqueline, WL
DOELL, Ms Christel, WL
DONCH, Ms Rosemarie, WL
DREWES, Mr. Manfred, ML, Evangelical Church in Germany—Lutheran
DULL, Mrs. Birgit, WL
ECKERDAL, Ms Ingrid Vera, WL, Church of Sweden
EPPS, Rev. Dwain C., MO, The United Presbyterian Church in the USA
EVDOKIMOFF, Mrs. Tomoko, WL
FELLER, Mrs. Ruth, WL, Swiss Protestant Church Federation
FISCHER, Mr. Jean, ML, Swiss Protestant Church Federation
FRIEDLI-DOBELL, Mrs. Shelagh, WL
GADSBY, Miss Philomena, WL, Roman Catholic Church
GALLIN, Ms Elizabeth, WL, American Baptist Churches in the USA
DE GASPAR, Dr. Diogo, ML, Roman Catholic Church
GHELFI, Miss Arlette, WL

GILL, Rev. David, MO, The Congregational Union of Australia
GODDARD, Miss Sandra, WL, The Church of England
GOSCH, Mrs. Ingeborg, WL, Evangelical Church in Germany—Lutheran
GREEN, Miss E. Rosemary, WL, The United Reformed Church in England and Wales
GREGORIADES, Mrs. Gisela, WL, Evangelical Church in Germany— Lutheran
GRUHN, Mrs. Colene, WL, United Church of Christ
HAMMERSTEIN, Dr. Franz, MO, Evangelical Church in Germany—United
HENDERSON, Miss Anne, WL, The Church of England
HILKE, Mr. Juergen, ML, Evangelical Church in Germany—Lutheran
HOFFMANN, Dr. Gerhard, MO, Evangelical Church in Germany—United
VAN HOOGEVEST, Miss Geertruida, WL, Netherlands Reformed Church
HOPPE, Miss Anneliese, WL, Evangelical Church in Germany—United
HORTON, Miss Angela, WL, The Church of England
IGWE, Rev. Dr. Egemba, MO, Methodist Church, Nigeria
IMBESCHEIDT, Miss Erika, WL, Evangelical Church in Germany— Lutheran
ITTY, Mr. Chirapurath, ML, The Orthodox Syrian Church, Catholicate of the East
JENKINS, Rev. Canon David, MO, The Church of England
KEIM, Miss Renate, WL
KENNEDY, Dr. William, MO, Presbyterian Church in the United States
KERKHOFF, Ms. Cornelia, WL
KINZEL, Miss Gerda, WL
KNOOIHUIZEN, Mr. Nicolaas, ML, The Reformed Churches in the Netherlands
KOEHLER, Mrs. Irmela, WL, Evangelical Church in Germany—Lutheran
KOILPILLAI, Mr. Victor, ML
KOK, Mr. Jan, ML, The Reformed Churches in the Netherlands
KOSHY, Prof. Ninan, MO, Church of South India
KROKER, Mr. Bruno, ML, Lutheran Church in America
KUNANAYAKAM, Miss Tamara, WL
KUNZLI-DOY, Mrs. Annie, WL, Swiss Protestant Church Federation
LEWIS, Rev. Arthur, MO, The United Reformed Church in England and Wales
LONG, Rev. Charles, MO, The Episcopal Church
LOWE, Miss Yvonne, WL, The Church of England
LUNT, Mrs. Carol, WL, The Church of England
LUSCHER, Mrs. Frieda, WL, Swiss Protestant Church Federation
MAEDA, Ms Frances, WL, The United Presbyterian Church in the USA
MAIER, Miss Franziska, WL
MAKHULU, Rev. Walter, MO, Church of the Province of South Africa
MANDWEWALA, Mrs. Jayashree, WL
MARIAN, Mrs. Marie-Louise, WL
MBITI, Prof. John, MO, Church of the Province of Kenya
MCGILVRAY, Mr. James, ML, The Episcopal Church
MELLOR, Miss Anne, WL, The Church of England
MEULSON, Miss Evelyne, WL
MEYER, Prof. Gerson, MO
MOREILLON, Mrs. Madeleine, WL, Swiss Protestant Church Federation
MULLER-FAHRENHOLZ, Dr. Geiko, MO, Evangelical Church in Germany—Lutheran

NIILUS, Mr. Leopoldo, ML
NORTHAM, Mr. Frank, ML, The Methodist Church
NOVOTNY, Mrs. Michelle-Claude, WL
PARK, Mr. Sang Jung, ML
PATELOS, Mr. Constantinos, ML, Greek Orthodox Patriarchate of Alexandria
PATER, Miss Margaret, WL, The Methodist Church
PICARAT, Mr. Marc, ML
POTTER, Rev. Dr. Philip, MO, Methodist Church in the Caribbean and the Americas
POTTIER, Mrs. Francoise, WL, Swiss Protestant Church Federation
RAISER, Dr. Konrad, MO, Evangelical Church in Germany—Lutheran
RANDRIAMAMONJY, Mr. Frederic, ML
RAY, Miss Sheila, WL
REBER, Mrs. Adrienne, WL, Swiss Protestant Church Federation
REICHEN, Mrs. Irmhild, WL
REILLY, Miss Joan, WL, The Church of Scotland
REUSCHLE, Mr. Helmut, ML, Evangelical Church in Germany—Lutheran
RICHARD, Miss Sylvie, WL
ROGERS, Miss Ginny, WL, The Church of Sri Lanka
SAMARTHA, Rev. Dr. Stanley, MO, Church of South India
DE SANTA ANA, Dr. Julio, ML, Evangelical Methodist Church in Uruguay
SAPSEZIAN, Rev. Aharon, MO, Armenian Evangelical Church/Brazil
SAUNDERS, Mrs. Phyllis, WL, The Church of England
SBEGHEN, Mrs. Renate, WL
SCHMIDT, Miss Sabine, WL, Evangelical Church in Germany—Lutheran
SCHNEIDER, Mr. Andreas, ML
SCHOT, Mr. Willem, ML, The Reformed Churches in the Netherlands
SCHWEIZER, Mr. Ruth, MO, Swiss Protestant Church Federation
SEVILLA, Miss Rosalia, WL, Roman Catholic Church
SJOLLEMA, Mr. Baldwin, ML, Netherlands Reformed Church
SMITH, Ms. Frances S., WL, The United Presbyterian Church in the USA
SMITH, Miss Irene, WL
SMITH, Miss Pauline, WL
SONG, Rev. Dr. Choan-Seng, MO, The Presbyterian Church in Taiwan
STALSCHUS, Ms. Christa, WL
STRAATHOF, Mr. Rudolf, ML, Roman Catholic Church
STRONG, Rev. Robbins, MO, United Church of Christ
STUNT, Miss Heather, WL, The Church of England
SUTANTO, Mr. Sutanto, ML
TAYLOR, Dr. John, ML, The Methodist Church
TAYLOR, Mr. John, ML, The United Methodist Church
TITTERINGTON, Miss Glynis, WL
TODD, Mr. George E., MO, The United Presbyterian Church in the USA
TRAITLER, Dr. Reinhild, WL, Evangelical Church A.U.H.B. in Austria
TSETSIS, Rev. Georges, MO, Ecumenical Patriarchate of Constantinople
VAZ, Miss Veronica, WL, Roman Catholic Church
VERSCHUEREN, Miss Francoise, WL, Roman Catholic Church
VISCHER, Dr. Lukas, MO, Swiss Protestant Church Federation
VAN VREDENBURCH, Miss Machteld, WL, Netherlands Reformed Church
DE VRIES, Rev. C. Michael, MO, Evangelical Lutheran Church
WEBB, Mrs. Muriel S., WL, The Episcopal Church

WEBER, Dr. Hans, MO, Swiss Protestant Church Federation
WEHRLE, Miss Luzia, WL
WEIL, Mr. Luiz Carlos, ML, Presbyterian Church/Brazil
WELSH, Dr. Robert, MO, Christian Church (Disciples of Christ)
WHITTLE, Mr. Stephen, ML, Roman Catholic Church
WIESER, Dr. Thomas, MO
WILKIE, Miss Linda, WL, The Congregational Union of Scotland
WILLIAMSON, Miss Anne, WL
WOLF, Miss Kunigunde, WL
YOUNG, Mr. Ralph, ML, The United Church of Canada
ZARRAGA, Mrs. Tatjana, WL

15. CO-OPTED STAFF

ABRECHT, Mrs. Audrey, WL, American Baptist Churches in the USA
ANFINOGENOV, Mr. Nikolay, ML, Russian Orthodox Church
ARNOLD, Rev. Canon John, MO, The Church of England
BACHMANN, Miss Anne, WL
BARTH, Mrs. Marie-Claire, WO
BASSILI, Father Iskandar-Alex, ML, Melkite Catholic Church
BEAUME, Rev. Gilbert, MO, Reformed Church of France
BENES, Mrs. Dorothea, WL
BEST, Mr. Kenneth Y., ML, Episcopal Church/Liberia
BINGLE, Dr. Richard, ML, The Methodist Church
BIRCHMEIER, Rev. Heinz, MO, Swiss Protestant Church Federation
BUSS, Mr. Theodore, MO, Swiss Protestant Church Federation
CARTAGENA, Mrs. Anita, WL
CATCHINGS, Mrs. Rose, WL, The United Methodist Church
CHAMBRON, Pastor Marc, MO, Reformed Church of France
CHIMELLI, Mrs. Claire, WL, Swiss Protestant Church Federation
COLEMAN, Mrs. Elisabeth, WL, The Church of England
CONWAY, Mr. David, ML, The Church of England
CRAIG, Mr. David, ML, The Church of England
CULLOT, Miss Martine, WL
DANIEL, Rev. Henry Felix, MO, Church of South India
DAY, Mr. John ML
DELFORGE, Pastor Frederic, MO, Reformed Church of France
DELMONTE, Mrs. Elisabeth, WL, Evangelical Church of the River Plata
FAERBER, Prof. Robert, ML, Evangelical Church of the Augsburg Confession of Alsace and Lorraine
FISCHER, Mrs. Nicole, WL, Swiss Protestant Church Federation
FREYGANG, Mr. Peter, ML
FRIEDEBERG, Miss Ilse, WL, Evangelical Church in Germany—Lutheran
FUETER, Pastor Paul, MO, Swiss Protestant Church Federation
GALLOWAY, Mr. Gilbert, ML, The United Methodist Church
GARCON, Ms Elsa, WL
GARRETT, Rev. John, MO, The Congregational Union of Australia
GARRETT, Mrs. Roberta, WL, Methodist Church of Australasia
GASSMANN, Mrs. Ursula, WL, Evangelical Church of the Augsburg Confession of Alsace and Lorraine

GAUTIER, Mr. Gerard, ML, The United Church of Canada
GINGLAS, Miss Roswitha, WL
GORINA, Miss Nataly, WL, Russian Orthodox Church
GOULDING, Ms Sarah, WL
GURNEY, Mr. Robin, ML, The United Methodist Church
HACKEL, Rev. Dr. Sergii, MO, Russian Orthodox Church
HART, Mr. Norman, ML, The United Reformed Church in England and
  Wales
HAWKE, Mr. Chris, ML, Roman Catholic Church
HEINS, Mr. Lester, MO, American Lutheran Church
HENKYS, Mr. Reinhard, ML, Evangelical Church in Germany—United
HENRIET, Pastor Marcel, MO
HES, Dr. Jan, ML, Netherlands Reformed Church
VAN HILTEN, Miss Cora F., WL, Netherlands Reformed Church
HOPMAN, Miss Saskia, WL, Roman Catholic Church
HUGGEL, Mr. Felix, ML, Swiss Protestant Church Federation
IDAROUS, Mr. Nat, ML, Presbyterian Church of East Africa
IRELE, Mrs. Elise, WL, The Church of the Province of West Africa
JAMESON, Mr. Victor, ML, The United Presbyterian Church in the USA
JONAS, Miss Ingrid, WL
JONSON, Rev. Dr. Jonas, MO, Church of Sweden
JUBERT, Mrs. Cosette, WL, Swiss Protestant Church Federation
KARANJA, Ms Rachel, WL, Church of the Province of Kenya
KAREITHI, Mr. Munuhe, ML
KIPLAGAT, Mr. Bethuel, ML, Church of the Province of Kenya
KIRILLOFF, Mr. Arian, ML, Russian Orthodox Church
KOBIA, Mr. Samuel, ML, The Methodist Church in Kenya
KUSIMBA, Miss A. Mary, WL, Church of the Province of Kenya
LADENBURGER, Ms Solange, WL, Evangelical Church of the Augsburg
  Confession of Alsace and Lorraine
LAMBERTZ, Mrs. Renate, WL, Roman Catholic Church
LASSERRE, Mrs. Nelly, WL
LAUTENBACH, Pastor Hugo, MO, Swiss Protestant Church Federation
LEAR, Mr. Robert, ML, The United Methodist Church
LEE, Mr. Soo Jin, ML, Presbyterian Church/Singapore
LEHTONEN, Rev. Risto, MO, Evangelical-Lutheran Church of Finland
LEMA, Dr. Anza, ML, Evangelical Lutheran Church in Tanzania
LESCAZE, Miss Marie-Claire, WO, Swiss Protestant Church Federation
VON LOWIS, Miss Andrea, WL, Reformed Church of France
DE LUZE, Pastor Bertrand, MO, Reformed Church of France
MALLET, Miss Beatrice, WL, Swiss Protestant Church Federation
MARTENSEN, Dr. Daniel, MO, Lutheran Church in America
MATTFELDT, Ms Ulrike, WL
MCVEIGH, Dr. Malcolm, MO, The United Methodist Church
MOBBS, Pastor Arnold, MO, Swiss Protestant Church Federation
MODEAN, Mr. Erik W., ML, Lutheran Church in America
MOIR, Ms Lillian, WL
MOLLER, Mr. Carsten, ML
MULLER-ROMHELD, Dr. Walter, ML, Evangelical Church in Germany—
  United
MULLER, Mr. Mauricio, ML
MULLER, Miss Christina, WL, Russian Orthodox Church
MUREITHI, Ms Charity, WL, Presbyterian Church of East Africa
NALPANIS, Mr. Anatole, ML, Russian Orthodox Church

NTOULA, Mr. Revelation, ML, Church of the Province of South Africa
NUNN, Rev. Roger, MO, The Baptist Union of Great Britain and Ireland
OGUEY-FROMMES, Mrs. Re'sy, WL
O'HARA, Mr. William, ML, Roman Catholic Church
OKITE, Mr. Odhiambo, ML, Church of the Province of Kenya
OMBIMA, Mr. John, ML
OMEDI, Miss Leah, WL, Church of the Province of Kenya
ORLOV, Rev. Ilia, MO, Union of Evangelical Christian Bapitsts of the
  USSR
OSBORNE, Miss Gertrude, WL
PATON, Rev. Canon David, MO, The Church of England
PEREZ-RIVAS, Rev. Marcelo, MO, Evangelical Methodist Church of Ar-
  gentina
PETERSEN, Mr. Niels Bryde, ML
PHILIBERT, Mrs. Janine, WL, Reformed Church of France
PRAGER, Mr. Friedrich, ML
RAKOTONIRAINY, Pastor Josoa, MO, Church of Jesus Christ in Madagas-
  car
REY, Mr. Daniel, ML, Swiss Protestant Church Federation
RICHTERICH, Ms Anita, WL
ROMANOVSKI-MALINE, Mrs. Irene, WL, Russian Orthodox Church
ROTHERMUNDT, Dr. Jorg, MO, Evangelical Church in Germany—
  Lutheran
DE ROUGEMONT, Miss Genevieve, WL, Roman Catholic Church
SALGADO, Mr. Sebastio, Jr., MO
SCHINDLER, Mrs. Micheline, WL
SIMONS-FISCHER, Mrs. Baerbel, WL
SMITH, Miss Irene, WL, Russian Orthodox Church
SOMMERFELD, Miss Sigrid, WL, Evangelical Church in Germany—
  Lutheran
SPAE, Rev. Joseph, MO, Roman Catholic Church
SPAULDING, Rev. Dr. Helen, WO, Christian Church (Disciples of Christ)
STEINIG, Ms Frances, WL
STENZL, Miss Catherine, WL
STRECKER, Mrs. Renate, WL, Evangelical Church in Germany—United
VON STRITZKY, Miss Dores, WL
TAWIL-SAAD, Mrs. Marie-Helene, WL, Roman Catholic Church
TESTA, Dr. Michael P., MO, The United Presbyterian Church in the USA
THALER, Miss Brigitte, WL
THOMSEN, Pastor Jens J., MO, The Church of Denmark
VALDIVIA, Rev. Gerard E., MO, Pentecostal Church of Chile
VANDEYAR, Rev. Edwin, MO, Methodist Church in the Caribbean and
  the Americas
VOIGT, Ms Helga, WL, Evangelical Church in Germany—Lutheran
VOSKRESENSKY, Mr. Mstislav, ML, Russian Orthodox Church
WAGNER, Mr. Christophe, ML
WANGALWA, Mr. Philip, ML
WEGENER, Mrs. Hildburg, WL, Evangelical Church in Germany—Lutheran
WEIL, Mrs. Joanne, WL, Presbyterian Church/Brazil
WIESER, Dr. Marguerite, WL, Swiss Protestant Church Federation
WIK, Mr. Boris, ML, Russian Orthodox Church
ZABEL, Miss Helga, WL, Evangelical Church in Germany—United

16. STEWARDS

AGWU, Mrs. Comfort O., WL
AKHURA, Mr. Levi, ML
ANDREWS, Mr. Harold, ML
D'ANGELO, Mr. Dominic, ML, Roman Catholic Church
APOLOT, Miss Dina, WL, Church of Uganda, Rwanda, Burundi and Boga
    Zaïre
ASHAMALAAH, Miss Nagwa A.E., WL, Coptic Orthodox Church
AUGUSTINE, Mr. Patrick, ML, The Church of Pakistan
BAAS, Miss Geertruida, WL, Netherlands Reformed Church
BAGLIO, Mr. Daniele, ML, Evangelical Methodist Church of Italy
BAGUMA, Mr. Agabus, ML, Church of Uganda, Rwanda, Burundi and
    Boga Zaïre
BARNES, Mr. Michael, ML, The Congregational Union of Australia
BARTHOLOMEUSZ, Mr. Darryl, ML, The Anglican Church in Sri Lanka
BASKARAN, Mr. Pitchai, ML, Federation of Evangelical Lutheran
    Churches in India
VAN BEEK, Mr. Huibert, ML, Church of Jesus Christ in Madagascar
BENICHOUX, Miss Catherine, WL, Reformed Church of France
BENJACK, Miss Doris, WL
BERNOULLI, Mrs. Gertrud, WL
BLACK, Miss Susan, WL, The United Presbyterian Church in the USA
BOMBO, Miss Batsiki, WL
BOREL, Mr. Christian, ML
BOTO, Mr. George, ML
CABALLERO, Mrs. Belen, WL, United Church of Christ in the Philippines
CABALLERO, Rev. Carmelito, MO, United Church of Christ in the
    Philippines
CHAN, Miss Grace, WL
CHIPENDA, Miss Selma, WL
CLEGHORN, Rev. John, MO, The Presbyterian Church of Australia
COSBY, Mr. Stuart, ML, The Episcopal Church
DORAI, Miss Stella, WO, Evangelical Lutheran Church
DREYER, Miss Melissa, WL, The Episcopal Church
ESABWA, Mr. Naftali, ML, Salvation Army, Kenya
FAARVANG, Mr. Svend, ML
FARIA, Rev. Lineu, MO
FELBER, Mr. Peter, ML
FILIP, Miss Marta, WL
FILO, Rev. Julius, MO, Slovak Evangelical Church of the Augsburg Con-
    fession in the CSSR
GACHANGO, Mr. Moses, ML
GAERTNER, Mr. Thomas, ML, Evangelical Church in Germany—United
GLENSOR, Mr. Peter, ML, The Methodist Church of New Zealand
DA COSTA GOMEZ, Miss B., WL, Roman Catholic Church
GOROG, Rev. Tibor, MO, Lutheran Church in Hungary
HERMANS, Mr. Vincent, ML
HILL-ALTO, Mrs. Louise Ann, WL, Reformed Church in America
IIJIMA, Mr. Makoto, ML
INDALO, Mr. Peter, ML
INGTY, Miss Angela, WL, Church of North India

INOUYE, Miss Satsuki F., WL
IRUNGU, Mr. Bernard, ML
ISABIRYE, Mr. Bezalel Y.B.N., ML, Church of Uganda, Rwanda, Burundi and Boga Zaïre
ISMAILJI, Mr. Chanajit, ML, The Church of Christ in Thailand
JACOB, Dr. Sara, WL, Mar Thoma Syrian Church of Malabar
JANSON BRUNDIN, Miss Carola, WL, Church of Sweden
JARVIS, Ms Anna, WL, Christian Church (Disciples of Christ)
JUMA, Mrs. Rose, WL, The Methodist Church in Kenya
KAHL, Miss Susanne, WL
KAMANYIRE, Rev. Eustace, MO, Church of Uganda, Rwanda, Burundi and Boga Zaïre
KATAHWEIRE, Rev. Ernest, MO, Church of Uganda, Rwanda, Burundi and Boga Zaïre
KENNEDY, Ms Katharine, WL, Presbyterian Church in the United States
KENTISH, Miss Joyce, WL
KHOYA, Mr. Samuel, ML
KIHIKO, Mr. Francis N., ML, Presbyterian Church of East Africa
KIKAFFUNDA, Mr. James R., ML, Church of Uganda, Rwanda, Burundi and Boga Zaïre
KINOTI, Rev. Nahashon G., MO
LAISER, Miss Namnyak L., WL
VAN LANEN, Rev. James, MO
LANGTON, Rev. Barbara, WO, The United Church of Canada
LAZERUS, Mr. Andre, ML, Evangelical Church of the Augsburg Confession of Alsace and Lorraine
LEHR, Mr. Michael, ML, The Church of England
LEMOPOULO, Mr. Yorgo, ML, Ecumenical Patriarchate of Constantinople
LOVELL, Mr. Samuel, ML, Methodist Church in the Caribbean and the Americas
LUMB, Ms Fiona, WL
LUMB, Mr. Peter, ML
MAHESA, Miss Margaret, WL
MAKOKO, Mr. Juda, ML, Roman Catholic Church
MANOHARAN, Rev. Ponniah, MO, Federation of Evangelical Lutheran Churches in India
MBURU, Rev. Jackson, MO, African Christian Church and Schools, Kenya
MCDONALD, Miss Anne, WL
MCTAIR, Miss Claudia, WL
MERBOLD, Mr. Fred, ML
MFULA, Mrs. Martha, WL
MICUNGWE, Miss Deborah, WL, Church of Uganda, Rwanda, Burundi and Boga Zaïre
MIRITI, Mr. Robert, ML
MOGOT, Miss Becky Mbehena, WL
MONDAL, Mr. Provash, ML, Church of Bangladesh
MOROENG, Mrs. Rosey, WL
MUCHAU, Rev. Joseph, MO, African Christian Church and Schools, Kenya
MULWA, Rev. Samuel M., MO
MUMBA, Mrs. Christine, WL
MUNNICH, Mr. Udo, ML
MUNSHI, Mr. Simon, ML, Baptist Union/Bangladesh

MUTHAMIA, Mr. Festus, ML
NDAMBUKI, Miss Ruth M., WL
NGAHYOMA, Miss Neema, WL
NGOMA, Mrs. Elizabeth V., WL
NISHONGWANA, Mr. Bernard, ML
NJOROGE, Mr. Henry, ML
NOAH, Mr. Arun, ML, Church of North India
NTHIWA, Mr. Edward, ML
OBALLIM-OMEN, Mr. John W.C., ML, Church of Uganda, Rwanda, Burundi and Boga Zaïre
OBRACAI, Miss Christa, WL
OLOO, Mr. Wilfrid O., ML, Church of the Province of Kenya
ORDONEZ-RUEDA, Mr. Ricardo, ML
OTIENE, Miss Rosemary, WL
OVERTON, Mr. Grenville, ML
OWINO, Mr. Fred, ML
OWINO, Mrs. Roselyne, WL
OWOUR, Mr. Kenneth O., ML
PANITZ, Mr. Sunny, ML
PARDEDE, Miss Ria Budi Wenny, WL, Protestant Christian Batak Church
PATTERSON, Miss Margaret, WL, The Presbyterian Church in Ireland
PEEL, Mr. David, MO, The United Reformed Church in England and Wales
PETERSSON, Mr. Arne, ML
PHIRI, Mrs. Christine M., WL, Church of the Province of Central Africa
PHIRI, Miss Ruth, WL
POPE, Mr. John W., ML, The United Presbyterian Church in the USA
POWELL, Mr. Jeffrey, ML, The United Presbyterian Church in the USA
PUN, Mr. Isaiah, ML, Church of Christ in China
PURCE, Mr. Roger, ML, The Presbyterian Church in Ireland
PURWANDAYA, Mr. Budhi, ML, Christian Churches of Java
REID, Mr. Duncan, ML
REILING, Ms Dory, WL
ROBBINS, Rev. Bruce, MO, The United Methodist Church
ROLLASON, Mr. Russell, ML, The Church of England in Australia
RUEFFER, Mrs. Lydia, WL
SAFARI, Mr. Benjamin Z., ML
SAIKI, Miss Wako, WL, The United Church of Christ in Japan
SANGA, Mr. Wellington, ML
SCHOT, Miss Jacoline, WL
SENTURIES, Mr. Alvado, Jr., ML, United Church of Christ in the Philippines
SETLABA, Mrs. Jacobina, WL, Lesotho Evangelical Church
SHINAVENE, Mrs. Loide, WL
SHOREY, Miss Norma, WL, Moravian Church, Eastern West Indies Province
SIKUNYANA, Mr. Isaiah, ML
SILVA, Mr. Jayasinghe K., ML
SIMIYU, Mr. Timothy, ML, Salvation Army, Kenya
SINABULYA, Mr. George, ML, Church of Uganda, Rwanda, Burundi and Boga Zaïre
SJOLLEMA, Miss Inge, WL
SMART, Mr. Alan, ML, The Church of Scotland
SMITH, Miss Kathe, WL

SMITH, Mr. Michael, MO
SODERLUND, Miss Linnea, WL
SOLT, Miss Sharon, WL
SONG, Miss Myung Rae, WL
SOVIK, Ms Liv, WL
SSERUNKUMA, Mr. Michael, ML, Church of Uganda, Rwanda, Burundi
and Boga Zaïre
SUGUNARAJAH, Miss Shiranee, WL, Church of South India
TAKERNGRANGSARIT, Mr. Pradit, ML
TATCHELL, Mr. Mark, ML, The Angelican Church of Canada
THAI, Miss Nesamani, WO, Evangelical Lutheran Church
THOLLEY, Mrs. Mary, WL
THORNE, Miss Dorothea, WL, The United Congregational Church of
Southern Africa
TJORHOM, Mr. Ola, ML
TODD, Mr. John, ML
TOEBE, Miss Maria, WL
TRAUMUELLER, Mr. Wolfgang, ML
TREMEWAN, Mr. Christopher, ML
TROCH, Mrs. Lieve, WL
UTTER, Rev. Jeffrey, MO, United Church of Christ
VAN SICHEM, Mr. Frederic, ML, Reformed Church of Belgium
VISCO-GILARDI, Mr. Arnoldo, ML
VOGELAAR, Mr. Hubert, ML, Protestant Church of Belgium
VUNINGOMA, Mrs. Joy, WL
WASPADA, Mr. Iketut, ML, Protestant Christian Church/Bali
WHITE, Mrs. Benedicte, WL, Roman Catholic Church
WHITE, Mr. Robert, ML, Lutheran Church in America
WHITTAKER, Rev. Peter, MO
WILDBOLZ, Miss Katrin, WL
WILKINSON, Miss Aneeta, WL, Church of North India
WOKABI, Miss Grace, WL
WOOD, Ms Bertrice, WL
YING, Miss Tam, WL, Roman Catholic Church
ZAGLOL, Miss Sozan, WL, Coptic Orthodox Church

Appendix 14
Constitution of the Conference
on World Mission and Evangelism
and the Sub-Unit and Commission on
World Mission and Evangelism

A. CONFERENCE ON WORLD MISSION AND EVANGELISM

1. THERE SHALL BE A CONFERENCE ON WORLD MISSION AND EVANGELISM OF THE WORLD COUNCIL OF CHURCHES

2. AIM

Its aim is to assist the Christian community in the proclamation of the gospel of Jesus Christ, by word and deed, to the whole world to the end that all may believe in him and be saved.

3. GOVERNING PRINCIPLES

(a) The main task of the Conference is to provide opportunities for churches, mission agencies, groups, and national and regional councils, concerned with Christian mission, to meet together for reflection and consultation leading to common witness.

(b) The Conference shall normally meet once between Assemblies of the World Council of Churches. It shall be convened at the call of the Commission on World Mission and Evangelism with the approval of the Central Committee.

(c) The Conference shall review the work and the accounts of the Commission. It shall set guidelines for the work and financing of the Commission in the coming period. The results of the Conference's work shall be communicated to its constituency by the Commission on World Mission and Evangelism, and shall also be brought to the attention of the Assembly and Central Committee of the World Council of Churches through that channel.

(d) Administrative and executive responsibilities of the Conference shall be carried out by the sub-unit and Commission on World Mission and Evangelism with the approval of the Central Committee.

4. MEMBERSHIP

(a) The membership of the Conference shall consist of not more than 250 persons named in the following ways:

(i) Not less than 50% shall be appointed by Councils affiliated to the Conference in accordance with a schedule prepared before each regular meeting of the Conference by the Commission and approved by the Central Committee.

(ii) The remainder shall be appointed by the Central Committee on the recommendation of the Commission through the Unit Committee, to ensure that those areas, concerns, groupings, and emphases not adequately represented by members appointed by Affiliated Councils are represented. Members of the Commission not appointed under (i) shall be appointed under (ii).

(b) The members of the Conference shall serve until appointments have been made for the next meeting of the Conference, or until their successors have been appointed.

(c) Members of the Conference shall seek to promote in their Councils and churches the aims and findings of the Conference, and the work of the sub-unit on World Mission and Evangelism. They shall draw to the attention of the Commission matters with which they feel it should be concerned. They shall seek to promote support for the work of the sub-unit.

(d) Consultants and observers may be invited to meetings of the Conference by the Commission and the Unit Committee.

5. AFFILIATION AND CONSULTATIVE RELATIONS

(a) All Councils affiliated to the CWME under the previous Constitution shall be regarded as affiliated to the Conference under this Constitution, unless they notify to the contrary.

(b) Other National Councils or Regional Conferences which accept the aim of the Conference may become affiliated to the Conference. Churches in countries where there is no affiliated National Council may apply for affiliation to the Conference. A group of churches organized for joint action for mission in a country where there is an affiliated National Council, or such an international or intercontinental group of churches, may also apply for affiliation. Applications for affiliation shall be considered by the Commission. If the application is supported by a two-thirds majority of the members of the Commission present and voting, this action shall be communicated to the affiliated members of the Conference, and unless objection is received from more than one-third of them within six months, the applicant shall be declared affiliated. There shall be consultation with the member churches of the WCC in the area concerned, except in the case of Councils already in association with the WCC.

(c) National or Regional Christian Councils which do not desire to become affiliated with the Conference, and churches and other groupings, may, if they accept the aim of the Conference, request a consultative relation with the Conference. Action on such requests shall be taken by the Commission. Councils and other groupings in consultative relation may send consultants to meetings of the Conference, who shall be entitled to speak but not to vote.

6. OFFICERS

(a) The Moderator and Vice-Moderator of the Commission on World Mission and Evangelism shall be the Moderator and Vice-Moderator of the Conference.

(b) The Conference, at each meeting, may appoint a Steering Group to meet with the Moderator and Vice-Moderator for the conduct of that meeting of the Conference.

7. QUORUM

One-third of the members of the Conference shall constitute a quorum at any given session, provided that those present at the session come from at least three continents and represent at least one-third of the Affiliated Councils.

8. AMENDMENT OF THE CONSTITUTION

The Constitution of the Conference may be amended, subject to the approval of the Central Committee, by a two-thirds majority of the members of the Conference, provided the proposed amendment shall have been reviewed by the Commission and notice of it sent to the Affiliated Councils not less than six months before the vote is taken. The Commission as well as the Affiliated Councils shall have the right to propose amendments.

B. COMMISSION ON WORLD MISSION AND EVANGELISM

1. THE COMMISSION ON WORLD MISSION AND EVANGELISM SHALL BE A SUB-UNIT OF THE PROGRAMME UNIT ON FAITH AND WITNESS.

2. AIM

Its aim shall be, in line with the basis of the WCC, to carry out the aims of the Programme Unit on Faith and Witness and the Conference on World Mission and Evangelism.

3. FUNCTIONS AND ACTIVITIES

(a) To assist the churches and councils and groups in common reflection on the content and meaning of the gospel and the manner of its proclamation and witness.

(*b*) To promote and carry out biblical and theological studies on the nature of the Christian life and witness, as demand arises from the life of the member churches in their encounter with the contemporary world, and from the concerns of the various branches of the ecumenical movement.

(*c*) To help churches, mission agencies, and groups to discern the range and character of the ongoing evangelistic task and the opportunities and priorities for mission in different cultural and social circumstances; to encourage them to attempt new forms of mission and to plan and share their resources for joint action in each place, and on a wider scale, in such ways as will manifest more fully the unity of the Church.

(*d*) To publish such literature as may be necessary for the work of the sub-unit and the Conference.

(*e*) To provide any administrative or executive services that may be needed by the Conference.

(*f*) To raise and administer, within the guidelines set by the Conference and according to the procedures of the WCC, funds that are needed for the work of the sub-unit and the Conference.

(*g*) To sponsor and undertake the initiation and administration of such programmes and agencies as may be required for carrying out the functions of the sub-unit, and to appoint with the approval of the Unit Committee the necessary sub-commissions and advisory groups.

(*h*) To participate fully in the life and work of the Programme Unit on Faith and Witness.

(*i*) To maintain close working relations with other Units and activities of the WCC and particularly with the Secretariat for Relations with Regional and National Councils.

(*j*) To call meetings of the Conference which shall review its work, accounts, and budgets.

4. COMMISSION

(*a*) The Commission on World Mission and Evangelism shall report through the Unit Committee on Faith and Witness to the Central Committee and the World Council of Churches Assembly. It shall keep the affiliated members of the Conference informed of its work.

(*b*) The Commission shall consist of twenty to twenty-five persons appointed by the Central Committee, plus the moderators of sponsored agencies and of sub-commissions or advisory groups, providing the total number is not more than thirty. The Commission shall consult affiliated bodies for names of persons that can be proposed for appointment to the Commission.

(*c*) The Commission shall elect from among its members those persons who, with the Moderator and Vice-Moderator, shall represent it on the Programme Unit Committee.

(*d*) The Commission shall ordinarily meet once a year. The Commission shall name its own Executive Committee which shall act for the Commission between meetings.

(*e*) The Commission shall, subject to the approval of the Unit Committee, appoint such advisory and executive groups as it deems necessary to carry out its work.

(f) The Commission shall prepare an annual budget, along the guidelines set by the Conference and in conformity with the financial procedures of the World Council.

(g) The Commission shall nominate its Moderator and Vice-Moderator for appointment by the Central Committee.

(h) The Director of the Commission shall be nominated by the Commission in consultation with the staffing committee of the Executive Committee and shall be appointed in accordance with the rules and procedures of the World Council. The staff shall be appointed in accordance with the rules and procedures of the World Council, on the nomination of the Commission.

(i) One-half of the membership of the Commission shall constitute a quorum.

(j) The Constitution of the Commission, subject to the approval of the Central Committee, may be amended by a two-thirds vote of the members of the Commission.

Appendix 15
By-Laws of the Commission of the Churches on International Affairs

Appendix B to Report of Policy Reference Committee I

I. NAME

The Commission shall be called Commission of the Churches on International Affairs, Commission des Eglises pour les Affaires Internationales, Kommission der Kirchen für Internationale Angelegenheiten.

II. ORGANIZATION AND RELATIONS

1. The Commission of the Churches on International Affairs is an agency of the World Council of Churches, constitutionally responsible to the Central Committee of the World Council of Churches. It is a sub-unit in Programme Unit II on Justice and Service, together with the sub-units on Inter-Church Aid, Refugee and World Service, Churches' Participation in Development and the Programme to Combat Racism.

2. Special relations may be negotiated from time to time by the World Council of Churches with world confessional bodies, other international Christian bodies, and with regional and national Councils of Churches to the end that the Commission shall assist them in their approach to international affairs and be assisted by them.

III. AIMS

It shall be the task of the Commission to witness to the lordship of Christ over human beings and history by serving people in the field of international relations and promoting reconciliation and world community in accordance with the biblical testimony to the oneness of human beings by creation; to God's gracious and redemptive action in history; and to the assurance of the coming Kingdom of God in Jesus Christ. This service is demanded by the Church's participation in the continuing ministry of Christ in the world of priestly intercession, prophetic judgement, the arousing of hope and conscience and pastoral care. This task necessitates engagement in immediate and concrete issues as well as the formulation of general Christian aims and purposes. In seeking to fulfil this task the Commission shall:

1. Serve the World Council of Churches, its units and sub-units, the member churches, the national and regional Christian councils with which the World Council of Churches is related and such other international Christian bodies noted in Chapter II, as a source of information and guidance in their approach to international problems, as a medium of counsel and action, and as an organ in formulating the Christian mind on world issues and in bringing that mind effectively to bear upon such issues.

2. Call the attention of churches and councils to problems which are especially claimant upon the Christian conscience at any particular time and to suggest ways in which Christians may act effectively upon these problems in their respective countries and internationally.

3. Encourage

(a) the promotion of peace with justice and freedom;

(b) the development of international law and of effective international institutions;

(c) the respect for and observance of human rights and fundamental freedoms, special attention being given to the problem of religious liberty;

(d) the international control and reduction of armaments;

(e) the furtherance of economic justice through international economic co-operation;

(f) acceptance by all nations of the obligation to promote to the utmost the welfare of all peoples, and the development of free political institutions;

(g) the advance towards self-government of still dependent territories;

(h) the international promotion of social, cultural, educational, and humanitarian enterprises.

IV. FUNCTIONS

1. To encourage in each country and area and in all the churches and councils the formation of organs through which the consciences of Chris-

tians may be stirred and educated as to their responsibilities in the world of nations.

2. To gather and appraise selected studies and materials on the relationship of the Christian faith to public, international, and world affairs, including the work of faculties and institutes, of other units of the World Council of Churches, of world confessional bodies, of related international Christian bodies, of regional and national Christian Councils, and of the various churches, and to make selected material available to the constituency and to the various units of the World Council of Churches.

3. To arrange for or promote research on selected problems of international justice, world order, and peace, and to utilize the results in furtherance of the work of the Commission.

4. To cultivate relationships in study and action with non-member churches and independent agencies sharing aims similar to those listed in Chapter III above.

5. To organize or participate in conferences in the cause of justice and peace.

6. To maintain and provide for the maintenance of contacts with international bodies such as the United Nations and its agencies, including regional bodies, which will assist in the attainment of the aims described in Chapter III, para. 3 above.

7. To represent the World Council of Churches or to provide for its representation and the co-ordination thereof, before these international bodies, as may be specifically arranged. The Commission may also represent, facilitate, and help co-ordinate the representation of member churches, related international Christian organizations, and non-member churches before such international bodies.

V. MEMBERS

1. Members of the Commission shall be termed Commissioners.

2. The Commission shall be composed of thirty Commissioners and its Director who shall be *ex-officio* a member of the Commission.

3. The Commissioners shall be elected by the Central Committee of the World Council of Churches on the basis of nominations by the Commission and in accordance with the general policies of the World Council of Churches.

4. In making nominations the Commission shall ensure adequate representation of the bodies in the categories listed in Chapter II, 2 above, and the bodies concerned shall be consulted in the nomination of the Commissioners representing them.

5. Christian knowledge and commitment and technical competence in international affairs and related subjects shall be the chief qualifications sought in all commissioners. An emphasis on laymen and lay women as members of the Commission and a proper balance of the membership in respect of geography, age, race, culture, and confession shall be sought.

6. The task of a Commissioner shall be:

(*a*) to correspond with the officers of the Commission, drawing their attention to matters which, in his or her view, should occupy their attention and advising them of the relevant data;

(*b*) to co-operate with recognized councils and church agencies and committees in educating public opinion or in making representation to authorities on matters in the international sphere of concern to the Christian conscience;

(*c*) as far as may be possible, to attend or to be represented by an alternate at duly convened meetings of the Commission.

7. The General Secretary of the World Council may sit with the Commission and shall also determine from time to time Directors of such units and sub-units who by reason of their duties and the issues to be considered should sit with the Commission.

VI. CORRESPONDING COMMISSIONERS

The Commission shall appoint, subject to approval by the Central Committee of the World Council of Churches, Corresponding Commissioners in number not more than forty, with tasks similar to those of the Commissioners and with the rights of the Commissioners except the right to vote at meetings of the Commission and the right to require convening of a meeting of the Commission.

VII. OFFICERS AND STAFF

1. The officers of the Commission shall be the President, at least one Vice-President, Director, and such other officers as the Commission may decide. These officers, except the Director, shall be nominated by the Commission subject to approval by the Central Committee of the World Council of Churches.

2. The Director shall be the chief administrative officer of the Commission to carry on its work in accordance with its aims and functions, and subject to the directives of the Commission. The Officers shall be assisted by a staff. The Director and the staff shall be appointed and employed according to the rules of the World Council of Churches after appropriate consultation with the Officers of the Commission.

VIII. REPRESENTATIVES

Such world bodies and ecumenical organizations with which the more organic relationships provided for in Chapters IV and II have not been negotiated may be invited by the Officers to send a representative to meetings of the Commission in a consultative capacity.

IX. MEETINGS OF THE COMMISSION

1. The Commission shall normally meet once a year at a place and time to be determined by the President in consultation with the Director. A minimum notice of three months shall be given for meetings except in cases of emergency.

2. Any ten members of the Commission or the General Secretary of the World Council of Churches may require a meeting to be convened for any purpose within the aims of the Commission and the President shall forthwith convene a meeting with due notice of the purpose of it.

3. The members of the Commission or those persons who shall sit with the Commission may propose alternates to attend meetings of the Commission, provided a fortnight's notice of the intention to do so and the names of the alternates are given to the President and he approves. Alternate members are entitled to vote.

4. The quorum for meetings of the Commission shall be one-third of its members.

5. The Commission in session shall determine the general policies to be followed by the officers and staff in fulfilment of the aims of the Commission. The Commission in session may also approve statements proposed for general publication in the name of the Commission, but in this case such statements are subject to the relevant rules of the World Council of Churches.

X. THE BUDGET

1. The Commission shall operate a separate budget under the rules of the World Council of Churches.

2. The Commission may

(a) request and receive grants-in-aid from the general budget of the World Council of Churches, and from the budgets of those world, regional, and national bodies with whom special organic relationship has been agreed (according to Chapter II); and further from other appropriate budgets of the World Council;

(b) subject to agreed World Council of Churches procedures, request and receive subscriptions and donations from corporate bodies and foundations, and individuals;

(c) subject to agreed World Council of Churches procedures, request and receive legacies;

provided that no conditions are attached which are incompatible with its aims.

XI. CONTACTS WITH THE CHURCHES

The Commission may encourage the formation of, and enter into relationship with, national or regional bodies of churches in fulfilment of the functions described in Chapter IV.

XII. CONTACTS WITH GOVERNMENTS AND INTER-GOVERNMENTAL BODIES

A. GENERAL PRINCIPLES OF CONTACT

1. (a) The Commission may negotiate directly in its own name and in the name of the World Council of Churches with the United Nations and other international bodies.

   (b) In making representation to national governments or other national entities to advance a Christian view on any problem in accordance with its aims, the Commission shall do so ordinarily with the concurrence of the national or regional committee and in consultation with the Commissioners and Corresponding Commissioners in the country or countries.

   However, in exceptional circumstances the Commission may make such representations without such consultation and even when national or regional committees do not concur. In this event it is understood that the national or regional committee will not be in any sense responsible for such action.

2. In formulating policies for representations to governmental agencies, the following procedures may be employed:

   (a) The Commission may, when meeting, formulate policies, or the President or Director on its behalf, following postal communication wherein a substantial and representative agreement has been expressed, may also formulate policies.

   (b) The officers in their official capacities may formulate policies, provided that it is in agreement with the Commission's policy as provided in its aims and after consultation with the General Secretary of the World Council of Churches and the Moderator of the Central Committee, and with their concurrence.

   (c) A national or regional committee or commissioner or corresponding commissioner may not act in the name of the Commission or of any of its officers or committees unless specific authorization has been given.

(*d*) The Commission may, in addition, prepare and recommend statements to the World Council of Churches for its consideration and to any appropriate assemblies or conferences meeting under the auspices of the World Council of Churches and to such bodies with which organic relationships have been agreed under the provisions of Chapter II.

B. PROCEDURES OF CONTACT

In accordance with the arrangements provided by the United Nations and its Specialized Agencies, the administrative officers of the Commission are empowered to seek and maintain on behalf of the Commission and the World Council of Churches the following contacts:

1. Official registration with the United Nations Department of Public Information.

2. Consultative status with the United Nations, its Specialized Agencies and other inter-governmental organizations.

3. Such contacts with other organs and specialized agencies as the officers may determine necessary to accomplish the Commission's aims.

4. The Commission shall, with the approval of the General Secretary of the World Council of Churches, be responsible for facilitating and arranging such direct contact with organs and specialized agencies of the United Nations as may be requested by other sub-units or Units of the World Council of Churches, and by bodies with which special relations have been agreed under the provisions of Chapter II.

XIII. CONTACTS WITH OTHER ORGANIZATIONS

As a general principle, the Commission will not establish organic relations with organizations, except as provided for in Chapter II, but, where deemed advisable, may co-operate with other bodies in such ways as will permit the exchange of information and promote action by the Commission in accomplishing its aims.

XIV

These by-laws may be amended by the Commission, provided that due notice has been given, subject to the approval of the Central Committee of the World Council of Churches.

Appendix 16
By-Laws of the Faith and Order Commission

1. MEANING

In these by-laws:

The Commission means the Commission on Faith and Order of the World Council of Churches and includes both the Plenary Commission and the Standing Commission.

The Officers of the Commission mean the Moderator and Vice-Moderators of the Plenary Commission and Standing Commission.

The Secretariat means the Secretariat of the Commission on Faith and Order.

The Council means the World Council of Churches.

The Assembly means the Assembly of the World Council of Churches.

The Central Committee means the Central Committee of the World Council of Churches.

2. AIM AND FUNCTIONS

The Aim of the Commission is to proclaim the oneness of the Church of Jesus Christ and to call the churches to the goal of visible unity in one faith and one eucharistic fellowship, expressed in worship and in common life in Christ, in order that the world may believe.

The Functions of the Commission are:

(a) to study such questions of faith, order, and worship as bear on this task and to examine such social, cultural, political, racial, and other factors as affect the unity of the Church;

(b) to study the theological implications of the existence and development of the ecumenical movement and to keep prominently before the Council the obligation to work towards unity;

(c) to promote prayer for unity;

(d) to study matters in the present relationship of the churches to one another which cause difficulties or which particularly require theological clarification;

(e) to study the steps being taken by the churches towards closer unity with one another and to provide information concerning such steps;

(f) to bring to the attention of the churches, by the best means available, reports of Faith and Order meetings and studies;

(g) to provide opportunities for consultation among those whose churches are engaged in union negotiations or other specific efforts towards unity.

The Commission, in pursuing its work, observes the following principles:

(i) It seeks to draw the churches into conversation and study but recognizes that only the churches themselves are competent to initiate steps towards union, by entering into negotiations with one another. The work of the Commission is to act, on their invitation, as helper and adviser.

(ii) It will conduct its work in such a way that all are invited to share reciprocally in giving and receiving and no one is asked to be disloyal to his convictions nor to compromise them. Differences are to be clarified and recorded as honestly as agreements.

3. ORGANIZATION

(a) The Faith and Order Commission is constitutionally responsible to the Central Committee. It is part of Programme Unit I on Faith and Witness together with the sub-units on Church and Society, on World Mission and Evangelism, and on Dialogue with Peoples of Living Faiths and Ideologies.

(b) The Faith and Order Commission shall consist of a Plenary Commission and a Standing Commission.

(c) The Plenary Commission will have as its primary task theological study, debate, and appraisal. It will initiate the programme of the Faith and Order Commission, lay down general guidelines for it, and share in its communication to the churches.

(d) The Standing Commission will have as its task to implement the programme, to guide the staff in the development of Faith and Order work, and to make administrative decisions on behalf of the Faith and Order Commission, to supervise the ongoing work and to act on behalf of the Commission in between meetings of the Plenary Commission. It shall represent the Commission in relation to the Programme Unit I Committee and the Council generally.

(e) The Plenary Commission shall consist of not more than 120 members (including the Officers and the other members of the Standing

403

Commission). The Standing Commission shall consist of a Chairperson and not more than 30 other members.

(f) Both the Plenary Commission and the Standing Commission shall be appointed by the Central Committee, in the following manner:

(i) The Plenary Commission, at its last meeting before the Assembly, shall appoint a Nominations Commiteee to prepare a list of names for the election of a new Standing Committee by the Central Committee.

(ii) The Central Committee shall appoint the Moderator and the members of the Standing Commission, who will hold office until the following Assembly of the World Council of Churches. The Standing Commission shall elect not more than four Vice-Moderators from among its members. The Chairperson and the Vice-Chairpersons shall be the Officers of both the Standing Commission and the Plenary Commission.

(iii) The Standing Commission shall submit to the Central Committee a list of candidates from which shall be chosen the members of the Plenary Comission, who will hold office until the next Assembly.

(iv) Vacancies on the Plenary Commission and the Standing Commission shall be filled by the Central Committee on the nomination of the Standing Commission.

(g) Since the size of the Commission precludes full representation of member churches of the Council, appointment shall be made on the basis of personal capacity to serve the purposes of the Commission. At the same time, care shall be taken to secure a reasonable geographical and confessional representation of churches on the Commission and among the Officers and Secretaries. The Plenary Commission should include in its membership a sufficient number of women, young and lay persons.

(h) Persons who are members of churches which do not belong to the Council but which confess Jesus Christ as God and Saviour are eligible for membership of the Commission.

(i) Before any candidate is nominated for appointment by the Central Committee, steps shall be taken to ensure that his name is acceptable to the church to which he belongs. A member should be willing to accept some responsibility for communication between the Faith and Order Commission and his church and ecumenical bodies in his country.

4. THE SECRETARIAT

(a) The appointment and reappointment of members of the Secretariat shall be made by the Central Committee or the Executive Committee of the Council upon nomination by the Standing Commission and after due consultation with the General Secretary of the Council. These Secretaries shall be employed by the Council, normally on a full-time basis.

(b) A sufficient number of Secretaries shall be appointed for the adequate performance of the work of the Commission.

(c) The Secretariat shall maintain full consultation and co-operation with the General Secretariat of the Council, with Programme Unit I, and as required with other Units of the Council.

(d) The Secretariat shall be responsible for ensuring the continuation of the work of the Plenary Commission, in accordance with the policy agreed at meetings of the Plenary Commission or Standing Commission. To this end the Secretariat shall keep in regular contact with the Officers and other members of the Commission.

5. WORLD CONFERENCES

(a) World Conferences on Faith and Order may be held when, on recommendation of the Standing Commission acting in the name of the Commission, the Central Committee so approves.

(b) The invitation to take part in such conferences shall be addressed to churches throughout the world which confess Jesus Christ as God and Saviour.

(c) Such Conferences shall consist primarily of delegates appointed by the churches to represent them. Youth delegates, special advisers, and observers may also be invited.

(d) Careful attention shall be given to the communication of the reports and recommendations of World Conferences to the churches.

6. MEETINGS OF THE COMMISSION

(a) The Plenary Commission shall meet at least once between Assemblies, but may be convened at any time by the Standing Commission after clearance with the Executive Committee of the Council.

(b) The Standing Committee shall normally meet every year but may be convened at any time by the Moderator in consultation with other Officers of the Commission or at the request of not less than one-third of the members of the Standing Commission.

(c) The Secretariat will be responsible for giving due notice of meetings of both the Plenary Commission and Standing Commission, for keeping its minutes and other records, and, in consultation with the Moderator, for preparing its agenda.

(d) A member of the Plenary Commission, by advance notice to the Secretariat, may name a proxy acceptable to his church to represent him at any meeting at which he is unable to be present.

(e) A member of the Standing Commission may name a person to represent him at any meeting at which he is unable to be present but such a person may not vote.

(f) Other persons may be invited to be present and to speak, if the Moderator so rules, but not to vote. In particular, in order to secure representation of its study groups, members of these may be invited to attend either body as consultants.

(g) The Moderator of the Commission or, in his absence, one of the Vice-Moderators, shall preside at such meetings. In the absence of these officers, the meeting shall elect its own Moderator. One-third of the total membership (including proxies) shall constitute a quorum.

(h) The Commission shall normally conduct its business according to the rules of procedure of the Central Committee. Questions arising about procedure shall be decided by a majority vote of those present and voting.

(i) If, at any time when it is inconvenient to hold a meeting of the Standing Commission, the Moderator and Secretariat shall decide that there is business needing immediate action by that Commission, it shall be permissible for them to obtain by post the opinions of its members, and the majority opinion thus ascertained shall be treated as equivalent to the decision of a duly convened meeting.

7. FAITH AND ORDER STUDIES

(a) The Standing Commission, giving due attention to the general guidelines laid down by the Plenary Commission (see 3c), shall formulate and carry through the study programme.

(b) The Secretariat, as authorized by the Standing Commission, shall invite persons to serve on the study groups and consultations. They shall pay particular regard to the need to involve members of both the Plenary Commission and the Standing Commission in the study programme, whether by membership of study group, consultations, or by written consultation. Due regard shall be paid to special competence in the fields of study concerned, and to the need for the representation of a variety of ecclesiastical traditions and theological viewpoints.

(c) Study groups shall normally include both those who are, and those who are not, members of the Commission. They may also include persons who do not belong to member churches of the Council.

(d) In planning such studies, all possible contact shall be sought or maintained with allied work already in progress under such auspices as those of regional or national councils or of individual churches, or of ecumenical institutes and theological faculties or departments.

(e) Study groups shall prepare reports, as requested, for discussion in the Commission, at World Conferences on Faith and Order, or at Assemblies. Any such report should bear a clear indication of its status.

(f) The publication of such reports and of other Faith and Order papers shall be the responsibility of the Secretariat, provided that adequate financial resources are available.

8. FINANCE

(a) The normal working expenses of the Commission and its Secretariat shall be borne by the general budget of the Council. The Secretariat shall be responsible for drawing up an annual budget of expenditure for submission, through normal Council procedures, to the Finance Committee of the Central Committee.

(b) There shall be a financial report annually to the Standing Commission.

(c) The Standing Commission shall be responsible for deciding the allocation of available funds to particular studies, and the Secretariat shall communicate such decisions to the officers of study groups.

9. REVISION OF BY-LAWS

These by-laws may be amended by the Standing Commission subject to the approval of the Central Committee. Any proposed amendment must be circulated in writing to the members of the Plenary Commission not less than three months before the meeting at which it is to be considered for adoption and, for adoption, requires the approval of two-thirds of the members of the Standing Commission present and voting.

10. COMMUNICATION WITH THE CHURCHES

The Plenary Commission and the Standing Commission shall be concerned to facilitate communication with the churches. They shall make generally available results of studies where such studies are formally communicated to the churches through the Central Committee. In certain studies, the Commission may invite a formal response from the churches.

Index

DATE DUE

MAR 28 '79			
FEB 7 '80			
FEB 28 '80			
JUL 30 '86			

DEMCO 38-297